W9-DFT-212

SECOND ACT TROUBLE

Behind the Scenes at Broadway's Big Musical Bombs

STEVEN SUSKIN

APPLAUSE THEATRE & CINEMA BOOKS ■ NEW YORK

Second Act Trouble
Behind the Scenes at Broadway's Big Musical Bombs
by Steven Suskin

Book design by Mark Lerner

Library of Congress Cataloging-in-Publication Data

Suskin, Steven.
  Second act trouble : behind the scenes at Broadway's big musical bombs / by Steven Suskin.
     p. cm.
  Includes index.
  ISBN-13: 978-1-55783-631-1
  ISBN-10: 1-55783-631-0
  1. Musicals—New York (State)—New York—History and criticism. I. Title.

  ML2054.S96 2006
  792.6'45'097471—dc22

                          2005024707

Applause Theatre & Cinema Books
19 West 21st St.
New York, NY 10010
Phone: (212) 575-9265
Fax: (212) 575-9270
Email: info@applausepub.com
Internet: www.applausepub.com
Applause books are available through your local bookstore, or you may order at www.applausepub.com or call Music Dispatch at 800-637-2852

SALES & DISTRIBUTION

North America:
Hal Leonard Corp.
7777 West Bluemound Road
P. O. Box 13819
Milwaukee, WI 53213
Phone: (414) 774-3630
Fax: (414) 774-3259
Email: halinfo@halleonard.com
Internet: www.halleonard.com

Europe:
Roundhouse Publishing Ltd.
Millstone, Limers Lane
Northam, North Devon EX 39 2RG
Phone: (0) 1237-474-474
Fax: (0) 1237-474-774
Email: roundhouse.group@ukgateway.net

for my wife Helen

and

for Johanna and Charlie

CONTENTS

Introduction

What is more exciting than a big new Broadway musical hit? Broadway's legendary masterworks—shows like *Oklahoma!, My Fair Lady, Fiddler on the Roof, A Chorus Line, Annie,* and *The Producers*—serve as milestones of popular culture, traversing America and circling the globe, earning accolades and millions along the way.

But things don't always work out as intended. The musical is one of the most collaborative of arts; songwriters, book writers, directors, choreographers, producers, stars, and others all contribute. When disparate elements don't gel, panic sets in. With the clock running out, and the bankroll running low, and superegos running amuck, strange things can happen. And do. Once in a while, the creators miraculously pull it off; but the Broadway graveyard is full of disheartening salvage heaps.

If Broadway musical hits are exhilarating, the backstage tales of Broadway failures are tantalizing soap operas in miniature. What went wrong, theatregoers wonder? How could things get so bad? The authors and directors and producers were all competent professionals, mostly. How could they not have known that their spanking new baby was a stinker?

The answer is complicated, and at the same time simple. Any number of things can go wrong, and do; musicals, the old adage goes, are not written but rewritten. One of the true skills of creating Broadway musicals is the ability to analyze and fix things on the fly. But the greatest show doctors are not invincible, for the simple reason that no two patients are the same. What should work, and worked yesterday, and always worked within memory, today stubbornly refuses to work. *Now* what do you do?

The general theatregoing public, of course, cannot slip inside the stage door and experience what really happens. If only we could sit with the creators in the rehearsal halls, at dress rehearsals and tryouts, in late-night hotel-room production meetings, and at after-the-fact recriminatory gripe fests. But, alas. No self-respecting producer would invite an outsider inside the room while everybody fights and fires and flings lawsuits.

Or would they?

Yes, it turns out.

There are numerous accounts in circulation detailing the trials and triumphs of Broadway's greatest hits, some of which the reader of this volume has no doubt encountered. For the exercise in hand, though, I've chosen to compile true-life sagas of shows that didn't make it. I do not mean to dwell on the negative, mind you. Many of these shows, for reasons understandable, tend to be overlooked and forgotten; and they all have tales to tell. Yesterday's hits can bring us heart-warming memories, sure; but failures—nay, disasters—are fascinating, inherently instructive, and in some ways ever so much more interesting. Some of these chronicles, too, bring along a "you are there" immediacy that might well have at least a few readers chewing their nails.

Hundreds of books have been written about musical theatre, including a dozen or so by myself. In the course of research, I've come across some especially vivid first-hand accounts of the creation of musicals. Going back to them again and again over the years, it struck me that these yellowing accounts—mostly from daily newspapers and weekly magazines, which went out-of-print the day or week after they were published—tell pretty convincing tales in themselves. Why not gather the best of them together, and put them in context, I wondered? Thus, *Second Act Trouble*.

Twenty-eight pieces have been selected, discussing twenty-five fallen musicals. (I've seen fit to include relevant follow-up pieces in two of the chapters; in another, I've reprinted a leading lady's letter to the editor rebutting the facts of the case.) These shows have been selected not because they were the worst or the biggest flops of all time, mind you; I decided to work only from original sources, and not all the biggest flops had a resident fly on the wall (or hot-on-the-trail reporter). Other accounts proved unavailable for reprint. Even so, the selections herein are representative.

Every flop follows just about the same trajectory. Things start on a note of extreme optimism. As rehearsals progress, hidden worries arise. The tryout exposes flaws, and tensions as well. Everybody agrees on what to fix and how to fix it, or everybody *disagrees* on what to fix and how to fix it. They try—oh, how they try—and the show seems to improve. (Replacing a lousy song with a decent song will make that four-minute section of the show quantifiably stronger, and lift everybody's spirits. But what about the *other* six lousy songs?) A second round of bad reviews in the next city, en route to Broadway, sends everyone into severe panic. And that's when the fun really begins.

If the saga is the same, the specifics vary. Some shows are done in by the material; some by the deficiencies or demands of the star. Others are overwhelmed by a battling of egos. (Or should we say superegos?) Sometimes factors from the outside world intrude, to the extent that the material itself is pushed into the background.

And then there are shows, quite a few of them, where simply everything goes wrong. Nightmares to live through, without question. But they make entertaining reading. If some writers, directors, producers, actors, etc. are caught in the spotlight (and unfavorably so) let us consider a few truths.

Nobody, and I mean nobody, sets out to write or direct or produce a bad show. Intentions don't count for much when the curtain finally goes up, but some theatregoers seem to take poor theatre as a personal affront.

Musical theatre, for various reasons, has developed into a highly collaborative art. All of the collaborative elements are not assembled, in one place at one time, until a couple of days prior to the first performance. (If all the elements are ready, that is; due to unforeseen delays, some shows find themselves before an audience without having finished a single dress rehearsal.) It is a given that some of the elements will not combine seamlessly. This is why we have pre-Broadway tryouts and/or New York previews, during which adjustments can be made.

Many elements are easily (or not so easily) fixable. There are four key steps: Recognizing the problem; deciding what to do about the problem; figuring out how to accomplish the solution; and successfully putting it on stage. This is standard operating procedure for new musicals, and eminently workable, provided that the creators and producers agree, and time and money hold out.

However, there are times when solutions are not so practical. Major production elements, especially in concept musicals, are not so easily replaceable. You can throw out a song, or a set of costumes, and rush through replacements. You can throw out scenery, though not as easily as in the old days when the sets were mostly canvas and paint. You can fire the director or the choreographer, or the director *and* the choreographer, or an actor or three, although the cost in buyouts, new costumes, and overtime rehearsal time are especially steep.

While it is standard practice to cut and replace songs that do not work, it is almost impossible to cut a significant portion of the score; the songs provide the underpinning of a musical. And the person who in more than a few instances is the true culprit, and clearly needs to be given a bus ticket back home, is *never* replaced. I speak, of course, of the producer....

But let us look with pity on these poor, struggling souls. And struggle they do, the novice playmakers working on their first effort and the legendary veterans with their ribbons and medallions. (Tony Award medallions, that is.) There is nothing worse than being stuck with a show that stubbornly resists improvement. With a stage full of people, and a team of collaborators, and a brace of backers, looking to you with desparate eyes for salvation. Worst of all, perhaps, is standing in the back of the theatre watching a paid-in-good-faith audience file in, knowing that they will within moments be presented with something that you, yourself, would walk out on.

There's an old story about a producer during a tryout of a massive musical extravaganza. There he is, standing impatiently at the box office window, haranguing the treasurer. He expresses his annoyance and exasperation, at length. Finally, the well-dressed gentleman on line behind him says, "Excuse me, sir, if you don't like it, you can get your money back."

The producer turns to the gent. "I wish I could, mister. I truly wish I could."

The material reprinted in this book comes from newspapers, magazines, and books. (Nine of the pieces were originally published in the *New York Times*, four in *New York* magazine.) Many of the newspaper and magazine pieces were written by reporters on assignment; in several cases, they were covering the show with the approval and cooperation of the producers.

While the producers and press agents presumably looked at these articles as potential publicity, some of the reporters were clearly on the prowl, smelling blood in New Haven or Boston. These items make for remarkable reading, especially when the reporter gets a hold of someone who was fired two days earlier. And the reporters in question, bless them, made sure they did! *Second Act Trouble* also includes a handful of autobiographical pieces. These I generally take with a grain of salt, as self-protective memory can play funny tricks. The pieces selected, though, are candid and outspoken enough to have the ring of truth. While the contents of this book were selected for their theatre-related interest, I was glad to find that many happen to be extremely well written. The contributor list includes such respected writers as Patricia Bosworth, Chris Chase, William Gibson, John Gruen, Lewis H. Lapham, and Ellen Stern. Listed in alphabetical order, naturally.

Virtually all the original articles are presented intact and unedited, the exceptions being a couple of the autobiographical pieces that interspersed non-show-related personal matters. Typographical errors have been corrected; stylistic choices and alternate spellings, too, have been adjusted as necessary. Each is prefaced by, and concluded with, brief notes. All of the pieces include references that the theatrically knowledgeable reader would have instantly picked up on at the time, but might well be unfamiliar forty or more years after the fact. I have thus annotated the pieces with information that is pertinent, or will shed light on the discussion. I would ideally prefer not to interrupt the flow of text; the use of footnotes, however, proved even more disruptive. The annotations have been inserted in their place, but in a different typeface. The intention is not to edit the original pieces, but fill in the gaps of time.

A volume of this sort cannot be compiled without the cooperation of the original authors, agents and publishers. The rights holders were in every case cooperative, understanding the educational value of the project. The authors with whom I spoke were especially happy to see their material back in print. To them all, a word of thanks. Much of the research on this book was done at the Billy Rose Theatre Collection of the New York Public Library for the Performing Arts. The collection, and its knowledgeable and helpful librarians, might well be the Broadway historian's most valuable resource.

Most of the material used for illustrations was provided by Max A. Woodward and Richard Kidwell, to whom I am (as ever) grateful. While I have heretofore assiduously avoided the use of autographed material, the signatures and greetings herein bring a special fascination. They were mostly accumulated well after the fact. Thus, the victim returning to the scene of the crime, with good humor and sometimes even a smiling face.

As I was formulating this book, I took the liberty of contacting

Geoffrey Block (who had compiled a somewhat similar volume, the excellent *Richard Rodgers Reader*). While Mr. Block and I didn't know each other, he nevertheless outlined the entire procedure, and invited further requests for advice. It goes without saying that I am highly appreciative of his guidance. I also thank my publisher, Michael Messina, and our designer, Mark Lerner, for taking my necessarily wordy manuscript and transforming it into such a pert and stylish package.

Once upon a time, back in 1965, the producers of a new Broadway musical saw fit to grant full access to a budding journalist from the *Saturday Evening Post*. The musical turned out to be *Kelly*, which startled Broadway by closing the night it opened with a mind-numbing loss of $650,000. Reporter Lewis H. Lapham sat by with his notebook as the producers fired actors, replaced songs, replaced the authors, battled the authors' lawsuits, and read the woeful out-of-town reviews. They even invited Lapham—since 1976, editor of *Harper's* Magazine—to ride along with them in the limousine to Philadelphia. While the *Kelly* article is not the earliest in this book, it served as model for most of the in-depth "making of a musical" pieces.

"With any luck," one of the producers told Lapham, "you will be able to write a textbook on how to produce a play in the American musical theatre." Indeed.

Read 'em and weep and laugh, and drop your jaw in amazement.

Cast of Characters (and List of Victims)

George Abbott a director (*Fade Out–Fade In, Tenderloin*) and a show doctor (*How Now, Dow Jones*)

Lee Adams a lyricist (*Golden Boy*)

Jerry Adler a stage manager-turned-director (*Hellzapoppin*)

Richard Adler a songwriter (*Kwamina*) and a producer (*Rex*)

Edward Albee an unlikely librettist (*Breakfast at Tiffany's*)

William Alfred an out-of-place librettist on crutches (*Cry for Us All*)

Richard Altman an observer with a notebook (*Tenderloin*)

Barbara Andres a featured player (*Rex*)

Brooks Atkinson a critic who retires (*Subways Are for Sleeping*)

Robert Alan Aurthur a librettist (*Kwamina*)

Robert Avian an assistant doctor (*Seesaw*)

Christine Baranski a featured player (*Nick & Nora*)

Howard Bay a designer with a lumbering set (*Cry for Us All*)

Norman Bel Geddes another designer with a lumbering set (*Flying Colors*)

Michael Bennett a doctor (*How Now, Dow Jones, Seesaw*) and a doctor who chooses not to doctor (*The Act, Rex*)

Sarah Bernhardt an act to follow (*Flying Colors*)

Leonard Bernstein a friend of the court (*Hallelujah, Baby!*)

Kermit Bloomgarden a producer (*Illya Darling*)

Jerry Bock a composer who writes new songs (*Tenderloin*)

Barry Bostwick a leading man (*Nick & Nora*)

Ben Boyar a general manager (*Flying Colors*)

Bertolt Brecht an inspiration (*Kelly*)

Alan Brien a friendly observer (*Hallelujah, Baby!*)

Mel Brooks a mad doctor (*Kelly*)

Rocco Bufano a director who is replaced (*Dude*)

Peter Bull a featured player who writes a letter to the editor (*Pickwick*)

Carol Burnett a Star with a contract (*Fade Out–Fade In*)

Ralph Burns an orchestrator hoping for laughs (*Illya Darling*)

Abe Burrows a director who departs (*Breakfast at Tiffany's, Hellzapoppin*)

Truman Capote an unhappy author of source material (*Breakfast at Tiffany's*)

Kevin Carlisle a replacement choreographer (*Hallelujah, Baby!*)

Diahann Carroll a potential Star replacement who answers the phone (*Breakfast at Tiffany's*)

Ralph Carter a child actor who replaces the adult lead (*Dude*)

Terry Carter a leading man who can't kiss the leading lady (*Kwamina*)

Dick Cavett a potential Star replacement who cracks jokes (*Hellzapoppin*)

Richard Chamberlain a Star from TV-land (*Breakfast at Tiffany's*)

Gower Champion a director/choreographer (*Mack & Mabel*) and a doctor (*The Act, Irene*)

Moose Charlap a composer who is replaced (*Kelly*)

Martin Charnin a director/librettist who is replaced (*I Remember Mama*)

Paddy Chayefsky a doctor who declines (*Golden Boy*)

Jill Choder a friend of the Star (*Hellzapoppin*)

Peter Coe a director who is replaced (*Golden Boy*) and who disappears (*Pickwick*)

Richard Coe an out-of-town critic who criticizes (*Mack & Mabel*)

Alexander H. Cohen a producer with grand ideas (*Hellzapoppin, I Remember Mama*)

Nathan Cohen an out-of-town critic who criticizes (*Kwamina*)

Cy Coleman a composer (*Seesaw*)

Edward Colton a theatrical lawyer who makes a match (*Rex*)

Betty Comden a lyricist (*Fade Out–Fade In, Hallelujah, Baby!, Subways Are for Sleeping*)

Noël Coward a lifeline (*Flying Colors*)

John Cullum a replacement for the Star who can sing (*On a Clear Day*)

Grover Dale a choreographer who is replaced (*Seesaw*)

Joe Darion a lyricist (*Illya Darling*)

Jules Dassin a director/author/producer/husband-to-the-Star (*Illya Darling*)

Sammy Davis, Jr. the Star (*Golden Boy*)

Alfred de Liagre a producer (*Kwamina*)

Agnes de Mille a choreographer (*Kwamina*) who is replaced (*Flying Colors*)

Billy de Wolfe a Star who quits (*Irene*)

Joan Diener the Star and the director's wife (*Cry for Us All*)

Howard Dietz a lyricist (*Flying Colors*)

Charles Dillingham a producer who absconds (*Flying Colors*)

Stanley Donen a replacement director (*The Red Shoes*)

Nat Dorfman a loyal press agent (*Kelly*)

Michael Dunn an actor who is given a reprieve (*Dude*)

Cyrus Durgin a critic who went to a concert (*Subways Are for Sleeping*)

Fred Ebb a lyricist (*The Act*)

Herb Edelman the Star's retainer (*Hellzapoppin*)

Hillard Elkins a scrambling producer (*Golden Boy*)

Lehman Engel a musical director who throws up his hands (*Illya Darling*)

Maurice Evans the Star (*Tenderloin*)

Louis Falco a choreographer who is replaced (*Dude*)

Cy Feuer a producer (*The Act*) and a director/producer (*Skyscraper*) and a replacement director (*I Remember Mama*)

Ron Field a potential doctor (*The Act*)

Dorothy Fields a lyricist (*Seesaw*)

Carrie Fisher the Star's daughter (*Irene*)

Lynn Fontanne a passing-by Star (*Flying Colors*)

Don Francks a Star who isn't discovered (*Kelly*)

Walter Fried an embattled general manager who is banned from backstage (*Irene*)

Penny Fuller a featured player (*Rex*) and a potential leading lady (*Mack & Mabel*)

George Furth a librettist who sues (*The Act*)

Helen Gallagher a former Star whose featured role is diminished (*Cry for Us All*)

Kelly Garrett a leading lady who is replaced (*Mack & Mabel*)

Kevin Geer an actor who is replaced but leaves his image behind (*Dude*)

Peter Gennaro a choreographer who is partially replaced (*Irene*)

George a man who pushes the button (*Cry for Us All*)

William Gibson a playwright who helps out (*Golden Boy*)

John Gielgud an icon who is fired (*Irene*)

Anita Gillette a featured player looking for her break (*Kelly*)

Joanna Gleason a leading lady (*Nick & Nora*)

Justice Samuel Gold an arbitrator (*Kelly*)

Fred Golden an adman with a secret (*Subways Are for Sleeping*)

James Goldman one of two book-doctor brothers (*Tenderloin*)

William Goldman the younger book-doctor brother (*Tenderloin*)

Cliff Gordon a vaudevillian who follows Bernhardt (*Flying Colors*)

Max Gordon a producer who jumps (*Flying Colors*)

Adolph Green a lyricist (*Fade Out–Fade In, Hallelujah, Baby!, Subways Are for Sleeping*)

Robert E. Griffith a producer (*Tenderloin*)

John Gruen a reporter on the trail (*Breakfast at Tiffany's*)

A.L. (Pete) Gurney an out-of-place librettist who is replaced (*Nick & Nora*)

Karen Gustafson an assistant conductor (*Illya Darling*)

Manos Hadjidakis a Greek composer (*Illya Darling*)

Halston the Star's designer (*The Act*)

Carrie Hamilton a newborn who holds up production (*Fade Out–Fade In*)

Joe Hamilton the Star's husband (*Fade Out–Fade In*)

Marvin Hamlisch a songwriter who dropped out early (*The Act*)

Dashiell Hammett an author of source material (*Nick & Nora*)

Sheldon Harnick a lyricist (*Rex, Tenderloin*) and a potential lyricist (*Nick & Nora*)

Barbara Harris a Star who can sing (*On a Clear Day*)

Julie Harris a Star who *can't* sing (*Skyscraper*)

Leland Hayward a producer who keeps quiet (*Subways Are for Sleeping*)

Audrey Hepburn a Star who isn't in the show (*Breakfast at Tiffany's*)

Jerry Herman a songwriter (*Mack & Mabel*)

Adela Holzer a producer (*Dude*)

Lena Horne a Star who walks (*Hallelujah, Baby!*)

Ken Howard a leading man who isn't replaced when everybody else is (*Seesaw*)

Sally Ann Howes a leading lady and the composer's wife (*Kwamina*)

Ron Husmann a featured player who is told where to move (*Tenderloin*)

Betty Hutton a Star replacement who doesn't sell tickets (*Fade Out–Fade In*)

Margaret Illman a leading lady who can't sing (*The Red Shoes*)

Dr. Max Jacobsen a man with a needle (*On a Clear Day*)

Raymond Jessel a replacement lyricist from *The Love Boat* (*I Remember Mama*)

Nunnally Johnson a librettist who is replaced (*Breakfast at Tiffany's*)

Louis Jourdan a Star who is replaced (*On a Clear Day*)

John Kander a composer (*The Act*)

Lawrence Kasha a producer in trouble (*Seesaw*)

Lainie Kazan a Star who is noisily replaced (*Seesaw*)

Sally Kellerman a featured player with radical rewrites (*Breakfast at Tiffany's*)

Kevin Kelly an out-of-town critic who criticizes (*Breakfast at Tiffany's, Hellzapoppin, Subways Are for Sleeping*)

Patsy Kelly a featured comedienne who mugs (*Irene*)

Sean Kenny a designer far away (*Pickwick*)

Jerome Kern a passing-by composer (*Flying Colors*)

Michael Kidd a choreographer (*Breakfast at Tiffany's*) and a director-choreographer (*Subways Are for Sleeping*)

Dorothy Kilgallen a columnist who stirs up trouble (*Skyscraper*)

Joseph Kipness a producer (*Seesaw*) who is squeezed out (*Mack & Mabel*)

Lisa Kirk a featured actress (*Mack & Mabel*)

Irwin Kostal an orchestrator who stands up to the director (*Rex*)

Terry Allen Kramer a replacement producer who throws her weight around (*Nick & Nora*)

Heidi Ettinger Landesman a set designer (*The Red Shoes*) and the wife of a theatre operator (*Nick & Nora*)

Rocco Landesman a producer who calls himself a real estate man (*Nick & Nora*)

Burton Lane a composer who wants his songs sung correctly (*On a Clear Day*)

Arthur Laurents a librettist (*Hallelujah, Baby!*) and a director/librettist (*Nick & Nora*)

Eddie Lawrence a lyricist-librettist who laughs at his own jokes (*Kelly*)

Eugene Lee a designer (*Dude*)

Michele Lee a replacement Star (*Seesaw*)

Carolyn Leigh a lyricist (*How Now, Dow Jones*)

Mitch Leigh a composer/producer who noshes (*Cry for Us All*)

Jack Lemmon a Star across the street (*Tenderloin*)

Alan Jay Lerner a lyricist-librettist-producer who summons his doctor (*On a Clear Day*)

Edwin Lester a theatre operator (*Mack & Mabel, Pickwick*)

Joseph E. Levine a producer in alligator shoes (*Kelly*)

Jerry Lewis the Star (*Hellzapoppin*)

Robert Lewis an ineffective director (*Kwamina, On a Clear Day*)

Ron Lewis a choreographer who is replaced (*The Act*)

Howard Lindsay a celebrated man of the theatre (*Skyscraper*)

John V. Lindsay a mayor playing a cameo (*Seesaw*)

Ella Logan a Star who is fired (*Kelly*)

Joshua Logan a director who declines (*Breakfast at Tiffany's*)

Louie a scene-stealing pooch (*Hellzapoppin*)

Edmund Love an eccentric author (*Subways Are for Sleeping*)

Lar Lubovitch a choreographer with a good ballet (*The Red Shoes*)

Alfred Lunt a passing-by Star (*Flying Colors*)

Gillian Lynne a choreographer who is replaced (*How Now, Dow Jones*)

Galt MacDermot a composer (*Dude*)

Richard Maltby, Jr. a lyricist (*Nick & Nora*)

Man with shovel a gravedigger (*Kelly*)

Albert Marre a director (*Cry for Us All*)

Ernest H. Martin a producer (*The Act, Skyscraper*)

Groucho Marx a man with golf clubs (*Flying Colors*)

Harpo Marx an eccentric visitor (*Flying Colors*)

Marlyn Mason a leading lady with too much makeup (*How Now, Dow Jones*)

Samuel Matlovsky a musical director (*Kelly*)

Elizabeth I. McCann a peace-making producer (*Nick & Nora*)

Thomas Meehan a librettist (*I Remember Mama*)

Daniel Melnick a producer who thinks it's getting better(*Kelly*)

Linda Rodgers Melnick a producer's wife and composer's daughter (*Kelly*)

Melina Mercouri the Star (*Illya Darling*)

David Merrick a producer who stirs things up (*Breakfast at Tiffany's, Hallelujah, Baby!, How Now, Dow Jones, Mack & Mabel, Pickwick, Subways Are for Sleeping*)

Bob Merrill a composer/lyricist (*Breakfast at Tiffany's*) and a ghost lyricist via fax (*The Red Shoes*)

Sidney Michaels a book doctor (*Pickwick*)

Liza Minnelli the Star (*The Act*)

Jerome Minskoff a producer with his own theatre (*Irene*)

Maggie Minskoff a producer (*Hellzapoppin*)

Mary Tyler Moore a star from TV-land (*Breakfast at Tiffany's*)

James M. Nederlander a producer (*Nick & Nora*)

Barry Nelson a leading man with little to do (*The Act*)

Phyllis Newman a featured player (*Subways Are for Sleeping*) and an innocent bystander (*Nick & Nora*)

Kwame Nkrumah an inspiration (*Kwamina*)

Marsha Norman a partially replaced lyricist-librettist (*The Red Shoes*)

Elliot Norton an out-of-town critic who criticizes (*Cry for Us All, Hellzapoppin*)

Clifford Odets a librettist who dies (*Golden Boy*)

Tom O'Horgan a replacement director (*Dude*)

Lester Osterman a producer who fighst his Star (*Fade Out–Fade In*)

Hugh Panaro a featured player (*The Red Shoes*)

Hildy Parks a producer's wife and co-producer (*Hellzapoppin, I Remember Mama*)

Arthur Penn a replacement director (*Golden Boy*) who is replaced (*How Now, Dow Jones*)

James Pentecost a budding producer (*Nick & Nora*)

Bernadette Peters a Star (*Mack & Mabel*)

Brock Peters an actor who doesn't get the lead (*Kwamina*)

Jane Powell a Star replacement (*Irene*)

Robert Preston a Star (*Mack & Mabel*)

Harold Prince a doctor (*Rex*) and a producer (*Tenderloin*)

James Rado a passing-by lyricist (*Dude*)

Gerome Ragni a lyricist/librettist out of control (*Dude*)

William Redfield a featured actor who is puzzled (*Dude*)

Lynn Redgrave a Star (*Hellzapoppin*)

Rex Reed a journalist who spreads the bad news (*Breakfast at Tiffany's, Irene*)

Roger Rees a leading man who is replaced (*The Red Shoes*)

Charles Nelson Reilly an actor who chews the scenery (*Skyscraper*)

Debbie Reynolds the Star (*Irene*)

Cathy Rice the director's chorus girl-girlfriend-turned-assistant choreographer (*Hellzapoppin*)

Martin Richards a producer who declines (*Nick & Nora*)

Harry Rigby a producer with expensive sweaters (*Irene*)

Marcia Rodd a leading lady who is replaced (*Mack & Mabel*)

Eileen Rodgers an actress in despair (*Kelly*)

Richard Rodgers a composer (*I Remember Mama, Rex*) who declines (*On a Clear Day*)

Herbert Ross a director/choreographer (*Kelly*) and a choreographer (*Golden Boy, On a Clear Day*)

Harvey Sabinson a long-suffering press agent (*Breakfast at Tiffany's, Fade Out–Fade In, Subways Are for Sleeping*)

Maximilian Schell a passing-by actor (*Kwamina*)

Johnny Schlesinger a friend who puts up the money (*Kwamina*)

Jack Schlissel a hardnosed general manager (*Pickwick, Subways Are for Sleeping*)

Gerald Schoenfeld a producer (*The Act*)

Susan H. Schulman a director who is replaced (*The Red Shoes*)

Arthur Schwartz a composer (*Flying Colors*)

Martin Scorsese a director who smokes a cigar (*The Act*)

Harry Secombe a Star with mumps (*Pickwick*)

Fred Segal an adman with pity (*Kelly*)
Albert Selden a producer (*Irene*)
Janie Sell an understudy who doesn't go on (*Irene*)
Doris Shapiro a production assistant and confidant (*On a Clear Day*)
Sparky Shapiro a reluctant princess (*Rex*)
Irene Sharaff a designer with questions (*Hallelujah, Baby!*)
Mickey Shaughnessy a loyal actor (*Kelly*)
Edwin Sherin a director who is replaced (*Rex, Seesaw*)
Burt Shevelove a director (*Hallelujah, Baby!*)
Neil Simon a visiting doctor (*Seesaw*)
Oliver Smith a designer (*Kelly, On a Clear Day*)
Stephen Sondheim a friend of the court (*Hallelujah, Baby!, Tenderloin*)
Leonard Spigelgass a librettist who is replaced (*Mack & Mabel*)
Martin Starger an embattled producer (*The Red Shoes*)
Joseph Stein a replacement librettist (*Irene*)
Leonard Stern a book doctor (*Kelly*)
Adlai Stevenson an inspiration (*Kwamina*)
Michael Stewart a librettist (*Mack & Mabel*) who departs (*Seesaw*)
Sandy Stewart a composer's wife (*Kelly*)
Peter Stone a librettist who rewrites (*Skyscraper*)
Charles Strouse a composer who writes more songs (*Golden Boy, Nick & Nora*)
Paul Stryker a pseudonymous lyricist (*The Red Shoes*)
Jule Styne a composer (*Fade Out–Fade In, Hallelujah Baby!, Hellzapoppin, The Red Shoes, Subways Are for Sleeping*) and a friend of the court (*Breakfast at Tiffany's*)
Charles Suisman a budding producer (*Nick & Nora*)
Dan Sullivan an out-of-town critic who criticizes (*The Act*)
David Susskind a producer from television (*Kelly*)
Tommy Tune a replacement actor/choreographer (*Seesaw*) and a doctor (*Hellzapoppin*)
Leslie Uggams a budding Star (*Hallelujah, Baby!*)
Liv Ullmann the Star (*I Remember Mama*)
Theadora van Runkle a designer who is replaced (*The Act*)
Robin Wagner a designer (*Seesaw*)
Ethel Watt a critic's wife with a canny idea (*Seesaw*)
Clifton Webb a Star who takes care of himself (*Flying Colors*)
Robert Weede a Star who loses his watch (*Cry for Us All*)
Jerome Weidman a librettist (*Tenderloin*)
Hugh Wheeler a librettist who leaves for a better musical (*Irene*)
Jesse White a featured comic who talks back (*Kelly*)

Stone (Bud) Widney a general factotum (*On a Clear Day*)
Nicol Williamson the Star (*Rex*)
Freddy Wittop a designer with rags of chiffon (*Kelly*)
Sherman Yellen a librettist (*Rex*)

When Everything Goes Wrong

The Act

Seesaw

Breakfast at Tiffany's

Dude

PLAYBILL

MAJESTIC THEATRE

"the Act"

The Act (1977)

Sweat and Sequins, Shine It On

Liza Minnelli started out in show business as the daughter of Judy
Garland, but the matter was definitively settled in 1973 when
Minnelli won an Oscar for *Cabaret* and an Emmy for *Liza with a Z*. This
was followed up by two poor films, *Lucky Lady* (1975) and *Somewhere
in Time* (1976, directed by her father Vincente Minnelli). A third
screen disaster, the monumental *New York, New York*, opened two
weeks before the first performance in Chicago of the show that
became *The Act*.

Minnelli's fame was nevertheless undiminished, and at the time
she was arguably the biggest box office name along Broadway. *The Act*
was a custom-fitted vehicle for Liza. The score was in the trusted
hands of John Kander and Fred Ebb, who wrote Minnelli's 1965
breakthrough musical *Flora, the Red Menace* (for which she nabbed her
first Tony Award) as well as *Cabaret* and *Liza with a Z*. Broadway
wiseacres dubbed her new show "Liza with a Zero," and they didn't
mean Mostel. But let's go back a few steps with journalist Cliff Jahr,
who followed the tryout for the *New York Times*.

Liza reached town with a new title and new artwork, by Joe Eula.

"In *The Act*, The Drama Backstage Is Not An Act"
by Cliff Jahr

Next Saturday night Liza Minnelli's new musical *The Act* opens at the Majestic, thus bringing to a close one of the most rumored and casualty-prone road tryouts Broadway has seen in several years—a tryout, ironically, that can boast not one but two backstage melodramas, the first one played on-stage, the second one, off.

Since the show's single dress rehearsal on the Fourth of July in Chicago, casualties have included two actors, an assistant choreographer, $92,000 worth of costumes and their designer, some $80,000 worth of scenery, one marriage, two titles (*Shine It On*, and before that, *In Person*), three songs, and most of the book. Plus the director, which is a story we'll get to.

With a ticket advance of $2 million, and half of its $1 million cost already paid back on the road, what New York critics will say may not matter much, especially since Miss Minnelli is contracted to play *The Act* for only 39 weeks. [The financial picture was not so rosy, as discussed below.] Before director Gower Champion quietly came in to doctor the show during its final month in Los Angeles—"unofficially" replacing Martin Scorsese—no one was betting *The Act* had much chance with the critics, anyway. That is, not beyond an expectation that they will admire Minnelli's razzle-dazzle performance. By closing week, however, Mr. Champion was said to have worked substantial changes and all bets are now off.

Produced by Cy Feuer and Ernest Martin (*How to Succeed in Business Without Really Trying*), the show brings home some realities. [Feuer and Martin's last two musicals had been *Skyscraper* (1965) [see page 234] and *Walking Happy* (1966). Their five Broadway shows following *How to Succeed* all failed.]

Item: Rising costs have pushed its Saturday night orchestra seats to a record $25. [This broke *Annie*'s $20-top.]

Item: Partly because regional and subscription theatre have grown while the influence of drama critics has diminished, *The Act* has been able to play a longish 15-week sellout tour through Chicago, San Francisco and Los Angeles, in the face of poor notices. (KNBC-TV in Los Angeles said, "After three hours, not only does the show need a new book, you need a new backside.") Two-thirds of the audience in San Francisco and Los Angeles was made up of Civic Light Opera members who were locked in months ago when they renewed their season's subscription. [Feuer and Martin ran the Civic Light Opera, which explains the unusual pre-Broadway route of *The Act*. Feuer and Martin were billed as producers, while the Shubert Organization—which shared financial responsibility—was billed as presenters.]

Item: While Hollywood is gingerly trying out movies like *Julia* and *Looking for Mr. Goodbar*, which speak to feminist concerns for more films about women, the new season's first likely musical hit offers the biggest, brassiest woman's role since *Hello, Dolly!* Bigger. Miss Minnelli plays Michelle Craig, a monomaniacal, sexually self-confident woman, who belts out 12 of the show's 13 songs. With a token assist from Barry Nelson and the company of 10, she dominates center stage, ducking off only twice all evening to change the color of her Halston pants outfits.

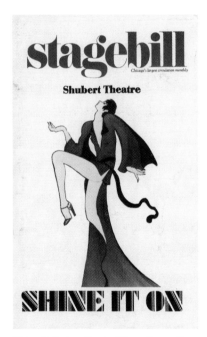

Shine It On has flop written all over it, don't you think?

If there's a point *The Act* underscores most, it's that Miss Minnelli on Broadway has incomparable star power, her box-office pull recalling the days of Ethel Merman and Mary Martin. Film and nightclub stars like Shirley MacLaine, Debbie Reynolds and Bette Midler fill seats, but so far they have chosen to play Broadway once or twice, while this is Miss Minnelli's fourth time up. She won the Tony for *Flora the Red Menace*, in 1965, played a two-week sellout concert at the Winter Garden in 1973, and reversed the slipping grosses of *Chicago* two years ago when she stepped in for an ailing Gwen Verdon.

Miss Minnelli is a manic overachiever, and *The Act* is an attempt to synthesize everything she's done so far: sing, dance and act in a vehicle which is both a concert and a book musical, with its settings in Hollywood and Las Vegas, mobilized on a Broadway stage. Half of the show is a straightforward Vegas act, written by John Kander and Fred Ebb, which portrays the nightclub debut of Michelle Craig, a 32-year-old former star of early 60s movie musicals. The other half by George Furth (*Company*) is a backstage saga told in flashbacks of her rise to and fall from fame, complete with a comeback, accomplished with varying degrees of help from a producer-husband, a lover and a song-writer confidant.

If the Craig biography is too scrambled to come off as unabashed *roman à clef*, its art still imitates the life of several recognizable stars.

SHUBERT THEATRE
Gerald Schoenfeld, *Chairman* 🄰 A Shubert Organization Theatre Bernard B. Jacobs, *President*

THE SHUBERT ORGANIZATION
presents
A FEUER & MARTIN PRODUCTION

LIZA MINNELLI
in the New Musical Play
"SHINE IT ON"
also starring
BARRY NELSON
with
LEONARD GAINES   GAYLE CROFOOT
and
MARK GODDARD

Claudia Asbury   Christopher Barrett   Wayne Clinato   Carol Estey   Michael Leeds
Roger Minami   Laurie Dawn Skinner   Albert Stephenson   Brad Witsger

Book by
GEORGE FURTH

Music by   Lyrics by
JOHN KANDER   **FRED EBB**

Scenery Designed by   Costumes Designed by   Lighting Designed by
TONY WALTON   **THEA VAN RUNKLE**   **THARON MUSSER**

Musical Direction   Orchestrations   Dance Arrangements   Vocal & Choral Arrangements
STANLEY LEBOWSKY **RALPH BURNS** **RONALD MELROSE** **EARL BROWN**

Miss Minnelli's Hairstyle   Sound Design   Production Stage Manager
SYDNEY GUILAROFF   **ABE JACOB**   **PHIL FRIEDMAN**

Choreography by
RON LEWIS

Directed by
MARTIN SCORSESE

6

Liza's billing is more prominent than the title. The first featured player, costume designer, and director were all gone by the time the show hit Broadway.

Mostly it calls to mind Miss Minnelli, or Shirley MacLaine, or Ann-Margret, all vaguely by way of Judy Garland. As it is smorgasbord, you can take your pick. Two years ago, when Mr. Furth was showing the book around to producers, working then with songwriter Marvin Hamlisch (*A Chorus Line*), the part was for a 40-ish woman and any number were mentioned, including Mary Tyler Moore, Doris Day, Debbie Reynolds and Cloris Leachman. Finally, it was offered to Shirley MacLaine.

But in mid-1976 when Miss Minnelli was filming *New York, New York,* for director Martin Scorsese, she asked for the part and got it. It seems Mr. Kander and Mr. Ebb were lined up to do the score now, and over the years they had written some 17 shows and acts for her, including *Cabaret,* for which all three won Oscars, with Mr. Feuer and Mr. Martin producing. [This was the film version of *Cabaret.* Harold Prince, who produced and directed the 1966 stage version, rejected Kander and Ebb's choice for Sally Bowles, because she didn't seem British and he thought she sang too well to play the not-very-talented character.]

It looked to be clear sailing again for the old team. The part was made younger, 32, Miss Minnelli's age. Also she wanted Mr. Scorsese to direct, and the team went along. Mr. Scorsese is one of the hottest film directors around since *Mean Streets* and *Taxi Driver,* but he lacked theatre experience and admitted he hadn't even seen much of it. His youth had been spent in movie balconies.

Rehearsals began in Los Angeles last May and it was tough going from the start. While Miss Minnelli worked on Kander and Ebb's songs and the dances created by Las Vegas choreographer Ron Lewis, Mr. Scorsese's time was split three ways: final polishing of *New York,*

New York, editing a rock documentary called *The Last Waltz*, and directing the show.

Designers despaired of having too little time with Mr. Scorsese to discuss their plans—only 15-minute meetings on the run—so it came as no surprise when their uncoordinated efforts at the Chicago opening were roundly disliked. In time the sets and lighting would be worked out, but Theadora Van Runkle's costumes seemed so misguided that they were scrapped at once. [This was the first and only Broadway credit of film designer Van Runkle, who did the costumes for *New York, New York*.] One critic described them as "sadistic," no doubt thinking of her crepe gown with a cutout circle exposing one side of Miss Minnelli's short waist—not her best feature. Or another that wrapped in gathers at the waist, when it wasn't unwrapping.

Halston was quickly summoned to redo all the costumes, as meanwhile Miss Minnelli got by on stage with Halstons out of her closet. The new designs costing $100,000 (plus fee) are simple and monochromatic, with all of Miss Minnelli's clothes shimmering with sequins.

But the show faced much tougher problems, stemming in part from Mr. Scorsese's overall conception. Early on, he had toyed with the idea of shaping *The Act*'s Michelle Craig as a continuation of *New York, New York*'s Francine Evans, the big-band vocalist role Miss Minnelli played. "It picks up the singer 10 years later," he said, "when she's alienated from the people around her. She ends up alone, but she's still working." Although he came to abandon the idea, partly because it would have Craig/Minnelli nearing age 50, Mr. Scorsese clearly meant to carry over the film's nearly operatic gloom. ("Now he thinks he's a stage auteur," one observer sniped.)

The flashbacks, as painful memories, were played downstage before backdrops on a black-painted floor. At one point he spoke of having Barry Nelson and the other actors in black leather, but settled for dark fabrics. Since these dimly lighted scenes dealt with quarrels, a fistfight, abortion, infidelity, bankruptcy, death, and so on—all of them totally unrelated to the nightclub act they interrupted—audiences came to dread them. Moreover, since Michelle Craig sometimes pattered to her audience as if they were in a Las Vegas nightclub, people got lost trying to sort reality from flashback.

The *Chicago Tribune*'s Linda Winer wondered if Miss Minnelli hadn't better things to do. Two weeks later the *San Francisco Examiner*'s Stanley Eichelbaum saluted Miss Minnelli, but called for "major overhauling." [The decision had already been made to change the title from *In Person*—which indicated a personal appearance rather than a new, fullscale musical—to *The Act*. San Francisco's American Conservatory

Theatre is commonly referred to as the A.C.T., so the producers opted to use *Shine it On*—a song-title—for the Frisco engagement.]

On opening night in San Francisco, two men slid into side aisle seats in the 23d row after the house-lights dimmed. They were directors Michael Bennett (*A Chorus Line*) and Ron Field (*Applause*). They had been invited by the Shubert Organization, major backers and owners of the Majestic where *The Act* would play, to have a look and quietly return comment. At intermission one of them was recognized, which next day prompted Mr. Feuer and Mr. Martin to invite them for a chat. Both agreed, and after the initial meeting, there followed six friendly bull-sessions in Mr. Bennett's hotel suite attended by the star, director, writers, choreographer and producers. Mr. Bennett and Mr. Field extemporized ways to brighten up the show, with the meeting ending up in hugs and kisses as dawn came in the window. Afterward Mr. Scorsese is said to have remarked, "Gee, this is so painful," to which someone cheerfully replied, "Marty, a wise man once said that if Hitler were alive today, they wished he were out of town as the director of a musical in trouble." [This was not some "wise man," but playwright/librettist Larry Gelbart. When Bob Fosse was fired in Washington from *The Conquering Hero* (1961)—a show which he directed, choreographed, and came up with the idea for in the first place—Gelbart said, "If Hitler's alive, I hope he's out-of-town with a musical."]

In the following weeks, though Mr. Scorsese installed some cuts and laughs, lightened the show's mood a bit, even painted the floor red, his meticulous cinematic work methods weren't fast enough to please anybody. "He's a terrific little guy," said Mr. Feuer in his Los Angeles office last week, "a film genius, but, um, this is theatre."

By now Mr. Feuer and Mr. Martin had eyes on other directors, especially Michael Bennett or Bob Fosse (*Cabaret* and *Chicago*) but Miss Minnelli stood firmly behind Mr. Scorsese. "If Marty goes," she reportedly said, "I go too," though she flatly denies this. While Miss Minnelli is known for being fiercely loyal to friends, especially her directors, in the case of Mr. Scorsese there have been rumors of a romance that dates back to the early days of shooting *New York, New York*. Now gossip-column reports of hand-holding in San Francisco restaurants and private film screenings in Berkeley only added to the company's growing unease about a lack of control and expertise at the top. There were mutterings at rehearsals, especially about Mr. Scorsese's absence at performances. [Scorsese was said to spend performances not in the house, taking notes with a sharp pencil, but in the star's dressing room with a long cigar.]

Still there was hope. On closing night in San Francisco, after Mr.

Scorsese had spent six weeks of hard trying, critic Stanley Eichelbaum on a second look found things "tighter, springier, and more enjoyable."

Then two bombshells dropped. The morning after the Los Angeles opening, the *Los Angeles Times* critic, Dan Sullivan expressed the general consensus when he wondered if he had just seen "the dumbest backstage musical ever, to the point where you figure they've got to be kidding." [Sullivan also said that *The Act* "looked more like the rehearsal."]

On the very same day it was announced that Julia Cameron, Scorsese's wife, had filed suit for divorce.

Beset by difficulties and other commitments from all sides, now, the director had to think of stepping down. Three weeks later when he was laid up with asthma, director Gower Champion was hired on with both Mr. Scorsese's and Miss Minnelli's agreement. A low-key announcement was given to the trade press citing the illness. "It was handy," notes Mr. Feuer, "so we used it."

Mr. Champion caught the Saturday matinee and evening shows Sept. 24, rehearsed the company on Sunday, and inserted several changes Monday night. Gone suddenly were eleven minutes worth of the overture, the abortion scene, a scene where Michelle Craig is slapped around by her lover until she subdues him with karate, and a pair of scenes in which she twice loses the Academy Award. At the same performance Mr. Champion put in a new opening, a tag on the second act show-stopper "City Lights," and a number of minor adjustments to lighten and simplify. Though he has

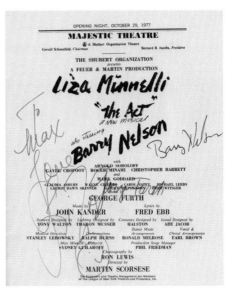

Martin Scorsese retained credit as director, although it was common knowledge that he was replaced by Gower Champion.

taken full charge and continues the process, his name will not appear in the credits. As this article goes to press, Mr. Scorsese is in Rome discussing a film about street gangs, with plans to return to New York for the opening. [The film discussion was apparently about *The Gangs of New York*, which took more than twenty years to get before the cameras.] He and Mr. Champion have closed ranks and refuse interviews. "I inherited a sick child," said Mr. Champion, "and I can't talk about it right now."

"So what's the big secret?" said an observer. "Directors are replaced every day. The way he's hiding out, you'd think Scorsese had committed mass murder or something."

"I had nothing to do with Marty going," Liza Minnelli is saying, stretched out on her dressing-room sofa in Los Angeles. "Marty did it. He came in. He said, 'I know you're going to trust me. I will not let you open in New York as anything less than superb. You've never worked with Gower, but we need help. It's a technique I know nothing about, but nobody is telling me. Gower can add something terrific. I want the very best for you.'" She takes a cigarette from her orange terry robe and lights it slowly. "It's not like Marty stormed off somewhere in an Italian rage. The show is still on his mind. Everything is very amiable, and the vibes are very, very good. He's even giving a cast party in New York."

Why, then, so much secrecy? "Everybody is rumor-shy now," she says. "This goddam production. You can't make a move, and they turn it into a big Federal deal. I've never seen publicity on a Broadway show like this, have you? About those rumors. There's a wonderful line in *Cabaret*: 'Sex always screws up a friendship.' Marty is my closest friend in the world, my closest ally—besides my husband—and guiding force and I wouldn't want to destroy that." She takes a long drag from the cigarette and looks into the mirror. "Six days. Six days to New York."

The Act opened October 29, 1977 at the Majestic Theatre to mixed-to-unfavorable reviews. It closed there July 1, 1978 after 233 performances, with a sizable loss.

And so *The Act* finally made it to Broadway. Feuer foresaw the Broadway reception: "I'm going to go there and get the hell kicked out of me by all of the newspapers and then do great business anyway." Librettist Furth was also outspoken. "Don't blame us for the shape the show is in, it's all Scorsese's fault," he said. "Gower has had only three weeks to repair the damage Scorsese did."

This didn't prevent Furth from suing the producers for a cool million, protesting an involuntary royalty reduction to help pay for Champion. Furth, Kander, Ebb and Minnelli, meanwhile, were sued for two million by Hollywood director Stanley Donen, who claimed that he had brought them all together for the project. [see *The Red Shoes*, page 302]

Champion did not, indeed, take director billing on the show, but the word around town was that he followed Scorsese in more ways than one. Gower ultimately stepped in to play Minnelli's husband—not her real husband (Jack Haley Jr. who soon divorced her), but her stage husband Barry Nelson (in a hapless role). Liza's next real-life husband was the assistant stage manager of *The Act*; his father had been the assistant stage manager of *Flora, the Red Menace*, read into that what you will.

As mentioned in Cliff Jahr's article, *The Act* managed to accumulate tryout profits of approximately $450,000, which appears to equal half of its $900,000 capitalization. But out-of-town fixings don't come cheap. The non-stop tinkering with the show, not to mention a completely new set of expensive costumes, added an additional $320,000 to the production costs; thus, *The Act* came to Broadway with $770,000 left to recover. Which it well might have, given smash business at the new $25-top.

But Minnelli was in erratic shape (which will come as no surprise to anyone who reads the tabloids). The star started missing performances; all told, she missed twenty-six shows, more than ten percent of the entire Broadway run. To accommodate Minnelli, the work week was cut from eight to seven performances, and then to six. And then there were none. "This is one the Shubert Organization is not going to get rich from," said Shubert Chairman Gerry Schoenfeld.

Even so, and despite it all, Liza won that season's Tony Award for Best Actress. Her only real competition was Madeline Kahn, of *On the Twentieth Century* across the street. Kahn, who also missed performances on a wholesale basis, was more expendable than superstar Minnelli. Despite rave personal reviews, the producers replaced Kahn with Judy Kaye. They unsuccessfully petitioned the Tony Award committee to make replacement Kaye eligible in place of Kahn. This move, not surprisingly, destroyed Madeline's chances and sent the votes to Liza. At least, she was still appearing in the show. Usually.

PLAYBILL
MAGAZINE

URIS
THEATRE

seesaw

Seesaw (1973)

It's Not Where You Start

A seesaw, by definition, has its ups and downs. The musical *Seesaw* underwent an almost total overhaul en route to Broadway. A Herculean job was done by Michael Bennett and his associates, and duly appreciated by the critics and the industry. But were the root problems fixable? Was the transformation, a painfully torturous and wildly expensive procedure, worth it? Patricia Bosworth told the tale—laced with quotes from the parties in question, taken in the heat of the battle—in the *New York Times*.

Nebraska lawyer Jerry Ryan balances on a crazy seesaw opposite dancer Gittel Mosca and other barefooted New York artistes in Frederic Marvin's artwork.

"The Fight to Save *Seesaw*"
by Patricia Bosworth

The new Broadway musical, *Seesaw*, opened at the Uris Theatre Sunday, March 19, to a standing ovation from the audience and solid reviews from the critics. But the next morning producer Lawrence Kasha sat in his office chewing on valium while his partner, Joseph Kipness, also known as "Cryin' Joe," cried. Then they did what they had to do—they posted the closing notice for *Seesaw* on the backstage bulletin board. It would close the next Saturday, after nine performances.

Since November 1972, Kasha and Kipness had spent one million dollars on *Seesaw*. Now there was not a penny left to run the show; not even money set aside for posters or "quote" ads to inform the public that, as critic Martin Gottfried said, "*Seesaw* is the kind of Broadway theatre that can't be duplicated on movie or television screens."

That glum Monday it looked as if *Seesaw* would become another in the increasing number of Broadway shows that open and close almost instantaneously, their producers unwilling or unable to fight, despite the real merits some of the shows possess. So far this season, seventeen have folded after twelve or less performances.

[The list: *From Israel with Love* (10), *Hurry, Harry* (2), *Pacific Paradise* (5), *Mother Earth* (12), *The Lincoln Mask* starring Eva Marie Saint and Fred Gwynne (8), *Lysistrata* starring Melina Mercouri (8), *Ambassador* starring Howard Keel (9), *Via Galactica* (7), *Tricks* (8), *Let Me Hear You Smile* starring Sandy Dennis (1), *Warp* (8), and *Status Quo Vadis* (1). This is only twelve, although you get sixteen if you include shows that lasted up to sixteen performances (two weeks), the additional items being *Dude* (see page 56) (16), a revival of *Purlie* (14), *No Sex Please, We're British* (14) and Tennessee Williams's *Out Cry* (13). And there were two additional musicals that closed during pre-Broadway tryouts, *Halloween* and *Comedy*.]

"Theatre people don't have the commitment to legit the way they used to," says an oldtime press agent. "It's too expensive."

However, some producers are still committed to Broadway—Larry Kasha and Joe Kipness among them. [Kasha and Kipness had coproduced the 1970 hit *Applause* and the 1972 flop *Inner City*. Kasha was a stage manager (*How to Succeed*) turned director (*Bajour*), who had served as associate producer of *She Loves Me*. Kipness was a garbage man turned restaurateur, known for Kippy's, Joe's Pier 52 (which was given a plug in a *Seesaw* song "My City," albeit sung by hookers), and his mob connections. *Seesaw* was his sixteenth of twenty-five productions, with three hits (*High Button Shoes*, *La Plume de Ma Tante*, and *Applause*) sprinkled among the flops.] This is the story of how these two producers fought to keep *Seesaw* open—with the help of their cast, their crew, not to mention the management of the Uris Theatre. "We just couldn't let that beaut of a show die," exclaimed Kipness. [Kipness and Kasha were only two of the four producers given equal billing above the title, the other two being moneymen James M. Nederlander and his sometime-partner George M. Steinbrenner III.]

So early on Tuesday morning he sold one of his $30,000 shares in the show, taking an immediate loss of $10,000 to raise cash to pay some pressing production bills. Meanwhile Kasha got on the phone to backers.

Raising new money to keep *Seesaw* alive wasn't easy. The show had originally been budgeted at $750,000 but had gone $400,000 over the budget. It needed to take in $60,000 a week to break even, and in its last week of previews had taken in only $17,539. But *Seesaw* lyricist Dorothy Fields put up $30,000 of her own money so that the Saturday night closing notice could come down and *Seesaw* director Michael Bennett, a 29-year-old former chorus boy who's been called "the new Jerry Robbins," rallied business associates in his apartment and they also started manning phones. Together with *Seesaw* composer Cy Coleman, they scraped up $6,000 to do spot commercials of Rex Reed's glowing tribute to *Seesaw* on radio.

By Wednesday the *Seesaw* company got involved, and just before the matinee, led by dancer Tommy Tune, they performed numbers from the musical in front of the Uris Building on Broadway, while stagehands and musicians passed out *Seesaw* flyers to pedestrians. "Stagehands demonstrating to keep a show open—can you believe?" Joe Kipness demanded, and he cried afresh. The fight to save *Seesaw*, greatly aided by the boosts given it by Earl Wilson every day in his *New York Post* column, culminated in a brilliant publicity gimmick thought up by Ethel Watt, wife of *Daily News* drama critic Douglas Watt, and a staunch admirer of the show. She asked Mayor Lindsay to appear on stage during the Friday night performance. Amid cheers from the audience, the Mayor made his entrance with *Seesaw* star and Lindsay-look-alike Ken Howard on the gaudy Times Square set. As the chorus went into its rousing first number, "My City," Lindsay stood center stage and made quips at the dancers strutting about as Broadway streetwalkers.

Afterwards, TV and news cameras were backstage to catch the Mayor telling reporters he was at the theatre to promote Broadway and tourism—"and I had a good time doing it." (The stagehands, who must be present and paid when anyone is photographed inside a theatre, forfeited their $3,000 fee. Several of them said they were doing it because their wives loved *Seesaw* and wanted to see it last.)

The morning after the Mayor's appearance, the Uris Theatre had an encouraging line at the box office, and the phones rang incessantly. "We did $21,000 worth of ticket orders that morning," composer Coleman said.

In its first week of performances *Seesaw* grossed $55,241, a big jump from the dismal last week of previews. In its second week, the gross was $60,794, at last topping the $60,000 breakeven figure. [*Seesaw* would prove unable to maintain that pace, alas, as discussed below.]

When I asked Coleman why this particular musical had prompted such strong support, from stagehands to producers, he smiled and said, "We had all worked so long and so hard. It seemed ridiculous to give up just because we needed more dough. Out of town we had real problems—problems—and we solved them. Why couldn't we solve this? The main reason *Seesaw* has succeeded artistically, and now commercially, is that six weeks ago a group of us banded together and worked with love and complete trust. No egos were involved. The behind-the-scenes story of *Seesaw* is terribly corny," he went on. "Like an MGM musical circa 1948. It's hard to believe that what happened in Detroit and during previews could happen, particularly in this day and age when everybody is so cynical and out for himself. It's been a very profound experience for all of us."

And with that, he and Larry Kasha and Michael Bennett proceeded to tell me what happened.

Seesaw, starring *zaftig* nightclub singer Lainie Kazan as bohemian dancer Gittel Mosca and Ken Howard as WASP Nebraska lawyer Jerry Ryan, began rehearsals under Edwin Sherin's direction on November 20, 1972. It was, of course, based on *Two for the Seesaw*, the 1958 dramatic hit by William Gibson in which Anne Bancroft and Henry Fonda were Gittel and Jerry—and the play's entire cast. According to Kasha, Miss Kazan had trouble learning her lines so Sherin spent hours working with her on the part. [Kazan, a singer in *The Happiest Girl in the World* (1961) and *Bravo Giovanni* (1962), attracted notice when she stood by for Barbra Streisand in *Funny Girl* (1964), a show on which Kasha served as assistant director.] In time, they quarreled violently over interpretation. While this was going on, Ken Howard was virtually ignored, as were other important aspects of the production, such as integrating musical numbers with the story, and allotting time for orchestrations.

Four weeks into rehearsal, Kasha and Kipness knew something was wrong. "Nothing was coming together," Kasha said. "I don't want to knock Ed Sherin," he continued, "he's a big talent and he did a great job on *The Great White Hope*. But he'd never done a musical before. The technical stuff was mammoth. It snowed him." [For Sherin's next musical, see *Rex*, page 290.]

Eventually the cast got edgy, spirits were anything but bright. "Let's be frank about this," a singer told me. "We were depressed out of our minds." Then, three days before the show went out of town, a representative from Columbia Records (Columbia was to record the show) came to rehearsal, uninvited. He watched a few numbers and also happened upon an ugly fight between Miss Kazan and Sherin. The following day Columbia bowed out of the record deal. "It was a low blow and totally unprecedented," Coleman said. "No show has ever been judged creatively or musically at that stage of the game."

By the time *Seesaw* opened its tryout at the Fisher Theatre in Detroit last Jan. 16, half the company had London flu; hysteria and confusion reigned. The show was praised for its energetic dancing and "suavely eclectic" music but criticized for its length (Act One had twenty-three scenes). The direction "lacked variety," said the *Detroit News*, and the *Windsor Star* called Lainie Kazan "totally miscast" as Gittel. The consensus of opinion was that she didn't look like a dancer or move like a dancer. She was also some 40 pounds overweight.

"When we cast Lainie, she promised she'd lose those 40 pounds," Coleman recalled. "She said she'd have it written into her contract that if she didn't lose the weight, we could fire her. Unfortunately we never checked to see if that stipulation was in the contract."

After much deliberation with Coleman, bookwriter Michael Stewart and lyricist Dorothy Fields, co-producer Kasha decided Miss Kazan must go. "She was working like a demon but she never totally learned her role," Kasha said. "Also I knew nobody in New York would believe she was a dancer." He phoned Michele Lee to see if she'd be interested in taking over as Gittel. Miss Lee, a slender feisty brunette who'd been in both the stage and screen versions of *How to Succeed in Business Without Really Trying*, said maybe. She'd catch the show on her way from Los Angeles to New York to do an Ed Sullivan special.

While Miss Lee was considering, Kasha phoned Michael Bennett.

Bennett was in California doing preparatory work on a new musical but he agreed to fly to Detroit and give his opinion. After seeing the show, he refused to take over as "artistic director." "Absolutely not. Not enough time. I will not, under any condition."

He kept saying no throughout a series of emotionally charged meetings with Kipness, Sherin, Coleman and Michael Stewart. At the last meeting, Kipness suddenly broke down and sobbed, "Every time a Broadway show dies, Broadway dies a little more. If you really care about Broadway, you'll take over *Seesaw*. It's your duty."

Bennett wavered. "I'm a sucker for Broadway too," he admitted to me. "That razzle-dazzle fantasy, that incredible promise of entertainment. The laughs. Since I knew precisely how to stage a singing and dancing show, I finally said yes."

However, he set two conditions. The only way he could save the show was by starting fresh. New cast, new sets, new orchestrations, new costumes. And he insisted on complete artistic control. "I'm the boss."

His terms were instantly agreed upon by everyone, whereupon Ed Sherin bowed out as director. As Kipness put it, "You cannot have two kings on one horse."

In between these sessions, Kasha flew to New York and during a five-hour dinner convinced Miss Lee to play Gittel. So now it was up to Michael Bennett to fire Lainie Kazan. "Actually, everybody agreed she must go. It wasn't solely my decision." However, when told her weight had proved the biggest problem, Miss Kazan threw a tantrum that Bennett will not soon forget.

After Miss Kazan left, "we discovered Joe Kipness had been too gallant to put the weight clause in the contract," Coleman said. "So we were stuck with paying her $3,000 a week for the run of the play."

At that point the production had no money to spare. Hence Coleman, Stewart, Fields, and Kasha have each been paying a fourth of her salary. "We didn't have to," Coleman said. "We didn't have to do a lot of things we did. Thank God, she's gone into another show. Now we only have to fork out $1,500 a week!" [Kazan went into Morton Da Costa's ill-assembled star-studded revival of *The Women*, but withdrew during rehearsals.]

Once in rehearsal, Bennett maintained that his only obstacle in revamping *Seesaw* was time. It was now Jan. 22; the musical was scheduled to open on Broadway March 3. "I did in six weeks what would ordinarily take me a year to conceive. I worked a year on *Follies* with Hal Prince, a year on *Company*. When I choreographed *Coco*, I lived in Paris for months watching Chanel work. Even at eighty-eight she was totally obsessed with her work. I'm totally obsessed."

Those last two weeks in Detroit, Bennett moved like a whirlwind, concocting a new *Seesaw* in hotel rooms around the city. "He had brought his three assistants from New York," Kasha recalled. "Everything was organized down to the second. Michael knew exactly what he wanted to do."

"The show had to move," Bennett said. "To be as fluid as a movie. That was my image. Film. No conventional exits or entrances. Everything was integrated, blending together. I even cued in the graffiti and neon sign projections like dances. Part of Sherin's concept had been to have the chorus push fake brick sets on and off the stage. That slowed down the musical's pace terribly. So I had Robin Wagner build new sets which glided on and off so softly you hardly noticed them. [Bennett and Wagner had first experimented with choreographed scenic moves on the 1968 musical *Promises! Promises!* Wagner served as a critical part of Bennett's team on his three remaining musicals, *A Chorus Line, Ballroom, and Dreamgirls.*] I also wanted a specific visual look so Ann Roth designed new costumes—all white for the first number, beige for the second, deep red for the third." The new sets cost $100,000; the new costumes cost about $80,000.

Subsequently Bennett fired 10 members from the chorus, replacing them with dancers he'd worked with in other musicals, dancers who "looked right" for the show. "*Seesaw* had to have a very specific New York look." He then phoned Tommy Tune, whom he'd worked with in A *Joyful Noise*, and asked him to help choreograph *Seesaw*. I said, 'You're going to have to do everything in a week. It's like stock.'"

URIS THEATRE
Under the direction of James and Joseph Nederlander and Gerard Oestreicher

JOSEPH KIPNESS and LAWRENCE KASHA
JAMES NEDERLANDER, GEORGE M. STEINBRENNER III and
LORIN E. PRICE

present

**MICHELE KEN
LEE HOWARD**

IN

seesaw

A NEW MUSICAL
Book by
MICHAEL STEWART
Music by
CY COLEMAN
Lyrics by
DOROTHY FIELDS
Based on the play "Two For The Seesaw" by
WILLIAM GIBSON
with

JOSHIE JO ARMSTEAD   TOMMY TUNE

Scenic Design by   *Costumes by*   *Lighting by*
ROBIN WAGNER   ANN ROTH   JULES FISHER
Musical Director   *Media Designs*
and Vocal Arrangements by   *Orchestrations by*   *and Photography by*
DON PIPPIN   LARRY FALLON   SHEPPARD KERMAN
Hairstyles   *Sound*
ERNEST ADLER   JACK SHEARING
Production Associate   *Production Stage Manager*
CHARLOTTE DICKER   ROBERT BOROD
Associate Choreographers
BOB AVIAN & TOMMY TUNE
Co-choreographer
GROVER DALE
Entire Production Directed and Choreographed by
MICHAEL BENNETT

The early New York program previews still credited librettist Michael Stewart.

The 28-year-old Tune is a 6-foot-6-inch dancer who's considered "the best tapper in the business," according to Bennett. "Tommy had just finished directing Adolph Zukor's 100th birthday party show in Hollywood so he was full of ideas. But I wanted him to perform, too. He's such a theatrical presence on stage. I decided he should play David in the show. He could be the bridge between the reality of Gittel and Jerry's love and the fantasy of the musical numbers."

The first night he was in Detroit, Tune stayed up till 4 A.M. tapping out "Chapter 54, Number 1909" in his hotel room. The crisp rhythm of the words (about a law statute) is now the basis of a show-stopping routine Tune performs in clogs. He also created an exuberant number to fit the show's prophetic song, "It's not where you start but where you finish." ["It's Not Where You Start" was a trunk song. Dorothy Fields had written an earlier version of the song in 1954, with altogether different music by Arthur Schwartz; it was cut during the tryout troubles of a long-forgotten musical called *By the Beautiful Sea*. "Sometimes you fly, sometimes you flop," sang a small-time vaudeville performer, "it's not where you start, it's only where you finish, and you're bound to finish on top." The Coleman-Fields version was written for *Eleanor*, an unproduced 1969 musical about the former first lady.]

The opening billing promotes Tommy Tune to the first featured slot (on a line by himself), with Michael Bennett receiving "written, directed and choreographed by" billing.

Using hundreds of colored balloons, he directed the dancers to career and whirl about the stage, each one wearing countless balloons. "Balloons are always on the brink of bursting, you never know when they are going to go pop," Tune said. "Those balloons gave the number a giddy silliness but an urgency, too." Walter Kerr called "It's Not Where You Start," "the nuttiest—and maybe just plain funniest—number I have ever seen in a musical."

Meanwhile, Bob Avian, Bennett's assistant and close friend for the last eight years—ever since they worked together as dancers in a European tour of *West Side Story*—rechoreographed some numbers while Grover Dale, *Seesaw*'s original choreographer, reworked others. Bennett would tell them what he wanted and they'd do it and then he'd edit and cut.

"He spoke to them in dance language," Kasha recalls. "Mainly communicating by looks. Or he'd say, 'Do a Betty Grable step here,' 'a lift there.' I didn't know what the hell they were talking about but I'd come back at the end of the day and there'd be three fantastic new numbers."

Bennett also managed to get the score re-orchestrated and, whenever he could, he stopped by Cy Coleman's hotel suite. [The new orchestrations were mostly by Larry Wilcox, although Larry Fallon retained sole billing.] The composer was suffering from the London flu but he and lyricist Dorothy Fields were busy writing new "character" songs for the show.

The new version of *Seesaw* cost the producers $200,000, so that at the end of the Detroit run there was not enough money to move the production to Washington, D.C., to continue the tryout. "We were forced to preview in New York, which was the worst thing we could have done," Bennett said. "Everybody in the business talks—we had terrible word of mouth in the beginning. Don't forget we'd been rehearsing the new version for only two weeks when we had that first preview at the Uris on March 2 and every show business vulture was in the audience to tear us apart."

To make matters worse, writer Michael Stewart walked out, saying he'd lost all perspective. "Which I thought was shocking," Bennett said. "It showed he had no faith in what we were trying to do. He could have waited for a few more previews."

Stewart later refused to take credit for the book in the program so finally Bennett did, although he says, "everybody rewrote—Michele Lee, Ken Howard, Cy Coleman, Dorothy Fields, myself."

But the book was still impossibly long. Enter Neil Simon. The playwright is an old friend of Bennett's and Coleman's. [Coleman had collaborated with Simon on *Little Me* (1962) and *Sweet Charity* (1966), while Bennett had choreographed Simon's *Promises, Promises* (1968).] During the first week of previews, the two men phoned Simon and asked him to see the show. "Why?" Simon purportedly asked. "Because we need you to help us cut." Simon answered, "I'd love to. Nobody cuts a show better than I do."

Simon came to one performance but his appearance caused a great deal of gossip. "As soon as Neil enters a theatre, it's assumed he's there to rewrite," Coleman said. "But he didn't. He went to Michael's apartment the following day, took the script and told him what should go and what should stay. He also said the character of Jerry's wife, who appeared in one scene in the play, should be cut. But he didn't rewrite one line of dialogue."

"By the end of the second week of previews, *Seesaw* suddenly clicked," Coleman said. "Audiences began to really relate, to identify with the characters on stage. Suddenly the new songs, the new dances, the special sound equipment Michael and Dorothy and I had insisted upon and paid for ourselves, the sliding sets, the media projections of New York streets, suddenly every element melted together and rushed at us like some gorgeous, happy Technicolor musical. It was magic. What had been stiff and lifeless came bursting alive. The company was joyful. I've never seen anything like it. And we'd done it together—all of us had done it together without a tantrum—or complaint."

There was one grim note. Money had become a crucial problem. By delaying the opening—it was to have been Feb. 27 but was set back nearly three weeks—and redoing the show, Kasha and Kipness had spent one million dollars. There was nothing left. The musical was to open Saturday, March 17, when Bennett realized, "Saturday's death night. If a show opens Saturday, it can close the same night. That way the producers avoid paying the cast and crew another week's wages." Bennett personally paid the Nederlanders, who run the Uris Theatre, $15,000 so that *Seesaw* could open Sunday, March 19, which would at least enable it to last a week.

"I did it for the company," Bennett said. "I couldn't stand the thought of a closing notice backstage on opening night." To help the show further, Bennett also refused his $5,000 fee as director. "Oh well," he shrugged, "we're not in this for the money. It must be love. Wasn't it Moss Hart who said, 'The theatre is not an occupation, it's a disease?'"

Now *Seesaw* has lines at the box office and a solid advance sale. Michele Lee has settled into a new apartment with her family, Ken Howard is fighting off female fans and Michael Bennett is planning to direct more musicals and produce them as well.

Larry Kasha sits in his pink and blue office, munching on tranquilizers. He feels calmer now. If he had *Seesaw* to do over again, what would he do differently? "Frankly, I'd get stars. Superstars. Stars are economically essential on Broadway now, and this has nothing to do with the enormous talents of Michele Lee and Ken Howard. Look at Debbie Reynolds. We got much better reviews than *Irene* [see page 104] but they have a million-dollar advance."

What about future plans? Any more musicals?

"Sure," says Kasha. I'm doing an original musical with Jerry Herman and Michael Stewart next season."

Michael Stewart, the book writer for *Seesaw*, who quit during previews?

"It'll be a new show," Kasha murmurs. [See Mack and Mabel, page 124.] Then he shrugs his shoulders in an eloquent gesture that seemed to say, "And that's show business."

The following rebuttal appeared in the *New York Times* three weeks later.

"Lainie's Seesaw Side"

To the editor:

Having read Patricia Bosworth's article on *Seesaw* in the *Times* of April 8, I feel duty bound to make some reply to it.

First, let me state that I couldn't be more pleased with the success of this wonderful show, if for no other reason than the affection I feel for the entire company of actors, singers and dancers.

It is seldom that I have read a more self-serving, hypocritical collection of quotes, with their innuendoes, half-truths and distortions which have to rank with the worst kind of yellow journalism. I find this inconsistent with the fairness and impartiality of The *New York Times*.

I was chosen for the role of Gittel Mosca last November by the unanimous approval of the production and creative staff of *Seesaw*. For me, it was the realization of a lifelong dream. What could be more perfect than for a Jewish girl from Brooklyn to play a Jewish girl from Brooklyn? So much for my being "miscast."

We started rehearsals in December and what followed were, for me, some of the happiest moments I have spent in my chosen profession. This was in spite of the unrelenting pressures of 16- and 17-hour days which included mornings of dance lessons before rehearsals began, singing lessons during my lunch hours, costume fittings whenever they could be squeezed in and, after a day's rehearsal (ending as late as 10 or 11 p.m.), being massaged and "wrapped," to help me (along with a rigid diet) to successfully lose the weight I had gained during my pregnancy and recent illness.

Those days, with their high emotional content, occasionally boiled over into fierce arguments and disagreements. Reading Ms. Bosworth's article, the gentlemen quoted would have one believe that such occurrences were something new in their experiences in the theatre. As if it were possible to collect in one place a variegated group of talented, creative and temperamental artists and expect everything to be sweetness and light!

I was contracted to play in *Seesaw* for eighteen months (until June 1974). This was at the insistence of the producers, who would not accept me on the basis of only a one-year contract. The contract was signed in good faith by both parties. When the producers elected to replace me, they were legally bound to pay my weekly salary until the contract expired. They were not, as Cy Coleman so snidely put it, doing me any favors. The irony is that I was persuaded to make a settlement in lieu of my contract and I am still awaiting payment, forcing me into the undignified position of having to commence legal proceedings. So much for the dignity of the theatre.

I have never blamed people for beating their own drums, having done it myself with some success for the past few years—but not, as in this case, to the detriment of other people. The implication that an argument during a rehearsal could influence a recording executive's decision for or against the recording of an original cast album is beyond my comprehension. It is common knowledge that the decision of a record company to record an original cast album is usually predicated on the quality of the musical score.

The tantrum which Michael Bennett was witness to must have taken place in the "twilight zone." The only meeting we had—at my request—lasted approximately 10 minutes, wherein he informed me that he considered me unsuitable for the conception he had of the role and I, in my turn, told him how much I wanted the part and asked if he would keep an open mind and see as many of the performances as I still had to do. It should be noted that I continued to play Gittel for two weeks after I had been given my notice.

The references to Ed Sherin and Michael Stewart will surely come back to haunt the arrogant men who made them. With a callous disregard for all human decency, these gentlemen have indulged in malicious gossip, slighting those who were associated with the original show, which serves only to show their desperation in achieving their objectives regardless of cost or methods involved. We all pay homage to the maxim, "The play is the thing," but I cannot believe that the price we pay has to include the loss of human dignity.

Having suffered so much emotionally from the horrendous experience of *Seesaw*, I took a part immediately in another Broadway vehicle, *The Women*, for which I now feel I was totally miscast. Let me state that I left *The Women* for this reason and with mutual understanding and agreement between myself and producers Jeremy Ritzer and Joel Rice and director Morton Da Costa, and with a great feeling of good will.

Lainie Kazan, New York City

Seesaw opened March 18, 1973 at the Uris Theatre, to favorable-to-mixed reviews. It transferred to the Mark Hellinger on August 1, and closed there December 8, 1973 after 296 performances, with a total loss.

The picture presented in Patricia Bosworth's article, which was published two weeks after the Broadway opening, was on the rose-colored side. The cameo appearance by Mayor John Lindsay on March 23 generated a great deal of publicity and a moderate bounce at the box office, but the upturn was shortlived. As with *Skyscraper* [see page 234], the reviewers, taking the circumstances into account, tended to praise the better things while only lightly carping on the weaknesses. This did not fool the public, however, which spread a mixed- to negative-word-of-mouth.

Tony Award exposure might well have helped, but due to the delayed opening, *Seesaw* just missed that year's early cut-off date. *A Little Night Music*, *Pippin*, *Sugar*, and *Irene* battled it out for the awards in April. By the time *Seesaw* eventually won its two Tonys in 1974, for choreographer Bennett and featured actor Tommy Tune, it had been closed for five months.

Seesaw, which was originally capitalized at $750,000, cost about $1,100,000 to open. Grosses settled down to roughly break-even level, with every good week counterbalanced by a poor one. A forced move, to the Hellinger across the street, only added to the deficit. By the time Kasha and "Cryin' Joe" Kipness threw in the towel, *Seesaw* had a loss of $1,275,000—which appeared to have set a new record. For a short while, anyway.

**FORREST
THEATRE**

under the direction of
Messrs. Shubert

PLAYBILL

the national magazine for theatregoers

HOLLY
GOLiGHTLY

Breakfast at Tiffany's (1966)

Excruciatingly Boring

"Blockbuster!" *Breakfast at Tiffany's* shouted, in extra-bold letters. A new musical from the producer of *Hello, Dolly!*, the composer-lyricist of *Carnival*, the director-librettist of *How to Succeed in Business without Really Trying*, and the choreographer of *Guys and Dolls*. Plus two of the most romantic, personable TV stars of the day. And don't forget that million-dollar title, which brought with it goodwill and fond memories of Audrey Hepburn and "Moon River" (neither of which, obviously, could be expected to be in the Broadway musical).

But *Breakfast at Tiffany's*—Truman Capote's 1958 novella about, let's face it, a high-priced hooker—came bearing hidden hazards. As word of the troubled tryout drifted into town, reporter John Gruen of the *World-Journal-Tribune* headed to Boston. (The *World-Journal-Tribune*—lest you're wondering—was a brief attempt at salvaging three dailies on the verge of extinction, the *World-Telegram and Sun*, the *Journal-American*, and the *Herald Tribune*.)

Mary Tyler Moore and Richard Chamberlain in a rehearsal shot, presumably before they read the script.

"The Million-Dollar Misunderstanding"
by John Gruen

A girl I'm crazy about is sick, and I was very concerned. I even hopped a train to be close, and what happened? They slammed the door in my face! Is she dying? I asked. No, but she's on the critical list, I'm told, and if the patient sinks the loss will be severe—severe to the tune of one million dollars!

I was told the doctors are working overtime—that they had no time to talk to me. They've got to save her. They've got to save Holly Golightly—sweet, adorable, unpredictable and wildly expensive Holly Golightly: the girl Truman Capote put in his story *Breakfast at Tiffany's*, the girl Paramount Pictures put in a lavish Audrey Hepburn movie and the girl David Merrick, Broadway's aging *enfant terrible*, will unveil on Dec. 26 in one of the most-talked-about, worried-over, fussed-with musicals ever to shakily wend its way to the Big Stem. This most nervous of all nervous productions was initially titled *Holly Golightly*. But somebody up there must have wanted to draw some attention away from Holly—she was getting something of a bad name—and so they've renamed the show *Breakfast at Tiffany's*, as good and familiar a name as any.

It seems that out of town, poor Holly just didn't seem to pull through. Even now, new name or not, she's thrashing in pain in Boston, as she had earlier in Philadelphia. And when she showed what she could do, the critics there, expecting pure enchantment (for Holly, as Capote drew her, *is* pure enchantment) were, to put it mildly, disenchanted.

So I called *Holly*'s New York press agent, Harvey Sabinson. I told him I wanted to go to Boston and find out what was wrong. But he told me Mr. Merrick says NO, he doesn't want me there, and NO, I can't have a ticket to the show, and NO, I can't talk to Abe Burrows, the director. And NO, NO, NO, I absolutely could not talk to Mary Tyler Moore, cast as bewitching, bedeviled and, by now, bemused and befuddled Holly Golightly.

"In fact," Sabinson told me, "We've canceled two major stories on her—two big national weeklies were ready to shoot pictures, do interviews—the works. But word came from the boss to hold off the publicity."

Hold off the publicity? What does that mean? Even after that big splashy cover story on Mary Tyler Moore in the *Saturday Evening Post* had Merrick calling her "our next big musical comedy star"? And saying, "I must think well of her or I wouldn't have sunk $500,000 into this show."

Then adding, "But win or lose with this one on Broadway, Mary Tyler Moore is going to be the next Mary Martin. Mark my word. Who do we have in musical comedy now anyhow? Barbara Harris can't sing, and Streisand you can't get."

Hold off the publicity? Something is wrong here. Something doesn't jibe. Why, Mary Tyler Moore, the *Dick Van Dyke Show*'s perfect TV wife, she of the gorgeous gams and sexy voice of TV's *Richard Diamond*, the girl viewed and known by millions, should be given all the publicity she can get! [Moore first came to prominence in 1959 on the detective show *Richard Diamond*, playing the switchboard operator "Sam." Moore was shown—from the neck down—seated at her switchboard; her face was never visible, but her distinctive voice launched her career. *The Dick Van Dyke Show*, which began in 1961, went off the air in 1966.] To have nabbed a role like Holly Golightly as a first Broadway assignment is news—big show-biz news!

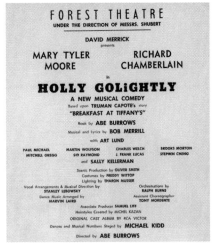

FOREST THEATRE
UNDER THE DIRECTION OF MESSRS. SHUBERT

DAVID MERRICK
presents

MARY TYLER   RICHARD
MOORE   CHAMBERLAIN

in

HOLLY GOLiGHTLY

A NEW MUSICAL COMEDY
Based upon TRUMAN CAPOTE's story
"BREAKFAST AT TIFFANY'S"

Book by ABE BURROWS

Musical and Lyrics by BOB MERRILL

with ART LUND

PAUL MICHAEL   MARTIN WOLFSON   CHARLES WELCH   BROOKS MORTON
MITCHELL OREGG   SID RAYMOND   J. FRANK LUCAS   STEPHEN CHENG
                  and SALLY KELLERMAN

Scenic Production by OLIVER SMITH
Costumes by FREDDY WITTOP
Lighting by THARON MUSSER

Vocal Arrangements & Musical Direction by   Orchestrations by
STANLEY LEBOWSKY   RALPH BURNS
Dance Music Arranged by   Assistant Choreographer
MARVIN LAIRD   TONY MORDENTE

Associate Producer SAMUEL LIFF
Hairstyles Created by MICHEL KAZAN
ORIGINAL CAST ALBUM BY RCA VICTOR

Dances and Musical Numbers Staged by MICHAEL KIDD

Directed by ABE BURROWS

The billing page for the Abe Burrows version. Note that the Forrest Theatre is misspelled.

Or is it possible the girl doesn't have it? That up there on that big, exposed, brutally revealing stage Mary Tyler Moore just doesn't come across as sweet, delicious, vulnerable, poignant Holly Golightly? Could it be that Mary Tyler Moore, viewed by millions, has turned out to be a million-dollar misunderstanding?

And what's this? Diahann Carroll's been to Boston to see the show? Stunning Diahann Carroll, the Negro beauty who had been a smash in *No Strings*, out there eying the most coveted starring role in many a Broadway moon? [Diahann Carroll won a Best Actress Tony Award for the 1962 Richard Rodgers musical, *No Strings*.]

So I hopped that train, checked into the Ritz Carlton (where all the principals are staying), rushed to the Shubert Theatre, where the matinee was in progress, and I spent nine dollars for a single ticket for the evening's performance of *Holly Golightly,* as it was called when I saw it. Then, quick as a flash, back to the hotel to call Abe Burrows on the house phone.

"So didn't Harvey Sabinson tell you *not* to come? So why did you come? You shouldn't have come!" Abe Burrows sounded wary on the phone. "I wouldn't be able to talk to you. Not now. I'm not ready to talk to anybody about the show. There's nothing to talk about yet. We're working on it. It needs work, a lot of work. And we're working. So why don't you go back? Come when the show is pulled together." Abe sounded worried. One million dollars worried.

"Diahann Carroll?" he said. "She's a terrific girl, a talented girl. She's doing a club date in Reno now. What? Replacement for Moore? Absolutely not. Moore sticks. She's opening the show. No question about *that.*

"You seeing the show tonight? It's not going to be the show we're coming in with. We're rewriting, we're restaging. Everybody is working like crazy. Please don't bother us. I can't talk to you anymore. Goodbye."

Funny Abe Burrows meant to be nice. Biggest show-doctor in the business. A pro writer. A pro adapter. A pro director. He's in trouble. [Burrows was best known for *Guys and Dolls* and *How to Succeed in Business without Really Trying,* on both of which he replaced other librettists (who retained full co-author credit). He was in great demand through the 1950s; among his patients were *Make a Wish, Three Wishes for Jamie,* and *Silk Stockings.*]

I figured I'd go back to the theatre when the matinee broke and try to see a few people backstage. Maybe Burrows will talk to me there. Maybe Mary Tyler Moore. Maybe Richard Chamberlain. That's right, Richard Chamberlain, another TV recruit—*Dr. Kildare* to millions. He's the co-star. Slim, agreeable, hard-working and—bland. Two TV kids in a million-dollar show. [Chamberlain's medical show, *Dr. Kildare* (1961–1966), had—like *The Dick Van Dyke Show*—just gone off the air, leaving Chamberlain and Moore available for Broadway.]

The show broke and I waited backstage. "Miss Moore can't see you. She's due for a new costume fitting, then she'll be rehearsing some more. She's not leaving the theatre. No, you can't go in. Miss Moore can't talk to the press. Sorry . . . sorry . . . sorry. No one can talk to you." The word was obviously out that someone was in from New York, snooping around. They slammed the door in my face.

I saw the show that evening. The house was near-capacity and when the stars appeared on stage they were applauded. It's a big show, all right—an expensive show. Everybody works very hard on stage.

During intermission the Boston folks smoke as much as the New York folks. And they chat about this and that. I couldn't help but overhear snippets of the chatter.

Tall matron to short matron: "I just can't work up any sympathy for that girl . . . ." Portly gentleman to gorgeous young thing: "She's real cute, that Tyler Mary Moore . . . that Mary Moore Tyler . . . How does that name go, anyway?" "It goes Vera Hruba Ralston, darling," says gorgeous young thing.

Then you hear it again—the joke that went around New York. Harvard type to Harvard type: "I hear Diahann Carroll is replacing Mary Tyler Moore and they'll change the name of the show to 'Holly Godarkly.'" Say! Maybe that's why they've decided to call it *Breakfast at Tiffany's*!

The second-act curtain goes up. After an hour or so, it comes down. The applause is not deafening. The people file out. Some say good things, some say terrible things, some say nothing, some look numb.

It started to rain in Boston. Again I went backstage. Again it's nix on talking to the stars—and Abe Burrows is nowhere to be seen. It's now past midnight. I went back to the Ritz. I picked up the house phone and asked for the stars. No go. They're too exhausted to talk. But I got Burrows back on the phone. "I'm in a meeting. Please, what can I tell you? I couldn't tell you any more than what I told you before. Look, I'm in a meeting. Breakfast? Impossible. I'm flying back to New York in the morning for a conference. But let me call you back later tonight, OK?"

OK, OK. But Abe Burrows doesn't call back. Protective, worried Abe Burrows!

Traffic between Boston and New York has been very lively of late. Lots of comings and goings. And some people are special enough to get flown in and out just to see the show and how it's faring. Take Truman Capote. Of course, that's hardly surprising since he's the author of the original story.

Yes, Truman Capote came, saw and said it. What's more, he said it in print—on a page one interview in *Women's Wear Daily*: "I don't like the score . . . or the leading lady. They followed the book more closely than the movie . . . Maybe they would have been better off patterning after the film. And I don't think the music is good enough." Cold-blooded Truman. Matter of fact, producer Merrick was reported to have said later that when the show opens on Broadway he might start billing, "David Merrick presents, In Cold Blood, *Breakfast at Tiffany's*."

[Capote began 1966 with the publication of the best-selling "nonfiction novel" *In Cold Blood*, about the murder of a Kansas family.]

Who else came to see poor *Holly*? Ah, yes. Edward Albee. *Edward Albee?!* That's right. He quietly stole into Boston to find a million-dollar baby turning bluer and bluer. America's leading young playwright called in to take Holly's temperature. Would he write a new adaptation? Could he pull it into shape? Could he do *anything*?

The release sent out by press agent Sabinson said it clearly enough. In so many words it officially announced Edward Albee as the new adapter of *Holly Golightly*. Everybody printed it. Everybody said *fantastic*. Until . . . another misunderstanding! Sabinson goes into a spin. He had sent out hundreds of releases to hundreds of papers only to learn that the deal was not complete. There was a hitch. Albee hadn't really signed to rewrite the show. Everything was too previous. And so, word went out that Albee was not the new adapter of *Holly Golightly*.

HOLLY GOLIGHTLY

This program used one of *Playbill*'s generic cover photos. The title was changed in Boston from *Holly Golightly* to *Breakfast at Tiffany's*.

Except that he is. Albee has been holing up in his Montauk retreat working, working on sick, sick Holly. And that's OK with Abe Burrows, who was supposed to have told Merrick, "After all, David, it's Albee. You're not sticking me with some schlump."

And then who came to Boston? Well, it's true. Lovely Diahann Carroll came to Boston, the girl Burrows said was definitely not replacing Mary Tyler Moore. "She's doing a club date in Reno," he had said. "She's a terrific and talented girl."

"Hello there, Miss Carroll," (I was on the phone calling Reno.) "I understand you were recently flown to Boston to have a look at *Holly Golightly*, now titled *Breakfast at Tiffany's*."

"Well, now," she says ever so calmly, "I've read in the papers that I was in Boston seeing the show, but that doesn't mean I was there."

"But people saw you there, Miss Carroll!"

"I don't know anything about that. And I can't tell you anything at all. I have no opinions on the show. But you should have some consideration for that very wonderful girl up there on that Boston stage. That girl is working very hard in a very strenuous role. When you've done writing your story, you can go to bed at night and forget it. But that girl has to go on every night and give a performance. I think you ought to give some thought to that."

"Are you going to replace Miss Moore?"

"I can't tell you that. Why don't you talk to Mr. Merrick. He's the man to talk to."

A lovely girl. An ambiguous conversation.

Meanwhile, other lovely girls are rumored to be standing by as replacements for Mary Tyler Moore, notably Tammy Grimes, Joey Heatherton and another three-named-wonder, Lesley Ann Warren.

When a show is in trouble, the people involved call on their friends in the business. Bob Merrill, *Breakfast at Tiffany's* composer and lyricist, is a close friend of Jule Styne. They've worked together on *Funny Girl*, and Styne is not a man to turn down a friend in trouble.

Friends just don't do that. For example, when director Gower Champion called on Jule Styne, Betty Comden and Adolph Green to come to the aid of Merrick's *I Do! I Do!*, then playing in Washington, D. C., they came to the aid (though their suggestions weren't heeded after all). Merrick flew them out, even though Merrick first optioned, then dropped, the incoming Styne-Comden and Green-Arthur Laurents musical, *Hallelujah, Baby!* [see page 134] Gower Champion was in trouble—he was a friend—and never mind hard feelings. [It was not Champion but Merrick who asked the songwriters for help with *I Do! I Do!* apparently at the behest of Mary Martin; the trio had successfully doctored the score of her *Peter Pan*. Merrick typically would say to the original authors, "Sure, you don't have to allow these new songs. But if you don't, I'm closing the show Saturday." In the case of *I Do! I Do!* Harvey Schmidt and Tom Jones—who had little love for Merrick—called the producer's bluff. With an eye on the large advance sale, he backed down. The four songs were quickly placed elsewhere, in the 1967 TV special *I'm Getting Married*, starring Anne Bancroft and Dick Shawn.]

So Jule Styne went to Boston, because a friend was in trouble. They say that Merrill wrote his songs and lyrics even before he read Abe Burrows' adaptation of the book. Then he had come in with a lot of material that when put with Burrows' story-line just didn't make much sense. Things were pretty lop-sided from the very beginning.

Obviously upset, Merrill asked Jule Styne's help. And Jule Styne saw the show and talked to Merrill. He told him what he thought was wrong. It had to do with making the character of Holly more lovable, more endearing, more sympathetic—all via the music and the lyrics.

Styne is a man you can talk to. He doesn't turn you down. And you learn things. For example, he was all set to do a musical out of *Breakfast at Tiffany's*, way before the movie was made, and he had terrific ideas for it.

"My plan was to start out with three or four brief vignettes showing Holly's background," he told me. "Her life with her hillbilly husband, her striving for better things, her rushing to Hollywood for a chance at stardom, and her eventual arrival in New York as a good-time-gal at 50 bucks-a-throw.

"That would all be shown very quickly, with music, but no songs. Only *then* would I go into my first big number—maybe the big party scene when Holly invites all her boyfriends to her apartment. The stage would be filled with guys doing a big number, and when that was over, Holly would make her first *real* entrance and go into some terrific song. That's how I would have begun it."

The fate of a million-dollar Broadway musical hangs in the balance. Should the New York critics find *Breakfast at Tiffany's* a dismal flop, there's still that million-dollar advance to keep it running for a few months. When the advance runs out, however, another musical comedy saga will have spelled heartbreak for a lot of talented and not-so-talented people. The books are full of such sagas. Monumental flops always leave a sickening, hollow gap in Broadway's dazzling though chancy firmament. Producer Leland Hayward's *Mr. President*, with an Irving Berlin score, had a $2.5 million advance some seasons back, but it was destined to be a flop. People just didn't buy tickets, once the advance ran its short course. [Berlin was joined on *Mr. President* by Howard Lindsay and Russel Crouse, librettists of *Call Me Madam* and *The Sound of Music*; and Joshua Logan, director of *Annie Get Your Gun* and *South Pacific*. All four were past their prime, never again to have success on Broadway.]

Although theatre tickets, once bought, are nonreturnable, producers who plan to stay in business in the future cooperate with theatre party groups to the extent of putting unsold tickets on sale at the box office, thus eating into their own additional sales. Also, individuals who have bought tickets in advance, knowing a turkey won't run too long, ask to have their seats changed for some far future date, and then get their money refunded when the show closes. In ways like that, the huge advance of *Mr. President* was dissipated, and after a few months' run, closed at a loss.

But *Holly Golightly, Breakfast at Tiffany's* or whatever the musical will ultimately be called, is getting the best, most expensive care in the world. Specialists, young and old, are handling the case, and for all anybody knows, when that curtain goes up later this month, it may turn out the biggest hit in Broadway history—and Mary Tyler Moore, if she hasn't been replaced by, say, Shirley Temple, may indeed turn out to be our next Mary Martin. David Merrick predicted it. And on Broadway David Merrick is God.

Breakfast at Tiffany's limped into town but closed during previews, as reported by Lewis Funke in the *New York Times*.

"Why Holly Went Badly"
by Lewis Funke

Although more than a week has passed since David Merrick closed *Breakfast at Tiffany's*, following four previews, because it was "an excruciating bore," his startlingly frank announcement continues to be discussed, argued, questioned. How did Truman Capote's novella, which provided the screen with a healthy bonanza, lead to one of the most spectacular disasters in the annals of the contemporary musical stage? What happened? Why?

The questions have a way of interlocking and Merrick, having donned the robes of Public Protector No. 1, also takes responsibility for the failure. "It was my idea and an impossible one," he says. "None of the blame should be attributed to the writers who had a go at it."

Considering the circumstances, he may be right. Agreement on what Capote's *Holly Golightly* should have been when she went to Broadway was virtually impossible to achieve. In the book she was regarded as a fey, kooky female, a girl with many of the problems of contemporary young people—sad, funny, lovable—a tramp, perhaps, whose assorted fantasies seemed to elevate her into a state of innocence. Hollywood, in its not-too-mysterious way, turned her into a kind of professional virgin, played with endearing charm by the enchanting Audrey Hepburn. When that concept was rejected for the stage in favor of a harsher approach, the road proved one big minefield.

Bob Merrill, the composer to whom Merrick first offered the idea, persuaded filmdom's Nunnally Johnson to try the adaptation. [Johnson was the acclaimed author of such celebrated films as *Roxie Hart* and *The Three Faces of Eve*. His three Broadway musicals—*Park Avenue*, *Henry, Sweet Henry* (with composer-lyricist Merrill), and *Darling of the Day*, were especially dire.] The decision to forget the film and strive for greater fidelity to the book resulted in a tougher Holly. Joshua Logan, who had agreed to direct, read the script. No, he said, the approach was wrong. You couldn't get away with that kind of Holly on Broadway. Johnson bowed out. Logan then was faced with a choice: wait for another adapter or take on *Hot September*, the musical version of William Inge's *Picnic*, the play with which he had scored a major directorial triumph several years before. He chose *Hot September*. [*Hot*

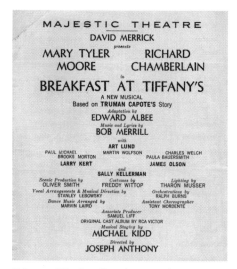

Patrons of the four Broadway previews received this billing sheet, with a new title; two new featured players (including Larry Kert); and a new librettist—Edward Albee!

September was produced by Leland Hayward and Merrick in the fall of 1965, a full year before *Breakfast at Tiffany's*. It closed in Boston. Logan also contracted to direct *Mame*, which opened in May 1966 and was thus more of a conflict with *Tiffany's*. In the end, Logan was fired from *Mame*—although he collected a sizable royalty.]

Enter Abe Burrows as writer-director, also inheritor of Merrill's songs and lyrics written to underscore Johnson's realistic treatment. Enter also trouble in the form of the dentist's chair. Burrows, before he could put his brain to work, found himself spending tortured hours and weeks at his dentist, unable even to talk. With the rehearsal date looming ever more menacingly on the horizon, Burrows finally managed to get a rough first draft on paper.

Merrill, reading the script, called Burrows. "I haven't known you well," he said, "but, by reading your script I can tell you are one of the sweetest men breathing. Only, the treatment is no good. You've softened up Holly." Merrill, concerned that his lyrics and music would sound discordant with Burrow's conception, apparently found support from Merrick. Burrows yielded.

Rehearsals began with a non-existent second act, Burrows figuring he could fashion it as he went along. Pressed by Merrill and Merrick, Burrow's Holly now emerged as something of a slut, a $50 hooker. Philadelphia critics were unhappy. Holly lacked charm. Members of the audience also seemed appalled at seeing and hearing Mary Tyler Moore doing things and saying the things she did. Miss Moore, a winsomely sweet young woman who had been treasured by television audiences as the lovely wife on *The Dick Van Dyke Show*, now was using four-letter words as freely as an enraged truckman.

Merrill ceased his campaign for realism. Burrows tried to soften Holly, work for greater entertainment values. Choreographer Michael Kidd stirred up some additional dance routines. Boston's critics weren't pleased. What had happened to Capote's book? A sweetened $50 hooker was unsatisfactory. Still, oddly enough, the show seemed to be working. According to at least one member of the company, it seemed to improve as the cast developed expertise with what it had. Audiences weren't screaming for refunds. Some sort of synthesis of the Philadelphia and Boston versions might turn the trick. Burrows was asked about bringing in another writer. He was agreeable. As director, he could work closely with the new man.

Then Merrick exploded a surprise. He brought in Edward Albee, author of *Who's Afraid of Virginia Woolf?* and this season's *A Delicate Balance*. Never before had the 38-year-old playwright tackled a musical. Merrick quipped, "Why drown in two feet of water? We might as well swim out and take our chances."

Albee, full of ideas and determined to see Holly as he believed Capote saw her, holed up in a Boston hotel. The last Sunday in Boston, with the company gathered onstage, Burrows read the first two scenes. Visibly upset, he said he could not direct them; this was not his kind of a show.

At this point someone came in with a copy of an interview in the *Boston Globe* in which Kevin Kelly quoted Albee as saying: "All those awful jokes will have to be thrown out and I hope to substitute some genuine wit. . . the characters, from Holly down, will be redefined and she won't have any of those Borscht-circuit lovers she's saddled with now." Burrows, badly shaken, said he was through. Everyone rushed to his side, all sympathy. Albee, evidently crushed and protesting that his confidences had been violated, begged Burrows to stay. Burrows was firm. With Albee clearly headed away from familiar musical entertainment and going toward a "serious musical comedy," Joseph Anthony, experienced with musicals and straight plays, was called in as director. [Veteran actor Joe Anthony became a director with *The Rainmaker* in 1954. Prior to *Tiffany's*, he had directed two musicals: *The Most Happy Fella* and Merrick's *110 in the Shade*, the musicalization of *The Rainmaker*.]

Meanwhile Albee, dissatisfied with his first writing efforts, had thrown them away and persuaded Merrick to delay the New York previews and opening long enough to enable him to do a completely new version. It cost Merrick reportedly close to $100,000. Albee required among other alterations the substitution of more naturalistic acting for the usual Broadway musical style. He didn't want singers facing the audiences to deliver their songs. He vetoed the brassy finishes the arrangers give songs—they sounded too much like a solicitation for applause. His specifications allowed for only a single group number. The ensemble was cut from 25 singers and dancers to a dozen.

When Merrill read the new version, he bellowed. "It was so ambitious," he says. "It called for an entirely different kind of stagecraft. From reality, it moved into fantasy. I realized that I would have to compose practically a new score. I didn't want to throw away a score that had taken two years to write. I went on strike. I didn't go near the theatre for three days. Then Albee visited me. I swear, he's the Knute Rockne of the theatre. He spoke and spoke and he embarrassed me into going back to work. I wrote six new songs. We kept five of the old ones." Altogether Merrill figures he wrote a total of 50 songs, lyrics as well as music. "I may not write good when I'm in a hurry," he says, "but I write fast." Actually, the score was praised on the road.

At the first preview, shock went through the theatre as Sally Kellerman, playing Mag Wildwood, came out and rendered an Albee soliloquy, winding up stretched out and sobbing on the stage. The grim reality and the four-letter words seemed to make the audience sink deeper and deeper into their seats. Merrick and Albee had come to the end of the road.

Albee is not at all discouraged. He's learned a lot, he says. He understands the conventions of the musical theatre better. "Audiences apparently expect a musical to be noisy, they expect to see people jumping up and down. Of course, it's difficult to overhaul the old elements. I think I could have done better starting from scratch. A musical book, even allowing for the conventions, can have three-dimensional characters. Too many are nothing but cartoons." Would he try another musical? Of course.

Merrill, musing on the wreckage, says, "You know, with his talent I wouldn't be surprised if he makes his ideas work. I have the feeling he might have licked *Breakfast at Tiffany's* if the clock hadn't run out on him."

Breakfast at Tiffany's began previews on December 12, 1966 at the Majestic. It closed there on December 14, 1966, prior to the scheduled December 26 opening, after four previews, with a total loss.

David Merrick issued this statement: "Rather than subject the drama critics and the theatre-going public—who invested one million dollars in advance ticket sales—to an excruciatingly boring evening, I have decided to close the show. Since the idea of adapting

Breakfast at Tiffany's to the musical stage was mine in the first place, the closing is entirely my fault and should not be attributed to the three top writers who had a go at it."

Merrick's next musical was *How Now, Dow Jones* [see page 196]. His program bio read, in its entirety: "Mr. Merrick is best known as the distinguished producer of the musical *Breakfast at Tiffany's*."

The
Broadway
Theatre

PLAYBILL
the magazine for theatregoers

Dude (1972)

Mud in the Valley (at a $15-top)

Once or twice every decade, a Broadway musical comes along that crosses the line from the theatre page to the news page. These are not necessarily the longest running shows (although many are), nor are they necessarily the best. But they are social happenings, events that must be seen—even by non–theatregoers.

Oklahoma! in 1943, might have been the first; *My Fair Lady* (1956) and *Hello, Dolly!* (1964) succeeded *Oklahoma!* in turn, taking over the number one long-run slot. Other titles in the newsworthy series include *A Chorus Line* and *Rent*. They were all events, and they all made news. When *The Producers* opened in 2001, it merited headlines in Chinese newspapers, in China. Not a traditional touring stop.

Hair, too, was an immense hit when it opened in 1968; a front-page, must-see event. Moreso than any of the other titles (except *Rent*), it also had cultural impact. While all of the aforementioned shows drew vast audiences of non-theatregoers, *Hair* was almost specifically geared toward the non-theatregoing crowd; all those under-thirties who wouldn't be caught dead in a Broadway theatre. The show's strength—carefully hidden beneath the controversy it courted with its anti-establishment, war protesting, foul-language-and-nudity banners and its inflammatory statement of "peace, love, freedom, flowers"—was that Galt MacDermot's score was filled with

The model is actor Kevin Geer, who was fired during rehearsals and replaced—in the title role—by 11-year-old Ralph Carter.

glorious melodies that Beatles fans, musical comedy fans, and grandparents could embrace.

And an immense moneymaker it was, too. *Hair* could not match the blockbuster musicals in weekly gross, as it was playing at the small-sized Biltmore. But with a cast of twenty-three (as opposed to forty-five at that season's Gower Champion musical, *The Happy Time*), a band of nine (against twenty-six), and a unit set calling for minimal stagehands, *Hair* coined cash. And unlike the reigning hits of the day, which typically sent out a national tour or two plus a bus-and-truck company playing split-week engagements, *Hair* was able to set up open-ended, sit-down companies in cities that would typically host only a four-to-six week run.

The *Hair* goldmine, needless to say, quickly resulted in a chain of rock musicals. The New York Shakespeare Festival—which originated *Hair*, although its rights lapsed before the show reached Broadway—set MacDermot and John Guare to work on Shakespeare's *Two Gentlemen of Verona*. This interracial, anti-Vietnam War protest piece was a popular hit, transferring from Joe Papp's free Shakespeare-in-the-Park to the house of *Dolly* (A.K.A. the St. James). *Two Gents* went on to win the 1971 Tony Award for Best Musical, forever disenfranchising *Follies* fans who think they wuz robbed. (The *Follies* score is unparalleled, but *Two Gents* had it beat in terms of both entertainment and clarity of message.)

But *Two Gents* was it; other rock-based musicals came and landed with a thud. Two of the most prominent, and most impossible, came from the same Galt MacDermot—within a seven–week period. *Dude* and *Via Galactica* offered incontrovertible proof that *Hair* was one-of-a-kind. Patricia Bosworth described the *Dude* debacle in the *New York Times*.

"*Dude* . . . An $800,000 Disaster: Where Did They Go Wrong?"

by Patricia Bosworth

Right after the opening night performance of *Dude*—which may go down in theatrical history as Broadway's most monumental disaster—its author, Gerome Ragni, huddled in a taxi clutching his 7-year-old son, Eric, to his bosom.

He kept rocking the little boy back and forth, chanting, "Nureyev loved it, booboo, Nureyev loved *Dude*. He told me."

Nobody else in the taxi responded so Ragni continued. "An' John Huston was there an' Ed Sullivan an' Lennie Lyons . . ."

He smiled. It was the same eager, goofy grin he'd worn all during those frenzied weeks before *Dude*'s opening—when the original director, choreographer and costume designer were fired, when the exhausted cast threatened insurrection and the producers swore they would close the show unless Ragni wrote a second act.

Ragni's battered clown grin has been a kind of trademark—along with his tangled Medusa locks. He used them both to supreme advantage in *Hair*, the fabulously successful "love-rock" musical which he co-authored and performed in and which turned him into a millionaire. It also inspired him to write *Dude*.

So he kept that grin tight across his cheeks until the taxi pulled up to the opening-night party at Tavern-on-the-Green. Then his expression changed to anguish. "The critics are going to destroy my musical," he prophesied. "The critics won't understand what I'm trying to do."

Weeks before the show went into rehearsal, even the people most closely associated with *Dude* couldn't understand what Ragni wanted to do. They began expressing their worries, often after pre-production meetings. The talk invariably came back to his book.

"It was chaotic, disorganized," said a production associate who prefers to remain nameless. "We kept telling each other *Hair* had no plot either. Finally we convinced ourselves *Dude* would be the son of *Hair*."

"The songs were great but the script remained a mass of undoable nonsense," said actor William Redfield, one of *Dude*'s stars. "I'm very fond of Ragni but the truth must be told."

"I never knew who Dude was," confided composer Galt MacDermot who wrote the music for the show as well as for *Hair* and *Two Gentlemen of Verona*. "Early on I accepted *Dude* as a totally illogical musical. But you know what? I liked that!"

Ragni described *Dude* as an "Off-Broadway Broadway show." He said as much in January 1972, when he and MacDermot dropped by Peter Holzer's east side townhouse lugging the 2,000-page manuscript of *Dude*.

Holzer, a 44-year-old shipping tycoon, is president of American Transport Inc.; his redhaired Spanish-born wife, Adela, has big land holdings in Spain, South America and the Orient. Together they were principal backers of *Sleuth* and *Lenny*. Earlier their $50,000 investment in *Hair* had earned them a $2-million profit.

Now they wanted to produce a Broadway show. As soon as they heard the creators of *Hair* had a new musical, they investigated.

Ragni had been laboring over *Dude*—subtitled "the highway life"—since 1968. Friends say he carried bulging *Dude* notebooks everywhere and scribbled dialogue and lyrics in them between meals at Max's Kansas City.

"We first discussed *Dude* after the L.A. opening of *Hair*," MacDermot recalled. "But we didn't start working together until I finished composing *Two Gents*. In the fall of '71 Gerry and I collaborated on 50 songs."

That night last January at the Holzers, MacDermot sang most of those numbers, accompanying himself on an antique spinet. His small audience loved the score. "It was exciting, brilliant," Adela Holzer recalled. "It combined Broadway tunes, jazz, rock, country and western, even soul."

She and her husband were also intrigued with Ragni's concept for the physical production. He wanted to have the interior of the Shubert Theatre scooped out and turned into a free-wheeling environmental theatre in the round which would represent heaven and hell.

The Holzers were interested in everything about the musical except the prospect of sifting through the unwieldy script. So they offered Ragni a room and a secretary in their offices and for the next month he worked there, cutting the 2,000 pages down to 200.

"Then I read it and responded," said Mrs. Holzer. "Although it had no plot line. That worried me a little. I see now it should have worried me more. Basically *Dude* was Everyman. Everyman who loses his innocence and fights to regain it. But *Dude* was also Gerry Ragni's own life. His memories. Temptations. His fears. His struggle to create. He's one of ten children from a poor Italian family in Pittsburgh, you know. When he was five years old, he began painting crazy beautiful pictures all over the walls of his family's house and his parents couldn't stop him. Even then he believed he was a genius. That belief has made him tireless.

"I knew *Hair* was a traumatic experience for him. He became famous—a rich man. But his marriage broke up and he fell in with a strange crowd. This was all spelled out in *Dude*. Although names were not named, a lot of the dialogue had angry personal references to Mike Butler [producer of *Hair*], and James Rado [*Hair*'s co-author]. He described how he felt when he and Rado were arrested after walking nude down the aisle during a performance of *Hair*. Gerry's basically a very conservative person. The first question he ever asked me was, 'Do you smoke pot?' He seemed relieved when I said no."

In April 1972, the Holzers optioned *Dude*. They decided to open early this fall—mainly because Ragni had asked them to. The pro-

BROADWAY THEATRE

ADELA and PETER HOLZER
present

DUDE
The Highway Life

| *Music by* | | *Book and Lyrics by* |
| GALT MacDERMOT | | GEROME RAGNI |

starring

| WILLIAM REDFIELD | RAE ALLEN | MICHAEL DUNN |
| SALOME BEY | ALLAN NICHOLLS | RALPH CARTER |

| EUGENE LEE | *Production Designed by* ROGER MORGAN | FRANNE LEE |

Musical Arrangements and Orchestrations by HORACE OTT

Musical Direction by THOMAS PIERSON

Assistant To The Choreographer and Director JENNIFER MULLER

Production Stage Manager MICHAEL MAURER

Choreography by LOUIS FALCO

Directed by ROCCO BUFANO

ORIGINAL CAST RECORDING ON COLUMBIA RECORDS

This handbill, listing director Rocco Bufano, was used for the early previews.

duction was budgeted at approximately $800,000, toward which Columbia Records put up $100,000.

"After raising $300,000, we put in around $400,000 of our own money," Mrs. Holzer admitted. "It was hard to get investors for *Dude* because the show sounded pretty experimental. Some of our friends got cold feet."

Understandably, Ragni's grandiose scheme for reconstructing the Shubert Theatre—and it *had* to be the Shubert—would cost $110,000. Nevertheless the Holzers went about arranging this with good-natured enthusiasm. Negotiations took weeks. [With Broadway in the midst of a dire period for new musicals, The Shubert Organization's flagship theatre was all too available. The long-running *Promises! Promises!* closed on New Year's Day, 1972. The Shubert hosted three quick flops that year, remaining dark for forty weeks. It finally returned to the hit column in February 1973, with *A Little Night Music*.] Finally, after agreeing on terms which included the cost of restoring the theatre to its original dimensions when *Dude* closed, Mrs. Holzer phoned Ragni, crying, "We got the Shubert!" His reply:

"Now I want the Imperial." Mrs. Holzer was unable to find out why he changed his mind.

Since *Pippin* was already booked into the Imperial, the Holzers eventually settled on the Broadway, the biggest house in the theatrical district and considered a "death house" by many performers because so many flops have originated there. [Fiddler on the Roof played its final nineteen months at the Broadway, which was then Broadway's largest-capacity house. Dude was the Broadway's only tenant from Fiddler's closing in July 1972 until Hal Prince's Candide in March 1974.]

For a while there was a delay in getting a permit from the city to reconstruct the interior of the theatre until Ragni personally phoned Mary Lindsay and asked her to put a rush on it. [Mary Lindsay was the wife of then-mayor John Lindsay.] In July, architect Leslie Cortesi and set designer Eugene Lee began work on the job of reconstruction. The seats in the orchestra floor of the Broadway were torn out. The action of *Dude* would take place in a circus-like arena in the center of the auditorium, with the audience sitting on all sides of the action. [If Dude was a disaster all around, it managed to launch the career of designer Lee. Candide transformed the Broadway into the same sort of environmental arena as Dude, making Lee the obvious choice to design that show. Prince has used Lee on five occasions, including Sweeney Todd; other credits include massive musicals like Ragtime and Wicked.]

Meanwhile the Holzers were trying to get Peter Brook or Tom O'Horgan to direct but both were unavailable. So Rocco Bufano was signed. Bufano had done some Off-Broadway shows but never any on Broadway. "His inexperience worried me," Mrs. Holzer said, "but he was charming and a good friend of Gerry's. He seemed to understand Gerry's vision for *Dude* and this was vitally important."

Bufano hired modern dancer Louis Falco as choreographer. The title role of *Dude* was to be played by Kevin Geer, also a close friend of Ragni's. Geer's muscular back still adorns the *Dude* display ads and posters.

With the exception of Michael Dunn, Bill Redfield and Rae Allen, the 33-member cast consisted mainly of youthful refugees from *Hair* as well as *Jesus Christ Superstar*. In August, the company went into rehearsal at the Ukrainian National Home on East 9th Street.

The Holzers soon realized that Geer couldn't sing—"He's probably a talented actor but this was the major singing role." They insisted he be replaced. Ragni exploded and disappeared into his rooms at the Chelsea Hotel.

Eventually the producers and Bufano convinced him a singer was essential. However, nobody quite remembers how they decided on

11-year-old Ralph Carter (who is black) to replace 23-year-old Geer (who is white). After more rehearsing, they realized that Carter could never sing numbers meant for the mature Dude. So singer Nat Morris was hired to play what was henceforth called "big Dude."

By this time, Allan Nicholls, a talented Canadian rock singer who had made a strong impression last season in *Inner City*, was brought in to play "33," a God-like figure in *Dude*. [*Inner City* was another one of the failed post-*Hair* rock musicals. Conceived, directed, and co-produced by Tom O'Horgan, it played 97 performances and lost a whopping $479,000.] Ragni, who says he is 33, had written "33" for himself. But the producers reminded him he had too much writing and rewriting to do. There was still no real second act.

Still he yearned to play "33," particularly on opening night. He kept reminding Nicholls of this until the rock singer told him quietly, "If you want to play '33' so much, Gerry, why the…don't you?" This silenced him momentarily.

During most of the rehearsals, choreographer Falco concentrated on movement. "It was like the Decathlon," Redfield said. "We sprinted, we climbed, we tumbled, we ran. God, how we ran! I thought I was going to have a heart attack. We also rehearsed a lot of the musical numbers but the show was never completely blocked. And we didn't dare discuss the script. How could we? There was none."

"By the fourth week of rehearsal, the producers, director, cast and choreographer had stopped communicating," said Nicholls. "And Bufano couldn't control anybody—least of all Gerry."

The burly Ragni simply would not complete the necessary work on the book. Instead, he conferred with his sister, Irene Ragni, who sat in on most of the rehearsals, recording the actors' gripes on a small tape recorder. He also made demands, phoning Adela Holzer at 2 A.M. to say he wanted a hundred butterflies let loose into the audience before each performance. No? Well then what about having a couple of oinking pigs and chickens run down the aisles at intermission?

Once inside the Broadway Theatre, technical problems arose. At the first runthrough, the stage, filled with two tons of top soil, filthied the actors and dumped dirt on everybody sitting in the first ten rows. People sneezed from the dust fumes; clouds of dirt rose into the air, making it difficult to see.

At the second runthrough, the stage was watered down. Naturally, the dirt turned into mud. "Actors will do anything to get ahead, but this was too much," Redfield said. "We phoned Equity and threatened insurrection." Eventually the stage was filled with thousands of brown felt scraps to simulate dirt. But the felt went, too, to be replaced by plastic.

Then Bufano called a company meeting which turned into a therapy session. "We became hysterical," Redfield said, "and released all our hostilities about the show, our fears. 'When was Gerry going to write some new dialogue?' we screamed. Later we began yelling about our careers and what the theatre meant to us and what life on earth meant to us…"

[Redfield was a respected Broadway veteran, who made his debut at the age of ten in 1937 and took his final Broadway bow in *Dude*. Among his credits were the Cole Porter musical *Out of This World*, and as Guildenstern to Richard Burton's *Hamlet*. Ragni also appeared in the latter, carrying a spear and understudying Horatio.]

BROADWAY THEATRE

ADELA and PETER HOLZER
present

DUDE
The Highway Life

Music by
GALT MacDERMOT

Book and Lyrics by
GEROME RAGNI

starring

| WILLIAM REDFIELD | RAE ALLEN | MICHAEL DUNN |

| SALOME BEY | ALLAN NICHOLLS | RALPH CARTER | NAT MORRIS |

Production Designed by
EUGENE LEE · ROGER MORGAN · FRANNE LEE

Musical Arrangements and Orchestrations by
HORACE OTT

Musical Direction by
THOMAS PIERSON

Production Stage Manager
MICHAEL MAURER

Directed and Staged by
TOM O'HORGAN

ORIGINAL CAST RECORDING ON COLUMBIA RECORDS

Dude resumed previews under the supervision of Tom O'Horgan. The role played by third-billed Michael Dunn was subsequently written out.

Ragni's sister taped the proceedings and Ragni ultimately inserted some of the confessionals into the show. Michael Alpert, *Dude*'s beleaguered press agent, recalls, "I came to a performance and suddenly Michael Dunn is giving this dramatic monologue about what it means to be a dwarf and an artist and I think, 'Where did that come from?' I asked Gerry and he just smiled." [The 3' 10" Michael Dunn was indeed a dwarf. He gave memorable performances opposite Colleen Dewhurst in the 1963 Carson McCullers play *Ballad of the Sad Café* (Tony nomination) and the 1965 film *Ship of Fools* (Oscar nomination).] The confessionals were subsequently dropped from the show, as were Ragni's personal references to *Hair*.

At the first preview on September 11, "the audience wanted to kill," according to Bill Redfield. "They kept yelling 'rip-off!' Worst of all, they could neither hear nor understand us."

The acoustical problems at the Broadway were caused by the new placement of the musicians—another Ragni brainstorm. One full orchestra clustered in a balcony high above stage left. A country and western band stood on a ramp stage right. Musical director Thomas Pierson conducted from a seat which jutted out some 100 feet above the audience's heads.

In performance, the score—melodic and driving though it was—simply melted into the air. The sound had nowhere to bounce.

Ultimately, engineers from M.I.T. tried to solve the problem by draping one wall of the theatre with heavy velvet. They also brought in so much electronic equipment the set began to look like a recording studio. All the actors wore portable mikes and had batteries strapped inside their costumes. And still the audience had difficulty hearing the lyrics.

By the third preview, *Dude* seemed a shambles. At this point, Bufano and Falco bowed out and the controversial Tom O'Horgan, who had directed *Hair* and *Jesus Christ Superstar*, took over. He could only stay with the show three weeks because he had to direct a Dory Previn TV special in Hollywood October 11. But he believed he could save *Dude*. [There was no replacement choreographer.]

The cast rallied as soon as the ponytailed O'Horgan appeared. "The audience thirsts for a story in *Dude*," he told them. "For one tiny thread to connect your gorgeous songs. We're going to make connections and enjoy ourselves while we're doing it."

Previews were shut down and the company went back into rehearsal with renewed energy. O'Horgan ordered new sets and costumes, and he let Michael Dunn go "because his talents were being wasted." He also abolished the show's semi-nudity. The actors now wore flesh-colored longjohns.

In the following days, O'Horgan's gaudy theatrical stamp came down on everything. From the trapdoor he ordered built in the stage so that little Dude could spring up as if emerging from Rae Allen's womb, to the hole gouged in the theatre's ceiling so that "33" could be resurrected on a trapeze and swing majestically into heaven.

But the flamboyant visual effects were not enough. Ragni would not come up with the necessary rewrites to make the book intelligible. The first act held—but just barely. Act Two was still in chaos.

Finally, O'Horgan met secretly with the producers and principal actors. He told them despairingly, "I cannot get Gerry to make any crucial decisions. I just want to run. What shall I do?"

They decided to go to Ragni in a body and give him an ultimatum: Either he rewrite certain key scenes or the show would close. "Gerry creates best under this kind of pressure," Adela Holzer said. "I think he realized we meant what we said."

Even so, Redfield and Rae Allen (who played Adam and Eve) were forced to write some of their own dialogue. "We had to. It was either write it or stand mute in the confusion."

Suddenly another problem arose. One of Gerry's brothers began attending rehearsals. Richard Ragni is a priest but he was in mufti so nobody paid any attention to him until his spiritual ideas were relayed to O'Horgan.

A supposed authority on Catholic dogma, Richard believed *Dude* should contain more religious overtones. O'Horgan rejected his suggestions but Richard continued to barrage the production staff with religious ideas. He was finally barred from the theatre.

Dude wasn't frozen until two nights before opening. The cast performed, rehearsed, tried on new costumes and attempted to memorize the new lines Ragni was scribbling in his notebook. Numbers in the first act were shifted to Act Two. Other numbers were dropped one night, only to be put back the next. An accurate program could never be printed.

However, by the last preview on Oct. 8, a great improvement was seen by those who'd followed the show since its inception. Now it moved with energy and joy and there was a definite flow between songs. But the audience still complained it made no sense: "It was entertaining sometimes, yes. The music was great, yes. But what's *Dude* all about?"

Critics asked the same question and drew harsh conclusions. Arriving at the party at the Tavern-on-the-Green, Ragni, the Holzers, their angels and actors watched the reviews come in on TV—all of them devastating. And the morning papers were no better. Described as "boring," "infantile," "shapeless" and "much ado about nothing," this eagerly awaited musical took in only $500 at the box office the day after its premiere.

The Holzers were angry at the critics, insisting they were "very unfair." "It's an audience show," they said. "Audiences love it. Word of mouth is terrific."

They took out a brave ad, announcing "tickets on sale until January 6, 1973"—a sign that they meant to fight. But last Monday night, as *Dude* started its second week, they put up the closing notice backstage. At press time, the show was scheduled to close last night after 16 performances—a loss of $800,000, and some say it may be a million.

The Holzers say they are finished with the theatre forever. "The Broadway system is a lousy system," Peter Holzer observed bitterly. "A bunch of stone-faced old men should not have the right to make up the public's mind."

"It's a shame the Holzers are through with the theatre," said George Thorn, a general manager of *Dude*. "They believed in *Dude* and they were committed to sticking with it. To making it work. The theatre needs people like that."

"When an innovative musical like *Dude* fails, it makes it 95 per cent more difficult to get fresh experimental stuff on," Tom O'Horgan said. "*Dude* was different—but it was a good show. It's very depressing."

And what of Gerry Ragni? Attempts to interview him were unsuccessful. But two days after the opening, he was running backstage at the Broadway Theatre with that eager, goofy grin on his face.

He could be heard assuring everyone, "We're gonna make it, boo-boos! This little show is gonna make it!"

Dude opened October 9, 1972 at the Broadway Theatre, to universal pans. It closed there October 21, 1972 after 16 performances, with a total loss.

The cast list was divided into "The Theatre Stars," "The Shubert Angels," and "The Theatre Wings." The Broadway was transformed into an environmental arena, with the audience seated in valleys ($15-top), foothills, mountains, trees and treetops. Can you imagine what would have gone on at ticket brokers if *Dude* had been a hit? "I've got a good pair in the foothills on the aisle. . . ." Gerry Ragni's vision permeated every angle of the production, it seems, and that vision was mighty dazed.

Producer Adela Holzer, who later wound up serving multiple stretches for things like fraud and immigration scams, blamed it on the critics. "They all missed the point. It's a new thing and it goes over old people's heads. I admit the book was not the greatest, but in a musical you can't spell out the story. It's not Ibsen."

During one of the final performances, Ragni was spotted in the lobby during intermission, barking "Go back to your seat" at theatregoers trying to flee. "Just go sit down and suffer with everybody else. Suffer!"

Star Turns

Hellzapoppin

Fade Out-Fade In

Illya Darling

Irene

Hellzapoppin (1977)

Fits and Fights and Feuds (and Egos)

Producer Alexander H. Cohen had long been looking for the big hit musical that would validate his public image of himself as a twentieth century Barnum. *Hellzapoppin*, Ole Olsen and Chic Johnson's "scream-lined" revue, was an immense hit when it opened in 1938; it was only the second musical to break the 1,000-performance barrier, setting a record run of 1,404 performances (which held until *Oklahoma!*). It also spawned three similar-but-less-successful entertainments, *Streets of Paris*, *Sons o' Fun*, and *Laffing Room Only*.

Hellzapoppin was the reigning hit when Cohen came to Broadway in 1941, and he long harbored plans to renovate it. Cohen presented TV-comic Soupy Sales in *Hellzapoppin' '67* at the Montreal Expo '67 World's Fair, which failed to wow them and never made it south of the border. Ten years later, Cohen tried again. Cliff Jahr recorded the opening—or, rather, the non-opening—for *New York* magazine.

Jerry Lewis looks quite happy in this photo, presumably taken prior to rehearsals. Note the elevated shoes.

"Hellzafloppin"

by Cliff Jahr

People who don't like Jerry Lewis are apt to look upon the recent closing of *Hellzapoppin* with feelings of apathy or even I-told-you-so. For Lewis fans, however, and there still are some, the musical's demise came as a sad surprise. Not that since Thanksgiving, when tryouts began, there hadn't been talk about a sluggish box office, unhappy critics, and—especially since Christmas—strained relations in the company. Word that Jerry Lewis and producer Alexander Cohen were fighting only confirmed the Shubert Alley predictions that two such giant egos would eventually either have to kill each other off or take a house in the Hamptons.

Lewis could have used a Broadway hit. When demand for him as a performer and film director dipped in the late sixties he rechanneled some of his driving energy into other areas like overseas concertizing and playing the visiting elder statesman at film schools. Oddly enough, his popularity today in parts of Europe may rival the frenzy he and ex-partner Dean Martin whipped up in the fifties. There is still his annual Labor Day telethon, of course, which now rivals the Miss America contest as institutionalized kitsch. It is probably watched as much for all those Vegas types caught in naked moments as it is for its tour-de-force bad taste.

Lewis could have used a Broadway hit. But *Hellzapoppin* proved to be aptly named. When the show closed January 22, it represented a $1.3-million loss and put 70 people out in the cold. Technically it was only being closed for general repairs and cast changes. Cohen said: "*Hellzapoppin* is for sale to anyone who wants to buy." And sure enough, in a dramatic closing-night curtain speech at Boston's Colonial Theatre, Jerry Lewis vowed to do just that. "I plan desperately in the next few days to keep the show together," he said, "and bring it to New York. I think it's terribly important to be uningenuous at moments like this." As of the middle of last week, Lewis's unheard-of plan awaited further developments.

How the show failed is a sort of "Lullaby of Broadway."

Rehearsals of the full company began on October 25. They were held in studios upstairs in the Minskoff Theatre, where it was expected *Hellzapoppin* would return to begin previews in exactly three months. Into the third week, director Abe Burrows stepped aside. [*Hellzapoppin* was Burrows's final Broadway attempt. (*see Breakfast at Tiffany's*, page 42) He died in 1985.] He and Jerry Lewis plainly lacked chemistry. Burrows, the funnyman of words, was a stickler for stage discipline—speaking every line as written—while Lewis, the funny-man of visual action, liked to stay loose and wing it.

Into the director's spot Alexander Cohen elevated the show's production stage manager, Jerry Adler, who in recent years had been his favorite second-in-command (under the director) on any number of shows. But he lacked heavyweight directing experience, and it was said in Shubert Alley that Cohen would handle the directing with Adler's assist and they still would have their hands full with a volatile star like Lewis.

Cohen planned to give the show his particular attention. This was his third attempt to revamp the Olsen and Johnson original. He had managed to leverage a tidy $350,000 investment from NBC, which wanted to use Lewis's Broadway debut for *The Big Event*, its new series of 90-minute specials. The plan was to broadcast some of the February 13 Minskoff opening live, preceded by pretaped sequences of auditions, rehearsals, and the like, with Flip Wilson as host.

"This kind of cross-pollination between theatre and television," said Cohen over a drumroll of NBC ballyhoo, "is long overdo."

MORRIS A. MECHANIC THEATRE

In association with Maggie and Jerome Minskoff
ALEXANDER H. COHEN
presents

JERRY LEWIS

in

HELLZAPOPPIN

A Musical Circus

co-starring

LYNN REDGRAVE

Written by
ABE BURROWS

BILL HEYER   HANK BEEBE

Based on a Format by
Olsen and Johnson

Music by   Lyrics by
JULE STYNE   CAROLYN LEIGH
HANK BEEBE   BILL HEYER

Music for "Bouncing Back" by CY COLEMAN

with

HERB EDELMAN   JOEY FAYE   BRANDON MAGGART

Robert   Tom   Mace   Justine   Bob
Fitch   Batten   Barrett   Johnston   Harvey

THE VOLANTES   BOB WILLIAMS AND LOUIE   LEONARDO

and
JILL CHODER

Scenery and Lighting by   Costumes by   Hair Designs by   Sound Designed by
ROBERT RANDOLPH   ALVIN COLT   JOE TUBENS   JACK SHEARING

Musical Supervision by   Orchestrations by   Dance Music by   Musical Conductor
ELLIOT LAWRENCE   RALPH BURNS   GORDON LOWEY HARRELL   JOHN LESKO

Co-produced by HILDY PARKS and ROY A. SOMLYO

Choreography by
DONALD SADDLER

Directed by
JERRY ADLER

The original billing page, from Baltimore.

It was to be a first, and some media watchers were left wondering whether the network had ever heard of the theatre's high mortality rate on the road.

Cohen visualized this new production as a lunatic vaudeville show, "choreographed chaos," he called it, a great big swell affair mixing flat-footed comics with leggy show girls, variety acts, and liberal dashes of mayhem kept clean as Disney for TV and for Lewis's young fans.

Lewis brought to *Hellzapoppin* an emotional investment. His father, Danny Lewis, a retired Catskills comedian, liked to remind his son that although he had conquered films, clubs, and TV, Jerry still had not made it in "legit." Lewis was persuaded that a Broadway hit would "complete the 360-degree spectrum."

At first, Lewis & Cohen seemed destined to make great vaudeville. "Each thought the other was the greatest genius in the world," notes Adler. "It was a big romance but, as they say, it was too hot not to cool down."

In rehearsals, relations between the two men were sometimes animated, but by the time of the first opening in Baltimore just before Thanksgiving, there was general harmony. When disputes broke out over how best to get a laugh, Lewis would often reach for his wallet and slap a $100 bill on the table. "*There!*" he'd say. "Now you put a quarter—that's 400-to-one odds—not bad—and we'll see who's right."

"I hated to take his money so often," said a smiling Alex Cohen in his Shubert Alley office last week, "and I always gave it to Muscular Dystrophy."

For a star with Lewis's presumed drawing power, sales were disappointing. The out-of-town breakeven figure was $140,000. In Baltimore it hit that figure only one week out of three. The show's reviews were not much better, though critics admired Lewis's tamed-down style. At the beginning he agreed to forget the spastic ad-libbing, stick to the script, and work ensemble with a fine group of stage veterans that included his pal actor Herb Edelman and old-time sketch artist Joey Faye.

According to *Variety*, *Hellzapoppin* was "only half the fun it could be," needing "work, tons of it," but it added, in the lingo of a Vegas M.C., "Lewis is once more a man funny in his own time." As for co-star Lynn Redgrave, she made a "valuable contribution" despite the weak material she had to work with. This weak-material criticism was to dog the show all the way to Boston.

Critics didn't take much notice of Jill Choder, a pretty redhead who is Lewis's protégée. Since she played opposite him in a sad-clown skit taped for his 1974 Labor Day telethon, she and Lewis have been close. Having plenty of Broadway experience, Ms. Choder was given a plum featured role that Lewis conceived in which she played a stagestruck usherette who unendingly *nudzhes* him. At the end of the show, he brings her up from the audience to do a song about this big-break experience called "A Miracle Happened." It was the show's only thread of a story line, a neat star-is-born role with seven entrances, and Ms. Choder was having difficulty with it. [Choder's "experience" consisted of playing one of the young girl "urchins" (and understudying the featured Sally Smith) in the 1965 musical *The Roar of the Grease-paint—The Smell of the Crowd*, and a small role in the 1975 one-week flop *Boccaccio*.]

Opening in Washington, D.C., two weeks before Christmas, amid snowstorms and a cold snap, the show was greeted frostily by Richard Coe of the *Post*. Echoing the Baltimore critics, he liked the first act "almost as it is"; admired Lewis, Redgrave, and Jule Styne's Broadway rhythms; but as for the material—he loved the dog act. Bob Williams and his spaniel Louie (named for Lewis) were stealing the show with the dog's sleepy disregard for his master's cheery commands: "C'mon, boy, sit up," whereupon Louie's backbone would turn to rubber.

Alarm was beginning to creep on little turkey feet into rehearsals and production meetings. A few days after the Washington opening, Lewis called management to a meeting in his suite at the Watergate Hotel, where he read them his memo outlining how to fix the show. The bottom line was that Redgrave must go.

There had been friction between the co-stars, but this was war. Some said Lewis wanted Redgrave out because her crisp charm threatened Jill Choder's audience impact. Others said it threatened Lewis. Redgrave's only musical solo had always offended him, a big sassy production number with her playing a zoned-out Eighth Avenue streetwalker who settles for Park Avenue in Vuitton hot pants. The number made hay of her screen role in *The Happy Hooker*, and one lyric in particular, "I miss the gang I used to bang," made Lewis, the overprotective father of six boys, quake in his dressing room each night. For Alexander Cohen, a strong voice in the drive to clean up Times Square, it was something of an embarrassment as well, but he didn't want to drop "Eighth Avenue" before getting a reading from Elliot Norton, the Boston *Herald-American*'s critic. Anyway, a clause in Redgrave's contract called for at least one musical solo.

The way management saw it, what the show needed was some good new material, less of Jill Choder, more of Lynn Redgrave. Even more important: Lewis and Redgrave had to get together onstage. As the show was then structured, the co-stars did not converge until the second act, doing a sketch that spoofed the [Barbara] Walters-[Harry] Reasoner news show, and they did nothing together musically—all of which goes against theatrical convention. So a new duet was written for them called "Butterflies." Since Choder's "Miracle" could stay and

"Eighth Avenue" would go out if he liked "Butterflies," Lewis reluctantly agreed to run through the song with Redgrave. This he did lying flat on the floor at a Christmas-morning rehearsal in a lounge of Washington's National Theatre. "It's cute," he said of it later, "like the second stanza of the national anthem," and with that, refused to do it.

"Every time I scheduled a 'Butterflies' rehearsal," said director Adler last week, "Jerry said 'We're not doing it. No way.' He was willing to do the number with Jill, but not Lynn. He just went too far with Jill. Finally it became the *burning issue*. It went beyond 'Butterflies,' beyond the show. It got into the area of discipline. Was *he* going to run the show or were we?"

If the question could have been decided by popularity, Lewis might well have won. Despite Cohen's handsome Christmas Eve cast party in a Georgetown restaurant and the little presents that he passed all around, Lewis warmed the company's heart the next morning, with Gucci key rings for the chorus and Vivitar cameras for the principals, left on the doorstep with a handwritten note. Maybe the show was in trouble, but the feeling was that somehow Jerry would pull it through. Besides, they were locked into *The Big Event* on February 13. How could they *not* open?

With show-doctoring stalemated, management acquiesced when Lewis wanted to put in a comic turn he'd used in clubs, a record pantomime set to Leroy Anderson's "Typewriter." Since Baltimore he had already introduced a monologue of Little Jerry, the five-year-old in knickers, who hates it when his fat Aunt Jean buries his face in her "cushions" and warns us, "You could die from that."

If *Hellzapoppin*'s backstage shenanigans were like something out of *42nd Street*, another complication—one more reminiscent of *All About Eve*—was the director's girl friend.

Cathy Rice, a comely ash blonde in the chorus line, had a friendship with Jerry Adler that aroused no end of resentment in the chorus, especially when they kissed in rehearsals or when she called him "Baby Cakes." It was widely believed Ms. Rice routinely sat in on production meetings and passed along chorus-room confidences. "She's a little snitch among us," said one dancer, "and this show hasn't got *enough* hassles?"

On New Year's Day, at the end of *Hellzapoppin*'s four-week Washington engagement, critic Richard Coe took it upon himself to re-review the show and deliver a stern lecture: "Redgrave is a comedienne with proven potential . . . and what's more she's beautiful. Were she playing the usherette who barges into a scene of her own, she'd give glamour and sparkle to what continues to be chintzy and time-consuming. How ridiculous to find a performer with such style relegated to 'second woman.'"

What Coe was most lathered up about was the lack of any change or improvement during the run: "The changes are minimal, " he said. "The pacing is a drag and co-star Lynn Redgrave, despite vows that she'd have more to do, is absurdly wasted."

Alexander Cohen was so disturbed by Coe's unusual action that he telephoned the critic to complain, but also to learn more. Cohen came away doubly determined to do surgery on the show. That day, he was painfully aware that the show had done only $304,000 in its four weeks in Washington instead of the $560,000 it needed to break even—an all-time record loss of about $260,000. The last desperate hope now was the Boston press preview on January 6.

"*Hellzapoppin* NEEDS MORE 'POPPIN," bannered Elliot Norton's review. "There is some fun . . . But the pace is slow . . . and the stars don't really have enough fine first-rate material." He didn't like the Little Jerry *shtik* or Jill Choder's voice but he loved Louie, "the funniest pooch in town." Of Redgrave's "Eighth Avenue" number, he made no mention.

While Norton is considered the dean of American critics, Kevin Kelly of the *Globe* is the one whose larger circulation can make or break a show in Boston. Kelly savaged *Hellzapoppin*: It "flays around like a has-been clown frantic for a comeback." He noted that "A Miracle Happened" could have been "a showstopper if Jill Choder had real magnetism."

So much for any box-office help from the critics, and the next night Cohen cut "Miracle" and "Eighth Avenue" out of the show.

"Something big is coming," Cathy Rice gloated to a friend later. "I can't tell you, but in 48 hours, you'll see."

Thursday night Tommy Tune was spotted in the audience. Director Michael Bennett had recommended the six-foot, six-inch dancer-choreographer to Cohen as a show doctor, and on Friday he was introduced to the assembled company as someone to help spruce things up "in all areas." [Tune had danced in three Bennett musicals; he served as well as associate choreographer on *Seesaw* (1973, see page 28), for which he won a featured actor Tony Award. Tune gained further acclaim as the director of the 1976 off-Broadway play *The Club*; he would finally become a major player in 1978, as co-director/choreographer of *The Best Little Whorehouse in* Texas.] Tune began by explaining he would be tied up all that day in meetings, but he had been working up some steps with "Catherine," who was going to show them a new opening number. Catherine? With that, Cathy Rice stepped forward to take charge and teach the ensemble a new opening of her own devising.

"Every other word out of her mouth was 'kiddies' or 'loveys' or 'honeys,'" groused one chorus girl. "I could gladly have strangled her."

By the end of an exhausting four hours, Cathy gushed, "Thank you, kiddies, for this wonderful birthday present of your hard work." One dancer burst into tears and ran off. There was polite applause for Cathy and Adler's compliments, but her new number was not used.

The next day Alexander Cohen dined at the Ritz-Carlton with four of Jerry Lewis's representatives, two from the William Morris Agency, a lawyer, and a business manager, who had flown from California at Jerry's request to press his case against having to do "Butterflies" with Lynn Redgrave.

Midway through the meeting there was a phone call for Cohen from the theatre. Hildy Parks, Cohen's producer wife, took it and returned with a message from Lewis. He was, she said, furious about the plan to make yet another cut in Jill's part and he was walking out on the matinee's second act, about to start. Moreover, he warned, Cohen had better not come to the theatre because he had a gun in his dressing room and it was loaded.

Cohen sent no reply. His mind was already made up about something. Meanwhile, backstage, members of the chorus were caucusing as to what to do about Cathy Rice's uppitiness. They voted to invite Jerry Adler to a meeting to "clear the air," and set about composing him a note.

The next day, Sunday, January 16, while Tommy Tune ran the ensemble through the paces of his new opening number, Alex Cohen was meeting again with Lewis and three of his men from California in Suite 533 of the Copley Plaza. The meeting lasted two and a half hours. While Lewis maintained he would be glad to rehearse another number, he would not do so with Redgrave. The only thing he would do with her, he said, would be to take out his c—k and p—s on her.

Cohen announced what he was about to do: For the good of the show and all concerned, Jill Choder must be released from her contract.

Lewis sobbed, then, regaining control and accepting the inevitable, said quietly, "Let me tell her. . . ."

Lewis would not speak to Cohen or Adler most of the week that followed. Monday night Tune's new opening number went over big and, while doing it, some cast members noticed Flip Wilson in the theatre. He had come to see "the big event" for himself.

The following night six men sat unnoticed in the theatre. Alexander Cohen had invited them to see the show in order to support or challenge his decision to close it.

Two of the men were NBC brass, four were producing colleagues, and all agreed with Cohen. The show had grossed only $69,000 the first week in Boston and $87,000 the second. The writing was on the wall.

The next morning in New York came Alex Cohen's crisp announcement to the press saying *Hellzapoppin* would close with its last performance in Boston Saturday night.

The closing notice had already gone up on the Colonial Theatre's bulletin board. Caught short, the Sunday *Daily News* had to cancel its four-color, four-page story.

At the matinee Jerry Lewis looked red-eyed and puffy. He played a sketch with Lynn Redgrave in the first act in which he was meant to take a sip of water and then, choking with surprise, spritz it out in a spray. This day, Lewis aimed for Redgrave.

"I don't want to talk about the show," says Lewis, not looking up from his reading. There is a long moment. "If that's what you want to talk about, our meeting's over. When the story is told it will be a doozy. Oh, I got plenty to say. After what I've been through, a civil-service job sounds appealing...."

For the next five days, Lewis and I have glancing meetings in his suite at the Copley Plaza in Boston, backstage, and in his New York office. He has shut out the press clamoring to know, What's the story, Jerry?

Up close Lewis is handsome; the famous face with the cleft, jut-jaw still uncreased and looking about 40 instead of 50. He cuts

National Theatre
In association with Maggie and Jerome Minskoff
ALEXANDER H. COHEN
presents
JERRY LEWIS
in
HELLZAPOPPIN
A Musical Circus
Written by
ABE BURROWS
BILL HEYER   HANK BEEBE
Based on a format by Olsen and Johnson

Music by — JULE STYNE / HANK BEEBE; Lyrics by — CAROLYN LEIGH / BILL HEYER; Music for "Bouncing Back" by CY COLEMAN

with

HERB EDELMAN   JOEY FAYE   BRANDON MAGGART

Robert Fitch   Tom Batten   Mace Barrett   Justine Johnston   Bob Harvey

The Volantes   Bob Williams and Louie   Leonardo

and

JILL CHODER

co-starring

LYNN REDGRAVE

Scenery and Lighting by ROBERT RANDOLPH; Costumes by ALVIN COLT; Hair Designs by JOE TUBENS; Sound Designed by JACK SHEARING

Musical Supervision by ELLIOT LAWRENCE; Orchestrations by RALPH BURNS; Dance Music by GORDON LOWRY HARRELL; Musical Conductor JOHN LESKO

Co-produced by HILDY PARKS and ROY A. SOMLYO

Choreography by DONALD SADDLER; Directed by JERRY ADLER

Co-star Lynn Redgrave has been given enhanced billing in the Washington playbill, her name larger and more prominently positioned.

his own hair in an individual style, slicked back in some places, crew cut in others, an extension of his Big Jerry-Little Jerry persona. A half-inch triangle where the part meets the hairline has been carefully shaved back to a four-day stubble, maybe to mow down a cowlick.

"Would you consider doing a revamped *Hellzapoppin*?"

"No thanks," he says. "Irrevocably no. I think when I get to New York, if things happen as I suspect, I will be ready to talk to you. Be patient, my young friend."

Later on the tape, Lewis sounds uncannily like a young Frank Sinatra—all the crooner's inflections, the swagger, the sweet-tough cool.

At the Saturday matinee everything is terminal euphoria. Word sweeps backstage that in the audience are the Shuberts, Maggie

Minskoff, and Dick Cavett. [The Shubert Organization, headed by Bernard Jacobs and Gerry Schoenfeld, was a major backer of the show. Maggie Minskoff and her husband, builder Jerome Minskoff, were associate producers of the show and owners of the Minskoff Theatre, where it was headed (see *Irene* page 104). Cavett was a popular talk-show host. He would make his Broadway debut several months later, as replacement for Tom Courtenay in Simon Gray's *Otherwise Engaged*.]

At the intermission Cavett looks like he's chuckling inside about something; I introduce myself, and he invites me to slide into the next seat. We kibitz the first part of the second act until Leonardo the plate-spinner comes on and Cavett sits up.

"Oh," he says drolly, "I'm going to like this."

It is obvious Leonardo is out of sorts today. He drops six plates.

"A strange, awful moment, isn't it?" says Cavett. "I don't know what I'd do with it yet but I'll think of something...."

"We kept Jill's goddamned number in for weeks after it should have been cut," Jerry Adler is saying over drinks at the hotel. "If Jill and Herb Edelman were not in the show, not only would we not be closing, we'd have a better show."

Adler, a great, soft huggy-bear of a man, glances over at Cathy Rice.

"Why didn't he go along with letting other people tell him, how to do it?" he continues. "It's just his own craziness. He could have been *fabulous* but he had to change the image a little. He had to mess himself up. Get out of the tuxedo. Get down with the people. People just aren't going to pay $20 to see the same old Jerry Lewis. Very sad, the way he is a victim. The biggest thing we all try to do in show business is never to be the victim."

"How about Cathy's infamous day as a choreographer?"

"I have been hated ever since," she says brightly. "Look, I'm a chorus member, I always was, and I always—I mean—I was terribly hurt."

"Who do you see to replace Lewis?"

"Just about anybody who is personable," Adler says. "Lucille Ball is toying with it. The Smothers Brothers, Steve Allen, Flip Wilson, Bill Cosby, Jack Paar—Alex even likes Milton Berle. Also Dick Cavett. Cavett was at the matinee, y'know, and he hates Lewis. He said, "You think I should go backstage and tell Jerry I love the dog act?" [Cavett served as Lewis's writer for a two-hour 1963 TV special, *The Jerry Lewis Show*.]

A notice is posted on the theatre bulletin board moments before the curtain goes up on the final performance. Cast members gather around and send up a whoop of joy. The news is right out of Andy Hardy, where Mickey Rooney says, "Gang, I've got it! We'll take the show to New York!" Signed by Cohen, the notice begins: "I have been informed that Mrs. Minskoff has offered to put up the money to take *Hellzapoppin* to New York City. . . ."

Maggie Minskoff liked what she saw at the matinee enough to propose buying the show away from the Cohen organization, something Cohen was only too happy to do.

Afterward the cast gathered onstage and Lewis gave details. "The show isn't good enough for the critics," he began, "but we have a show that is terrific for the people. I'm not making any promises. I'm only telling you I'm going to give it one hell of a try."

With Mrs. Minskoff and probably other prior backers, Lewis was into a large undertaking—buying up a $1.3-million production to save it from closing—and no one remembered anything like this ever having been attempted. Lewis returned to New York to go about making his grand gesture a reality.

The final billing page, incorporating the designed title treatment.

Some said saving *Hellzapoppin* was an impossible task, partly because of the production's recent troubles, and partly because Cohen—and Lewis—were right. It was not a critics' show.

Early in the week Lewis agreed to another meeting with me.

His Seventh Avenue office on the twenty-seventh floor in the Muscular Dystrophy headquarters looks much like that of an account supervisor except for the 100 or so photos, cartoons, and drawings of Lewis that cover the walls. There are none of his family.

Lewis looks at home in his business surroundings. His pal Herb Edelman is on the love seat, wearing a black nightclub suit. Clearly he means to stay for the interview.

"Nothing I can discuss with you relative to the show," Lewis says. "I will have lawyers bust you in the mouth if you get me to say anything. You want the story that will give me a lawsuit. I don't need your f—king story that badly."

"Are you pi—ed off at me or something?"

"No, I'm pi—ed off with life. In 48 hours we'll either be in New York with the show or I'll be in Los Angeles."

"Does the whole experience seem worthless now?"

"No, not at all. Anytime you stand up before an audience it's all the same. But I have never been in this position where the work you do will be judged by one critic and that will have an effect on the continuation of said performing. One guy can rap it and it's in the toilet. Jesus Christ almighty, when are people going to start judging a man on a series of performances rather than just one?"

"How would you have fixed the show, Jerry? What all did you want to do in that memo at the Watergate meeting?"

"When I called that meeting, I thought I was talking to rational people. But even one of Alex Cohen's own attorneys calls him a Hitler. Alex Cohen, the Hitler of the theatre."

"Did you suggest a replacement for Lynn Redgrave?"

"No, I didn't. I suggested a replacement of material. Nothing's wrong with Lynn and I. We had a great working relationship. I said to Alex, how could you demean this artist by giving her s—t? She's supposed to be a co-star. You call that a co-star entrance? They had her flying in on a f—king balloon. They tried everything. And Cohen could never understand—I said my name is above the title of the show. Anything that goes on on that stage is under my name. I want her to come off like a class performer. You got her doing chicken s—t that chorus girls could do."

"What about the difficulty with Jill Choder?"

"That's personal. But if you think that had anything to do with the show, forget it. The moment the star of the show has other friends, Cohen sabotages them."

"He was sabotaging Jill?"

"He took 25 slashes at her. Every slash at her was material I had written."

"Did you write 'Miracle'?"

"I wrote the whole premise leading up to it."

"But it was a good song and, after all, wasn't Cohen interested in a hit show?"

"NO! He doesn't want a hit! He wants to hang out with Richard Burton and ride around in his f—king Cadillac. Sick man. He's a star f—ker. Do you understand the word megalomania? Look it up. I had to. Cohen wanted to control me. And when he gave my attorneys an ultimatum—Jerry will do what I tell him! He will sing what I tell him! Stand where I tell him—I sent my people back to tell him to stick the show up his ass."

"You make it sound like he was obsessed with Jerry Lewis."

"Of course. You want to hear a statement he made to one of my staff members? 'I'm going to make Jerry Lewis a global star.' And one of my staff members said, 'You f—king idiot, he is a global star. Has been for a long time. Maybe you mean you want to be a global producer?' You know what he said to Donald Saddler [the choreographer]? 'There's only one way I'll get that son of a bitch out of this show and that's close it.' I'm giving you the facts!"

"They're the facts," says Herb Edelman, nodding his head, "just the way Jerry gave them to me, and I'm his brother."

"In the end wasn't it really a duel between two successful showmen?"

"No. Uh-uh. No," says Lewis, "I'm the only one that's the successful showman. He's a fraud. A con man. You think Hitler wanted to rule the world? S—t, he was a f—king pygmy. But with the name 'Cohen,' God willing, we'll have six or seven trees uprooted in his name from Israel."

"You see," says Edelman, "these are the facts of some of the events, but you still don't have the truth. His performance and the way he handles himself, that's the truth. So all you have is just a bunch of material."

"You can call the story 'Broadway S—ks!'" says Lewis with a chuckle, and Edelman roars. "Not really," Lewis adds, "you can't blame Broadway."

Turning to the windowsill behind him, Lewis holds up a yellowing copy of the *Village Voice* with a back-cover headline that explains JERRY LEWIS IS NOT A SCHMUCK.

"I allude to the *Village Voice*," Lewis says, beginning to snap the fingers of his free hand in a kind of waltz beat. "See that headline? I just want you to remember that."

"Well, it's a great headline but a lot of people still think Jerry Lewis is a schmuck."

"I've got 80 million people that don't think so," says Lewis. "All the people you're talking about, well, these are the things they hate most." Lewis reaches for his memo paper and starts writing a list as he speaks, "...truth, courage, talent, competence, point of view, tolerance of them, and, most of all, multifaceted. The people you're talking about wouldn't like to know Jerry Lewis in person either because then they'd lose somebody to rap. They need that to get through their f—king little timid lives."

With both hands Lewis holds up an eight-by-ten color photo, his elbows resting on the desk, and moves it slowly toward me. It is Frank Sinatra. "One of the greatest human beings that ever lived on the face of God's earth," Lewis says. "You want to talk about cheap shots?"

"Sinatra is the mayor of cheap-shot city," says Edelman. "He really is."

"You want to hear who else they take cheap shots at?" says Lewis, reaching again for memo paper and beginning to write, "...George C.

Scott, Barbra Streisand, Paul Newman, Dustin Hoffman, Bob Redford, Frank Sinatra, Jerry Lewis, and about ten more. But you know who those people are? They're all honest, outspoken, serious-minded, perfectionlike artists that care desperately about what they do.

"The man that does nothing makes no mistakes—I will not live this life without making mistakes."

Hellzapoppin began its tryout tour November 22, 1976 at the Mechanic Theatre in Baltimore. It closed at the Colonial Theatre in Boston on January 22, 1977, with a total loss. The February 13, 1977 Broadway opening at the Minskoff was cancelled.

Like almost all shows that close under similar circumstances, all talk of remounting *Hellzapoppin* soon fizzled and everyone—including the scene-stealing spaniel Louie—went along home.

If Lewis was outspoken in his assessment of Alexander H. Cohen, a fair share of Cohen's competitors and one-time investors would no doubt have wholeheartedly agreed with the sentiments expressed. Cohen was a showman, all right, with many dozens of plays, musicals, and television spectaculars to his name. But his record as a theatrical producer of quality productions was spotty, to say the least.

While Cohen continued producing on Broadway until his death in 2000, at the age of seventy-nine, he was to attempt only one other big budget, can't miss, luminary-crammed major musical: *I Remember Mama*, which was a story in itself [see page 204].

Colonial
Theatre

PLAYBILL

the magazine for theatregoers

May 2 1964

FADE OUT-FADE IN

Fade Out–Fade In (1969)

Disposition and Indisposition

The star vehicle has been an important component of the Broadway theatre since Edmund Kean played *Richard III* at the Park Theatre in 1820. Producers aim for an entertainment of such quality that people will line up in droves. (Most producers, that is; I've come across some who just want to make a quick buck.) The presence of a star, at least, provides a certain invulnerability. In theory, that is; these pages are littered with star vehicles that failed as surely as shows starring Joe Nobody.

A good show can be enhanced by a star presence, certainly. Like *My Fair Lady*, with or without Rex Harrison. A mediocre show can get an enormous boost, like Lauren Bacall's *Applause*. A truly bad star vehicle, truth be told, is likely to stink in any event. (Editor's note: That should be *sink* in any event.)

Our next essay concerns a star vehicle done in by its star, but with a twist: The lady was wildly able, but—for reasons unrelated to the material—unwilling. Press agent Harvey Sabinson explains in his 1977 memoir, *Darling, You Were Wonderful*.

New mother Carol Burnett looks happy to be starring in a Broadway musical.

"Starlight, Starfright"
by Harvey Sabinson

Jack Gaver, a writer for United Press International, called the Carol Burnett caper "a case unique among all of the odd things that have happened on Broadway." An exaggeration, perhaps, but he said it, I didn't.

It all started innocently enough when Lester Osterman and Jule Styne, the composer, got together to produce an original musical called *A Girl to Remember*. [Osterman had produced two 50s musicals with Styne, *Mr. Wonderful* and *Say, Darling*. In 1962 they founded On Stage Productions, which—with funding from ABC—presented three unsuccessful musicals two years later, *High Spirits, Fade Out-Fade In*, and *Something More*.] Betty Comden and Adolph Green were writing the book and lyrics, and Styne, the music. George Abbott, just turned seventy-five, was engaged to direct. The show was to star Carol Burnett—then a burgeoning television personality—as an usherette who, through mistaken identity, is picked for Hollywood stardom.

Characterized by the *Times* as "an interesting hybrid of one part 'American-as-apple-pie-girl-next-door'—a veritable pandowdy of wholesomeness—and one part amiable klutz," Miss Burnett confessed to the interviewer, "There's no doubt that theatre is the prestige medium. It's a bigger challenge to a performer. And doing eight shows a week is exhausting in some ways, exciting in others. You get the chance to experiment."

I announced the salient facts about *A Girl to Remember* to the theatre world and then I waited, and waited . . . and waited. I must have waited a year and a half before the money was raised, the script and score were completed, and the show was ready to go. Or at least I thought it was ready to go.

During that time, Carol did not twiddle her thumbs. She kept adding to her admirers through repeated appearances on the Garry Moore television show. It was only a question of time before she had her own TV show.

In the winter of 1962, Osterman advised me that his production would open on November 23, 1963, at the Mark Hellinger Theatre. Preparations continued through the rest of that winter and well into the spring. Several supporting actors were signed, as well as most of the singing chorus. Designers were commissioned, advertising was planned, dates were allocated to theatre party groups, a major record company agreed to do the original cast album. A serene air of optimism prevailed.

The COLONIAL THEATRE
OWNED AND OPERATED BY
JUJAMCYN THEATERS — SAMUEL H. SCHWARTZ
WEEK OF APRIL 27, 1964
LESTER OSTERMAN and JULE STYNE
present
CAROL BURNETT
in
FADE OUT - FADE IN
A New Musical Comedy
Book and Lyrics by
BETTY COMDEN and ADOLPH GREEN
Music by JULE STYNE
Also Starring
JACK CASSIDY
with
DICK PATTERSON   TINA LOUISE   MITCHELL JASON
REUBEN SINGER   VIRGINIA PAYNE   TIGER HAYNES
AILEEN POE   DAN RESIN   DON CRICHTON   FRANK TWEEDELL
and
LOU JACOBI
Dance and Musical Numbers Staged by ERNEST FLATT
Settings and Lighting by
WILLIAM & JEAN ECKART
Costumes by   Hair Styles by
DONALD BROOKS   ERNEST ADLER
Musical Direction   Orchestrations by
COLIN ROMOFF   RALPH BURNS & RAY ELLIS
Vocal Arrangements by   Dance Music Arranged by
BUSTER DAVIS   RICHARD DE BENEDICTIS
"I, 2, IN QUEST OF HIS YOUTH" — ORCHESTRATED BY ROBERT PRINCE
Directed by GEORGE ABBOTT
Original Cast Album by ABC - Paramount Records
An ABC - Paramount-On-Stage Recording

The billing page from the Boston tryout.

That feeling was short-lived. Early in June, a worried Lester Osterman called me. "You won't believe this," he said, "but the show's off until May of next year. Burnett's pregnant."

"Pregnant?" I yelled in shock. "By whom?"

"Her husband, of course," he replied.

I had forgotten that a few months earlier, Carol had married a television producer named Joe Hamilton, the father of eleven children by his first wife. Rehearsals, Lester said, could probably start in March 1964.

"What about an abortion?" I asked.

"Her husband won't buy that," said Lester. "He's Catholic, I think."

"Terrific," I said. "He doesn't believe in abortion, but he believes in divorce?"

My engines had been all revved up, and now I was being told to go back to the hangar. Breathlessly, I released the information about Carol's confinement to an unsuspecting world of theatregoers, embellishing my announcement with some pertinent statistics: $1,000,000 in group sales was being returned, twenty Equity contract holders would each receive a two-week salary settlement in lieu of steady work, the Hellinger Theatre would be paid a nonrefundable $20,000 rental guarantee, and some $6,000 would be required for additional miscellaneous expenses incurred by the postponement. Miss Burnett's baby was going to be expensive—for Osterman and Styne.

During the gestation period, the show's title was changed from *A Girl to Remember* to *The Idol of Millions*, and finally to *Fade Out–Fade In*. Perhaps it should have remained *A Girl to Remember*. In December, Carol gave birth. [Carrie Hamilton, Burnett's first child, was born December 5, 1963. She became tabloid fodder during her stormy adolescence. Burnett and Hamilton later collaborated on the memory-play *Hollywood Arms*, which was produced shortly after Hamilton's death in 2002.] Two months later, the picture of rosy good health, she reported for rehearsals, a bit reluctantly, it should be said, since the astronomical fees being offered her by the networks made Broadway inconsequential by comparison. Certainly she no longer needed the show as a steppingstone.

Burnett in costume, as a movie usher who finds herself the unlikeliest of movie stars.

Rehearsals and the pre-Broadway engagement were, from my viewpoint, successful and pleasantly uneventful. My relationship with Miss Burnett was not as warm as the one I enjoyed with Lucille Ball. [Sabinson had represented the 1960 musical *Wildcat*, which closed after six months when Lucy, the star and the producer-in-fact, became ill.] Carol tolerated me politely, and that was good enough. *Fade Out–Fade In* was a slightly better show than *Wildcat*. It provided its star with funnier material. It opened at the Hellinger on May 26, 1964, to mixed notices, but it became a solid hit, soon surpassing the box office records achieved by *My Fair Lady* at the same theatre.

In mid-June an abdominal ailment sidelined Carol for a few performances, and her understudy, Carolyn Kemp, took over. Although the producers had had the good sense to take out an insurance policy to cover Carol's absences, it paid them only $2,500 nightly, hardly enough to make up for the refunds.

In July, forewarned that their star would require a week off for minor surgery, the producers secured the services of Betty Hutton, a Hollywood luminary in limbo. They wanted to offer ticketholders a "name" as a replacement. Nevertheless, business that week slumped alarmingly. [The gross plummeted from $64,000—more than competitors *Hello, Dolly!* and Styne's *Funny Girl*—to $18,000.]

Carol's appearances in *Fade Out–Fade In*, following her return from the operation, were sporadic. Claiming that "a very serious neck and back injury," incurred five years earlier, had been aggravated in July when a cab in which she was riding stopped short, she was ordered by her doctors (you and I have a doctor; a star and an ex-president have doctors) to spend most of every day in traction. The producers acceded to a request that her most difficult numbers in the show be curtailed, but they voiced skepticism about her ailment.

In late August, Carol missed another five performances because of the neck injury. Her absence resulted in more refunds.

Osterman and Styne's skepticism was increased in mid-September when it was announced by Bob Banner Productions, a television producing firm, that their star had been signed to appear simultaneously in a new TV variety series entitled *The Entertainers*, to be produced by her husband, Joe Hamilton. "I've missed the tube," she told Val Adams, the *Times* television columnist. "Television is my first love. It makes me furious when I hear television called the illegitimate child of show business."

Carol admitted that she had asked to be released from *Fade Out–Fade In*, but denied a rumor that she had offered a huge sum to buy up her contract. Osterman and Styne, however, admitted privately that her manager had proposed a $500,000 settlement, which they were forced to refuse when the authors objected. ["The authors" had to mean Betty and Adolph, as Jule was one of the producers.] After the Hutton experience, they were also aware that their show was Burnett's, and that a replacement star wasn't feasible. In turn, they sought an injunction to prohibit Carol's television appearances.

Battle lines were rapidly being consolidated as each party engaged high-powered legal advisors. The producers retained Theodore Kheel; Miss Burnett hired Edward Costikyan.

The most explosive salvo yet was fired by Carol when, on October 13, she issued a statement that she must immediately cease all professional activity and enter a hospital for treatment of her back and neck. The doctors had recommended an indefinite period in traction, according to her personal press agent.

Four days later, she was admitted to the Hospital for Joint Disease. Camera bulbs flashed on her arrival at the hospital entrance. Osterman and Styne asked a logical question: when would she be able to return? They received no definitive answer. "We'll run the show as long as we can," Osterman said with feigned determination. "If we can't, we will store the production pending her recovery. We say that she can't work in any other medium until she fulfills her contract with us."

Headlining Mitzi Welch, a new understudy, *Fade Out–Fade In* limped along to ever dwindling grosses until November 14, when, in the face of financial disaster, it was forced to close.

In reply to another request from the producers for the date of her return, Carol, now out of the hospital, wrote: "I have no idea when, if ever, I can return to the type of physical activity I was doing before I went in the hospital—simply because the doctors themselves do not know. I am sorry I got sick. I am sorry the play had to close because I was sick. I am sorry you don't think I'm sick."

Al Hirschfeld provided this preliminary artwork, making the most of Burnett's features.

Aware that she owed an explanation to the cast, Carol sent a message that was posted on the backstage bulletin board: "Just wanted to let you know how sorry I am about the whole mess. Someday, when it is all over, I'd like to tell all of you and the public about the producers and their play." She claimed that a doctor recommended by Osterman had warned her in September that she "would risk serious injury if I didn't cease all activity." She said she had no idea when she could go back to work and "that is why I could not let our producers know."

Osterman and Styne promptly brought charges against Carol at Actors Equity Association, requesting disciplinary action. She had refused to submit the matter to arbitration, and now it had become Equity's hot potato. Carol, in turn, filed counter-charges against the producers, asking Equity to "deprive Osterman and Styne of their right to act at producers in the theatre for attempting to destroy me as a performer and for attacking my personal and professional integrity." Equity had no choice but to reject her allegation. Instead it appointed a committee to consider the producers' charges.

The situation was exacerbated further by Carol's continued appearances on *The Entertainers,* even though these had been filmed prior to her hospitalization. Adolph Green expressed surprise at seeing her hit in the face with a pie and having a door fall on her head on the TV show. At a press conference in her apartment, Carol, wearing a surgical collar, attempted to refute this accusation by explaining, "The thing with the door was done with a camera angle and a sound effect. And I'd like to say to Adolph that I've never been hit with a pie in my life."

She admitted that she was "unhappy and dissatisfied with the musical long before last July," and acknowledged that she tried to buy her way out "for as high as I could have afforded. Right now I'm mad at all of them. They are harassing me in an attempt to get a money settlement, although the show has closed through no fault of my own. I don't like to fight. You know what? Jule Styne is still my favorite composer, though I should bite my tongue for saying it." She added that she would call a truce if an agreement could be reached "with some degree of reasonableness—but I don't think these people are capable of reasoning."

The Equity committee began to hold a protracted series of hearings. More than ten such sessions were held. While these were going on, Carol, much improved, returned to *The Entertainers* on December 28. I gave up all hope that she would ever come back to *Fade Out–Fade In*.

Then, in early February, almost three months after the suspension of performances, Osterman called to say that Carol, at the urging of Equity, had capitulated. She had agreed to return to the show in a few days. Although it would cost an additional $100,000, he and Styne were determined to reopen. He asked me to coordinate an announcement with Carol's representative, which I cheerfully did. In a matter of hours I issued the following statement from her:

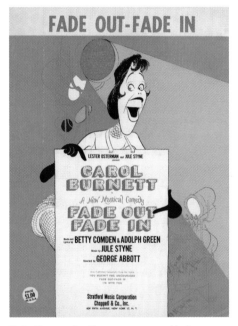

Note the new teeth, nose, eyes, and hair on Hirschfeld's revised art.

"My doctors, including an orthopedic specialist, will now permit me to return, although they said there is, of course, a risk of recurrence of my neck injury. The doctors said that the choice of returning to the show was mine to make. I have always told Lester Osterman that I would return as soon as the doctors would permit me to. Accordingly, I informed Lester that if he wants to reopen *Fade Out–Fade In*, I will do my utmost to perform in it."

It was not a statement to inspire the confidence of theatregoers, but it was the best I could do since it was virtually dictated to me by the legal experts.

Frantic preparations were made for a February 15 resumption at the Hellinger. As part of the settlement, the authors agreed to clarify and trim the story about the unknown who accidentally becomes a movie star. Carol agreed to take a cut in salary to make possible the engagement of comedian Dick Shawn to replace her former leading man, Jack Cassidy, who had grown tired of waiting and taken another job. [Featured actress Tina Louise left as well, to make a TV pilot called *Gilligan's Island*.]

In an attempt to renew interest in this battered property, I composed a brazen ad whose bold-lettered headline read: "CAROL BURNETT IS COMING BACK!" I followed this with what I thought was a persuasive message:

"When *Fade Out–Fade In* was forced to close because of Miss Burnett's illness, it was playing to capacity audiences. Tickets were difficult to obtain. This situation is no longer true. Right now, you have first choice. There are no longer theatre parties. There is no 'million-dollar' advance sale. All tickets are available to the public on a first-come-first-served basis. The opportunity to get GOOD tickets for a HIT musical for current dates is unprecedented."

I did not win an award for copywriting that year.

The *Times* of February 16, 1965 reported: "Peace reigns at *Fade Out–Fade In*, which resumed last night after a 13-week shutdown. After a contractual dispute, the settlement restored employment for 171 persons." Osterman was quoted as saying, "We are trying to avoid acrimony. We want everybody to kiss and make up."

This story does not have a happy ending. Despite my energetic promotional efforts, the box office reaction was disappointing. The events of the previous few months had made the public wary. Theatregoers felt that purchasing tickets was too much of a gamble. On April 17, Osterman and Styne, weary from the fray, and having failed to balance the budget, closed *Fade Out–Fade In* forever after 271 performances, at a loss of $500,000.

A week after the closing, while engaging in informal athletic activity with her husband's children, Carol Burnett tripped and broke an ankle. I cannot say that the news provided much cheer for Osterman and Styne, but I doubt if they ever sent her a "get well" card.

Fade Out–Fade In opened May 26, 1964 at the Mark Hellinger Theatre to favorable reviews. Performances were suspended November 14, and resumed February 15, 1965. The show closed April 17, 1965 after 271 performances, with a total loss.

The *Fade Out* affair did not damage Burnett's career. *The Entertainers* was followed by *The Carol Burnett Show* (1967–78), during the course of which zany comedienne Burnett transformed herself into one of America's best-loved performers. She remained persona non grata on Broadway, perhaps, but no harm done. (And I can't believe that she wasn't regularly solicited by Broadway producers, despite *Fade Out*.) During her 1973 hiatus, she toured in the musical *I Do! I Do!* with Rock Hudson, doing land-office business everywhere she went but avoiding New York.

It wasn't until 1995—at the age of sixty-two, and thirty years after *Fade Out*—that Burnett finally returned to Broadway. Her talents were undiminished, but her diminished ticket-selling power was not enough to withstand the weaknesses of *Moon over Buffalo*. (The play did result in a fascinating 1997 documentary, *Moon over Broadway*, which preserves the backstage poison of a Broadway show in severe trouble.) Burnett made yet another visit in 1999 with the Stephen Sondheim revue *Putting It Together*, but star and show met with public apathy and a disappointing three-month run.

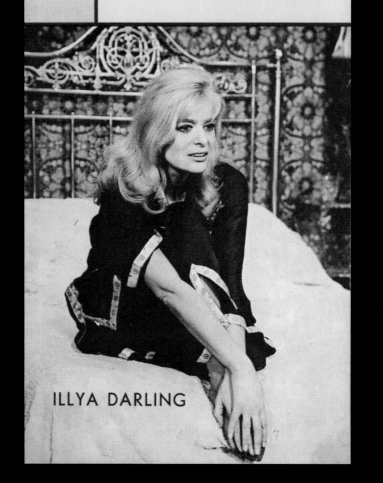

ILLYA DARLING

Illya Darling (1967)

The One-Eyed Prostitute

Lehman Engel (1910–1982) came to Broadway in 1934, working initially as composer of incidental music for such plays as Sean O'Casey's *Within the Gates* and T.S. Eliot's *Murder in the Cathedral*. After wartime service, he returned in 1946 as musical director of Harold Rome's "mustering-out" revue, *Call Me Mister* (the first of eight shows he did for Rome). By 1950 he was working almost exclusively as musical director, picking up Tony Awards for Gian-Carlo Menotti's *The Consul* and Leonard Bernstein's *Wonderful Town*. By 1966 he had conducted about two dozen Broadway shows, including *Fanny*, *Li'l Abner*, *Take Me Along*, and *I Can Get It for You Wholesale*.

Engel's recounting of his experience on *Illya Darling*—taken from his autobiography, *This Bright Day*—offers a cautionary tale of working with international star-producers and their international director-librettist-producer husbands.

Melina Mercouri graces the cover of the Broadway program.

from "This Bright Day"

by Lehman Engel

I spent the summer of 1966 in New York. In June, Jules Dassin, whom I had known twenty-five years earlier, called me. He was to write and direct a musical based on his charming film *Never on Sunday*. I invited him to dinner, where I cautioned him that in my opinion this translation from film to stage would be very difficult and urged him to think carefully about it before starting. I advised the making of a subplot because of the single-mindedness of the only plot in the film and the creation of some suspense, and most of all I thought the subplot on stage was necessary because, in the film, Melina Mercouri (his wife) was in nearly every frame. She could not physically (I thought) be in every scene, and the use of a subplot would not only be a relief for Melina but also for the audience.

Julie said he thought this was all very interesting and promised to think about it. (He did nothing about it and Melina was in nearly every scene.)

When Julie returned to New York with Melina and Manos Hadjidakis, the composer, we had more meetings than any pharaoh ever dreamed of while building a pyramid. And at all of them everybody, in every department, was asked be present. The wasted time was prodigious.

Hadjidakis is a very fat man who looks much older than he is. A number of upper front teeth are missing and others are a "bright canary yellow." ["Bright Canary Yellow" was a Rodgers and Hammerstein song cut from *South Pacific*. (It has been used on several occasions since Hammerstein's death, under the title "Loneliness of Evening.") Hammerstein used the descriptive phrase in "A Cockeyed Optimist," which begins "When the sky is a bright canary yellow...."] He speaks more English than he admits and usually tries to hide behind his French. He is enormously talented and shy.

I was invited often to Julie and Melina's apartment, where a Greek servant fixed marvelous dishes. There was music, gaiety, dancing, and singing. Melina was all Greek except for figure and wardrobe, which were Paris. She was chic, knowing, charming, petulant—a gracious hostess, sometimes a child but more of the mother of everyone else.

Julie always had Hadjidakis play his latest song, and I found all of them very pretty, but I was disturbed by their similarity, gentleness, prettiness, nontheatricality, and their lack of real endings. I spoke of this frankly and was finally able to include into the score of *Illya Darling,* as it came to be called, Hadjidakis's old hit song "Never on Sunday." [This was the title song of the film.] It turned out to be the only successful song in the whole show.

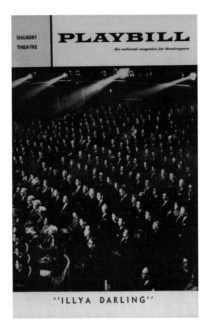

"ILLYA DARLING"

This program used one of Playbill's generic cover photos. Theatregoers don't dress the way they used to.

Everyone was kept busier with the preparation of this show than with anything I had ever done before. We interviewed many bazouki (the Greek mandolin) players. Few read any music, and all were arrogant since they had well-paying café jobs, which they were reluctant to leave for the pre-Broadway tour of *Illya Darling.*

Julie had two production ideas which were quite impracticable: he wanted Melina (near the start of the show) to dive into the orchestra pit followed by a number of men! (It was to be the Aegean Sea.) Everyone protested. It was dangerous. Also the pit would have to be cleared. Thirty or forty minutes would be required to install and connect music stands, place chairs, distribute music, and seat the players before there would be any playing. Julie was very slow to believe this, and indeed he never quite abandoned the idea.

The other idea was to "fly" four bazouki players on a platform festooned with flowers. Their music would comprise the overture. There were several versions of this, and in the end they were mildly effective. [Orchestrator Ralph Burns's note on the score for his final version of the Overture: "At this point shipyard noises and Illya's laugh etc. should come in if not before, as without them the audience will have left the theatre!!"]

I made simple vocal arrangements as requested by Hadjidakis, who approved them all. They were taught to the male chorus (singers and dancers), but Julie wanted only unison or two-part singing. There were arguments and much wasted time. One day it was one way; another day, another.

Everyone connected with this production was doing musical theatre

SHUBERT THEATRE
OWNED AND OPERATED BY
JUJAMCYN THEATRES   SAMUEL H. SCHWARTZ

KERMIT BLOOMGARDEN
in Association With UNITED ARTISTS
presents

MELINA MERCOURI
in
"ILLYA DARLING"
a new musical based on
"NEVER ON SUNDAY"
Co-starring
ORSON BEAN
with
TITOS VANDIS   NIKOS KOURKOULOS   DESPO
RUDY BOND   HAL LINDEN   WILLIAM DUELL

Music by   Lyrics by
MANOS HADJIDAKIS   JOE DARION

Scenic production by   Lighting by   Costumes Designed by
OLIVER SMITH   JEAN ROSENTHAL   THEONI V. ALDREDGE
Musical Direction and Vocal Arrangements by   Orchestrations by   Dance music arranged by
LEHMAN ENGEL   RALPH BURNS   ROGER ADAMS
Assistant Choreographer   Associate Conductor   Production Stage Manager
TOMMY PANKO   KARON GUSTAFSON   DON DOHERTY
Dance and Musical Numbers Staged by
ONNA WHITE
Book and Direction by
JULES DASSIN
Original Cast Album on United Artists Records

The Philadelphia billing page. Lehman Engel is credited for musical direction and vocal arrangements.

for the first or (in Julie's case) second time. [*Illya* was Dassin's third musical. *Magdalena*, a Wright & Forrest operetta, lasted 88 performances in 1948. *Two's Company*, an especially troubled revue starring Bette Davis, lasted 90. On the latter, Dassin worked with choreographer Jerome Robbins—who at one point had "entire production under the supervision of" billing.] Much money was wasted. Almost from the start of rehearsals, we worked overtime an hour a day. After the opening in Philadelphia we never rehearsed *without* the scenery, which meant paying a full stage crew—an unheard of extravagance in the theatre because of its prohibitive cost.

Julie engaged Joe Darion (*Man of La Mancha*) as lyricist against much advice to the contrary; he then became so dissatisfied that he spoke of sending for a Greek poet who spoke English!

Schedules were seldom made for the next day until after the cast had been dismissed. The stage managers spent many late hours telephoning everyone.

Ralph Burns (orchestrator) was nearly frantic at not getting songs early enough to orchestrate. Theoni Aldredge (costume designer) said there would be *no* costumes if precise personnel were not selected for each scene and measured at once. (Julie shifted personnel in nearly every ensemble number almost daily.)

I complained that it was impossible to train a chorus with shifting personnel, shifting arrangements, missing lyrics, and unfinished songs. (Even the *finished* songs sounded unfinished.)

There were meetings all the time. I never knew who to take orders from since Hadjidakis (composer) and Dassin (director) were always at odds with one another and each gave conflicting orders.

From time to time all the principals except leading man Orson Bean suffered from laryngitis.

After rehearsing two and a half weeks, the ensemble still did not know what to do, what notes to sing, or which lyrics were being used. Dassin nightly promised me more rehearsal time, but the next day, plans were changed and I usually ended up with none.

As I had predicted, there was too much Melina, although her charm was obvious. The part of the romantic leading male was too unimportant and there was—as we found—no second act.

Hadjidakis wanted me to conduct everything slowly, while Dassin wanted it fast. They argued and, as always, left me with no clear direction.

My orchestra rehearsals began January 9 in Philadelphia. (We had begun stage-rehearsing December 5.) As I had no interference, everything went smoothly. While this was under way, the late Jean Rosenthal, the very talented lighting designer, was setting her cues in the theatre. However, when Dassin arrived in Philadelphia he categorically and petulantly declared, without seeing what Jeannie had spent several days working out, that he would do his own lighting.

We opened January 16. Nothing was good. The only musical number the audience bought was "Never on Sunday." It stopped the show, and we did an encore.

About the middle of our Philadelphia engagement James Felton of the Philadelphia *Bulletin* asked me for an interview, which appeared prominently in his paper on the Sunday of our departure for Toronto. The headline of the article was, "Retiring from Rat Race: No More Pit Stops for *Illya* Conductor?"

In the piece I was quoted as saying:

"I've had it," says Lehman Engel, music director of 160 Broadway shows. [This figure was vastly exaggerated.] At 56, he's still moving forward, but he doesn't plan on swinging a baton anymore after *Illya Darling* runs its course. He's musical director of the show, which ended its tryout run here yesterday, and is headed for New York via Toronto and Detroit.

MARK HELLINGER
THEATRE

KERMIT BLOOMGARDEN
in Association With UNITED ARTISTS
presents

MELINA MERCOURI
in
ILLYA DARLING
a new musical based on the film
"NEVER ON SUNDAY"

Co-starring
ORSON BEAN

with
TITOS VANDIS   NIKOS KOURKOULOS   DESPO
RUDY BOND HAL LINDEN WILLIAM DUELL HAROLD GARY JOE E. MARKS

Lyrics by   *Music by*
JOE DARION   MANOS HADJIDAKIS
Scenic production by   *Lighting by*   *Costumes designed by*
OLIVER SMITH   JEAN ROSENTHAL   THEONI V. ALDREDGE
Musical Direction
KAREN GUSTAFSON

Orchestrations by   *Dance music arranged by*
RALPH BURNS   ROGER ADAMS
Assistant Choreographer   *Production Stage Manager*
TOMMY PANKO   DON DOHERTY
Dance and Musical Numbers Staged by
ONNA WHITE
Book and Direction by JULES DASSIN
Original Cast Album on United Artists Records

The final billing, with Broadway's first female musical director Karen Gustafson. Note that lyricist Joe Darion and composer Manos Hadjidakis have switched positions from Philadelphia.

"It takes too much time, and I have better things to do than to run bad shows," he explained in his hotel suite the other night, taking a hard look at Broadway with soft eyes.

Then I spoke of my book (*The American Musical Theatre: A Consideration*), which was by then in the editing stage. In connection with this, I was further quoted:

"A good show will work when all of its elements are equally good— libretto, characters, music, lyrics, choreography. *Oklahoma!* and *West Side Story* are good because they work on every level. And they'll go on being good shows. That's the difference between a hit that might run on Broadway for a year or two and the shows that will become staples.

"What we need is a theatre of feeling. Who can identify with the grotesque, middle-aged women who star in some of the big shows today? It's hard to feel much for a one-eyed prostitute in Turkey."

This latter remark was taken personally, but I was not to learn about it for a few days.

Rehearsals in Toronto in the enormous O'Keefe Centre went along fairly well, but Manos's presence slowed things down. He wanted many, many changes and because of his inarticulateness and his language problems, rehearsals often nearly came to a standstill.

We opened on Wednesday and got very bad reviews. Two days later Kermit Bloomgarden (the nominal producer) called me into his suite. He told me he thought I had been stupid in giving the Philadelphia interview, that Julie and Melina were upset because of my reference to "grotesque, middle-aged women." (I know that I had intended it only as a reference to a growing trend in the American Musical Theatre.) However, I could certainly understand their feeling. (Had I done it intentionally?)

Kermit said that since I was unhappy, they would release me at once. I agreed that I was extremely unhappy, but inasmuch as I had put in so much work I was not willing to quit: my contract however could be bought. Kermit made me an offer, and we finally reached settlement. I was asked *not* to conduct that evening. My assistant took over.

I stayed in my hotel room that evening, as there was no flight to New York. William Little of the *Toronto Sun* came to interview me and wrote a piece that appeared the following Monday. Again I had—but sincerely unintentionally—offended. The headline read: "Bored Conductor of *Illya* Quits, Is Replaced by Woman."

During the following six weeks, I had letters and phone calls from many of the show's people (but none from my assistant, who had replaced me). [Engel's departure resulted in Karen Gustafson becoming—as far as I can tell—the first woman to serve as musical director of a new musical. A very few women, including Gustafson, had conducted as assistant or replacement. Women conductors on Broadway remained a rarity for another twenty years.]

At the New York opening *Illya Darling* got a poor press, but Melina contrived to draw audiences for a number of months. All that I foresaw that could be wrong with it was wrong. I was tired of playing Cassandra and felt the time had finally come when I expected never again to become involved in a Broadway production.

Illya Darling opened April 11, 1967 at the Mark Hellinger Theatre to unfavorable-to-pan reviews. It closed there January 13, 1968 after 320 performances, with a partial loss.

Jules Dassin began his career as an actor at the Yiddish Art Theatre on Second Avenue. He directed his first (of six) Broadway shows in 1940, his first film in 1941. In Hollywood, he specialized in film noir, with such movies as *Naked City* (1948) and *Night and the City* (1950). His career was cut short when he was named before the House Un-American Activiites Committee as a Communist. (Dassin was named by Edward Dmytryk, director of *Murder, My Sweet*, *Crossfire*, and *The Caine Mutiny*.) He moved to France, where his career picked up with foreign films like *Rafifi* (1955) and *Topkapi* (1964).

Never on Sunday (1960) was Dassin's biggest hit; besides directing it, he starred opposite—and coproduced it with—Melina Mercouri, whom he married in 1966. The musical version of *Never on Sunday* (with lyrics to be written by E.Y. Harburg) was first announced in 1962 by producer Kermit Bloomgarden, a supportive friend of many blacklist victims. The international success of *Topkapi* (starring Mercouri) made *Illya* a reality, with full funding from United Artists. Lyricist Joe Darion (recently of *Man of La Mancha*) and writer John Patrick (of *Teahouse of the August Moon*) came along, although Patrick eventually departed to, in his words, "avoid a conflict with the author of the original story."

As Engel indicated, *Illya* was indeed an ending. He continued to conduct around the country and as far afield as Tokyo (where he served as musical director of the Harold Rome-Joe Layton *Scarlett*, based on *Gone with the Wind*). But *Illya* was his final Broadway musical—or would have been had he not departed in Toronto. Engel had already embarked on a new career as a teacher. In 1961, he started meeting with young Broadway-bound songwriters under the auspices of Broadcast Music Inc. (BMI), the music-licensing organization.

As Engel restricted his conducting activities, he began to focus more and more attention on the BMI Musical Workshop. The Workshop has been the starting point for such writers as Maury Yeston, Alan Menken, Howard Ashman, Stephen Ahrens and Lynn Flaherty, and more. Engel's role in the writing of *A Chorus Line* caused him to be posthumously immortalized (?) as a musical comedy character in Ed Kleban's *A Class Act* (2001).

SHUBERT
THEATRE

PLAYBILL
MAGAZINE

IRENE

Irene (1973)

That's How the Money Goes

If Ruby Keeler can headline a smash hit revival of the creaky old 1925 "Tea for Two" musical *No, No, Nanette*, why not Debbie Reynolds in the even creakier, even older 1919 "Alice Blue Gown" musical, *Irene*? And so, yet another Broadway adventure, as captured by Chris Chase in *New York* magazine.

This Philadelphia program features an early and somewhat ghostly version of the art by Hilary Knight.

"No, No, *Irene*"
by Chris Chase

They call it a Broadway show, but the company's been wandering the provinces—Toronto, Philadelphia, Washington—since last December, while the cast cleaned up its Irish brogues and the management just cleaned up.

Already this tryout tour of *Irene* has grossed more than a million dollars, and on March 13, with Debbie Reynolds starring, the revival of the 1919 musical hit about a poor girl from Ninth Avenue who falls in love with a Long Island millionaire will finally open at the Minskoff Theatre in New York.

The saga leading up to the opening night begins with three oddly-assorted producers. (A producer raises the money. Show biz makes strange breadfellows.) There's Harry Rigby. Harry is gaunt, white-haired, expensively sweatered. During rehearsals, he prowls the house, his sardonic laughter booming through the dark, confusing the actors who don't know what the joke is. He uses his hands like Jack Benny, sounds like a cross between Truman Capote and Selma Diamond, says what's on his mind, and has a passion for nostalgia which seems almost willfull. Having been jilted by *Nanette* (it was Harry's idea to revive N.N.N, it was Harry's idea to hire Busby Berkeley and Ruby Keeler, Harry had all the ideas; it was co-producer Cyma Rubin who threw him out, Cyma had all the money), he was nonetheless eager to try again with *Irene*.

There's Albert Selden. Selden is big, handsome, has nice manners and nine children. He brought Harry in on *Hallelujah, Baby!* [see page 134]; Harry brought him in on this one. Either Selden is so rich he doesn't give a damn, or he's supremely confident because, in the middle of February, he said "ta" to the troupe, and went off on an African safari.

The third man is contractor Jerome Minskoff. He and his family own the skyscraper (on West 45th Street) which houses the new Minskoff Theatre where *Irene* will be the first attraction.

Also involved from the start has been the 40-year-old Debbie, who left her shoe-magnate husband, Harry Karl, minding the store in California and came east to play. (Shoe biz makes estranged bedfellows? Nah, I just can't pass up a pun.)

But the rest of the cast could be listed in order of disappearance:

Sir John Gielgud, director. He was hired reverently—to bring class to American musical comedy—and he was let go the same way. (Remember Clark Kerr's crack, after his removal as president of the University of California at Berkeley? "I left the presidency as I entered it," he said, "fired with enthusiasm.")

Hugh Wheeler, the author. He wrote the book (from an adaptation by Harry Rigby, based on the original play by James Montgomery, says the *Playbill*), but the day—in Toronto—that the show opened, Hugh Wheeler closed. ("The man had an incredible contract," Debbie Reynolds marveled later. "He was already signed to do the new Hal Prince show. He worked with Sir John and Harry four, five weeks, whatever it was, and then he was through, he had to go. And everybody knew it but me. I said, "How can a writer leave the day you open out of town, and you have to begin to redo things?"") [The show in question was *A Little Night Music,* which—with *Irene*'s delayed opening—became Wheeler's first musical. It came to Broadway February 25, 1973, two weeks before *Irene* arrived across Shubert Alley.]

The cover from Washington, with a livelier and more modern Debbie Reynolds.

Billy De Wolfe, actor. The part of Madame Lucy (a couturier) in this revival was built around him. He came to the first four of five days of rehearsals, announcing from time to time that his doctor had advised against the effort. "I'm doing it for you," Billy told the company. On his 67th birthday, Debbie brought him a cake. He quit anyway. [The prissy character comedian was best known for his film and television work (often supporting Doris Day). He died one year into *Irene's* run.]

There was one real tragedy (Norman Norel, who was to have designed the costumes, died), and there were several minor injuries (the leading man, Monte Markham, sprained his ankle; the composer of incidental music, Wally Harper, got pneumonia; Patsy Kelly, who plays Debbie's mother, was out for a couple of days with an abcess), but even when the show was at its woolliest, out-of-town patrons flocked to lay their money down. Once again, Harry Rigby had dug up a work—and a star—people would come out to see.

Debbie, who prefers movies "but I'm not making movies; there isn't anybody rushing up to me with movie offers," had been saying no to Rigby for two years. Her kids were in school, she had a hot nightclub act (the Desert Inn, in Las Vegas, let her out of a contract so she could do *Irene*), she was busy with her Motion Picture Museum. Then, she says, one day it hit her. "I'm not a kid anymore. If I don't do this show, I won't do another."

That's John Gielgud's signature at the bottom, although you'd suppose that he'd want to disavow any connection to the endeavor.

She wanted Peter Gennaro to choreograph—"He did *Molly Brown* for me, his style is my style, if I have a style"—and she and Rigby were both excited by the idea of getting Sir John. "Everybody said oh, he'd never do it," Debbie remembers. Everybody was right. He didn't do it.

They opened in Toronto, a shambles. A show has to break in somewhere, but Canadian newsmen behaved as though Debbie had invited them to an exhibition of her dirty laundry. Then she lost her voice, and the heat was transferred to her understudy, Janie Sell.

"They locked her in a room," Debbie says. "I heard about the meeting, and I went there in my orange bathrobe, carrying a cup of tea. I couldn't even speak. I stood at the door and there were five people around this girl. All these leeches telling her she had to go on, and she was in tears. I told her to get up and leave, and a certain person said to her, 'Sit down, you have a contract!' and I walked over to him and I set my teacup down and I croaked, '*I* have a contract, and she isn't going on and make a fool of herself. *I'll* go on and make a fool of myself!'" Pause. "And I did."

Pantomiming her part, Sir John rambled through a long synopsis of the story, and some spectators booed, and 300 demanded their money back. Debbie got through the evening, only to discover that Rex Reed had been in the audience. Reed promised not to write about it. Then he went on television and told everybody what a ghastly experience it had been. He hadn't promised not to talk about it.

Even from New York, bad-mouthers were reaching out for Debbie. After CBS showed a special called *Opening Night, USA*, which included scenes from what purported to be *Irene*'s first performance in Toronto, the *Daily News* pronounced the offering superb. Except for Debbie. She gave new meaning to the term show-stopper, said the *News*'s reviewer, because "the show slowed and sputtered" each time she appeared. After which he talked about "her tinny singing," compared her unfavorably to Sammy Davis Jr. and Milton Berle, and wished her luck. Still, Canadians bought tickets.

Eight weeks after they first came together (one month's rehearsal, one month in Toronto), the *Irene* company headed for Philadelphia, tripping over rumors as they traveled.

Some of the rumors: that so many play-doctors (including Robert Benton and David Newman) were being implored to come down and patch up the book, they were bumping into one another on the Metroliner; that equal numbers of songwriters were being invited to create new songs; that Debbie had called Sir John "a hack;" and that Peter Gennaro had (1) quit (2) been fired (3) turned off his hearing aid.

An intrepid reporter checks everything out. I phoned Mr. Benton. [Benton and partner Newman wrote the script for the musical *It's Superman* and the screenplays for *Bonnie and Clyde* and *What's Up Doc*?]

"Gee, no, I don't want to talk about it," he said. Then I asked Ruth Cage, the show's press representative, if Debbie had called Sir John that bad name. Ruth said no, Debbie never. Then I found out that Sheldon Harnick *was* going to write a song for the finale (but I found that out a long time afterward) and that Peter Gennaro had neither quit nor been fired. I don't know if he turned off his hearing aid.

Two of the three Philadelphia newspaper reviews were terrible. One guy adored Debbie –"Almost singlehandedly, she manages to make the Cinderella drivel seem fresh"—but blamed Sir John for the "directionless, humorless, unglued staging." Another chap didn't like the direction or the star. Only the *Evening Bulletin*'s man found *Irene* "a friendly and funny show."

That was enough for Harry Rigby. "Two bad, one good is fine. One for the box office, and the other two to get the cast up. If they'd got all raves, they wouldn't have done any more work."

He wasn't talking about Debbie, who doesn't know how to stop working, and who gazed, cold-eyed, at the people rushing back to tell her she had a smash. "I like to know the truth, I don't like all the b.s., all that 'Oh, that was wonderful, dear.' Opening night here everybody loved this show. I never heard such accolades. And I just stared at everybody and I came back to the hotel and had a drink by myself. I thought, well, it's good we got through it, but there's work to be done—why is everybody so happy?"

I met Debbie in Philadelphia, in the week between Christmas and New Year's. I'd been to the show. It rambled. You couldn't hear the singing, except for George S. Irving. (Irving plays Madame Lucy.) Patsy Kelly, desperate for laughs, had turned herself into a dog, climbing up Irving's shirt front, pawing, sniffing, barking, when she wasn't crossing herself, or offering a fellow actress two hands and both feet to be kissed. It was an outrageous display, and once you've said that, you also have to say the audience loved it. The audience filed out saying how much better *Irene* was than *Sleuth*, which had been the previous attraction at the Shubert. [This was presumably a touring company of *Sleuth*, the hit 1970 thriller.]

Late that evening Ruth Cage and I were invited to the living room of Debbie's suite. We found her sitting on a blue-and-green-plaid couch, sipping wine and smoking a cigarette. She's self-conscious about the smoking because her sixteen-year-old daughter, Carrie Fisher (who's working in the *Irene* chorus) doesn't approve. [Fisher, the daughter of Reynolds and Eddie Fisher, became a sudden movie star in 1977 with the release of *Star Wars*.]

Also in the room was Rudi Render, who is Bobby Short's cousin and Debbie's secretary, rehearsal pianist and friend. From time to time, Rudi would put in a word about Debbie's gifts—"Her forte is really dramatic, she doesn't quite accept it."

Despite her abiding public image—cheerleader, sprite, the madcap who goes on the Carson show and tears Johnny's clothes off—unrestraint is not Debbie's thing. Having come up at M-G-M, through a contract system which turned out iron maidens, starlets made of steel—"After us, no more, that was the end, television came in, and everything went out"—she believes in learning discipline (that's why Carrie's in the chorus) and says her old studiomates—Jane Powell, Ann Blyth, Leslie Caron, Vera-Ellen—were even less self-indulgent that she. "They lived on celery leaves, carrot sticks. I'd ask Janie why and she'd say, 'I have to keep my figure.' 'Keep it?' I'd say. 'You couldn't give it away, there isn't anyone wants it.' When I'm upset, I eat the world up."

Onstage, Debbie looks like a Madame Alexander doll, the great puffs of red-blond hair, the wide-spaced eyes under long glossy black lashes, the bright red mouth. Here, wigless and clean-faced, she looks even smaller, plucked, tired. Maybe she eats the world up, but odds are she hasn't had any mashed potatoes lately.

She says *Irene*'s big problem is with the book. "The music is there. 'Alice Blue Gown,' 'You Made Me Love You,' 'What Do You Want to Make Those Eyes at Me For?'"

"No one knows," says Rudi. "She's untapped talent."

After some pussyfooting around, the big question is put. Has Debbie become disenchanted with Sir John?

"I've never thought of another director," she says, "and he's never thought of leaving. It's all just a dumb rumor. I think he's fantastic, I love him, and that's the truth."

Is the show different from the way it was in Canada?

"Unfortunately, no," says Debbie. "But it will be."

She's more optimistic now because Joe Stein ("an old friend and a wonderful writer") who did the book for *Fiddler on the Roof*, has suddenly become available to work on *Irene*. "Today he gave us three major changes, and they're terrific."

Since she doesn't intend to face the New York critics—"When you come to Broadway from Hollywood, there's a kind of snobbery toward you the way there isn't if you're from New York or England or someplace like that"—until the show is "as good as we want it," Debbie has refused to be stampeded back to the Apple. She's insisting on extending the tour, and she's upsetting the management. She says she's been willing to try everything, out of town, but "the things I didn't like five weeks ago, I still don't like, and now they're going. I gave them the best chance I could. This is not my medium, and I bow to the experience of others."

Sometimes. Sometimes she fights—"for the proper material, for time for the people to write it, for time to rehearse it, for time to put it in front of an audience and let *them* decide."

"Debbie's name will sell tickets," Rudi says. "And it'll run. You know why? Word of mouth. By the time this show hits New York, it will have everything going for it, you're just gonna laugh and say oh, how marvelous."

From the lady who cleans the dressing rooms, and treasures an autographed picture of Debbie ("She's a lovely girl, she married a boy from the neighborhood," the cleaning lady says—for her time has had a stop, Eddie and Debbie are still young lovers), to the queues of people at the ticket window every morning, Philadelphians are wild to see *Irene*. Maybe Rudi Render knows something.

In the Barclay Hotel, which he likes because the people there are so polite, Sir John Gielgud is facing another morning.

Politesse is much on Sir John's mind. He says the girl who has just brought him a fresh light bulb is polite, and so is the woman who's taken away his laundry. He talks about Jackie Kennedy in the same way. "Charming girl," he says, "very polite."

This business of doing a musical comedy interests him—*Irene* appeals because "it's got a sort of fragrant charm" he remembers from the musicals of his youth—"but I wish I had a bit more control over it. There are three producers and all the other departments and everybody disagrees about what should be changed, and the actors find it difficult to play one version and rehearse another. And I, being an actor, am very sympathetic to the actors' problems and want to make them happy if I can. But the things you keep on telling them not to do they *will* do, because once the curtain's up you can't stop them."

He smiles a trifle wanly. "It all shakes down, and it's amazing how quickly one forgets the unpleasant things in life. Thank God. And if you can only bring a thing off at the end, you forget all your troubles—"

That afternoon, on the freezing cold stage of the Shubert, Sir John is trying to figure out a way to bring six chorus boys through a door, and not bring chaos with them. Huddled in a pale mink movie-star coat, black slacks and a warm hat, Debbie makes suggestions. Sir John seems like a great, weary bird, too refined, too gentlemanly to deal with the actor in front of him who is bickering about every syllable of a line of dialogue.

Out in the house, Harry Rigby slumps in a seat and sighs over the actor's intransigence. "I don't know whether he's a frustrated director or writer or what."

Rigby says he knew *Nanette* was a hit even before they had a second act, but about this one, "I just can't tell. The dress rehearsal was the worst I ever sat through, and that includes the one with Mrs. Rubin. [This refers to the notoriously difficult Cyma Rubin, the aforementioned controlling producer of the revival of *Nanette*.] Sir John was hysterical, the choreographer was hysterical, and then she came out—" he indicates Debbie—"and she said, 'If we all get upset we won't be able to do it.' Of everybody in the show, I have the best rapport with her. And she's the smartest."

A kid rushes up the aisle with a sheaf of contracts. "Thank God they found them," says Harry. "I thought I left them at the Woman's Exchange when I went to get some brownies."

He's watching Sir John make one more attempt to line up the six boys in some kind of order. "Messy," Harry says. "Messy."

A few days later comes the end of the Knight. Sir John is out. The company's going to stay an extra week in Philadelphia, and the first morning the new tickets go on sale, 200 are sold.

Albert Selden has sent for his friend, director Burt Shevelove, to fly in from London and take a look, and Debbie Reynolds has sent for her friend, director Gower Champion, to fly in from Malibu and take a look.

Now the pressure is on. Not only will Champion not allow any press at rehearsals, he won't allow any non-cast member whatsoever at rehearsals, and that includes producer's wives.

Albert Selden's wife doesn't care, she's going on a safari with her husband, but before they leave, Selden offers an opinion. "Champion's a cold fish," he says, "and I mean that as a compliment. He keeps his distance from the actors; they don't argue with him, they do what he says."

[Selden's first Broadway credit was as a composer of the 1948 revue *Small Wonder*, with direction by Shevelove; lyrics by Billings Brown (a.k.a Shevelove); and choreography by newcomer Champion.]

Time passes. From his pad at the Watergate in Washington, Gower permits the world one interview. It's with a woman named Gwen Dobson. "*Irene*," he tells Ms. Dobson, "can never really be my show because I didn't create it. The problem is vast, it is complex, it is an inherited illness."

Since Sir John is still listed in the Playbill as director, somebody suggests an ad which will say "production supervised by Gower Champion." Champion has a counter-suggestion: "Why don't we say salvaged by Gower Champion?"

A herald for Washington, offering Gielgud prominent placement.

In Washington, reviews are again mixed. One critic says Debbie doesn't have "what it takes to be a Broadway musical-comedy star," and adds that if somebody doesn't apply reins to Patsy Kelly, "she will mug her way out into the lobby." Another says it's a pure joy just to watch Deb move across the stage, and she's having a triumph. And again, mobs come, including celebrities. When Richard Nixon saw the play, he told reporters, "I think this will be a big hit in New York, perhaps not with New Yorkers, but with the out-of-towners."

The night I make it down to the National Theatre, I see Harry Rigby standing out front studying the gentry. "It looks like a Cadillac ad," I say. "Very glittery crowd."

Harry tosses his head. 'It's Washington," he drawls. "They're probably all coming from dinner at the Uruguayan Embassy." He's waiting for Ruby Keeler to arrive and give him a straight opinion.

Seventeen hundred people are there, having a hell of a time, and only a few are apologetic about it, like the guy I hear at intermission. "I think it's tremendous," he's saying, "but maybe I'm old-fashioned…"

To see the show in Washington, after having seen it in Philadelphia, is to believe. In Gower Champion and Joe Stein, particularly.

Suddenly, the book has logic, and there are funny lines ("Your father used to say, 'It's better to be relaxed and happy for a whole year than sick and nervous for one day,'" Patsy tells Debbie proudly, and then looks confused. "That's very deep.") And the musical numbers aren't just stuck in anymore, they come along as they're needed. And the love story is more convincing. You begin to understand what made Harry so sure he had something.

Like the Flying Dutchman, *Irene* is sailing with a ghost captain and a ghost first mate (Champion's name will *not* appear in the credits; neither will Joe Stein's), but she may, after all, reach the shore.

The wages of fixing a show on the road are steep, as detailed by Mel Gussow in this article published in the *New York Times* just after Reynolds left the show.

"*Irene* Trying the Patience of Angels"
By Mel Gussow

In the 11 months since the musical *Irene* opened in the new Minskoff Theatre, it has grossed about $6-million. It is taking in more money than any other show on Broadway. Last week, Debbie Reynolds's final week in the show—Jane Powell steps into the title role tonight—*Irene* grossed $149,542, for a Broadway record. But the 167 limited partners who made the show financially possible have not received one cent back on their original investment of $800,000 and it will probably be at least one more year—should the show run that long and continue to operate at close-to-capacity—before it even begins to turn a profit.

The primary question is: Can a smash hit be a fiscal fiasco? And—while such musicals as *Pippin* and *A Little Night Music* have quickly returned profits to backers—what does the case of *Irene* mean for a Broadway already caught in a stranglehold of ascending productions costs, strict union demands, high ticket prices and increasingly wary investors?

"It's the worst investment I ever made," said Robert M. Sloate, a restaurateur who has $8,000 in *Irene*. "It's the most uncontrollable. If the show had closed out of town, it wouldn't have bothered me as much. It would have been like playing the wheel in Las Vegas—and losing."

An investigation by the *New York Times* into the production reveals that *Irene* off-stage has become a drama filled with charges of mismanagement, accusations of bad faith and bad bookkeeping, and threats of legal action.

Despite the lack of profits, some people have profited financially from *Irene*. Royalties and salaries have been paid. Miss Reynold's income, under her contract, should come to about $500,000 for her Broadway engagement. Sir John Gielgud, the show's first director—he was discharged in Philadelphia—has been paid about $100,000 in fees and royalties.

David Rogers, who in the early stages worked on the book but whose final contribution to the show was so minimal that he gets no credit in the program, has made approximately $45,000.

Sixteen persons (producers, directors, writers and Miss Reynolds) receive a total of 24.75 per cent of the gross as royalties, and an additional $1200 a week goes to lesser creative contributors. Another 25 per cent of the gross pays for the rent of the theatre.

A group of backers has formed an ad hoc committee to seek explanations for the lack of a paycheck. The producers, Harry Rigby, Albert W. Selden and Jerome Minskoff, are divided about the backers' complaints, and about their own responsibility. Mr. Selden is allied with his general manager, Walter Fried. Mr. Rigby and Mr. Minskoff (together with Miss Reynolds) are, in different degrees, critical of the management of the show. In addition, Mr. Rigby leans towards the backers' viewpoint.

The principal reason for the musical's still not showing a profit is its costs, which soared during the out-of-town tryout from an initial capitalization of $800,000 to $1,492,000.

That $700,000 difference, which Mr. Selden said was necessitated by repairs on the road, was advanced to the show as a loan by two of the producers, Mr. Minskoff and Mr. Selden. While the backers' original investment has not yet been paid back, Mr. Minskoff and Mr. Selden have been paid off all but $50,000 of their $700,000. When the sum is complete, said the producers, the payback will begin to the backers. The backers call this "preferential treatment." Mr. Selden calls it normal business procedure. "A loan," he said, "never takes a back seat to an investment." Everyone agrees that it is legal.

But there still is some question as to why the show cost so much to bring to Broadway, why its weekly operating cost reaches $100,000, and where the income (an average of $120,000) is going.

With *Irene*, depending on one's point of view, virtually everyone else is a villain, except for one hero—or rather, heroine—Miss Reynolds. Rival parties—and *Irene* has almost as many rival parties as it has composers and lyricists—agree that more than anyone else Miss Reynolds is responsible for the show's success. On the road and in New York, she never missed a show, or a chance to publicize it. Affectionately the cast calls her "Mother."

Mr. Selden has other names for her, such as director, producer and costume designer. "She throws her weight around," he said.

"Do shows with stars," he vows for his future, "but make them partners."

Miss Reynolds indicated this week that she was not satisfied with the show's management, specifically excluding Mr. Rigby and Mr. Minskoff, and making it clear that she meant Mr. Selden and Mr. Fried.

"I feel they were incompetent," she said. "I would never work with either party again." At her request, during her run in *Irene*, Mr. Fried was banned from the backstage area.

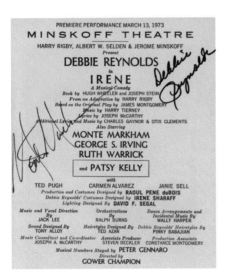

Gower Champion and Joe Stein ultimately decided on taking credit.

According to Mr. Rigby, last July 10, he and Mr. Minskoff, representing more than 50 per cent of the general partnership, attempted to dismiss Mr. Fried, but were dissuaded by Mr. Selden. Mr. Fried, a longtime producer (he co-produced the original *Death of a Salesman*) and general manager, suffered a heart attack last week and was not available for comment.

Mr. Selden said that charges of mismanagement are "totally unwarranted." About the ill feeling toward Mr. Fried, he said, "The general manager is essentially the hatchet man. He has to tangle with egos." He indicated that it was the producers who are responsible for the show, and admitted, "I obviously didn't do something right."

In contrast to *Irene*, last season's other two hit musicals—with much lower budgets—have proven to be excellent investments. *Pippin*, produced by Stuart Ostrow for $500,000, opened Oct. 23, 1972, paid back its entire investment Feb. 28, 1973, and has made $1-million profit. *A Little Night Music*, produced by Harold Prince for $600,000, opened Feb. 25, 1973, paid back its entire investment Sept. 24, 1973, and has made $650,000 profit.

Mr. Selden calls *Irene* a "cancer show," a Broadway term indicating a show that is lingering and unprofitable.

"There are two kinds of cancer shows," he said. "One is a show that grosses just enough to stay above the stop clause so that you can't close it." The stop clause says that if the week's grosses fall below a certain specified level—in the case of *Irene* around $90,000—the theatre can evict the show. "Then there is this kind of show, so overloaded with extra production costs that you can not recoup. It should-n't happen to investors or producers. When it happens, you're dead."

Those let out in the financial cold are the shivering angels. With investments from $500 to $100,000, they include bankers, bartenders, widows, stockbrokers and accountants. "Doctors are big investors," said Mr. Selden. "They love musicals." And some are more concerned than others about their investment. Carroll Rosenbloom, who owns the Los Angeles Rams, is one of the largest investors (with $32,000) and according to his New York representative, he is uninterested in the backers' dispute. In contrast, for some of the investors, even a small investment is enormous.

Annoyed at what they consider "cavalier" treatment of their investment, a group of backers met informally, and advised by a lawyer, Dennis P. Ryan, sent a letter to their fellow backers seeking support in asking the management for explanations.

"We got a 90 per cent return on our letter," said Mr. Ryan. Strong response came from around the country, and to forestall the Broadway equivalent of a stockholder's battle, the producers invited the angels to the Minskoff Theatre on Dec. 11 for a "pre-holiday drink" and answers to their questions.

It was, as one backer recalls, "organized chaos." The chief concern was the Minskoff-Selden loan.

The producers' answer was that without the loan *Irene* would have closed out of town and everyone would have lost their money. Some of the angels were mollified. Others left the meeting even angrier.

"All I received from *Irene*," says one woman who invested $8,000, "was one free cocktail and a record album."

Miss Reynolds, who has been sympathetic to the angels said, "It's one thing to lose, but this is a winner. One backer sent me a note, 'The show's a hit—where's the money?' I agree with them." So does Mr. Rigby. Last week he sent a letter to his partners suggesting they take no more money from the show until the investors' share is returned.

The root of the trouble goes back to the tryout. It is not unusual for a show to switch directors or undergo rewrites. Nor is it odd for a musical to find itself underbudgeted. But with *Irene*, the hirings and discharges, the changes of costumes and the changes of mind were, even her best friends would admit, absurd.

The show had two directors, Sir John Gielgud and Gower Champion (and a choreographer, Peter Gennaro, credited with staging the musical numbers); two costume designers, Raoul Pene deBois and Irene Sharaff; and 13 authors and composers (some of whom have since died).

"We had an entourage of creators attached to the show that would sink a ship," Mr. Selden said. "Everything doubled. The sets went from $200,000 to $395,000. Orchestrations should have been $60,000. They cost $120,000. We had no control. Once you've jumped off the diving board you can't change your mind midair." While he and Mr. Minskoff were trying to raise the additional $700,000 to save the show, "We were kiting bills like crazy," Mr. Selden said. "We were one step ahead of the sheriff all the way to New York. It was a most ghastly experience."

Debbie Reynolds surrounded by (from left to right) Ruth Warrick, Monte Markham, George S. Irving and Patsy Kelly.

Mr. Minskoff, a partner in the building firm of Sam Minskoff and Sons, agreed about the lack of communication, and added: "If you're building a building, you do not start until you have all the plans. Certainly you wouldn't put the roof on until you have the foundation. Errors were made on the show. It's one thing to pay overtime, but we had the whole show to do—and it was all overtime."

The picture is further complicated by the fact that the Minskoff Theatre is owned by Mr. Minskoff's firm and rented (for $200,000 a year) by Mr. Selden. The arrangement is not unusual, but it does mean that Mr. Selden as producer has to bargain with Mr. Selden as theatre manager. In addition to receiving money to pay the loan, Mr. Selden receives rent from *Irene*, approximately $30,000 a week.

Mr. Selden said that it cost about $29,000 to operate the theatre (a figure that Mr Rigby disputes; he estimates it at about $16,000) and that in addition he had to raise an extra $150,000 to open the theatre in the first place. The three producers also share the producer's fee (share of royalties), about $2,000 a week.

Several weeks ago Mr. Selden sent a letter to all those who receive royalties asking that everyone, including the three producers, take a 50 per cent reduction.

It is the nature of Broadway investment that backers are supposed to remain silent, and to wait, angelically, for a windfall. But *Irene*'s angels are agitated. Some think that the producers have made a killing (while they have not even made a tax loss).

But Mr. Minskoff and Mr. Selden say they "haven't made a dime."

During his 25 years as a producer Mr. Selden has had a number of failures and one big hit, *Man of La Mancha*, which he remembers more and more wistfully.

Besieged by his backers, shunned by Miss Reynolds, getting angry letters from Mr. Rigby, and with financial problems mounting—but with the Minskoff Theatre still filled with happy patrons—the usually jovial Mr. Selden looks at *Irene* with a jaundiced eye.

"It has been a draining experience—financially and emotionally," he says. My life would be easier if I never got involved with *Irene*."

"Fortunately, *Irene* was a hit," says Mr. Minskoff. "Unfortunately, it cost too much."

Irene opened March 13, 1973 as the inaugural attraction at the Minskoff Theatre, to unfavorable reviews (but SRO business). It closed there on September 8, 1974 after 594 performances, at a substantial loss.

Irene without Debbie Reynolds fell off, business-wise. Jane Powell headed the show through spring and summer of 1974, closing Labor Day. Reynolds took the show on the road, attracting sell-out crowds on tour as she had in town. By the time she was finished with *Irene* for good, the investors had recovered about 30% of their investment, leaving a loss of just under $600,000. Reynolds personally made about $750,000 for her efforts, but it is only fair to say that—good show or bad—her performance was well worth it.

The *Times* article helps illuminate a question that has been raised elsewhere in this book (notably in the discussions of *The Act* and *Seesaw*): How can a show sell tickets but still lose money? Mel Gussow carefully explains how the costs of fixing a show on the road can explode the budget; and, more importantly, how the percentage royalties paid to the new creators—on top of those contractually due the old creators—can saddle the ledger in quicksand. A normal musical comedy of the time might have had a royalty package of 16%; as new workers came and went—thirteen writers in all!—*Irene* exploded to 24.75%. Which meant that even though *Irene* easily met its weekly expenses, the upside was 9% slimmer than it should have been.

Still smarting from the experience, Reynolds determined to return to the scene of her triumph. The 1976 star-plus-dancers-in-sequins revue *Debbie* raised not a glimmer of interest, though, and folded after a mere 14 performances at the Minskoff.

Material Objection

Mack & Mabel

Hallelujah, Baby!

Kwamina

Cry for Us All

The John F. Kennedy Center for the Performing Arts
presents The DAVID MERRICK Production of

ROBERT   BERNADETTE
PRESTON PETERS

in

MACK & MABEL

Book by   Music and Lyrics by
MICHAEL STEWART JERRY HERMAN

Also Starring
LISA
KIRK

with

| JERRY DODGE | CHRISTOPHER MURNEY | TOM BATTEN |
| BERT MICHAELS | NANCY EVERS | ROBERT FITCH | STANLEY SIMMONDS |

and
JAMES MITCHELL

Musical Director and Vocal Arrangements	Orchestrations by	Dance Music by
DONALD PIPPIN	**PHILIP J. LANG**	**JOHN MORRIS**
Scenic Design by	Costume Designs by	Lighting Designed by
ROBIN WAGNER	**PATRICIA ZIPPRODT**	**THARON MUSSER**
Associate Choreographer	Production Supervisor	
BUDDY SCHWAB	**LUCIA VICTOR**	
Associate Producer	Based on an idea by	In Association with
JACK SCHLISSEL	**LEONARD SPIGELGASS**	**EDWIN H. MORRIS**

Original Cast Album by ABC Records

Directed and Choreographed by
GOWER CHAMPION

Mack & Mabel (1974)

Goodbye, Mabel!

A new musical from the composer, librettist, director-choreographer and producer of *Hello, Dolly!*—starring Broadway's own *Music Man*, Robert Preston—had all the earmarks of a new superhit for a Broadway starved for a good musical. But musical theatre is an inexact science; even the best of ingredients, as we've seen, don't necessarily combine when brought to a boil. Ellen Stern covered *Mack & Mabel* for *New York* magazine.

The Washington herald promises bathing beauties and Keystone Kops, which were only intermittently in evidence.

"*Mack & Mabel*: Getting the Show off the Road"

by Ellen Stern

A smile bursts across Gower Champion's face. He leaps from his front-row seat, bends his legs and crooks his arms, looks up at the cast on stage, and dances to their tune. He's just shown them some new steps, and the new steps work. It's midafternoon in mid-September, and he's got three more weeks in which to make the rest of the show work as well.

Mack & Mabel—the new musical about Mack Sennett and Mabel Normand…the new musical from the same team who gave the world *Hello, Dolly!* (composer-lyricist Jerry Herman, author Michael Stewart, producer David Merrick, and director Champion)…the new musical which received reviews ranging from fair to phenomenal in San Diego, Los Angeles, and St. Louis—has just bombed in Washington. "*Mack & Mabel* landed on the Kennedy Center Opera House stage Tuesday night with all the zip of a wet, very dead flounder," Richard Coe reported in the *Washington Post*. But he was wrong. *Mack & Mabel* is neither fish nor fowl. Yet.

It's had three years to make up its mind. Jerry Herman was the first to get involved—in 1971, when Ed Lester, managing director of the Los Angeles Civic Light Opera, suggested the project and the collaborator, Leonard Spigelgass. [Spigelgass did the screen adaptations of two fifties musicals, *Silk Stockings* (1957) and *Gypsy* (1962). His limited Broadway experience included the Gertrude Berg comedies, *A Majority of One* (1958) and *Dear Me, The Sky Is Falling* (1963), and one failed musical, the Jule Styne-Sammy Cahn *Look to the Lilies* (1970).] Herman said yes. "It was a composer's dream," he explains. "A poignant love story set against pies, cops, and craziness. The combination wouldn't let me say no." He did some research, wrote some songs, and lost Spigelgass to less musical pastures.

So Jerry Herman went to Michael Stewart. Stewart said yes. "Jerry handed me a neat bundle of Sennett books, reviews, and clippings, which was a break. When we did *Dolly*, I had to go to the library."

Together, they went to David Merrick. Merrick said yes. "I liked it. It entertained me. Why else does anybody produce a show?"

And then they went to Champion, who had most recently directed the saccharine *Sugar* and *Irene*. Champion said no. "I was going through a divorce, and I didn't want to leave California and my kids." So he did a movie instead, a turkey called *Bank Shot* with George C. Scott. And Herman, Stewart, and Merrick waited. They even offered to open the show in Los Angeles. Champion said yes. "That worked out fine for me," he says, "because I'm a home man."

The team signed the estimable Robert Preston to plays Mack Sennett. [Jerry Orbach, of *Carnival* and Merrick's 1968 hit *Promises! Promises!*, was originally signed. Preston—who had done *I Do! I Do!* (1966) for Merrick and Champion—expressed interest, and was too bankable a name to pass up. Orbach returned to Merrick, Champion and Stewart in 1980 for *42nd Street*.] But casting Mabel was a problem, a problem that Henry VIII would have appreciated. Actress Marcia Rodd was the first to come and go. As she recounts the experience: "My agent said there would be absolutely no auditioning; the role of Mabel was going to Penny Fuller. [Fuller had recently played Eve Harrington in the 1971 musical *Applause*, after serving as the original standby (and replacement) for the role of Sally Bowles in *Cabaret*. Fuller's next Broadway stint would be in *Rex* (see page 290).] The next thing I know, they're holding auditions. I hired a studio, hired somebody to teach me pratfalls, did the auditions, and more auditions, and some readings. They cried.

"Gower called and said, 'You're our choice, but we have to look at some big-name stars.' I understood that. I decided to wait it out. After five weeks, I got the part. And off I went to Bermuda to take a vacation, since I figured I was going to be in this big hit and tied up for two years."

It was then, presumably, that Champion saw Kelly Garrett in a show called *Words and Music*. [Sammy Cahn's songbook revue, featuring Cahn and Garrett, opened at he Golden in April 1974.] He liked what he saw, and liked it a lot better than what he'd already seen. He decided to fire Marcia Rodd. "She's a dynamite performer," he says, "but Mabel Normand had to have a broken-wing quality."

Opera House

John F. Kennedy Center for the Performing Arts

ROGER L. STEVENS
Chairman

MARTIN FEINSTEIN
Executive Director

JULIUS RUDEL
Music Director

THE KENNEDY CENTER presents
THE DAVID MERRICK PRODUCTION

ROBERT
PRESTON

BERNADETTE
PETERS

in

MACK & MABEL

The musical romance of
Mack Sennett's funny and fabulous Hollywood

Book by
MICHAEL STEWART

Music and Lyrics by
JERRY HERMAN

Also Starring
LISA
KIRK

with

JERRY DODGE   CHRISTOPHER MURNEY   TOM BATTEN
BERT MICHAELS   NANCY EVERS   ROBERT FITCH   STANLEY SIMMONDS

and

JAMES MITCHELL

In Association with EDWIN H. MORRIS

Scenic Design
ROBIN WAGNER

Costume Design
PATRICIA ZIPPRODT

Lighting Design
THARON MUSSER

Musical Director and
Vocal Arrangements
DONALD PIPPIN

Orchestrations
PHILIP J. LANG

Incidental and
Dance Music
JOHN MORRIS

Associate Choreographer
BUDDY SCHWAB

Production Supervisor
LUCIA VICTOR

Associate Producer
JACK SCHLISSELL

Based on an idea by
LEONARD SPIGELGASS

Hair Stylist TED AZAR

Original Cast Album by ABC Records

Directed and Choreographed by
GOWER CHAMPION

The Washington billing page for "the musical romance of Mack Sennett's funny and fabulous Holywood."

"I got back," Marcia Rodd continues, "and I got a call from Gower, saying, 'We're going to rehearse a week early.' That was weird. And from that second on, I knew something was wrong. You don't like to be paranoid, but he had been so warm to me—during negotiations, watching two-reelers, working with Jerry Herman—and now he was cold and terse. I knew I hadn't done anything wrong because I hadn't even started to work yet.

"The two days of rehearsals weren't really rehearsals, but setups so he could justify firing me. He thought he was being kind, and he was being just as cool as could be. He put the blame on me. He said he had no doubt that if I really *worked* at it, and so on, but I wasn't enough to build a show around.

"I was stunned. I've never been fired in my life. I couldn't say, 'Gower, I'll be the best Mabel you've ever seen.' It was the part I had worked and waited for all my life. The pain was incredible. When he wanted me, he could not have been nicer. He was kind of like an uncle; we had a nice, open relationship. But when he got scared, everything closed up."

Kelly Garrett replaced Marcia Rodd, but didn't last half as long. "It was such a fiasco," says Garrett's manager, "that as far as I'm concerned, it was *their* loss. I just don't have any respect for the way they handled it. It was really tacky." Says Champion: "That one broke my heart. That face, that voice. But this role takes a lot of deep acting." He hired Bernadette Peters, known best for her appearances off-Broadway and on television, and cynics began calling the show Mack & Maybe.

"I can understand why Bernadette got it," says Marcia Rodd. "She's a wonderful performer. She has a set of mannerisms I don't have. She's more a personality actress than I am, and more power to her. I only hope she has an ironclad contract."

Whether or not she has an ironclad contract, Miss Peters does have a poodle, who shares her room at the Watergate Hotel and her dressing room at the Opera House. Both have big eyes, fluffy hair, and a limited vocabulary. [Peters first appeared on Broadway (or thereabouts) at the age of ten in the 1959 City Center revival *of The Most Happy Fella*. Her breakthrough performance came in 1968, as the ingénue in the off-Broadway musical *Dames at Sea. Mack & Mabel* was Peters's third consecutive Broadway flop; or fifth, if you include two that closed before reaching town.]

"I didn't want to audition," says Bernadette, untying her bow mouth, "because I had moved to California. But I had to go to New York to do a game show, so I auditioned. I was ready to leave, I was on the plane, on the runway, and suddenly the engine goes *pffft* and we have to get off. I called my lawyer in California to say I'd be on a later flight, and while he was talking to me, his other phone rang. It was Merrick's office, calling to say I'd gotten the part. It was fate. I really believe that."

Lisa Kirk, an alumna of *Allegro* and *Kiss Me, Kate*, believes in luck. She first met Marge and Gower Champion in the late forties, when they were dancing and she was singing at the Bradford Roof in Boston. But Champion had never seen her dance, so when *Mack & Mabel* came along—with the featured role of Lottie Ames, a song-and-dance star who moves from vaudeville to Sennett's troupe to talkies—Lisa tucked her long red hair under a short, curly wig, put on a top hat, picked up a cane, and whirled through a number called "I Really Love to Sing and Dance," written for the audition by Fred Karger and her husband, Bob Wells. She got the part, and it will be her first time tapping on Broadway.

Rehearsals began in New York on May 6, and the show opened in San Diego on June 17. Reviews were good, not great. "I'll never open again in California," says Champion. "When you open in Boston or Detroit, people realize it's a show in progress. In California, your peers see it and expect it to be perfect."

It wasn't. Although critics were optimistic and audiences entertained, Merrick knew better. "We hit solidly in California and in St. Louis," he says, "but I wasn't entirely happy with it. And good reviews don't make writers and directors work very hard." Merrick has known this for a long time. When another musical, *Do Re Mi*, was on its pre-Broadway tour in 1960, he called critic Richard Coe. "I had him come in and give a bad review so the creators would get to work on it," he says. But while Merrick asked Coe for that bad review, he did not ask for this one.

On the program, *Mack & Mabel* is billed as "the musical romance of Mack Sennett's funny and fabulous Hollywood." Both aspects—the romance and the funny—are problematic. The Sennett-Normand relationship, in real life, was tempestuous and ultimately thwarted. While Sennett was known as the King of Comedy and considered himself ordained to make the world laugh, he was also a rough drinker, which didn't make Mabel laugh. "He may have given her a black eye once or twice in a lifetime," says Robert Preston, "but he really adored her."

Mabel died of tuberculosis in 1930 when she was 36. Mack sat back in his bathtub and read about it in the paper.

The love story in the show is being emphasized in several ways—restaging a rendezvous here, adding a midnight sail there—but the sharpest thorn in the creators' craw has been, since San Diego, the happy ending: a slapstick wedding fantasy fastened on to alleviate the gloom of Mabel's death. In Washington, they unfasten it.

"We're trying to get the negative drama reduced without changing the basic story," says David Merrick. "She died, and they *didn't* get together and walk off into the M-G-M sunset."

"We're going for reality instead of Disneyland," says Gower Champion.

Where he failed in love, Sennett succeeded in silent movies. His company of clowns (who were generally underpaid) included, in addition to Mabel, Charlie Chaplin, Gloria Swanson, Fatty Arbuckle, Chester Conklin, Buster Keaton, gaggles of bathing beauties, and a bumble of Keystone Kops. His filmic innovations included pies in the face, slow-motion collisions, and a form of bedlam that Kaufman and Hart found suitable to borrow some years later.

High-speed high jinks on the screen are one thing. On stage, they are nearly unattainable. In Washington, Champion is beginning to discover this. He is also trying desperately to fix it.

"I studied all those films," he says, pacing from piano to mirror to window in a rehearsal room high above the Opera House, "and what made them work were incredible mechanical gags—buildings falling down, horses riding through living rooms, cars going off piers. That was Sennett's madness. The biggest frustration is not being able to do it in this show. The mechanical age is what he used. And what do I have? One adorable fire engine. But I can't tip it over, and I can't run it through a wall."

To add to his dilemma, Champion has been dropping the scrim every now and then during the show and projecting a Sennett film pastiche. Aware of the comparison he risks, he now considers eliminating the clips altogether. "But if I did," he laments, plowing his fingers through his graying hair, "I still would be faced with the basic problem of trying to have life imitate art. I think Sennett's work is too internationally imprinted on the public's mind."

So instead of cutting Sennett's work, he cuts his own. "The other night we had twenty trims," says Preston. "I got *them* all right and got everything else wrong."

Out go the Keystone Kops. "If I had a Jerry Robbins ballet with the Kops," Champion says, "it still wouldn't work. [Champion is referring to Robbins's legendary "Bathing Beauty Ballet" in the 1948 musical *High Button Shoes*, which featured a bunch of Sennett-like cops.] In my play, the Kops are real, and they're not funny people onstage. Sennett's kinetic action is what makes them funny on screen."

Jerry Herman says he likes the Kops number because "it's kind of a nice statement, saying that Mack Sennett started screen violence." But he'll go along with the cut (he calls it an experiment) if it's good for the show. What's good for the show is good for him. [The number, "Hit 'Em on the Head," was reinstated for the 1995 London production.]

Herman just may be the most successful Broadway composer around these days, thanks to the popularity of *Dolly* and *Mame*, and the number of companies still doing them all over the world. But he's not popular with the critics. His biggest problem seems to be that his music is musical.

He expects to be knocked for the show's big *Dolly/Mame*-like number, "When Mabel Comes in the Room." "But I'm proud of it," he says, "and I'm going to keep writing this kind of song until I'm 85, because that's what's missing in musical theatre, that's what audiences can hold on to."

A few weeks ago, Gower Champion was quoted as saying he would have liked the "big Mabel" number killed. Herman read the interview and admits he was surprised. Champion says he was misquoted. "No, I wouldn't take it out of the show. I just said I'll never do a big-star number again because I did it in *Dolly*. I've done the best."

Hello, Dolly! was not the best on the road. It is, in fact, regarded as the theatre's most successful Band-Aid job. How does the team compare that show with this one? "I can't," says Merrick. "This has not been a disaster. *Dolly* was. It was really a mess. We rewrote it entirely."

Champion says that fixing *Dolly* was "not as tricky as this one."

Jerry Herman, who's most hurt by the rumors that his favorite *Dolly* songs were written by other people, considers *Mack &*

Robert Preston as Mack Sennett and Bernadette Peters as Mabel Normand.

Mabel more difficult technically, what with an intricately motorized set and a scrim as rippable as Kleenex. As for the doctors who attended *Dolly*'s birth, he says they haven't been summoned.

[When *Dolly* was struggling in Detroit, Merrick called in Bob Merrill, his composer-lyricist from *Take Me Along* and *Carnival*. Gower, meanwhile called in Lee Adams and Charles Strouse of *Bye, Bye Birdie*. (Stewart had worked with them all, on *Carnival* and *Birdie*.) Merrill's contributions included two songs, "Elegance" and "Motherhood March," both of which Herman completed. Adams and Strouse offered structural ideas as well as a song called "Before the Parade Passes By." Champion found this song unsuitable, and Herman wrote his own song, with the same title, for the slot. It was to become one of his biggest song hits.]

And Michael Stewart says, "Everybody must be replaced in this business someday, but if I'm fool enough to get myself in that position again, I promise you I won't go out with any dignity." [This is a reference to Stewart's prior show, *Seesaw* (see page 28). Stewart had signed a three-show deal with producer Joseph Kipness. The second show was *Mack & Mabel*, although the producer departed the project under mysterious circumstances. In a dispute over his participation, Kipness sent some fellas over to Merrick's office to slash the place up. This move backfired, as it gave Merrick added leverage over the negotiations. Kippy ended up with no billing and 10% of the non-existent profits. The only one of the three Stewart shows that proved profitable was *I Love My Wife*, although Kipness lost his share of that one as well.]

Stewart's first job was typing a manuscript for Robert Penn Warren. He'd like his next to be typing a novel of his own. Meanwhile, he's celebrating his fifteenth year in the theatre, having written the librettos for *Bye Bye Birdie*, *Carnival*, *George M!*, and *Dolly*.

He's itchy in Washington. "We've been on the road a long, long time, and I don't like that," he says, scratching his blond head. "I wouldn't mind so much if we changed cities more often. You're in one place for a few weeks, so you write for that city. And as sophisticated as L.A. or Washington are, they're not New York. In New York, people come because they want to be in that theatre. In Washington, or any subscription town, they're in the same seats every time, and they're not impressed with the Opera House any longer. It's become routine.

"I'm longing for the New York opening, to have it decided. I can't stand waiting for the jury. Come in, and say, 'Guilty,' or 'Not Guilty,' and get it over with."

While Jerry Herman says he's never made so few changes in a show, Stewart says he's never made so many. He does his writing early in the morning and puts a hotel towel under his typewriter so he won't wake the neighbors. "I have a packet of changes a foot and a half thick," he says. "I save them all, God knows why."

Team spirit is good. "We've changed, and cut, and rewritten," says Champion, "and we've never had a fight. We sit down and we figure it out."

"I'm usually pale, rundown, and terribly tense," says Herman, "but this time I'm not. The major reason is that Gower, Mike, and I are like a family at this point. That's very rare and very special. It cuts out the garbage. Merrick doesn't come to rehearsals. He simply calls and checks on our progress. We never feel that Big Brother is watching us. He's got his team back, and they know what they're doing."

Do they? Is the coach really all that confident? "No," says Merrick, "I never feel confident. Sure, they did it with *Dolly*, but I can think of other shows where they did not." [These include Champion's *The Happy Time*, *Sugar*, and *Irene* (the first two produced by Merrick); Herman's *Dear World*; and Stewart's *Seesaw*.]

Mack & Mabel opens at the Majestic on October 6. Will it be a hit? "Maybe it will, and maybe it won't," says Merrick, who has already laid out $850,000 and has more than big bucks to regain after his unrequited flirtation with Hollywood. "It used to be that you'd bring a show into New York, and if it got terrible reviews you closed it; if it got mixed reviews, it cost money to keep it running. I've done that with a lot of shows. But it can't be done anymore. Now it's hit or miss completely."

Mack & Mabel opened October 6, 1974 at the Majestic Theatre, to negative reviews. It closed there on November 30, 1974 after 65 performances, at a total loss.

Many theatregoers sensed that the traditional Broadway musical comedy was dying in the period that followed the opening of *Hair* in 1968. Stephen Sondheim and Harold Prince gradually developed a very different kind of musical, starting with *Company* (1970) and *Follies* (1971); but the early 70s saw one disappointing musical after another from former hitmakers like Rodgers, Lerner, Styne, Bock, Strouse, Herman, Kander, and Coleman. *Mack & Mabel*, by virtue of the presence of the *Dolly* team, was perhaps the most promising of them all. Its outright failure was almost a requiem for the old-style musical.

The night before the opening, I was sitting at a banquette along the eastern wall of Sardi's. (These prime tables were usually empty between the pre-show and after-show rushes, except for managers and producers dining after the count-up.) Merrick ducked in during the first act of *Mack & Mabel*, across the street at the Majestic, and sat at the next table.

"I could only get it about 80% where I wanted it," he said, shaking his head. "I hope that's enough."

It wasn't.

PLAYBILL

the national magazine for theatregoers

Hallelujah, Baby! (1967)

A Conclave of
Ego-Maniacal Children

What happens to a star vehicle when the star walks out? Lena Horne, for whom *Hallelujah, Baby!* was conceived and written, is not mentioned in the article that follows. But there is clearly a hole in the middle of the enterprise being observed by British theatre critic Alan Brien, a friendly observer who wrote this candid chronicle. It was printed prior to the opening in London's *Sunday Telegraph*, where it couldn't do any harm.

A simplistic logo by Paul Bacon, inspired by the song "When the Weather's Better" (which was cut in Boston).

"The Making of a Musical"
by Alan Brien

March 2

This morning I write to my old friend Burt Shevelove in New York from London confirming a suggestion I had put to him weeks before. Burt was one of the authors of the musical, *A Funny Thing Happened on the Way to the Forum* and the film *The Wrong Box*.

A formidable intellectual who can identify an obscure quotation from English literature with the speed of a computer, an insatiable book-collector with a rather unnerving special interest in witchcraft and monsters, a Jewish New Yorker with a passion for London, he has been living here for the past two years. Now he is back on Broadway directing a new musical *Hallelujah, Baby!*, the story in song and dance and drama of the Negro movement towards equality since the beginning of the century, which opens out-of-town in Boston on March 20.

I explain that I will be in New York in six day's time and would like his permission to drop in now and again on rehearsals to chronicle the long labor pains which accompany the birth of a Broadway show. I assure him I will be as tactful and inconspicuous as possible, but that I understand the presence of a Boswell, especially a Boswell with an intermittent urge to play Dr. Johnson, may not be welcomed by this prickly collection of talents.

March 7

The first thing I do after taking off my hat in the apartment is to telephone Burt at his home number.

"Mr. Shevelove's residence."

"Is that really Mr. Shevelove's residence, or his answering service?"

(Eveybody who is anybody in New York has an answering service which often intercepts calls when the subscriber is home but working or drunk or in a bad mood or otherwise engaged. They always answer in the assumed character of an old family retainer. A heavy outlay of sweet-talking persuasion is sometimes necessary to get them to disobey the subscriber's instructions.)

"You are not by any chance the famous answering service, 'The Bells,' about whom the Judy Holliday musical *Bells Are Ringing* was written, are you?"

"Why, yes we are. It's nice to be remembered."

"Well, now, you used to be my answering service 10 years ago in New York. My name is Alan Brien."

"Welcome back, Mr. Brien. I think Mr. Shevelove would like you to know he is rehearsing at the Martin Beck Theatre. This is the production office number."

I ring the number all day and much of the night. I ring in the middle of a drink. I ring ten times in a row. But it is always busy.

March 8

This morning I go down to the Martin Beck Theatre. *Hallelujah, Baby!* is already spelled out in lights high over the front. I am a little nervous about the stage doorman, often a far more peculiar and individual character than you are likely to see portrayed on the stage, but notoriously, as a breed, hostile to strangers trespassing beyond his glass sentry-box.

This one looks like an off-beat villain from an early Orson Welles thriller, with a lop-sided head, torch-bulb eyes and a pugnacious jaw. My English accent saves me from too prolonged an inquisition as he cannot understand a word I say—"You wha'? . . . you're who? . . . Aw, go in and ask fellah." I elude the tackle of several kinds of stage manager and rush for the production office where I spot Burt Shevelove and the author, Arthur Laurents. I am relieved to find that my proposition seems to have been accepted and both are friendly.

Most of the people involved in creating the show are gathered in an intimate group, like a cocktail party without drinks, and their talk seems to ascend in the air like a multiple stream of consciousness. There is always one of them on the telephone. I say I have heard the rehearsals are going very well. "It's going so well we just lost the choreographer—that's how well it's going." [Peter Gennaro, of *West Side Story* and *Fiorello!*, was replaced by newcomer Kevin Carlisle.]

"Our star's only been on the stage once before in her life—she played *The Boy Friend* in a tent in California."

"Irene says what initials do you want her to have sewn on the hat check girl's head band?" [Irene Sharaff, also from *West Side* (written by Laurents), designed the costumes.]

"That speech of the mother's in the second act is like a letter by Bertrand Russell."

Most of the day I sit in the darkened auditorium, just beyond the point where the eye-blinding glare of the dangling work-light onstage is cut off by a half-lowered curtain. Some of the team always choose to position themselves where the actors can see every movement they make and this annoys others in the team. The chilly, gloomy atmosphere of the empty theatre crackles with kidding insults, almost sotto voice, half jovial, half savage.

"Who do those two think they are—the Berkeleys of Broadway?"

"You mean Maria and Uriah Heep?"

"You've heard of a manic depressive? Well, he's a manic elative."

"I don't think he believed a show put on by eleven Jews could be anything but anti-Negro."

"So what changed his mind?"

Most of the time they are auditioning understudies, or possibly replacements, for some of the smaller roles. Nobody likes to be too specific and I'm afraid to ask.

"He's good."

"He's scary."

"I like him."

"Aren't you going to stay to see the other mothers?"

"Who's a mother-lover? I need some sleep."

March 9

A day off to write my article on what's wrong with Broadway and back for a day in the dark. I am getting to be unnoticed human lumber. Even the doorman looks right through me, which means I'm in.

Most of the cast are Negro and the non-white members seem to me a little out-faced and under-privileged. Robert Hooks, the male lead, is a handsome, clever, tough young actor who manages his own theatre. [Robert Hooks presented (and appeared in) *Happy Ending* and *Day of Absence*, by Douglas Turner Ward, at the St. Mark's Playhouse on November 15, 1965. The 504-performance run directly resulted in the Ford Foundation funding the Negro Ensemble Company, which Hooks and Ward founded in 1967.] He runs again and again through the same tiny scene with a kind of relaxed agility, the girl's part in the duologue is read by the stage manager, an ex-actor, who now puts his lines across with a good deal of passion and feeling.

"Bobby said the other day, 'My, they're going to hate us N——s at the end of this bit.'"

Leslie Uggams, the female lead with the defiantly un-Broadway name, is a television star with almost no previous acting experience. She has long lashes, teeth which snap in the tenderest of traps, and rather endearing legs which always threaten to knock. She spends a lot of the day walking her Great Dane upstage.

March 11

Saturday is no day off for the company or for me. The slow ritual repetitions of words and movements, advancing each time through the text at what seems a tortoise-pace to an outsider, have a soporific effect. I wake up to hear uproar in the aisles.

"Jule's lost his overture."

"He never brought it with him."

"Here it is, no it's not. It's a god-dam sandwich wrapping."

"Who is it who eats those egg sandwiches and leaves the crusts under the seats?"

"Jule's having a hemorrhage."

"Tell him to call home."

"Irene's on the phone. Is it 'I.C.' for 'Ivory Club' or 'E.R.' for 'Ebony Room' on the hat check girl's head band?"

"Jesus, does it matter?"

"Irene's designing the costumes. If it matters to her, then it matters."

"Tell her to make it '711.'"

The billing page from Boston.

March 12

My birthday. There is to be a run-through of the show for a small, hand-picked audience of friends and enemies at 6:30.

In the morning I watch the new choreographer, Kevin Carlisle, a taciturn young man with a large head of white hair teaching some new routines to the dancers. Sometimes they dance each other's roles. Having by now read the script, I can sort out the characters even when they double up. But there is no script for a dance and Carlisle has to imprint each movement by demonstrating it. Naïvely, I am surprised to see that dancers do tread on each other's toes, lose balance and bump head on.

The basic group in the auditorium is always the same—Jule Styne, composer of *Gypsy* and *Gentlemen Prefer Blondes*, small, restless, talking with a smile and rasp in his voice, sitting alone at the side. "Betty 'n' Adolph," whose names are pronounced as one, like "Rock 'n' Roll," who sit together like twins and do not need to finish their sentences. Arthur Laurents, implacable as a Red Indian brave, with an edge to each remark which would draw blood from a stranger. Burt Sheve-love, in a British sweater and white sneakers ("all my clothes are in England"), always proceeding down the aisle to make a quiet, mild suggestion, dropping jokes like birdseed.

They talk to and about each other, in each other's hearing, usually not noticeably listening, like old married couples. Sometimes it is show-biz news. "Hear *Gypsy*'s going to London—with Merman." "Who's putting it on—old Stinkie?" "Any ideas for director?" [*"Old Stinkie" was presumably Hugh "Binkie" Beaumont, managing director of H.M. Tennent Ltd. The question about director was apparently meant to taunt Gypsy-librettist Laurents, who had made it clear that he disagreed with some of the original staging by Jerome Robbins. Merman never took the show to London, but it was successfully produced there in 1973 with Angela Lansbury in the lead, Tennent as one of the producers, and Laurents as director.*]

Sometimes they discuss the state of the show as if it were the weather and entirely beyond their control. "This show is farther behind than any show I've ever worked on." Sometimes they savage other shows. "I saw that one the other day. Those two ageing adolescents being coy with each other and flitting about the stage and calling it dancing." "But the audiences love it." "That's what's so hateful about it. That and David Merrick making money." "I just love to hear you hating things." [*This is presumably Laurents discussing Mary Martin and Robert Preston in* I Do! I Do! *Laurents was especially angry that Merrick—who coproduced* Gypsy—*had dropped* Hallelujah, Baby! *(as discussed below).*] Sometimes they gossip about personal habits. Adolph Green gave up smoking five years ago and still compensates for the deprivation by compulsive chewing. "If you drew his personal expenditure like a pie, you know the way they do with the federal budget, there'd be eight per cent for rent, light, heat, food, clothes, holidays and 92 per cent for gum."

Sometimes the tension bypasses the principals out front and erupts in comical squabbles among assistants backstage.

Just before the runthrough I heard this lively double act.

"Quiet. That means you."

"Who told you to say, 'Quiet'?"

"My boss."

"Who's your boss?"

"He's my boss, there."

"Who told him to tell you to say, 'Quiet'?"

"Your boss asked my boss for quiet."

"Why did he?"

"You ask you're boss and you'll find out."

The best performance of *West Side Story* I ever saw (and I saw it four times) was at a runthrough. *Hallelujah, Baby!* too has a freshness, a bloom, an excitement like an initiation ceremony, which it will probably never quite recapture.

By now I have forgotten that I was ever a critic. There is a kind of transference which takes place in a company trapped into such intimacy which is like that which fixes a psychiatric patient upon his analyst. I see things I like and things I don't like, but the idea of changing them seems as impossible as rearranging my own features on my face. Fortunately, the people who create Broadway shows have learned to resist this auto-hypnotism. They watch their own work as if they are watching an operation under local anesthetic.

The audience of visitors is small but distinguished, including Arthur Laurents's two collaborators from *West Side Story*, Leonard Bernstein and Stephen Sondheim. I am introduced by mistake to Betty Comden, dark, attractive, rather Russian co-lyricist with Adolph Green, who looks as if she should play the Hollywood version of Stalin's daughter. "We know him," she said. "He's been here so long we were thinking of writing a song for him in the second act."

The official reaction is show-biz effusive. There are occasional corner-of-mouth mutterings in the lobby afterwards. The group do not appear unduly swayed either way. They know they have more time to serve and off they go afterwards like people determined to survive a sentence in the salt mines and discover diamonds. The next day they left for Boston.

March 20

I have been a week away from *Hallelujah, Baby!* Today I go backstage at the Colonial Theatre in Boston where the show has already had two previews and opens tonight officially for the local critics. I meet Burt Shevelove in the aisle.

"You know, your letter got forwarded and forwarded and I only read it this morning. So that's what you're doing here at rehearsals."

But nobody seems to mind this late revelation.

Sitting as if I had spent my life there, in the empty theatre, seeing the sets leap dangerously up and down and on and off, I ask Betty Comden whether this continual examination of your own entrails doesn't grow sickening.

"We're so used to it by now. But sometimes, after singing the songs over and over again with Adolph and Jule, I begin to feel we should just hire a lectern, book some halls and go on the road as a trio."

In the afternoon there is to be another full rehearsal of the second act with a new ballet. But everybody agrees that I should get the hell out of there and visit some museums in order not to spoil the effect of the opening night. So I leave.

At the opening, sitting at the back near the director, watching him dictate notes, leap from his seat to go backstage, I found the show seemed to go in and out of focus like a film on a draughty screen. I knew it too well and yet I seemed not to recognize what I knew.

But it is breaking no oath of secrecy to report that Leslie Uggams made an impact which at least rivals that of Barbra Streisand. The notices were mixed—ranging from a wild rave in the *Christian Science Monitor* to a sour pan in the *Boston Globe*. But everyone loved Leslie.

Another umbrella logo, this one an infinitely more stylish design by Hilary Knight.

Of all the collaborators, Arthur Laurents probably received the hardest blows. But as somebody said at the party afterwards, "The author always gets the most blame, but then he also gets the most money."

The group described themselves, implicitly and explicitly, in many ways during my stay. Perhaps the most colorful was, "a conclave of ego-maniacal children."

The striking difference between making a musical and playing in one could be seen after the second night. I met Leslie Uggams, Robert Hooks and several of the dancers enjoying themselves in a cocktail lounge, singing, dancing, parodying their lines, barracking the pianist, full of healthy disrespect for everything and everybody. They looked as if they would sleep well.

The makers of the musical looked as if they would never sleep again. Guilt hung in the air, but no one knew how it should be shared. "It must be the first time a song has ever been ruined by a dress," groaned somebody ironically. I thought of Stephen Sondheim's opening night telegram to Burt Shevelove—"If you can keep your head when everyone is losing theirs and blaming it on you, good luck."

Critics do not know when they have it easy. *Hallelujah, Baby!* opens on Broadway on April 26. Lots can and will happen to it before then. But I would not like to forecast one of them.

Hallelujah, Baby! opened April 26, 1967 at the Martin Beck Theatre, to mixed reviews. It closed there January 13, 1968 after 293 performances, at a substantial loss.

Material Objection

Fledgling producer David Merrick, with two-out-of-two hits in his pocket, announced a new Harry Belafonte musical for the fall of 1956. Harold Arlen and E.Y. Harburg set to work, and everything was in order until Belafonte was forced to drop out due to a detached retina. It took two years, and three operations, to save Belafonte's eyesight. Merrick was determined to go ahead, so he replaced Belafonte with Lena Horne, who was just then the toast of the town with her nightclub act at the Empire Room of the Waldorf.

How do you revise a Harry Belafonte vehicle for Lena Horne? With great difficulty. *Jamaica* was a shambles of a show by the time Merrick got finished with it, with the authors storming away in anger (while happily accepting royalties). Horne sizzled, as they say, which was more than enough to put *Jamaica* in the hit column.

Jamaica established Horne as an even bigger, more mainstream star. In 1965, Arthur Laurents fashioned a new musical for her, in which he was quickly joined by Styne, Comden, Green, and producer Merrick. *Hallelujah, Baby!* was to examine race relations in America through the decades, with Horne perhaps the only performer strong enough to carry the material past an audience that was still far from enlightened.

Laurents and Horne had been extremely close friends since the early 50s. In his remarkable 2000 memoir *Original Story By*, Laurents goes on at length about Lena, hinting at something to come that irreparably disrupted the relationship. When he gets to *Hallelujah, Baby!*—well, he never does get to *Hallelujah, Baby!* It is missing from the book altogether, as if a great big lawyer swept down from the sky and tore out the pages.

With Horne suddenly out of the picture, Merrick and director Gene Saks withdrew from the venture. "Every producer along the line has turned down something that eventually becomes a big hit," said Merrick, in an uncharacteristically diplomatic statement to the press. "I haven't made a big mistake like that yet. *Hallelujah, Baby!* may very well be my first one." To which Laurents responded, "I hope Mr. Merrick is right."

This was the end of *Hallelujah, Baby!* for all intents and purposes, although Laurents and his three songwriters went on to their doom. The property went through the hands of two more sets of producers before landing with Albert Selden and Hal James, just then flush with cash from *Man of La Mancha*. Selden brought in Shevelove, or Shevelove brought in Selden; Selden, in his days as a composer, had written two musicals with Shevelove. On the 1948 revue *Small Wonder*, Shevelove—who was making his Broadway debut as a director—wrote lyrics under the sly moniker Billings Brown. Their second musical, the 1951 Nancy Walker vehicle *A Month of Sundays*, closed in Boston.

Money troubles inevitably followed, the problem being: How do you do a Lena Horne musical without Lena Horne? Unless, maybe, you get Harry Belafonte? Or a young, bursting-to-be-discovered talent like the girl Styne had in *Funny Girl*? Leslie Uggams was unquestionably talented, and she had at least some prominence thanks to her TV exposure. But she couldn't hope to float *Hallelujah, Baby!*

As it happened, Uggams got a Tony Award for her efforts. So did Styne—who had never won, not for *Gentlemen Prefer Blondes*, *Gypsy*, or *Funny Girl*. *Hallelujah, Baby!* won the Tony for Best Musical, in fact, albeit against such lesser entertainments as *The Happy Time*, *How Now, Dow Jones* [see page 196] and *Illya Darling* [see page 96].

But by Tony Sunday, *Hallelujah, Baby!* was long gone and all but forgotten.

ORDINARY PEOPLE

Music and Lyrics by **RICHARD ADLER**

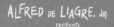

ALFRED DE LIAGRE, JR.
PRESENTS

KWAMINA

STARRING

SALLY ANN **HOWES** AND TERRY **CARTER**

MUSIC AND LYRICS BY
RICHARD ADLER

BOOK BY
ROBERT ALAN AURTHUR

DANCES AND MUSICAL NUMBERS STAGED BY
AGNES DE MILLE

PRODUCTION DIRECTED BY
ROBERT LEWIS

MUSICAL AND CHORAL DIRECTION BY
COLIN ROMOFF

Also Published Separately from the Score:
WHAT'S WRONG WITH ME?
ORDINARY PEOPLE
NOTHING MORE TO LOOK FORWARD TO
SOMETHING BIG
I'M SEEING RAINBOWS
ANOTHER TIME, ANOTHER PLACE

PRICE
1.00

SAHARA MUSIC, INC.,
Sole Selling Agent
CHAPPELL & CO., Inc.
609 Fifth Avenue, New York 17, N. Y.

Kwamina (1961)

The Rising Edge of Hysteria

Songwriters Richard Adler and Jerry Ross burst upon Broadway
with two musical hits within a year, the back-to-back Tony Award
winners *The Pajama Game* (1954) and *Damn Yankees* (1955). Both
topped the 1,000-performance mark, only the ninth and tenth
Broadway musicals to do so; they also contained an impressive
group of song hits in "Hey There," "Hernando's Hideaway," "Steam
Heat," "Whatever Lola Wants" and "Heart."

But Ross's health was deteriorating, and he died of leukemia in
November 1955, at the age of twenty-nine. Adler embarked on a
musicalization of W. Somerset Magham's 1915 novel *Of Human
Bondage*, working with lyricist Bob Merrill. (Like Adler, Merrill hailed
from Tin Pan Alley; he had not yet established himself on Broadway,
which he did in 1957 with *New Girl in Town*.)

After *Of Human Bondage* was abandoned Adler wrote and
coproduced two TV musicals in the fall of 1957, *Little Women* and
The Gift of the Magi. Starring in the latter was British musical
comedy star Sally Ann Howes, the prospective leading lady of *Of
Human Bondage*. Howes married Adler in January 1958, and the
following month she replaced Julie Andrews in the Broadway
company of *My Fair Lady*. Adler gave us a warts-and-all chronicle of
the birth and death of his next musical in "*You Gotta Have Heart*,"
his 1990 autobiography.

The witch doctor casts an evil spell on *Kwamina*.

from "You Gotta Have Heart"
by Richard Adler with Lee Davis

Sometime in 1959, buried on a back page of the *New York Times*, there was an article about the son of an African tribal chief who'd attended Oxford on a scholarship. A brilliant man, he'd spent seven years there, and had earned his M.D.

Then, his father died, and he was called back to Africa to assume the leadership of his village. He went, but by now, he was no longer a mindless practitioner of the ancient ways of his tribe. He'd absorbed not only the knowledge but the values of another culture. He brought modern medicine with him—and, by implication, a totally alien way of life. The *Times* article chronicled his fight to wrest the will of the people away from their witch doctor.

It was a fascinating tale, and something had clicked in me when I read it. The story had conflict—the basic ingredient of drama—on a multitude of levels. But more than that, it dealt with a contemporary problem. It had an exotic setting. It offered an opportunity for an entire smorgasbord of musical thoughts. If a love story were added, it could complicate the conflict and humanize it. And if the love interest were a *white* woman, that woman could be Sally Ann.

It was certainly unorthodox material for a musical, but then again *Of Human Bondage* wasn't exactly a backstage story, either. This story had all of the elements of riveting drama, and all the potential of being an exciting, different sort of show. I wasn't sure *how*, but I knew it had potential. And so, I'd put it on file.

Now, as if fate were taking a hand and determining my destiny once more, Sally Ann and I were invited to a cocktail party. One of my idols, Adlai Stevenson, was there. [Stevenson (1900-1965) served as governor of Illinois from 1947-1953. He ran for the presidency twice, in 1952 and 1956, losing both times to Dwight D. Eisenhower. Stevenson served as United States ambassador to the United Nations from 1961-1965.] I knew what Stevenson stood for, and I was thrilled to see him again. When I was first introduced to him, by my dear friend, the equally humanistic Mary Lasker, he'd just been defeated for the presidency, and had come back from the Belgian Congo, where he'd spent time observing tribal life. We discussed this at length.

Now, three years later, at Mary Lasker's, that first conversation came back to me, and I reminded him of it.

"Yes. The Belgian Congo," he said. "The most exciting area in the world, and full of contrasts. You can be in a modern city like Stanleyville one minute, and then, a few miles away, you can be in the most primitive village, where human sacrifice is still practiced."

I talked with Stevenson for a long time that night, and the next day, I began to sketch an outline of a musical that combined my story with some of his perceptions. I knew I needed a librettist. But I also knew that it was a show whose music and lyrics I would write alone.

And so, *Kwamina*, my first theatre piece without Jerry, was born.

My search for a librettist ended at another party. This one took place at the home of Robert Alan Aurthur, the playwright and television writer whose play *A Very Special Baby* hadn't won him any prizes, but whose television dramas *Man on a Mountaintop* and *A Man Is Ten Feet Tall* had garnered him two Sylvania Awards. [Aurthur was a prolific TV writer and producer. He never achieved success on Broadway; however, he served as Bob Fosse's producer and co-author on the 1979 film *All That Jazz*.] Sally Ann and I were there through the good offices of Mel Brooks, who, with his cohort Carl Reiner, performed, that evening, for the first time ever, their classic, excruciatingly funny routine, "The Two-Thousand-Year-Old Man."

When we'd dried our eyes from laughing, Robert Alan Aurthur and I got into a conversation about plots. I tried the African one on him, and he nodded his head enthusiastically. "I had a classmate in Graduate School at the University of Pennsylvania in 1946," he said. "Kwame Nkrumah."

"You mean the president of—" I said.

"Yes," he nodded. "He's the president of Ghana now, but then he was just a graduate student. And he had these glowing ideals. 'Change everything now!' he used to tell me. Then he became president, and he found he had to deal with the fetish men, the witch doctors." Aurthur sighed. "Now his philosophy is 'I won't bother you if you won't bother me.' They're powerful. The witch doctors. Supernaturally powerful." [Kwame Nkrumah helped wrest control of the Gold Coast from Britain in 1957, becoming president (and dictator) of Ghana until he was overthrown in 1966.]

It was a beginning, a tentative joining of interests, and in light of what happened afterwards, it probably should have ended right there.

But I was naïve. I loved *A Man Is Ten Feet Tall*, particularly in its expanded, movie version, starring Sidney Poitier. I felt that in it, Bob had shown that he had a thoroughgoing knowledge of the vision, sensibilities, and mental processes of Blacks. What I overlooked was that there was a world of difference between the thinking of Black Africans and Black Americans. And although Bob had a great depth of understanding of the American experience of Blacks, he would never wholly comprehend the *persona* of the Black African. And that would constitute a fatal flaw in our show.

Sally Ann Howes confronts Terry Carter.

Years before, Oscar Hammerstein had said to me, "Nothing can ever work, no matter how great the songs are, if the story isn't right, and the people don't ring true." He was talking about *Very Warm for May*, the flop he'd written with Jerome Kern. [Kern's final show underwent severe tryout turmoil when it was mounted in 1939, although it left behind a handful of fine songs including one of the best showtunes ever, "All the Things You Are."] Oscar had been uttering a universal theatrical truth.

Of course, I didn't know that it would eventually apply to our show in that spring of 1960. Bob and I began to meet, every day, on the same bench in Central Park, near the Metropolitan Museum of Art. More dimensions began to be added to the project, as he recalled a young Navajo Indian he'd met in New Mexico a few years earlier. The man had gone to the University of Chicago to study medicine, and came back with a non-Indian from Chicago as his bride. The oldsters in the tribe refused to accept either his bride or his new ideas. Everyone greeted him with hostility—except the children. "But the old people are dying off," he'd told Bob. "I just have to work with the children, and wait."

And so we had our theme. And each day, Bob would come up with new ideas. One time, he arrived excitedly, after having read Richard Wright's book *Black Power*, which talked about Wright's trip to a small village in Ghana, on the eve of that country's independence. He'd encountered fear and silence and revelation, as the village waited for the fetish men to pick ten human sacrifices to accompany their dead chief to paradise.

Our show would take place on the eve of an African nation's independence, too. And its main character—and its title—would be *Kwamina*, which was not only a variation on Kwame Nkrumah, the man who had brought he strands of the story together for us, but an

African word that meant "Born on Sunday."

It was a new beginning, then, in a host of ways. And it felt right, from the start. Sally Ann had been excited by the idea as soon as I'd told her about it. She, as much as I, felt that working together would bring us closer together.

And, as I plunged into the writing of the score, I found that it came easily. Astonishingly so. In many cases, the music and the words came together simultaneously.

I was enjoying myself, too. I was working, really working again. Ideas exploded. I determined to write two scores—one with an African feeling for the Africans; one with a Western feeling for Sally Ann and the other European character, called Blair. The music that emerged was like nothing I'd ever written before. It refused to follow set patterns of popular music, but, like the theatrical songs Jerry and I had written, it flowed smoothly, acquiring its shape from the shape of the scene in which it fit.

Other pieces began to fall into place, as if they'd been meant to all along. Some time after the book and most of the score had been written, I discussed the show with Johnny Schlesinger, a friend of mine and the head of one of the two wealthiest and most powerful families in South Africa. He questioned me carefully about the subject, about the production, about the music. The more questions he asked, the more excited he seemed to get.

"You've got to play me some of the music," he finally said.

I agreed, and invited him to come to my studio at 130 East 67th Street, where my pianist and musical secretary, Herbert Shutz, played the songs I'd written and I sang them.

Johnny seemed to be in heaven. "Do you want to be involved?' I asked him.

"Yes," he answered.

"How much of it do you want?"

"All of it."

I shook my head. "No, really, Johnny, how much?"

"All or nothing," he said.

He was a friend of mine. "It's a risk," I said, in spite of my belief in what I was doing. "It isn't a commercial type show. It's a message show. It has miscegenation in it. It's not going to be a money show. It's just something I want to do."

And there it was. While I was talking to him, a number of uncomfortable truths I'd buried came to the surface. This show was a personal crusade. It probably wouldn't be a big commercial success. And we were going to have to scratch around to get the $400,000 at which it would capitalize.

Johnny stood his ground. "I don't care what you say, I want this show. All the way. All or nothing," he said. "I think it's great."

And so, he committed for $400,000, and we were completely and instantly financed.

Now, with these pieces in place, finding a producer was no problem. His toughest task—raising the money—had already been accomplished for him. Still, we wanted the best, and we got him in the person of Alfred de Liagre, who had produced *The Voice of the Turtle*, The *Madwoman of Chaillot*, *The Golden Apple*, and *J.B.*, among a host of other adventurous and magnificent ventures.

Agnes de Mille, who, since *Oklahoma!* had become one of the most prestigious choreographers on Broadway, was hired to stage the dances. Tony Richardson, who had brilliantly staged *Look Back in Anger* and *The Entertainer* in London and New York, was our first choice for director, and he was eager to do the show, and gave us verbal assurances that he would. But film studios in London and Hollywood were already aware of his cinematic skills, and he had to beg off after a very juicy offer to direct the film version of *Look Back in Anger* turned up.

So, we hired Robert Lewis, who had done fine, sensitive work with *Brigadoon* and had staged an exciting Harold Arlen-E.Y. Harburg-Fred Saidy show called *Jamaica* the previous season.

Our musical director would be Colin Romoff, an extraordinarily gifted musician.

Will Steven Armstrong, who had designed a brilliant, suggestive set for *Carnival*, did the same for *Kwamina*. His thirty-two-foot turntable that, in various revolves, showed an African village and a clinic from several distances and perspectives, was hugely inventive. But it created its own set of problems. It made a hideous, grinding noise, always dissonant to what was being performed. In the early performances it was terribly distracting; later on, the grinding was softened, but it never reached the pianissimo that would have satisfied me. And I turned against revolving sets forever.

As we went into rehearsal in the summer of 1961, it felt like coming home, when home is a place of accomplishment and fulfillment. The score was met with enormous enthusiasm by the cast. I'd largely achieved what I'd set out to do. My African music sounded African, though it really wasn't any more than "Bali Ha'i" is a South Seas song. A little exploration of true African music had convinced me that even half an evening of it would have been very difficult for theatre audiences. So, although I used a five-tone scale for the welcoming chant and a Bantuesque approach for "Nothing More to Look Forward To," a plaintive duet, the music was designed merely to work in each given situation. That the situations were more numerous and varied than most musicals till that date was a challenge. But the solutions, I felt, were good ones. Or, at least, most of them were. Some didn't work.

And, from the time he first began to set his ideas to paper, Bob Aurthur had trouble with the book. Then, to add to that, there was the fact that he'd never written a musical before. He was dealing with a medium whose demands he really hadn't mastered. But he was a responsible, dedicated man. Looking back, I think that perhaps the very magnitude of the task crippled him. He wanted to make it human, to deal with the larger issues, to balance them, and—and here is where we probably all went wrong: to attempt to make it acceptable to American audiences of 1961, three years before the Civil Rights Act.

Miscegenation in a musical had always been a tricky subject. How far could we go with it? We had cosmic things to say. How many of them could we put onstage without the show becoming ponderous and pedantic? We were dealing with an exotic locale. How exotic could we let it become before it became inaccessible?

We were asking for trouble, but it was exciting trouble, and we entered the thickets of rehearsal with our eyes open. We had a marvelous cast of fifty Blacks and two whites. Johnny Sekka, a native African, had originally been cast as Kwamina. But the demands of the role had exceeded his skills, and we'd replaced him with Terry Carter.

I wanted Brock Peters to play Kwamina. He was a magnificent actor and a beautiful singer with a deep, rich, baritone voice. To me, he was interesting looking, and not at all the conventional leading man type. And unfortunately for that reason, nobody else liked him.

So, Brock Peters played the witch doctor, and Rex Ingram the tribal chief, and their power was palpable, from the very first readings. And Sally Ann was miraculous. She was beautiful, she read brilliantly and sang like a musically advanced angel. She was simply the best musical performer I had ever written for, and she loved my music. The show was working on a multitude of levels, for all of us.

And then, the trouble began.

From the first rehearsal, there was unrest and tension among the players, a simmering resentment that the vast majority of the cast was Black, and the production staff was white, with the sole exception of Albert Opoku, a Ghanian choreographer and dancer who was serving as technical consultant to Agnes de Mille, and James Wall, our general stage manager.

The dances were brilliant but the book still didn't work, and, as we dug into rehearsals, Bob couldn't seem to resolve its problems. Songs had to be moved, rewritten, written anew.

As we advanced further into rehearsals, I began to experience differences with Bobby Lewis. My training had been under George Abbott, and I was probably applying much of that perspective to the show. But I could clearly see that Bobby wasn't bringing the spectacle and the personal story into balance. The spectacle was swallowing up the story.

And, some of the songs I'd written just weren't working.

Well, that was what out of town was for, and so, at the end of August, we headed for Toronto and the O'Keefe Center. It was a terrific theatre. And Toronto was a very long way from New York—long enough away for us to work on the show in comparative privacy.

We were all nervous when we arrived there. We knew we had something—but it wasn't really a show yet. It was a bunch of separate parts, some of them brilliant. But a cohesive work it wasn't. We had four weeks in Toronto—a week of rehearsals and three weeks of performances—and then another three weeks in Boston to fix it. I'd been part of a team that had done just that with *Damn Yankees*, and I felt we could do it now.

So, we opened on September 3, 1961. It wasn't a good opening. The first act was too long. The applause was sometimes thunderous, particularly for Agnes's superb dances, and for some of the songs. But more often than not, it was merely polite; a danger signal.

The next day, the reviews were split in our favor: Two were favorable, one was negative. Hugh Thompson, of the *Globe and Mail*, bolstered Bob Aurthur and me by stating that "[*Kwamina*] has an overwhelming sincerity which carries impact... Authors Richard Adler and Robert Alan Aurthur have taken a dramatic safari into Africa and returned with a worthy trophy."

But our own sense of the show and the audience reaction was much closer to Nathan Cohen's opinion in the *Toronto Star*, that the show was "listing from bad basic construction and injudicious ornament. It needs a crisis repair job in the worst possible way."

I in fact had lunch with Cohen two days later, and found him to be an articulate, intelligent, and savvy man. He had good suggestions, some of which we utilized. He followed the show to Boston, and became one of our staunchest supporters.

But back in Toronto, it was crisis time. I rolled up my sleeves and went to work. One of the first songs I jettisoned was one of my favorites, "Barbarians." It was sung by the witch doctor, and was a twist on the accepted use of the word. In the lyrics, white Western civilization emerged as barbaric.

It was met with stony silence from the audience, and it was apparent that the hostility it engendered could damage the show from that point forward. The audience resented the comparison. By the time Bobby Lewis brought it up at the following morning's meeting, I'd already determined to cut it.

The mood was intense, as it generally is on the road, but there was also a slowly rising edge of hysteria that was beginning to insinuate itself about *Kwamina*. As days went by, changes were made . . . but were they for the better? This would have been the time that Mr. Abbott would have taken an iron hand to the proceedings. But Bobby Lewis had no iron hand. In fact, the further into trouble we got with the show, the further he seemed to move away from the center of it. And without that strong anchor of direction, the show began to founder.

Some of us began to assume directorial chores, and this was a mistake.

But a few of our ideas worked and the second week in Toronto, *Kwamina* began to improve. I had business to take care of in New York, so I felt comfortable enough with the situation to fly east for a couple of days—and I needed a little time away from the tension. I'd written seven songs in Toronto, to try to shore up the book.

Before I left, I'd personally set the opening number, "The Cocoa Bean Song," a choral piece written in five-part counterpoint. It was tough musically, but the chorus was singing it beautifully. Each of the five groups was cohesive and expressive, and when they were brought together, as the song built and built, it was thrilling, musically and dramatically, and got the show off to a rousing start. The audiences loved it, and so did I.

I got back from New York in time to catch the evening performance. It was horrifying. "The Cocoa Bean Song" was a shambles. The mounting excitement that had been in it when I left for New York was gone. And the reason was apparent to me from the first few notes. The number had been completely restaged. The vocal groups had been broken up and redistributed around the stage, and the entire musical impact, the rising crescendo of sound was dissipated and garbled because of it.

I was furious. I dashed backstage and demanded to know who had restaged the number. Agnes said she had. And she had done it with the best intentions, and within a system of "everyone for themselves" that had established itself in Toronto. I pointed out the damage the restaging had caused, and the next afternoon, we spent an hour putting everything back the way it was. It was wasted energy, and had consumed valuable time that should have been spent elsewhere, but it was typical of the compounding troubles of the show. What else could go wrong? I asked myself, as yet another partially happy, partially dissatisfied audience filed out of the O'Keefe Center.

Plenty, I was to discover, that very night.

We were all working under intense pressure, now. The Toronto run was ending, and we were still doing major rewrites, every night. Nerves were frayed; tempers were as raw as a January wind.

I was particularly tired, and when Sally Ann and I finally dragged ourselves up to our suite, I told her I was going to bed immediately. We'd agreed to sleep in separate bedrooms; she needed her rest to face the daily rehearsal and performance schedule; I worked best in the early morning. I didn't want to disturb her. We kissed each other good night and I crawled into my bed and fell asleep immediately.

About 5:00 A.M., I got up to go to the john. As I came out, I noticed that Sally Ann's bedroom door was open, just a crack. It was usually closed tight, to protect her from my work habits. I wondered if she was all right. I pushed the door open and entered her bedroom, and stopped dead in my tracks. The bed was empty. The front door was slightly ajar.

I sat in a chair facing the door, waiting.

Three-quarters of an hour later, she came in. She let out a little cry when she saw me, and then admitted, as rapidly and as straightforwardly as she had about Maximilian Schell, that she'd been with Terry Carter. [Howes had an affair with Schell when they appeared together in John Frankenheimer's 1960 TV adaptation of Ernest Hemingway's *The Fifth Column.*] It was something that was fairly common in the theatre, leading men and leading ladies getting together, but in our case it was more than that. It was, unconsciously, a monumentally destructive act. She'd practically carved a trail for herself. She could have shut the bedroom door before she left. She could have said to me that she'd gone out for a walk. But in some perverse way—again, I am certain, unconsciously—it seemed as if she actually wanted to be caught.

I was hurt, minimized, betrayed, cuckolded. I exploded. The problem was not only one of marital infidelity.

It was far more crippling than that. What about rehearsals now? A show in trouble brings the people in it close together. I'd have to face both of them every single day and night now, for the rest of the Toronto run and the entire Boston run. She wasn't only hurting me; she was hurting herself, and Terry Carter, and the show.

I was a wreck. I needed some advice about this, my latest crisis.

I phoned Dr. Bak, my analyst. He listened patiently, and then said, "It's one of the most destructive, and self-destructive acts I can imagine. You needed help. I think she does, too."

Sally Ann and I finished Toronto in polite silence. Each of us was a professional; each of us buried, as much as we could, the knowledge and the hurt, but it must have spilled over into the show.

On the flight to Boston, I turned to Sally Ann. "Look," I said, "I know this sounds crazy, but I still care about you. There's something I want you to do."

"What's that?" she asked.

"I want you to go into psychoanalysis," I replied.

She nodded. "All right," she said. And she did.

In retrospect, I can see that a large part of the blame for these acts should have rested on my own unprepared shoulders. Even though I was in my late thirties, I wasn't yet sufficiently emotionally mature to cope with the enormous demands of a husband-wife relationship, especially when both are theatre professionals. More than probably, my own insecurities and anxieties got in the way of the relationship. Instead of having a "we'll fix it" attitude, I clung desperately and defensively to my bruises.

Sally Ann completed her analysis in five years. And I know it helped her enormously.

But by then, we would both know that the marriage had really been over for years. It had been wounded in New York and it died in Toronto.

I will, however, always be grateful to

PREMIERE PERFORMANCE, OCTOBER 23, 1961

54th STREET THEATRE

Alfred de Liagre, Jr.
presents

KWAMINA

The New Musical

starring

Sally Ann   Terry
HOWES   CARTER

with

BROCK PETERS

REX INGRAM   ETHEL AYLER   NORMAN BARRS

MUSIC AND LYRICS BY   BOOK BY
Richard Adler   Robert Alan Aurthur

DANCES AND MUSICAL NUMBERS STAGED BY
Agnes de Mille

Setting and Lighting Designed by   Costumes Designed by
WILL STEVEN ARMSTRONG   MOTLEY

Musical and Choral Direction by   Dance Arrangements by
COLIN ROMOFF   JOHN MORRIS

Orchestrations by
SID RAMIN and IRWIN KOSTAL
ALBERT OPOKU, *Technical Consultant*
(Courtesy of the Government of Ghana)

PRODUCTION DIRECTED BY
Robert Lewis

The billing page from the opening night program.

Sally Ann Howes for the kind, tender, and adoring way she treated my two sons. She remained a mother to them for always, and when, later, Christopher became terribly ill, Sally Ann took leave of her devoted husband and came to live in New York City to be the supportive person she is intuitively. [Christopher Adler (1954-1984) was just starting to achieve success as a promising young lyricist. His most prominent credit was *Jean Seberg* (with composer Marvin Hamlisch), which Peter Hall directed and produced for the National Theatre in 1983.]

We postponed the Boston opening for a night, claiming mechanical troubles. But the troubles were deeper and more enduring than that, and the critics and audiences there were split, as they had been in Toronto. Two reviews were favorable, two were on the fence, and two were unfavorable. Elinor Hughes in the *Herald* called it "Big, colorful, and courageous," and it was that. But Elliot Norton, of the *Post*, turned thumbs down on us.

We toiled hard in Boston. I was strung out. Bobby Lewis seemed to be sleepwalking through his paces, and I was willing to give him the benefit of fatigue until one odd and disquieting evening.

I was in my hotel room, and I decided to phone Delly, as we called our producer Alfred de Liagre, in New York. For some reason, the phone lines crossed, and I came in on a conversation already in progress. Bobby Lewis was talking, and he was slaughtering me, running me into and below the ground to Delly.

Delly was defending me, and the more he defended me, the more Bobby Lewis bitched, and I mean exactly that.

On and on it went, while I listened, silently. They hung up, and I hung up.

The next day, I walked into rehearsal. Bobby was standing in the right wing, and I walked over to him. "Bobby," I said, "you don't like me, do you?'

His eyebrows elevated. "Oh no, Richard," he answered, "that's not true. I adore you."

And then I let him know that I'd heard his diatribe, heard his ten to fifteen minutes of verbal massacre. I never once raised my voice; it was all delivered in bittersweet tones with a dash of carbolic acid.

But when it was over, it was over, and there would be no love exchanged or lost between Bobby Lewis and me from that point onward. [Robert Lewis, in his 1984 autobiography *Slings and Arrows*, has a different take on the situation; he says that Adler specifically refused to allow Kwamina to kiss Eve (Howes), leaving the on-stage affair unrealistically tame and "hypocritical." Lewis, who at the time was drama critic for the *New Leader*, gave *Kwamina* a bad review. "When one aims high," he said, "the miss is more than a mile."]

And so, we'd all reached a new nadir. By October, when we were to open in New York, Bob Aurthur and I were fighting. Elinor Hughes had said, in the *Boston Herald*, "If *Kwamina* were as good as its best portions—namely, the Agnes de Mille dances and Richard Adler's songs—it would be a sure Broadway hit. Unfortunately, there's serious book trouble."

There had been book trouble from the very first day, and although it had improved since Toronto, the book was still weighing the show down. Looking back, I don't suppose Bob was given the kind of help he needed from the rest of us. Each of us on the production team was more knowledgeable about theatre than Bob. We could have helped him more.

But even if we had, we ourselves hadn't solved still another problem, and that was a major dilemma that had grown from our own emotional attachment to the material. We were dealing with something we believed in, and yet we also fervently wanted a hit in New York. And so, we didn't really resolve the issues at the end of the show. We copped out. Perhaps if we'd been grittier and more realistic, the thematic force of the show would have been great enough to carry it through. But we sent the two lovers—and the audience—off with the dream that, in another time, another place, it might have been different.

I didn't know when I wrote the song, "Another Time, Another Place" lyric that I'd be describing not only the relationship between the lovers, but also that between Sally Ann and me.

And so we opened in New York, at the 54th Street Theatre—later the George Abbott—on October 23, 1961. And flopped. Badly. We lasted for thirty-two performances, and closed on a very sad Sunday night.

It had been an embittering experience. Much has been said and written about flop sweat—the feeling you get before you fail. But not enough will ever be said about the feelings after. They're sometimes too terrible to record, and excavating the memoirs of that time almost amounts to masochism.

When it was over, I had more than the postpartum blues. I was blackly, deeply, despondent. I knew I'd written the best score of my life. And that was reinforced the week after the show opened, first by a laudatory article by *New York Times* music critic Irving Kolodin, then by a phone call from Harold Arlen, who said it was one of the finest scores he'd ever heard; and finally and most touchingly by my father, who, after the opening night performance came up to me, and said, "I haven't understood what you've been doing up till now. But I understand this. And I like it. You're a fine composer, a fine musician."

I put my arms around him, and hugged him and all of those contentions of the past disappeared like mist when the sun starts to shine. It was as if, with one accomplishment, I was no longer the young boy tagging along after my father as he strode, like Brahms, through the countryside of Karinoke. I'd caught up—in my mind and in his—and what a profound achievement that was. [Clarence Adler (1886–1969) was a concert pianist and a reknowned teacher, whose students included Aaron Copland and Richard Rodgers.]

And yet, all of this was being dulled by the failure of the show. I was angry at Bobby Lewis, at Bob Aurthur, at myself for not taking a still-stronger hand when I knew it was coming to pieces. I was angry at Sally Ann, angry at my naiveté and bad judgment in placing the burden of the salvation of our marriage on the show.

And I was angry at the public, which reacted much more hostilely than the critics at our audacity in portraying the love of a white woman for a Black man onstage. The hate mail roared in even before we opened in New York, and spit forth from the mailbox long after we closed. It was vituperative and vile, and Sally Ann had to bear the brunt of most of it. The very bottom was reached one day during the first week of the New York run, when she received a piece of used toilet paper in an envelope.

Kwamina opened October 23, 1961 at the 54th Street Theatre, to mixed-to-unfavorable reviews. It closed there on November 18, 1961 after 32 performances, with a total loss.

As Adler tells it, the failure of *Kwamina* was preordained. This despite a highly adventurous score; the African songs were especially interesting, and very much different than anything heard previously on Broadway. Adler received his third Tony nomination as composer, although he didn't win this time. Richard Rodgers took it for *No Strings*, which followed *Kwamina* into the 54th Street. Adler was in good company, sharing the runner-up slots with his mentor Frank Loesser (for *How to Succeed in Business without Really Trying*) and novice Jerry Herman (for *Milk and Honey*).

Adler's two final musicals followed *Kwamina*'s path. *A Mother's Kisses* (1968) had a tortured tryout, closing in Baltimore. (The title character was played by Robert Alan Aurthur's former wife, Bea Arthur.) *Music Is* (1976), with George Abbott of *The Pajama Game* and *Damn Yankees*, enjoyed a highly successful tryout; but Broadway, in the era of *A Chorus Line* and *Chicago*, wasn't interested in a pleasantly mild adaptation of *Twelfth Night*. That was a bad year for Adler, certainly; he produced not only *Music Is* but Richard Rodgers's *Rex* as well [see page 290].

The
Broadhurst
Theatre

PLAYBILL

the national magazine for theatregoers

"Cry For Us All"

Cry for Us All (1970)

A Little Turntable Music, Please

Composer Mitch Leigh had one of the more unrelenting careers among Broadway's one-hit wonders. A budding tycoon from the world of advertising jingles—"Nobody Doesn't Like Sara Lee" remains his most popular title, other than "The Impossible Dream"— Leigh determined to storm the world of Broadway. He provided incidental music (and, reportedly, financing) for two early 60s plays directed by Albert Marre. This experience (and, reportedly more financing) earned Leigh a Broadway musical assignment, on an unlikely musicalization of *Don Quixote*.

But one never knows. *Man of La Mancha* proved a smash when it opened in 1965, quickly earning a place on the list of Broadway's favorite musicals. Leigh's next offering, which had been intended as a companion-in-repertory with *La Mancha*, was picked up by innovative musical theatre producer Cheryl Crawford (of *Brigadoon*, *Johnny Johnson*, *Flahooley*, and more). *Chu-Chem*, "a Zen Buddhist— Hebrew musical comedy," starring Menasha Skulnick and Molly Picon, closed during its Philadelphia tryout in 1966.

Leigh, who had coproduced *Chu-Chem*, thenceforth determined to be controlling producer on his future musicals, all six of which were massive failures. Only one of Leigh's later scores displayed creative talent, *Cry for Us All*. Ellen Stern covered the tryout for *New York* magazine.

Cry for Us All came to town with this enigmatic ink-blot logo by Fay Gage.

"Case History of an Out-of-Town Tryout"
by Ellen Stern

In New Haven, George's motor stalled. Agnes Hogan died in Act I, but her ghost still hovered over Act II. The love interest was without love and without interest.

In Boston, George's motor hummed. Agnes Hogan was still haunting Act II. The love interest was still without love and without interest.

And then, the last night of the Boston tryout, after 38 days of on-the-road travail, the audience went wild. They loved the lovers. They cried bravo at the curtain calls. They even applauded the ushers. Mitch Leigh, the composer and producer, remembered a night in 1965 when the same thing happened to *Man of La Mancha*.

Now it may be happening to *Cry for Us All*, the twelfth big musical of the Broadway season, which, stepping gingerly over the corpses of *Buck White*, *Jimmy*, *Gantry* and *Georgy*, will make its bow at the Broadhurst Theatre on April 8. [The others were *La Strada*, *Coco*, *Purlie*, *Blood Red Roses*, *Minnie's Boys*, *Look to the Lilies*—and *Applause*, the only bonafide money-maker among the lot.]

Mitch Leigh is not only the successful composer of *Man of La Mancha* but chairman of the board of the enormously successful public company he formed, Music Makers, that has turned out thousands of enormously successful tunes for radio and television commercials. The Yale University School of Music Alumni Association awarded him a certificate of merit in 1967 (he studied at Yale with Paul Hindemith and received his B.S. in 1951, his M.A. in 1952). Artur Rubinstein says he's the most brilliant composer writing for musical theatre today. And Andrew Scott Leigh, who's 9, thinks his father's music is shaping up okay.

Like most other musicals, *Cry for Us All* is based on a proven success—in this case, the fragile tragedy *Hogan's Goat* by William Alfred, which opened in November 1965, ran for 607 performances off Broadway, and won the Vernon Rice Award for the best play of 1965-66. [*Hogan's Goat* is all but forgotten, remembered chiefly as the play that catapulted twenty-four-year-old Faye Dunaway to Hollywood and *Bonnie and Clyde.*] Like many other musicals, it will cost almost a million dollars to mount. And like any other musical, *Cry for Us All* has gone through the tortures of the damned, or the jinxed.

"We never do the same show twice," the musical director lamented one painful day during the Boston run. "I've never seen any show change as much as this one has." He could have been wrong. Other musicals just might have run into worse crises. But as this chronicle of its trials on the road illustrates, *Cry for Us All* surely had more grief than it needed.

New Haven

The formidable turntable set has emerged from the bowels of designer Howard Bay's laboratory. The set is balkier than a temperamental actor, bulkier than a carousel, and less predictable than a schizophrenic. Above the turntable, a Brooklyn street, home, front yard, bar and back room, and a staircase climbing high into the flies, revolve in a cycle of 360°; pushed beyond that, the cable will snap (and it has). "We all love the set," says the stage manager, "but we tend to call it things. Like the Mad Marvel." [Howard Bay was best known for his massive sets for musicals like *Up in Central Park*, *The Music Man*, and *Man of La Mancha*.]

The Mad Marvel is operated by a man named George, who stands in the wings at a control board, turning the set just so many degrees for each scene, anxiously peering at a gauge which tells him how close he is to 360° and potential disaster. At intermission, the cable must be rewound. But worst of all, the damned thing hums. Really hums. And it's a problem beyond the call of 3-in-1 oil.

On Wednesday, January 28, the world premiere of *Cry for Us All* has to be postponed when George's motor stalls. Thursday night's performance is also canceled, and a team of machinists and other exotic craftsmen, working all kinds of strange hours through a long week, collect $50,000. "Even *they* were embarrassed," Mitch Leigh sighs.

On Friday, the situation doesn't look great, but it looks good enough, and it occurs to William Alfred, the playwright, who happens to have a broken leg, that if he hobbles onstage on crutches, he might have a chance at winning the sympathy of a skeptical audience. But it seems a touch too obvious, so at the last minute an assistant stage manager rakes his fingers through his hair, walks onstage, smiles weakly, and reads the apologia Alfred has hurriedly written for the occasion:

> Ladies and gentlemen, your kind indulgence!
> If acts should stall or lights lose their effulgence

Or our game actors sometimes pantomime
Amazement at effects seen the first time;
For they're as fresh to parts of this as you,
Because our set was often loose a screw.

The curtain opens. It is spring of 1890 in the city of Brooklyn. Fighting to be heard over the hum of George's motor, striving to maintain their equilibrium on a turntable that doesn't always stop when it's supposed to, Matthew Stanton, a handsome young ward leader, competes with Edward Quinn, the crusty incumbent, for the mayoral nomination. Kathleen Stanton, Matt's new wife, regrets her civil-ceremony marriage and agonizes over her lost virtue. Agnes Hogan, once Quinn's mistress, then Stanton's, then nobody's, dies.

Pretty gloomy stuff. Relief comes chiefly through a tattered Greek chorus in the guise of street rats, who parody the action of the leading characters and, in effect, reinforce the plot. "I got the idea," says playwright Alfred, "from the book *Jacob Riis Revisited*, where I found a series of pictures of the street rats of the nineties. When I was young, my grandmother kept volumes of *St. Nicholas* magazine. My favorite story was "Teddy and Carrots"—kids on their own. New York apparently was full of them. I was eight, and I was fascinated. I still am."

While the tragedy huffs and puffs, counterpoint is provided by Scott Jacoby, Darel Glaser and tiny Todd Jones as they bound onstage from time to time to clear away the cobwebs and reenact what has just transpired with the grownups. Alfred sees them as a delegation from the audience. "Every audience arrives with reservations about consenting," he says. "The kids represent a cynical innocence, and the audience can say, 'We'll assent if you'll amuse us.' The children will always get it wrong when they re-enact the story because they're so brutally innocent they leave the feelings out."

"We're the narrators, and I feel we're pretty important," says Darel Glaser, 14, who is oldest of the three and their spokesman. This is a serious business, and he rarely smiles. "For people who find the play going on in a sad sort of color, we add the bright color."

Okay, but the problems are still clearly in view—problems in addition to the set, its whims and the *a cappella* hum of its motor. For one thing, there's no sympathy for Matt and Kathleen, the main characters, because nobody knows if they love or hate each other. For another, the secondary characters are threatening: Tommy Rall (as Boyle) and Helen Gallagher (as Bessie) perform "The Verandah Waltz" so effectively—and for so long—that the audience can't even remember who Matt is much less why he married Kathleen.

The Irish brogues are cluttering the poetry of Alfred's words, making them almost impossible to understand. And, finally, there is Agnes Hogan, who, by virtue of her absence, has become the indisputable heroine. The action centers around her: Stanton and Quinn hate each other because she loved them both; Bessie and Boyle are unswervingly devoted to her and resent anyone who isn't; "Cry for Us All," the show's most powerful musical number, is a dramatically sorrowful celebration of her death. Obsessed by Stanton's affair with Agnes, Kathleen provokes her own death. Final diagnosis: Agnes Hogan is just too important. The stage is overpopulated. The New Haven audience is baffled.

And then disaster strikes in the final scene: as Kathleen lies in Matt's arms, dying of a broken heart and neck, she manages to sing a few more lines. The audience laughs. Nervously, but they laugh.

"Even if the scene could have worked, it wouldn't have that night," Leigh is saying a few days later as he devours two hamburgers and sips black coffee in the Sizzleboard, across College Street from the Shubert. "Whether it was too melodramatic or not, I don't know. But we committed the cardinal sin of having our two main characters do nothing all night but sing, with the minor ones doing everything else. By the end, who gave a damn?"

Fifth-billed star Margot Moser—best known as a long-term Eliza Doolittle replacement—was written out of the show in Boston.

Kathleen's farewell aria is eliminated, and *Cry for Us All* is ready to face the press on Monday evening, February 2. The New Haven reviews are wondrously encouraging. "In this tryout condition," one critic writes, "*Cry for Us All* is an impressive, appealing, affecting musical drama. It is richly conceived, willing to be uncompromisingly serious in its major elements…. The important thing about the production—and the set—right now is that both show every promise of being perfected."

"I'm *amazed*," William Alfred whispers, his eyes opening wide. "I thought we were in a *very* sorry state."

So did somebody else, apparently. The title of the show is changed from *Cry for Us All* to *Who to Love?*

Boston

"Kathleen is a terrible complainer," says Joan Diener, who plays her. "There are very few scenes in which she isn't going through a conflict between Matt and God. I don't know how people tolerate her." [Diener, who gave a memorable and perhaps incomparable performance as Aldonza in *Man of La Mancha*, was the director's wife. Marre cast her in her four major Broadway roles, the other two being *Kismet* [1953] and Leigh's one-performance flop *Home Sweet Homer* [1976].]

"She's not clear," Leigh adds, "and what *is* clear about her is bad: she's a *nudge*."

It is painfully obvious that Kathleen and Matt have to be made more lovable, to each other as well as to the audience. Which means that first they have to become more visible.

Step one is to kill two characters whose only contribution has been to confuse the story line. Margot Moser, who plays one of them, goes back to New York; Ted Forlow, who plays the other, stays on as an understudy. Step two: Helen Gallagher and Tommy Rall get their roles trimmed, and, in the process, lose "The Verandah Waltz." They're not grateful.

"If subtractions help the show, they inadvertently help me, I guess," Miss Gallagher says bravely, but without conviction. "I'm sorry they cut Bessie. It's the first time I've ever had a part cut down. Usually, if the secondary characters can do their own stuff very well, they give you more—unless you're working with an Ethel Merman or someone who's afraid of you." [This appears to be a direct reference to leading lady Joan Diener. Gallagher had a Broadway career of ups and downs. A Tony Award-winning featured performance in the 1952 revival of *Pal Joey* brought her a full-scale star vehicle. *Hazel Flagg* (1953) failed, though, as did *Portofino*. As her career foundered, Gallagher returned to featured roles (most prominently as the star's friend and standby in *Sweet Charity* and as a replacement Gooch in *Mame*). She followed *Cry for Us All* with her final Broadway role, triumphantly taking a best actress Tony for the 1971 revival of *No, No, Nanette*. After which she turned to TV, with a fourteen-year run (and three best actress Emmys) for the soap opera *Ryan's Hope*.]

"Adding and subtracting songs and scenes," says Leigh, "is like having one marble that's the wrong shade in a jarful of marbles that are perfect. You know you have to remove the wrong one, but in doing that you upset the others."

Leigh says he writes for the plot, not the record charts, and he's still wondering why, out of context, "The Impossible Dream" from *La Mancha* is such a success. "We don't want gratuitous songs," he explains. "I don't say, 'Hey, let's have a song.' The play is so truly integrated, the only time you sing is when emotion gets too high to talk."

"The Verandah Waltz" is given to Matt and Kathleen, and it works beautifully. "A relationship like theirs can't exist except in a dance," says choreographer Todd Bolender. Expository sequences are clarified and strengthened. Kathleen stops wringing her hands and makes jokes now about her great transgression—that *civil* marriage. The Irish brogues are softened. By cuts and fills, Agnes Hogan's ghost is finally laid to rest. But it isn't enough. Kathleen still needs a song to introduce her, something equivalent to Matt's strong "End of My Race," which immediately proves him ambitious and confident. The writers confer. Why don't we just have Kathleen come down the stairs and say "Hello?" they say. So Mitch Leigh picks up one of his favorite expressions from the play, "How are you since?" and writes a song on it that does the trick.

"The phrase didn't exactly turn them on," he says, "and it's the first time I've ever pushed for a song nobody wanted to do. But I said, 'Let me just write a few bars, hear how it sounds.' I had to get it out of me."

The problem of Kathleen's entrance is solved. Now she descends the stairs, goes easily into "How Are You Since?" and she is welcomed by her husband's back-room supporters as they sing it with her. A few minutes later, she and Matt sing a romanticized reprise of the song to each other, and it's obvious, at least, that they're in love.

"She sees in him a strong, good-looking guy," says Leigh. "He sees in her the lady he wonders if he deserves. A lady to the manner born, come to down-home politics. He has vitality and charm. She has beauty and breeding. You've got to like them. Now you care about what's going to happen to them . . . positive or negative."

William Alfred and *Hogan's Goat* have gone through a meat-grinder. Alfred is a soft-spoken man, who smiles—when he smiles—a bit fearfully. He creeps about the theatre during rehearsals, his tall body slightly bent under a somber wool scarf he wears around his shoulders, and he looks as if he's afraid of being in the way as he searches for a quiet place to work on the revisions required of him. Alfred's play is based on events that really happened to his great-aunt and great-uncle in the early 1900s, in a house that is still standing on Second Place in Brooklyn. It's not easy to rewrite a heritage.

For a gentle man, whose greatest love is probably the Anglo-Saxon poetry he teaches at Harvard, the rigors of writing for Broadway are not easily borne. "I realized in New Haven that I knew very little about the musical form," Alfred says. "I am used to people talking to each other—I put everything I can into interchange—but I began to understand such niggling things as that you need lines to get characters from one room to another.

"But you have to be brutally objective," he says. "And what you have to be, you have to be. I've lost count of the rewrites I've done.

One scene has 18 versions. We're trying to strip every inch of fat out of it."

This is the first show for Alfred's co-lyricist, Phyllis Robinson, who's been working with words for 20 years as a vice president at Doyle Dane Bernbach. She's rewriting like she never did before, but says, "*Writing*'s the easy part..."

George's motor is in working order, but some of the lighting equipment hasn't arrived from New Haven, so just before the show opens at the Colonial Theatre on Wednesday, February 11, William Alfred weakens and again decides to apologize to the audience. He appears on stage—he got rid of his crutches in New Haven—and shyly announces that this will be an "unpaid performance," and that ticketholders can have their money back if they like, or get free tickets to a later performance. If this is an attempt to forestall reviews, the attempt fails. Next day, Elliot Norton of the *Record-American* says the production is "grievously melodramatic and often grievously dull."

A few days later, Mitch Leigh and William Alfred appear on Norton's television show on WGBH to discuss their play and his review. The guests put the host on the defensive. "I got him in such a way that he was grabbing his necktie," Leigh recalls. "He asked me questions, and I answered them for him. He said, 'What can we do to help the theatre?' and I said, 'Nothing. You're a newspaperman, you're not in the theatre. You write your Sunday pieces and say why don't new things happen in the theatre, and when we do something different, you damn us.' It would have been easy if I'd said, 'You son of a bitch,' but I didn't. He does his thing, I do mine."

The cast is assembled at the Colonial for yet another rehearsal, and time is running out. Director Albert Marre talks slowly and quietly; it's a strain to hear him. "When we get to New York," he says, "we won't be able to get into the Broadhurst when we want it, so we'll rehearse at the Winter Garden. We'll get into the Broadhurst the week of the 16th, and start previews on the 23rd. We'll have time to fix a lot of little things. Obviously, I'll cut a few moves, and we'll fix the set so it doesn't revolve so many times.

"And it develops," Marre continues, "that for a whole series of reasons that become almost comic, we're going back to the original title..."

Leigh twists around in his seat to elaborate: "We changed the title," he whispers, "because the 'experts' thought that *Who to Love?* would appeal more to the ticket-buying public. We had our doubts. We know that the title doesn't matter if the play's a hit. Ajax is hardly the most euphonious name. It sells like our play should only sell." He turns back to hear what Marre is saying.

"…and those scenes are in bad shape but that I can only clear up in New York. For the kids' scene after the steamer business, Mr. Alfred is on his way over with that, so, kiddies, hold on. You'll have a few more things to learn."

"*More* new lines?" murmurs one street rat's mother to another.

The cast disbands; some go on stage to work out "This Cornucopian Land," a riproaring song and dance that will go in tonight; some sit where they are, talking or reading the *New York Times*; several go out for coffee, and the boys run over to where their mothers are sitting and comparing credits. They empty crackling paper bags they've been gripping. Bagged laughter, playing cards and instant bouquets fall into the mothers' laps: the Greek chorus has discovered Jack's Trick and Joke Shop on Park Square.

On stage, the singing population of Brooklyn is learning how to dance. The assistant choreographer is leading them through their steps. "I like working with singers," says choreographer Bolender, as he keeps his eyes on the stage. "They have rhythm, and you don't have to teach them how to count."

Note that the actors are billed in six degrees of type, undoubtedly negotiated meticulously. Handwriting analysts can have their own holiday with this page; the monument on the left is the autograph of Joan Diener.

Herbert Grossman, the musical director, agrees. "If I have to deal with *dancers* who are learning to *sing*," he says, "I have to explain everything. When I work with these people, the shorthand is there. We speak the same language."

"In New Haven, we were in *good* shape," Leigh is saying, over lobster and beer at the Union Oyster House on Stuart Street. "Everything that could have happened, happened here."

He speaks the truth. George's troubles in New Haven were as nothing to the traumas of the cast in Boston. Especially afflicted are company members staying at the Bradford Hotel, a dreary warren with floors and floors of empty rooms and musty corridors. Leigh's assistant, Lucia Craycraft, reports: "I wanted to have Mr. Leigh's laundry done. Next to the phone there are 93 numbers to call for service, none of them the valet. So I dial, wait for 40 minutes, and then the operator comes on and I ask for the valet. And do you now what she says? 'I'm sorry, miss. The valet died.'"

It grows worse. William Alfred gets sick enough to be carried out of his house into an ambulance. He stays in the hospital for a day and a half with the flu.

Tommy Rall gets the flu and is out of the show for a week; when he returns, he isn't strong enough to sing his songs or do his two strenuous dances until the final night in Boston. Todd Jones, youngest Greek chorus member, is out one night with a sore throat.

Albert Marre gets the flu. Joan Diener, his wife, gets the flu. Robert Weede, once *The Most Happy Fella* and now Mayor Quinn, returns to his room with the flu, only to find that thieves have been there first, and have taken his money and a watch given him by the stagehands in *Milk and Honey*.

Scott Jacoby is hit on the head by a piece of wood one gusty Saturday between shows. He goes to the hospital. "They thought it was my brain," he reports happily. "They stuck all sorts of needles into me and touched me with feathers to see if I could feel anything." To his dismay, he can feel everything.

Dolores Wilson, who plays Maria Haggerty, walks into some scenery just before curtain time and can't go on.

Mitch Leigh has put on 40 pounds so far from non-stop nervous noshing. "If it's fattening, I want it," he is frequently heard to say.

Steve Arlen, who plays Matt, collapses in the middle of the second act one Monday night. "He just keeled over, and they schlepped him offstage," says Leigh. "We thought it was a heart attack, but he had an electrocardiogram and it was nothing. Thank God." [Arlen replaced opera singer John Reardon, who was originally signed for the role.]

The gregarious mothers of the three little boys are barred from the theatre during performances. "They're just too much *with* us," someone says.

The set defies George and gravity one night and pursues an uncharted course. "The set... the *set*," Leigh moans. "It'll end up eating us all."

The 1,800-pound tree falls while the set revolves and a perplexed audience watches. As the chief carpenter attaches himself to the trunk, trying to hold it down, the tree plunges into the wings where, miraculously, there is enough space to catch it.

George's motor drones on.

And then, in spite of it all, on Saturday, the final day of the run, after

9 performances in New Haven and 28 in Boston, it all works. The audience applauds the kids, and everyone else in sight. They relent toward Quinn and frown with compassion when he sings "Where Are All the Good Times Gone?" They stop the show after Boyle's manic lament in "Cry for Us All," after Bessie swings her bag in "Swing Your Bag," and after "This Cornucopian Land." They are outraged to see empty seats in the house. "It was the first time I felt *La Mancha* happening," Leigh says, relaxed at last, "and it felt pretty damned good."

Eleventh-hour bulletins:

Dolores Wilson, who was injured backstage the last night in Boston, did herself greater harm than anyone realized. She won't be able to go on in New York and will have to be replaced.

George's motor continues to hum. In the beginning, it hummed in B flat and, after all the repairs, went to B natural. Leigh will try to shorten its chain, raising the motor to a C, and will compose underscoring to cover it. He also plans to work on a new overture, write an entr'acte, and refine the dance music—three chores usually relegated by composers to their arrangers.

Before New Haven, there were 23 songs in the score. In New Haven, 18. In Boston, 16. By April 8, at least two more will have been added, bringing the total up to 18 again. (*Mame* has 12 songs; *Oklahoma!*, 13; *Hello, Dolly!*, 11, and *West Side Story*, 12.) "This is one of the lushest music shows I've ever worked with," says musical director Grossman. "With all the songs, plus underscoring, I never stop."

Leigh told himself it "didn't matter" when *Man of La Mancha* opened in 1965 (11 days after *Hogan's Goat*). Since then, he's been in analysis. Now he's eating a lot and puffing on his Punch cigars a lot and freely conceding that this time it *does* matter.

"I sure hope it's a hit," says one of the little boys. "My mother's had it up to *here*."

The worst, it would seem, is over. Leigh swears it's his last show. "The changes we've made were the right ones," he says, "and we're finally at the point where we'll win. *Kinahora*. [Which is Yiddish for, more or less, "let us be protected from the Evil Eye."]

"We've given people something to respond to. Our characters aren't bad people. They're not vicious. All they want to do is get out of their ghetto situation. Matt's ambition is not necessarily a simple ambition: it's for him and his kind. A vital culture, this Irish culture. It relates to Jews and blacks and all ghettoized people.

"It's a play about good people trying to better themselves. We all do it. We're all trying to get out of where we are. That's why it's called *Cry for Us All*."

"Cry for Us All?" gasps the lady at the League of New York Theatres, who keeps track of what shows open where. "I'm awfully glad you told me. I've had it down as *Cry for Saul.*"

Cry for Us All opened April 8, 1970 at the Broadhurst Theatre, to unfavorable reviews. It closed there on April 15, 1970 after 9 performances, with a total loss.

That last-minute lift from Boston, turned out to be illusory. The critic from the *New York Post* saw *Cry for Us All* as "ambitious" but "little short of disastrous"; the critic from the *Times* found himself "crying only for Mr. Alfred," upon whose play the musical was based; and *Women's Wear Daily* noted that the play "has been tilted so that Stanton's wife is the central figure; she also has many costume changes; she is played by the director and co-author's wife, Joan Diener. Miss Diener has a range of expression that can best be described as pancake makeup."

It might seem foolhardy to take such an uncompromisingly serious property and transform it to the musical stage. It worked for the Messrs. Leigh and Marre on *La Mancha*, yes; but *La Mancha* carried a theme as well as an "Impossible Dream" that were relevant to the social upheaval of the times. *Cry for Us All* was merely a poetic tragedy of corruption, greed, and murder. The experiment didn't work, despite what was easily the most adventurous musical score of an especially lackluster season. Until eighteen days later, that is, when *Company* opened at the Alvin.

Salvage Jobs

Golden Boy

Tenderloin

How Now, Dow Jones

I Remember Mama

SHUBERT
THEATRE

PLAYBILL

the magazine for theatregoers

"GOLDEN
BOY"

Golden Boy (1964)

Misbegotten but Alive

While serving as an actor in the early productions of the Group Theatre (from 1931 on), Clifford Odets began writing plays. *Awake and Sing!* (1935) thrust him to immediate fame, bringing a new voice to American drama. This was followed—a mere five weeks later (!)—with *Waiting for Lefty*. The Broadway success of *Golden Boy* (1937), and its 1939 motion picture version, kept Odets in Hollywood for most of the rest of his career. He made a half-dozen bittersweet visits back to Broadway, with only *The Country Girl* (1954) managing to find success. Odets died on August 18, 1963 at the age of fifty-seven. At the time of his death, he was story editor for TV's *The Richard Boone Show*. His final stage project, a musical version of *Golden Boy*, conceived as a vehicle for Sammy Davis, went into rehearsal in May 1964.

William Gibson met Clifford Odets in 1950, when the latter was organizing a playwrights' seminar at the Actors Studio. By 1953, Odets was a close friend to Gibson and his wife Margaret Brenman-Gibson (who later wrote *Clifford Odets: American Playwright* [1981]). William Gibson, like Odets, achieved notable success with his first two Broadway plays, *Two for the Seesaw* (1958) and *The Miracle Worker* (1959); he remained active five decades later, with the 2003 play *Golda's Balcony* enjoying a long Broadway run. Gibson wrote a chronicle of his part in the making of the musical *Golden Boy*, which was included as a preface to the published script. Given the personal nature of the writing, I have avoided the use of annotations; supporting information appears after Gibson's piece.

Sammy looks studious in this rehearsal shot. *Golden Boy*'s advertising campaign underwent numerous changes along the way to Broadway.

from "A Memento"

by William Gibson

We were among those he asked to see when he lay dying in a Hollywood hospital, and because we were on Cape Cod with an unlisted phone the message reached us a week late; I flew out that night. Clifford never knew I was there, he was heavily sedated the last three days and oblivious to this world, but all that week I lived in the rented Beverly Hills house he had occupied, and indeed continued to fill. Its every room was brimful of his voracious spirit, hundreds of masterwork records drowning the piano top and spilling into chairs, a thousand books overflowing the shelves onto tabletops and floors, and everywhere scraps of notepaper overrun by his handscript, jottings to himself in red ink about fictional characters, the conduct of life, women, art and artists, childhood and fatherhood, his own nature, and unsent letters, usually irate.

Paula Strasberg was there acting as housekeeper that month, being mother to Clifford's two teen-agers, and I loved her for it, and since it seemed part of my purpose was to familiarize myself with the legacy of problems every death leaves the survivors, I read all I could of what Clifford had last been working on; Paula brought me whatever she could find. In the garden—beside the alluring and baptismal font of moviedom, the swimming pool, used by no one in the household except a girlfriend of Clifford's secretary—I read the mimeographed draft of the *Golden Boy* musical with which Clifford had planned to return to the stage.

It was obvious that, at the least, much work remained to be done. The driving line of the original play was of course there; Clifford had once said to me that he "never thought much of that play" but after viewing some semipro staging of it years later he "knew they'll never break it down," and his sense of its line was still unerring. But music in the theatre creates a profoundly altered time-world in the audience, material which in straight drama requires ten minutes of preparation can in a musical context be attacked instantly, and the text was that of straight drama, as yet undistilled to the concentrate which music compels. And Clifford, still working on the page, had not been privileged to witness the physical fact onstage of a Negro boy talking to a white girl; Joe Bonaparte had been changed in name only, to Wellington at that. I rather disapproved of the whole project, which seemed a cashing-in upon the current scene, and it would be a year before I understood what Clifford's eye had seen in it. Nor did I understand the implications I have stated here, I knew only that if this text went into production a swarm of problems would arise and no writer's hand would be there to meet them, it lay dying on a hospital sheet. I had a brief fantasy at that swimming pool of offering my services to the producer Hillard Elkins, whom I did not know, but concluded that my expectation of being indispensable to him would not necessarily coincide with his; I thought if he wanted me he would call me, and a year later he did.

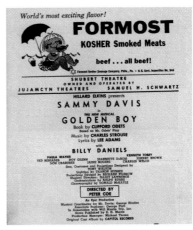

The billing page from the first stop of the tryout tour.

Two days after Clifford's body was cremated I flew back to Massachusetts and my own work. I could not shake his death, and a month later I sat for eight unhappy days over a tape recorder dictating every detail of it I had observed during my week in his house, as well as all I could remember of him in the years preceding, and put the tapes away for whatever interest the future might take in him as man and writer. In the next year we were much involved with his spiritual estate; my wife began the research for her biographical study, and we lived immersed in his papers and other people's memories of him. Some of his physical possessions were always in view around our house, his son had presented me with a few of his pipes and my wife with his silver cigarette case, and we had inherited a quantity of his unwanted books and 78-rpm records, and all winter on our enclosed porch there stood a certain old writing table. It was part of the shambles found in the New York apartment Clifford had lived in with his wife and children prior to her death at the age of thirty-three, and which he had continued to pay the rent on through his last nine years in Beverly Hills. The table was too shabby to be sold or given away, and it was to be junked; but when Paula told us it was dear to Clifford because on it he had written his first play, *Awake and Sing!*, my wife harassed me into roping it onto our station-wagon, and we drove it home to Stockbridge. That winter a builder was putting up a workroom for me in the woods by our cottage on Cape Cod, and in midsummer when I drove my family there the table was back on top of the station-wagon; it went into the new studio as my worktable.

We were hardly there when my wife answered the phone and said, "You want to talk to Hillard Elkins?" I knew *Golden Boy* was in Boston and what the conversation would be, and the next night my wife and I drove in from the Cape to see another show in trouble on the road. I was prepared to say two clever things to whatever writer was with it,

and then drive off again, my duty discharged. I was not prepared to find the book gutted of content, no writer present at all, the audience yawning, the director in the third week of a holiday at home in merrie England, and with its Broadway unveiling a month and a half off, the star in an impotent wrath that the production was saying nothing of what he knew it must say—if only for verisimilitude—on the most divisive issue of our time in this country. I told Elkins that from beginning to end the book, wherever it had a choice of materials, had made the wrong choice; Hilly said it had been a scissors-and-paste job put together by a committee of non-writers after Clifford's death. I was not astounded when that night he and Sammy Davis asked would I rewrite it, but I was deeply unready to say yes.

Sammy Davis and Paula Wayne in *Golden Boy*. Sammy's hand on Paula's shoulder was incendiary in 1964—as it was intended to be.

I had ten motives converging on me to push me in, all impure, but I made a virtuous effort to surmount them. I heard that another playwright whom I respected had been up to see the show, and when Hilly quoted his opinion, "It ain't nigger enough," I said I quite agreed and requested Hilly to phone him that moment to invite him to rewrite it, if he accepted I'd be off the hook; and I went into another room and read a newspaper until Hilly came in and said I wasn't, the other guy was in the middle of a play. I said I was in the middle not only of a play but of a book I had been working on for three years. I was much attracted to Hilly, a hybrid original of thirty-four with a fast wit and insinuating intelligence, part rocket, part goniff, part magus at the cradle of talent, who understood what Clifford meant to me, and I could not but admire a host with the chutzpah to invite a fly and say bring your own flypaper; from our first handshake we met each other on the level. And when I listened to Sammy's passionate tongue, which talked Clifford's language, I saw I was in the presence of another fast wit and an incisive mind, and an ego whose thousand-horsepower drive was in this hour of history married to the collective ego of twenty

Salvage Jobs

million Americans in their assault on the old order for an honorable place within it. I also met "the boys," the songwriters Charles Strouse and Lee Adams, who turned out to be another humorous pair; whatever the show might be lacking it was not extracurricular jokes, and I knew that to work with the company would be a pleasure. I could play savior, learn as a theatre man something of the nature of musical shows, impersonate my dead mentor—an act which contained some irrational overtones of resurrection—and by an assist towards the box-office success of the show repay his progeny some of my debt to him. Further, I could speak a few words on a social issue that moved me more to vehemence than anything had in two decades. When Sammy said he had "fused Clifford a bit" I quite believed it, because he fused me too, and now I understood not only Clifford's promise to him—"I'm going to write this play in your mouth!"—but his nonfiscal interest in the undertaking: Clifford's theme had always been the liberation of the soul from its social shackles, and the Negro now was the equivalent of his cab driver of the thirties. One of my deeper doubts was my capacity to write for and about Negroes, and when Hilly reminded me that we had "an expert consultant" in Sammy I said yes, the only way I could envision any white man daring to take pencil to this would be in collaboration with Sammy on every line; doing so would be to educate oneself on a sizeable segment of American life. Sammy's pitch was less abstract, he said pleasantly that if the show came in as the bookless dud it was he hoped I would blame myself, and to my wife his parting word was, "Help!"

The Broadway billing page. Despite heavy revisions, the production team was careful to leave the cast intact.

Yet my strongest desire to decline came when next morning I read for the tenth time Clifford's play. My musical taste is not identical with that of the populace, and I have never taken an interest in the musicalization of plays on which our theatre compliments itself as having created a new form; its accomplishment seems to me to consist mainly of replacing good writing with platitudinous music and dance. Half a million dollars was impotent to do anything more than denature the artwork Clifford's play had been written as, and rereading it brought tears to my eyes, partly because it was his own obituary, partly because the fire of that writing could still singe any perceptive reader. People in the show were saying his dialogue was "dated," simply untrue, it remained what it always was, the best dialogue ever written by an American; what they meant was that dialogue written for a white couple in 1937 was unbelievable in the mouths of a Negro youth and a white girl in 1964. Measured against

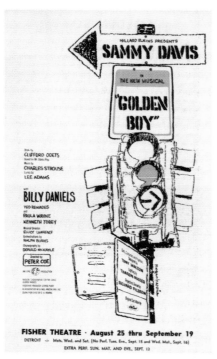

The original herald, with Morgan Harris's artwork reflecting the show's traffic light scenic motif.

what was onstage the play was such a towering act of genius that I decided there and then that I would say no, and that conscience—Clifford's or mine, it wasn't clear—was ordering me back to my own muse. Yet we stayed over to see the matinee, and during it I was working out in my head how to restore Clifford's story line to the stage, in the knowledge that if I didn't nobody would. My wife said nothing, and out of that silence I asked her, "Why do you want me to do this?" and she said, "I've been asking myself that question;" our thoughts were not dissimilar.

When we left for the Cape I told Hilly my final answer was I definitely didn't know, and he must proceed as though I'd said no; to redo the entire book in the time available seemed impossible. Still, I took a mimeographed script with me back to my studio. Hilly phoned the next evening and I said I was sitting with it, call again tomorrow, and the following day I told him it could be done and I was doing it, but by then I had rewritten a third of the first act for myself; what finally ensnared me was the joy of solving and wording. Endeavoring to write in Clifford's idiom for the sake of a consistent texture, I worked around the clock, keeping what was alive onstage, drawing much upon the original text, and inventing a new body of material for the love story out of a discovery about the play. Though the protagonist's dilemma—art or worldly success—was postulated as a social allegory, its turning point was individual, if the woman had not betrayed the boy the denouement would have evaporated, and this fact was fraught with meaning for a production whose new element was interracial love; for a Negro, to make good in the world implied the white world, and if the betrayal was of love, the allegory had willy-nilly changed into one of interpenetration of the races. As my wife said, the Southerners saw the issue with clarity as a sexual mat-

Salvage Jobs

ter, and my own view was that with the act of love acceptable the racial problem qua racial problem would vanish; if sex was taboo, so was sitting together at a lunch counter. Seeing the lovers thus as representatives of a larger story —I had no question it was how Clifford would have seen them—I rewrote the first act in five days and took my illegible pages back into Boston, to advise Hilly and Sammy that if they wished to go in this direction I would rewrite the second act and nothing was lost if they didn't.

A post-opening herald recognizes that the show's main selling point was Sammy Davis.

My reading of the pages was greeted by a collective sigh of relief—Sammy said he saw only one problem, "How you gonna teach Sidney Poitier to sing?" and Lee Adams said, "Come on, Sammy, he sings pretty good!"—and only the willingness of the director to collaborate was in question. When he flew in from London the next day I found he was not dissatisfied with his present script and he found he "basically disagreed" with mine; given a year I might have argued this through, but we had six weeks, and the next night at my request my almost brother Arthur Penn was in Boston to inspect the production. It oppressed him—walking from the theatre to the hotel he shook his head over the labor of "lifting" it—but he listened attentively to my third reading of my pages, and when Hilly asked him would he direct Arthur said simply, "Yes." I bestowed a kiss upon his right hand, and Sammy and I embraced so collisively that half of Sammy's drink baptized us both; from that instant, though I was to suffer moments of perplexity, I never doubted we would have a show. It was well after midnight, and a year to the day when, with his son at his bedside, I had touched Clifford's hand in farewell and felt its chill, an hour before his death.

The next afternoon I drove again to the Cape to rewrite the second act; in three days I was done, and when the following noon I rejoined the show it was to live with it until we brought it in. Hilly was now undertaking little less than a complete second production while performing the first, and the events of the subsequent weeks constituted a breakneck saga—Arthur threw the new book in its entirety onstage with a week's rehearsal, and most of the scenery was changed to fit, and Hilly hired an additional choreographer named Herb Ross who was invaluable in contributing half-a-showful of new dance to new songs composed by the boys, and I rewrote the book for the last time a week before opening night—all of which was so exhilarating that throughout I paid Hilly a dollar a day for the privilege of attendance. Day after day, pages that were in my typewriter at noon were on the stage that evening, it was a heroic and joyful company to work with, and it repaid us trebly for Arthur's initial decision to sustain its morale by firing nobody. It was never possible for us to bring in a truly organic show—the components we had to blend, music, book, casting, lyrics, dance, sets, were so disparate the union was not unlike a shot-gun wedding, and the daily revision to meet musical changes cost us much of Clifford's dialogue—and the reviews we garnered reflected its inner incompatibilities; but however misbegotten it was alive, and its successful delivery after such labors displeased none of us. Clifford's son was with us on opening night, and although after seeing it in Boston he had planned to picket it with a maledictory banner we rewrote his opinion too, which meant something to me.

People said that Clifford aloft must be smiling down upon us; I don't think so, I think the cloud around his feet is littered with unsent letters in red ink, all irate, most of them pointing out my inadequacies and the rest denouncing a higher authority for the omission of mail service earthwards. I must add that, in a way it embarrasses me to recall, I never felt Clifford's ghost was far off. It hardly escaped me that my baptismal chore at the table on which he had written his first play was the unfinished libretto of his last, and on the road my nightly relaxation was over some of his old records, three dozen of the more obscure Haydn and Mozart symphonies with the dates noted in his handscript, and any pipe I had in my mouth was one of the best I owned, those his son had given me. When one burned through I thought it a bad omen, and saw I had turned quite superstitious. In our second meeting Hilly said that Clifford like Moses "had been given the Tablets but not allowed into the promise land," and when the next day my wife received in the mail an Israeli solicitation for funds containing a tin miniature of the Tablets I appropriated it, and wore it pinned inside my shirt to every rehearsal and performance thereafter; the one afternoon I forgot it I felt stricken, though no evil ensued, and I gave it to Sammy an hour before our Broadway opening, saying I hoped it would work for him, and of course it did. Such hallucinations ended with the labors they subserved. Wishes persist longer, and the night the rewritten book first went onstage I received from Hilly the only telegram I was moved to keep; it read, "Thanks from those of us who are here and I'm sure those of us who aren't."

Golden Boy opened October 20, 1964 at the Majestic Theatre, to mixed reviews. It closed March 5, 1966 after 569 performances, with a partial loss.

First-time producer Hilly Elkins was one of those people who could talk his way into almost anything (although as time passed, he couldn't necessarily talk his way out). He started in the mailroom of William Morris, working his way into personal management; his major clients included Steve McQueen and Robert Culp.

The original director of *Golden Boy* was Peter Coe, who got the assignment on the basis of his direction of Lionel Bart's *Oliver!* (London, 1962; New York, 1963). Coincidentally, Coe also directed the 1961 London production of Gibson's *The Miracle Worker*.

Golden Boy began its tryout in Philadelphia, opening June 25, 1964 to poor reviews. The show then moved to Boston on July 29, meeting a second batch of bad notices. It wasn't until this point that Elkins called on Gibson for help. The "new" show played Detroit, opening August 25, before heading to Broadway.

The writer who came in before Gibson but turned them down, according to Elkins, was Paddy Chayefsky, author of *The Tenth Man* and *Gideon*.

Elkins also tells us that Arthur Penn arrived in Boston with Anne Bancroft, whose career was launched with two Tonys and an Oscar for Gibson and Penn's *Two for the Seesaw* and *The Miracle Worker*. The idea, apparently, was for Bancroft to take over the female lead. This did not happen, but it was not altogether farfetched; the production team behind *Gypsy* very much wanted Bancroft to play the title role, but she turned it down for *Miracle Worker*.

Gibson accurately describes the show's "inner compatibilities," inevitable perhaps given the patchwork fixing during the tryout. The results were flawed, yes; but the general consensus was that *Golden Boy* was "interesting" and "fascinating." The show's 569-performance run set a new record as the longest-running Broadway musical to lose money; as with several other shows discussed in this book, it was ultimately impossible to recover the excess costs of tryout revisions.

NOV 28 1960

46th St.
Theatre

PLAYBILL

a weekly magazine for theatregoers

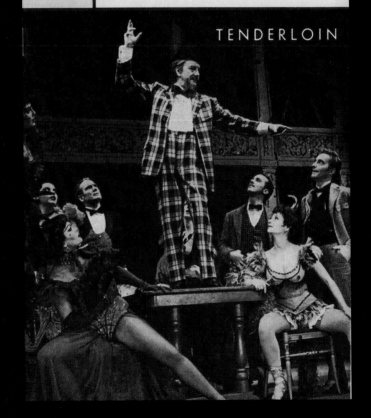

TENDERLOIN

Tenderloin (1960)

Any Suggestions?

Richard Altman served as assistant director to Jerome Robbins on *Fiddler on the Roof* (a position brokered through Carol Burnett, a UCLA friend of Altman). *Fiddler* had its own set of tryout troubles; for starters all but one of the second act songs were replaced by the time the show hit Broadway. The *Fiddler* saga was colorful enough for Altman (and co-author Meryn Kaufman) to fill a book, *The Making of a Musical*. Altman opened his book with a discussion of his first exposure to producer Harold Prince and songwriters Jerry Bock and Sheldon Harnick.

The intractable Maurice Evans—in a Cecil Beaton costume—lords it over members of the chorus.

"What's the Show About?"

by Richard Altman with Mervyn Kaufman

Jerry Bock and Sheldon Harnick's next effort after the Pulitzer Prize-winning *Fiorello!* was to reunite them with the *Fiorello!* team: co-producers Robert E. Griffith and Harold Prince, director George Abbott and his co-librettist Jerome Weidman. The project was an adaptation of the Samuel Hopkins Adams novel *Tenderloin*, a saga of New York's bawdy entertainment district in the late 1800s. The show was to be racy and razzle-dazzle, evoking a colorful bygone era. However, though the creators were the same, the formula that had successfully concocted *Fiorello!* fizzled. *Tenderloin* was a slick hodgepodge whose elements, many of them excellent, were totally at war with themselves. It was a decided disappointment and, coincidentally, my first opportunity to see Bock, Harnick and Prince at work.

In 1960 I received a Ford Foundation grant to observe the creation of *Tenderloin*. My specific assignment was to report on the way George Abbott built and shaped a Broadway show. Abbott was a legend by then, an unyielding and glacial wizard of Broadway know-how. He was incredibly fit for a man of seventy-three, and his towering height helped make him terribly imposing, but I was not fortunate enough to observe his work when he was at his peak. I quickly became disenchanted with his directorial methods, which to me seemed hopelessly mechanical. I was also surprised at his inability to come to grips with *Tenderloin*'s problem-ridden book early enough to make it work. He blindly followed his own rule of changing little or nothing until a show went out of town.

Another of Abbott's liabilities on *Tenderloin* was his lack of rapport with its star, Maurice Evans. It was obvious, for example, that the two of them had never agreed on an approach to Reverend Brock, the character Evans played. Evans, in his musical comedy debut, proved to be a less than engaging song-and-dance man—a surprise, considering that he was said to have been the first choice, *before* Rex Harrison, to play Professor Higgins in *My Fair Lady*. [Actor-producer-director Maurice Evans (1901-1989) was one of the most acclaimed interpreters of Shakespeare and Shaw at mid-century, famous for his full-length *Hamlet* in 1938, his wartime "G.I. Version" of *Hamlet*, and his 1947 *Man and Superman*. Fame being what it is, he is best remembered for playing the warlock Maurice, father of the heroine, on the 1964-72 sitcom *Bewitched.*]

Tenderloin's book was the primary source of trouble, however, and because of it life out of town was far more hellish for Bock and Harnick than it would be on *Fiddler*. If the book was a failure, the only thing that could possibly rescue the show was the score. The pressure was never off the composers to keep coming up with new and better material. They worked around the clock, and as a result five or six of the best songs in the show were inserted during the Boston run.

"The main problem with *Tenderloin* was that it was done too fast," says Sheldon. "The experience on *Fiorello!* had been so good and there was such euphoria among Abbott, Griffith and Prince, Jerry and myself, that I think even before *Fiorello!* opened we were talking about the next show. They had the rights to *Tenderloin*, and we just plunged right in. For myself it was an eye-opener, because I really had not paid

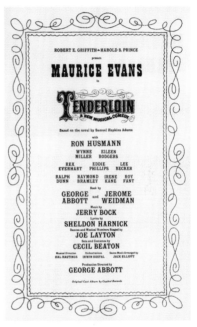

The billing page from the souvenir program.

much attention to the books of the shows I'd been involved with. In *Fiorello!* it was Abbott at his best; it was 'Daddy' taking care of all of us. So I figured he would do it again on *Tenderloin*.... Looking back on it, I can see that we didn't follow the original source closely enough. In the novel the minister is a small part, but we chose to make it the star role, which meant we couldn't shorten it out of town. And unfortunately, as it's been pointed out to us since then, the minister, though he was on the side of virtue and good, was a killjoy."

Cataloguing all of *Tenderloin's* various production woes—the intrigues, tensions, casting errors, personality conflicts, muddled points of view—it is easy now, with hindsight, to see that the show was doomed to failure. But, as with any show struggling to get on its feet, those involved were much too close to it at the time to realize how bad things really were. The book was being doctored, but not everyone connected with the show was certain exactly how—or by whom.

There were two brothers who were also "observers" of the production. At first, I couldn't understand why they were so pointedly chilly to me, but I later learned that, quietly and quite unofficially, they were working on the book, and no one was supposed to know about it. James and William Goldman survived the experience and, among other things, went on to write respectively *The Lion in Winter* and *Butch Cassidy and the Sundance Kid*. [While *Tenderloin* was ending its run, Prince co-produced James Goldman's play *They Might Be Giants* at Joan Littlewood's Theatre Royale Stratford, in London's East End. In January 1962, Prince was called to Philadelphia to try to salvage *A Family Affair*, a musical the Goldman brothers wrote with composer John Kander. The show was a quick failure, but it was Prince's first Broadway directing job. Nine years later, Prince directed and produced James Goldman's final Broadway show, *Follies*.]

A quote-ad herald, with artwork by Robert Graves.

To earn my grant, the Ford Foundation directors asked that I keep a detailed record of my observations. The following excerpts from my journal suggest, if nothing else, that *Fiddler* had smooth sailing compared to its predecessor. And my first entry, dated August 10, 1960, was ominous indeed: "I don't know why they're going into rehearsal with this wooden script."

Here are some other entries, starting with *Tenderloin*'s rehearsals and ending with its opening night in New York:

8/17—Abbott blocked huge crowd scene, juggling groups of twenty-five people extemporaneously. After twenty minutes everything was working, with much detail. Incredible!

8/22—I begin to think Abbott is definitely handling Ron incorrectly. He gives Ron line readings, but Ron parrots and doesn't know what he's saying or thinking or feeling. [Ron Husmann, a singer from *Fiorello!*, had his first major role as the reporter who goes undercover for a story on the Evans character.]

9/2—Am increasingly annoyed by Abbott's handling of Ron. In beach scene with Evans, Abbott told Ron to hang his head, pause, smile and turn—but never discussed what he should be feeling.

9/6—Run-through with audience. Score went over generally well, but audience not really with the show.... Book doesn't work; it's hokey, melodramatic. Everyone too pleased that Stephen Sondheim was positive and enthusiastic afterward. Are they getting a false sense of security? [Sondheim was already, apparently, intimidating to his friends. Lyricist for Prince's *West Side Story* and Merrick's *Gypsy*, he would make his composing debut in 1962 with the Abbott-Prince musical after *Tenderloin*, *A Funny Thing Happened on the Way to the Forum*.]

9/7—Arrived New Haven.... Evans seems tense and resigned.... Beaton is aloof and distant toward everyone. [This was the twelfth Broadway assignment for Cecil Beaton, who designed the sets and costumes.]

9/10—The orgy scene just laid there, as did Act I finale. Restlessness during Act II, little applause at end.... I don't see how they can ever make this book work.

9/12—Opening night... reaction very mild. Meeting held afterward: Prince seemed disturbed, no one else appeared to be. All were pussyfooting and discussing details until Abbott said: "Gentlemen, I had a concept for this show and it doesn't work. Any suggestions?"

9/13—It is increasingly obvious that the Goldmans are heavily involved.

9/14—*Variety* review appeared today: a pan.

9/16—Very little concrete improvement has been made in New Haven... will be the same show for Boston, with the same basic problems.

9/18—Boston. Evans apparently objecting to new prologue... much secret scurrying around, meetings and rewriting of prologue going on... Bobby Griffith to Prince, "Well, then, YOU get him to do it!" [*Tenderloin* was Griffith's sixth and final musical. He died six weeks after the show closed, on June 7, 1961.]

9/20—Opening night. Big improvement, thanks to new opening number.... If the rest of Act I could be strengthened with new numbers, there could be hope, though the book is still nowhere.

9/21—Boston reviews: three favorable, three pans... *Christian Science Monitor* accurately picking up the hollowness and the problem of trying to be on the side of virtue with vice being more entertaining. So much depends on new songs, IF show can be saved at all.

9/25—There seems to be a movement to place entire blame on Evans.... Neither Abbott nor Evans has ever been clear as to WHO Brock is or WHAT he is.

9/26—Evans depressed and couldn't (or wouldn't) learn lyrics.… Finally Abbott told him to carry the lyrics and pretend they're letters from parishioners.… Prince says Abbott afraid to make changes now because Evans such a slow study.

9/28—Act I Finale much better with "How the Money Changes Hands."

9/30—Everyone optimistic today. New song, "Dear Friend," sounds excellent. People feel they've got a hit. Hal says "the word" on the show from New York is good now.… Evans still flubbing his words but seems happier with his role and the show.

10/1—New York reviews of *Irma La Douce*, being good, depressed everyone… that show apparently deals with prostitutes and vice in a clever, original way, which can point up emptiness of *Tenderloin*. [David Merrick's transfer of the Paris-and-London hit was a moneymaking success, running 524 performances.]

10/3—"Dear Friend" into show. Charming. The number is a plus.… Trouble across the street with Jack Lemmon's *Face of a Hero*. Harold Clurman has taken over direction, with Alexander Mackendrick just sitting by.

10/4—Pepless performance tonight.… Clurman's first move after taking over *Hero* supposedly was to try and get rid of Lemmon. [Robert L. Joseph's *Face of a Hero* opened at the Eugene O'Neill on October 20, and closed after 36 performances. Lemmon remained with the show, with Mackendrick—best known as director of the films The *Man in the White Suit* and *Sweet Smell of Success*—retaining credit.]

10/5—Evans displeased with opening speech; wrote his own, which Abbott promptly discarded.

10/6—Very difficult to sit through show by now, or to be at all objective.

10/7—New orgy won't go in. Abbott, Griffith and Prince said no after looking at it. Layton now working on another approach to it that will enter the show in New York. [Joe Layton started his Broadway career as a dancer (and understudy to "Wreck") in Abbott's 1953 musical *Wonderful Town* (stage managers Griffith and Prince). Prior to *Tenderloin*, he choreographed *The Sound of Music* and Abbott's *Once Upon a Mattress*.]

10/11—First New York preview. Benefit audience—predictably quiet. Show definitely "off" tonight; technical errors, underrehearsed orchestra, pacing of numbers and scenes slow, and Evans flubbing his song lyrics.

10/14—Deadly audience tonight.… Evans and Ron panicked and barely got through confrontation scene. They changed all the lines.…

Second act was a shambles.... New orgy doesn't work.... There is an air of desperation around the theatre.

10/15—Matinee audience best ever... gave people hope for Monday's opening.

10/17—Opening night. Audience applauded numbers, relatively quiet during scenes.... Four curtain calls. After final call, Ron fainted.

10/18—The reviews: five negative (*Times, Tribune, Post, Mirror, Journal*); two affirmative (*News, Telegram*).

Tenderloin opened October 17, 1960 at the 46th Street Theatre to generally unfavorable reviews. The show closed there April 23, 1961 after 216 performances, with a substantial loss.

Unlike many of the examples in this book, *Tenderloin* was the work of top creators at the height of their creativity. Not the seventy-three-year-old Mr. Abbott, perhaps; but the authors were just off their Pulitzer-winning *Fiorello!*, with the songwriters moving directly on to *She Loves Me* and *Fiddler on the Roof*. And they had two of Broadway's most supportive producers of the era, Bobby Griffith and Harold Prince. Even so, *Tenderloin*'s problems were insurmountable.

In his unsurpassed 1968 chronicle of Broadway, *The Season*, William Goldman tells of a conversation with Sheldon Harnick during the tryout of a musical in trouble. Watching the actors rehearse a rewrite of an impossible scene, Goldman asked if Harnick thought it was better. Harnick agreed, unenthusiastically. "The trouble with washing garbage," he said, "is that when you're done, it's still garbage." Goldman doesn't identify the circumstances, but this exchange almost surely occurred during the doctoring of *Tenderloin*.

DAVID MERRICK

by arrangement with EDWIN H. MORRIS & CO., INC.

presents

A NEW MUSICAL COMEDY

HOW NOW, DOW JONES

starring

ANTHONY ROBERTS MARLYN MASON BRENDA VACCARO

with

GEORGE COE   SAMMY SMITH   MADELINE KAHN   CHARLOTTE JONES
ED STEFFE   JENNIFER DARLING   ARTHUR HUGHES

and

HIRAM **SHERMAN**

Book by   Lyrics by   Music by
MAX SHULMAN   CAROLYN LEIGH   ELMER BERNSTEIN

Based on an original idea by **Carolyn Leigh**

Scenic Production by   Costumes Designed by
OLIVER SMITH   ROBERT MACKINTOSH

Dance and Incidental Music
Arranged and Conducted by   Orchestrations by
PETER HOWARD   PHILIP J. LANG

Directed by

ARTHUR PENN

Dances and Musical Numbers Staged by

GILLIAN LYNNE

Associate Producer
SAMUEL LIFF

Original Cast Album by
RCA VICTOR

SHUBERT THEATRE

PHILADELPHIA

Tues. Eve. Oct. 10 thru Sat. Eve. Oct. 28

Opening Night 7:30; Other Evenings 8:30   Matinees at 2:00

Matinees 1st Two Weeks Thurs. & Sat.; 3rd Week Wed. & Sat.

A Theatre Guild-American Theatre Society Subscription Play

How Now, Dow Jones (1967)

The Doctor Is In

With the immense success of *Hello, Dolly!*, David Merrick went on a production binge, with half-a-dozen shows a year for the next five seasons. Financing was no problem; in addition to his usual clamoring investors, RCA-Victor—flush with profits from the cast recording of *Dolly*—gave Merrick a cool two million. (The dollars, alas, were sunk into *How Now, Dow Jones*, and three of the biggest failures of the decade: *Mata Hari*, *Breakfast at Tiffany's* [see page 42] and Broadway's first million-dollar loser, *The Happy Time*).

How Now, Dow Jones was Merrick's second of three attempts at a caustic, "business" musical comedy (the first having been the dark *I Can Get It for You Wholesale*, in 1962). The idea came from the talented-but-difficult lyricist Carolyn Leigh. Leigh (1926-1981) came to Broadway in 1954 with Mary Martin's *Peter Pan*; Martin liked her pop-song "Young at Heart" ("Fairy tales can come true…") and insisted she be hired despite her lack of theatre experience. Leigh and composer Moose Charlap's score was spotty; while some of it was very good ("I Gotta Crow," "Tender Shepherd"), the rest was jettisoned and replaced by new songs from Jule Styne,

Among the departed from this pre-Broadway herald are director Arthur Penn, fourth-billed Hiram Sherman, and three featured performers (including newcomer Madeline Kahn).

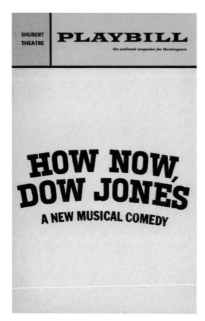

Producer David Merrick quickly retired his artwork logo and went simply with the title.

Betty Comden, and Adolph Green ("Never, Never Land," "Captain Hook's Waltz").

Leigh formed a partnership with composer Cy Coleman, which resulted in some top-rate pop hits ("The Best Is Yet to Come," "Witchcraft") and the unsuccessful musicals *Wildcat* and *Little Me*. (The latter might have lost money, but Leigh provided one of the best sets of comedy lyrics of the era.) Leigh was famously difficult; she dragged a street cop into the Erlanger in Philadelphia and tried to get him to arrest Cy Feuer and Bob Fosse when they cut one of her songs from *Little Me*. (When Fosse approached Coleman to write *Sweet Charity*, he bypassed Leigh in favor of Dorothy Fields, lyricist of the 1959 Fosse-Verdon Tony-winner *Redhead*.) Leigh's impossible behavior limited her opportunities; *How Now, Dow Jones* was her fourth, and final, show to reach Broadway.

When *How Now, Dow Jones* ran into tryout trouble, veteran play doctor George Abbott was dispatched to Boston. Edwin Bolwell, of the *New York Times*, caught up with him there.

"Dr. George Abbott Again Caring For a Broadway-Bound Patient"

by Edwin Bolwell

George Abbott is the kind of doctor a producer goes to when he has a show in trouble. He is perhaps Broadway's most renowned play doctor, a man who has restaged or rewritten more shows than he can remember.

At the age of 80, Mr. Abbott is performing his particular type of surgery once again. His patient is the musical, *How Now, Dow Jones*, trying out here at the Colonial Theatre before a Broadway opening scheduled for Dec 2.

How Now, Dow Jones is the 109th show Mr. Abbott has been associated with in one capacity or other. Besides doctoring plays, he has acted, written, directed or produced them in his own cause since 1913. His hits include *A Funny Thing Happened on the Way to the Forum*, *Never Too Late*, *Fiorello!*, *Damn Yankees* and *Pal Joey*. [Abbott's final two hits were *Forum* and *Never Too Late*, both in 1962. From then on, he directed fifteen more shows, including the unsuccessful musicals *Fade Out–Fade In* (see page 86), *Anya*, *Flora, The Red Menace*, *The Education of H*Y*M*A*N K*A*P*L*A*N*, *The Fig Leaves Are Falling*, and *Music Is*. His final production opened on the night of his 100th birthday; as general manager, I escorted him to Sardi's for the opening night party. Our revival of his seminal 1926 melodrama *Broadway* closed when he was one hundred plus two days old.] Mr. Abbott took over the staging of *How Now* about three weeks ago, after its original director, Arthur Penn, and its producer, David Merrick, parted company over what were termed artistic differences. At that stage, the show had rehearsed for several weeks in New York, had played one week in New Haven, and was in the throes of a two-week tryout in Philadelphia. [Arthur Penn was best known for directing the late 1950s dramas *Two for the Seesaw* and *The Miracle Worker*—although just before *How Now, Dow Jones* went into rehearsal, he catapulted to cinema fame directing *Bonnie and Clyde*. Penn's musical experience was minimal. In 1958, he had originated the idea for *Fiorello!*, although he withdrew—amicably, with continued participation—midway through the writing. Abbott replaced him, and the show went on to win Pulitzers for Abbott and his collaborators. Penn's second musical came in 1964, when he rushed in to help his close friend William Gibson salvage *Golden Boy* (see page 178).]

"There's usually a good deal of confusion when you take over a show on the road," Mr. Abbott remarked, as he talked about play doctoring in general after the Boston opening last week.

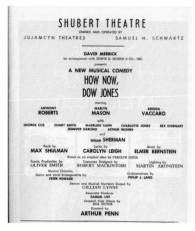

The Philadelphia billing page.

"There have been a lot of experiments to try to make things go well, and the first thing is to straighten out the story line. Then you accent your assets and minimize your liabilities."

In the case of *How Now*, this approach is leading to more razzle dazzle in the main production number, "Step to the Rear"; the replacement of two other numbers (one of which, according to a cast member, has already been changed five times), and other changes in the cast, choreography, dialogue and sets. [The new "razzle dazzle" came from a replacement choreographer. Just as *How Now, Dow Jones* was about to begin its tryout, Michael Bennett received superlative reviews for his work on the otherwise savaged *Henry, Sweet Henry*. Bennett was quickly shipped to Boston to replace Gillian Lynne, who in 1965 had choreographed *The Roar of the Greasepaint* and *Pickwick* for Merrick. Lynne remained away from Broadway until 1982, when she returned with *Cats*.]

"Of course, a musical depends on its numbers," Mr. Abbott went on. "If they don't go, the show won't. But it takes time to get new numbers written and fitted in properly. You may have to live patiently for two weeks with a number you know is wrong."

It was 10 A.M. and he was seated in his room at the Ritz-Carlton Hotel in blue pajamas, fawn dressing gown and black socks. He had gotten up three hours earlier to resume rewriting a scene he had put aside at 1 o'clock that morning.

The phone rang. It was a call from Carolyn Leigh, the show's lyricist, closeted elsewhere in the hotel. Mr. Abbott talked briefly with her about a new song, concluding: "Fine, but stay away from ideology. I don't want any more propaganda in this thing."

By noon, black socks mated with a neat blue suit, Mr. Abbott was at the theatre, rehearsing the cast in the rewritten scene. He had the air of a benevolent dictator. He smiled a lot, spoke softly and called the performers by their first names (even if sometimes it was only their stage first names), but there never was any doubt about who was in charge.

"Katie," he said gently, addressing Marlyn Mason, one of his two leading ladies, "your makeup today is lurid. You look like a woman who sucks blood."

As another actor tried to explain at some length how he thought a line should sound, Mr. Abbott quietly cut him short: "Let's be pragmatic—just show me."

During complete run-throughs of the rewritten scene, Mr. Abbott became a one-man show himself. Constantly uncoiling from a leg-hugging position on a bench seat, he played each of eight parts at some stage or another, demonstrating a desired stage movement or voice inflection.

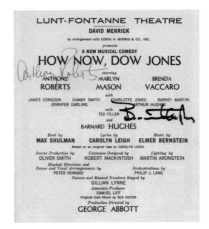

The Broadway billing page reflects the many personnel changes—but leaves replacement choreographer Michael Bennett uncredited.

"You're getting in the way of the action," he told one actress. "After you say your line, move over there and pour some tea." To an actor: "That's an unusual line but you're losing it at the end. Say, 'Sorry doesn't butter any parsnip.' Let's hear the last word."

The rehearsal lasted until after 1 p.m. As the actors scurried to prepare for the 2 p.m. matinee, in which they would incorporate the new dialogue, Mr. Abbott explained why he had agreed to restage *How Now*.

"First, I was free," he said, adding that two other shows he had been signed to stage this season—*Hellzapoppin '68* and *The Education of H*Y*M*A*N K*A*P*L*A*N*—had been delayed. "Second, I like Merrick and this will be my first show with him."

How Now, Dow Jones opened December 7, 1967 at the Lunt-Fontanne Theatre to lukewarm reviews. It closed there on June 15, 1968 after 220 performances, with a partial loss.

This was the first and only meeting of Abbott and Merrick. Abbott started producing his own plays in 1932 (*Twentieth Century*) and musicals in 1938 (*The Boys from Syracuse*). As he headed past sixty-five, he stopped producing while lending his weight (and his office) to the new team of Robert E. Griffith and Harold S. Prince (with *The Pajama Game*, in 1954). Bobby Griffith had been an Abbott stage manager since 1936, with Prince joining the team in the late 40s (and serving as assistant stage manager on *Call Me Madam* and *Wonderful Town*). Abbott directed all of the Griffith-Prince musicals except *West Side Story*, and shared an office with Prince for the rest of his (Abbott's) life. While Abbott worked for numerous other producers throughout his career, he was clearly in the Prince camp from 1954—and thus, far away from Merrick. But when *How Now, Dow Jones* came up, Prince was directing his own musicals and Abbott had been idle for ten months.

If the fixing of the show yielded minimal results, it did mark an important step for the up-and-coming Bennett. He went uncredited for his troubles, but his exciting work brought him his breakthrough assignment—on Merrick's third "business" musical, *Promises, Promises* (1968). Which led Bennett directly to *Company* (1970).

If *How Now, Dow Jones* was deeply flawed, it was blessed with one of Broadway's catchiest titles ever. This helped the show amass an advance sale of $500,000—somewhat astounding for a show with no stars, no star writers, and no star director. *How Now, Dow Jones* had already run through its advance when Actors' Equity Association went on strike in June 1968. Merrick, aware that the show's days were numbered anyway, used the strike as an excuse to close *How Now, Dow Jones* and the similarly fading *I Do! I Do!* Placing full blame for the closings, of course, on Actors' Equity.

IT IS NOT THE END OF THE WORLD
LYRICS by MARTIN CHARNIN   MUSIC by RICHARD RODGERS

ALEXANDER H. COHEN & HILDY PARKS
present

LIV ULLMANN
I REMEMBER MAMA

Also Published:

EV'RY DAY (COMES
SOMETHING BEAUTIFUL)

YOU COULD NOT
PLEASE ME MORE

TIME

Music by
RICHARD RODGERS
Lyrics by
MARTIN CHARNIN
Book by
THOMAS MEEHAN
Based on the Play "I Remember Mama"
by JOHN VAN DRUTEN
and Stories by KATHRYN FORBES
Directed by
CY FEUER

Rememba Enterprises, Inc. and
Sethwell Productions, B.V.

MCA Music, a division of MCA, INC., sole selling
agent, 25 Deshon Drive, Melville, N.Y. 11747

US 2245

$1.95

I Remember Mama (1979)

Fjord Every Stream

Here was what you might call a theatre-party special; a big-name
star vehicle based on a beloved property in four media (fiction,
drama, film and television). From the authors of *The Sound of Music*
and *Annie*, two of the most successful family musicals of all time.
But *I Remember Mama* proved to be all hype and no substance, and
went down swinging despite severe ministrations. Ralph Tyler
covered the process for the *New York Times*.

James McMullan's artwork graces this sheet music cover.

"The Doctoring of *Mama*—
Is She Now Fit for Broadway?"
by Ralph Tyler

After hitting an iceberg in Philadelphia and enduring one of the most drastic overhauls in theatrical history, the musical version of *I Remember Mama* will sail into its Broadway opening Thursday night at the Majestic with all flags flying. Liv Ullmann will be singing in her first musical, the orchestra will be playing the latest Richard Rodgers score, and somewhere in the counting houses the people who put up $1,250,000 to launch the show will have their fingers tightly crossed. The backers will be praying that *Mama* has been turned around sufficiently since it came under the fire of the Philadelphia critics to withstand the rigors of Broadway, which this season has already seen several likely musicals capsize. [These included *A Broadway Musical* (Charles Strouse and Lee Adams), *The Grand Tour* (Jerry Herman), *Home Again, Home Again* (Cy Coleman) and *Carmelina* (Burton Lane and Alan Jay Lerner).]

If *Mama* hasn't been changed for the better, it won't be for want of some pretty spectacular trying by Alexander H. Cohen, who produced the show with his wife Hildy Parks. The original director and lyricist, Martin Charnin, who had developed the idea for the show, was replaced by Cy Feuer, whose musical credits go back to the 1950's and such shows as *Silk Stockings*. A new lyricist, Raymond Jessel, was brought in from California. Nearly half the original songs were thrown out and fresh ones introduced. Some of the cast got their walking papers, a new choreographer took over, and the opening, originally set for May 3, was twice postponed. Meanwhile, the structure of the show was totally revamped, a narrative line inserted and the overall concept of the musical was shifted, in Mr. Cohen's words, "from shtik to spine" (by shtik he meant a vaudeville approach, by spine a truthful one). There's a significant story in the tryout ordeals of *I Remember Mama*, and Mr. Cohen himself suggested that the title of this account might be "The Making of Two Musicals."

Of course, there is nothing new about reworking a musical out of town, and some of the most utterly transformed shows have gone on to triumph. *Fiddler on the Roof* is a classic example: its pre-Broadway notices were abysmal but it pulled itself up by its bootstraps on the road. In fact, the highly successful *Annie*, which has lyrics by Mr. Charnin and a book by Thomas Meehan, who also wrote the book for *Mama*, was extensively reworked after its debut at the Goodspeed Opera House in Connecticut.

I Remember Mama is about a large family of Norwegian immigrants in San Francisco in the early 1900s. The father is a carpenter in the shipyards, money is tight, but the mother holds the family together with her earthy practicality and her tenacious dream of a better world for her children in the new land. *Mama* first appeared in the nostalgic recollections Kathryn Forbes published in *Reader's Digest* and then collected in her book, *Mama's Bank Account*, in 1943. As dramatized by John van Druten, *I Remember Mama* was produced on Broadway in 1944 by Richard Rodgers, who has now set it to music, and Oscar Hammerstein II. The play was made into a movie in 1948 with Irene Dunne starring in the role Mady Christians originated on the stage.

A reduced version of James McMullan's artwork for the show.

CBS adapted the property for television in 1949 with Peggy Wood as Mama, the series persisting for an amazing seven years. If the musical version is a hit, *Mama* may yet go through another movie metamorphosis, since Universal Pictures provided half of the show's financial backing.

The suggestion that *Mama* might make a musical was brought to Mr. Charnin about five years ago by Jane Chodorov, who was then his agent at William Morris. It was a period when he and Mr. Meehan were trying to drum up interest in a production of *Annie*. Between sessions with potential angels, Mr. Charnin worked on *Mama*, deciding which scenes could use songs and then developing them. Looking for a new project after the runaway success of *Annie*, he remembered *Mama*, and Mr. Meehan agreed to write the book. *Mama* is about something, Mr. Meehan, explained. "Without getting on a soapbox, it celebrates the American family and the immigrant family." Mr. Charnin's concept of *Mama* is roughly the same: "It's a valentine to the American family and to the simple yet elegant values that are so buried in society today that when they're presented on the stage they come out brand new."

Whether or not its values seem novel today, *I Remember Mama* is in some ways a throwback to the homespun musicals Mr. Rodgers used to create with Mr. Hammerstein in the 1940s and 1950s. The people behind *Mama* are banking on what they see as a shift toward sentiment. They also have noticed that *Annie* has attracted theatregoers who had been staying away from Broadway in droves because there were no family-oriented shows, and they hope *Mama* will have similar appeal. On the other hand, the question of how to handle sentiment in an age in which it doesn't come quite naturally may have been one of the reasons why the show took so much kneading and prodding to get in shape.

Things went with deceptive smoothness at first. Miss Ullmann, herself a Norwegian, said she was delighted when she was approached by Mr. Charnin in New York, where she was appearing in Eugene O'Neill's *Anna Christie*. She explained how she felt about the offer to star as Mama in a recent interview in her dressing room at the Majestic.

"I first felt complete astonishment," Miss Ullmann recalled. "I didn't see how anybody could figure me out as a musical person. What I have done is far away from musicals. But then I felt very great happiness and I didn't wait more than five minutes to say yes. Whatever the outcome, it is wonderful to be part of a musical that Richard Rodgers has written. I grew up on him. A lot of the things we sang and danced to and listened to on the radio were his."

In reply to a question about her singing voice, which she said has now replaced an earlier incessant question ("What is it like to be directed by Ingmar Bergman?"), she said: "I don't think Mama has to be a great singer. If we were doing *Hello, Dolly!* you would need a singer with a big voice. There is no excuse for singing poorly, but I think it's O.K. that Mama sings the way I do. If you sing a lullaby to your child you don't have to be an opera diva. I have another quality, an acting quality, with the music. It's another way of performing, and I do it my way."

Mr. Rodgers, as energetic as ever at 76 despite a laryngectomy five years ago, also accepted readily. He is never happier than when working on a Broadway musical (*Mama* is his 40th); he had teamed with Mr. Charnin in 1970 on *Two by Two* starring Danny Kaye, and *Mama*, to him, had the kind of warm, human characters that lend themselves to singable situations. Mr. Cohen, who had produced *Anna Christie* with Miss Ullman, also was enthusiastic about Mr. Charnin's concept and came in a producer. It was one big happy family. So what went wrong?

For a start, Mr. Meehan discovered that what Mr. van Druten had skillfully put together was a series of vignettes rather than a play. So Mr. Meehan proceeded to put in a strong narrative line, with a definite beginning, middle and end. This was rejected at an early story conference, however, on the grounds that he was straying too far from the van Druten version and leaving out too many incidents. He returned to the vignette approach, and that was what the Philadelphia critics panned. Later, when he went to work with Mr. Feuer to restructure the musical, he was to restore much of his discarded first draft.

"I have the soul of a book author and what I like is a book musical," Mr. Meehan explained while the show was previewing in New York. "It doesn't have to be a complicated story but it should have a kind of mythic, basic appeal. This is about a struggling family and about separation anxiety—when the father goes back to Norway. It's about love and money, which according to Jane Austen are the only things worth writing about. The musical that opened in Philadelphia had no dark parts. For example, the father didn't go to Norway, but only temporarily to Canada to earn money. It didn't show Liv Ullmann to best advantage. She's really an actress, but she was playing Julie Andrews."

The Philadelphia title page, boasting the "entire production directed by Martin Charnin." Note the message from Liv Ullmann.

Mr. Cohen, who fired Mr. Charnin as director on March 20, the day after *Mama* opened out of town, said a fundamental disagreement about how to do the play had already developed during rehearsals: "I believe Martin Charnin felt the production should be approached from the vaudeville or comic strip vantage point. I think he saw it as a show which had a Walt Disney quality. I saw it is a show in which every element had to be truthful. But I waited to see what would happen in Philadelphia. The critics said we were 'milding' them to death—it was so coy, so arch."

Mr. Cohen's remarks didn't sit well with Mr. Charnin, now cast in the role of ghost at the feast. "To call my approach 'comic strip' is expedient and unfair," he said. "Is it comic strip to make things incredibly theatrical and super-real? What I did in *Annie* was to take comic strip characters and invest them with the truth. The search for truth made *Annie* what it was. And I don't think it is possible to think of *Mama* as a cartoon. If that were the case my lyrics would have been of a cartooning character. I made them as human as I could write."

After Mr. Charnin was relieved as director, although kept on as lyricist (soon to be supplemented by Mr. Jessel), he fired off a telegram to the New York, Los Angeles and Detroit companies of *Annie* which said, in part: "Ms. Ullmann and I do not see 'I to I' about how musicals are made. To make a long and ugly story short, there's no longer a fjord in my future." Asked to expand on this, he said:

"Perhaps there was a fear on Miss Ullmann's part of being exposed in a musical and believing she was not getting the right sort of attention. It was my conviction from the beginning that while Mama was crucial to the play, it was an ensemble piece. I had to take into consideration the other 26 characters on the stage who could not be neglected.

"Miss Ullmann is a transient in the musical theatre," Mr. Charnin continued. "She will go on to do any number of films and straight plays and one-woman evenings. I make my living in the musical theatre. She was a newcomer to the process and perhaps was at the beginning overwhelmed by it. Her previous experience in the United States was with authors whose lines could not be changed—Ibsen and O'Neill didn't go to Philadelphia."

Miss Ullmann said she felt Mr. Charnin had "sort of stabbed me in the back" when he publicly blamed her for the rift. She insisted she was loyal to Mr. Charnin, although she couldn't defend what he was doing, when she sensed a division forming between the director and producer. Far from being responsible for his firing, she said it would have happened earlier but for her. And yet the fact that she is an actress who carries great conviction may have—unintentionally on her part—thrown the original concept of the show out of kilter. Mr. Cohen, after he called in Mr. Feuer for radical surgery, said, "Miss Ullmann's performance is the core. We are trying to strengthen everything else around it. She is the strength of the show and we are trying to match it."

Mr. Feuer assumed command March 2, a week after Mr. Charnin was dismissed. During that time, Mr. Cohen said, he invited "several friends" to Philadelphia to see if they confirmed his opinion of the show and its problems. Although the visitors included such high-powered directors as José Quintero, Elia Kazan, Robert Moore, Gerald Freedman, Craig Anderson and Arthur Penn, "in no case," Mr. Cohen said, "were they candidates to replace Mr. Charnin." The ideas of Mr. Feuer, who was also one of the directors asked to look at the show, "were so collateral with my own," Mr. Cohen said, "that I asked him if he would like to take over."

Although Mr. Feuer had other responsibilities this month, including openings in San Francisco and Los Angeles of the Civic Light

Opera, which he and his partner Ernest Martin co-produce, he welcomed the chance to come to *Mama*'s rescue. "I was supposed to be out in California when the fire bell went off. But there's always something challenging when you're told a show is in trouble out of town. You grab your hat and slide down the pole." [See *The Act*, page 18.]

Mr. Feuer is not unfamiliar with turning a show around. The Cole Porter musical *Silk Stockings*, which Mr. Martin produced and he directed, went out of town for four weeks of tryouts and stayed out for a 14-week going over. [Feuer and Martin produced *Silk Stockings*. When the show met with severe trouble, director-librettist George S. Kaufman (who had directed *Guys and Dolls* for Feuer and Martin) was replaced as librettist by Abe Burrows (who had been replacement librettist on *Guys and Dolls*). Feuer took over as director, in name at least.] "In that instance, the show made it," Mr. Feuer said. He is also an experienced play doctor, most recently with the black version of a Feuer-Martin hit of the 1950s, *Guys and Dolls*.

Mr. Feuer worked under the gun with *Mama*. The delay added several hundred thousand dollars to the cost of the show, which started with a payroll of 28 actors, 25 musicians, 23 stagehands and 30 on the production staff. He set up priorities, concentrating on the book first and then the music. The major change he made with the book was to return to the original van Druten concept of having one actress play both the 30-year-old woman who is remembering Mama and herself at 11. "Using two people in front of the audience and saying they were one person didn't work," Mr. Feuer said. "There was no emotional connection between the narration at the side of the stage and the drama. In fact, the older woman became more of an announcer than a narrator." (Incidentally, Mr. Meehan wrote a fifth child into the show to make a part for the young actress who was laid off when the roles were combined.)

When Mr. Feuer discussed the show with Mr. Meehan, they agreed that a narrative line was needed throughout, and it was then that Mr. Meehan brought his first draft out of the drawer. "The narrative line now is very identifiable—perhaps more conventional—but decidedly more satisfying," Mr. Feuer said. "In that way I was able to achieve my number one requirement, which was to create dramatic scenes and dramatic songs for Liv Ullmann."

To expand Miss Ullmann's dramatic opportunities, Mr. Meehan wrote in a new scene in which she expresses both her anger at, and her need for, her husband Lars after he leaves for Norway. It was a straight dramatic scene at first, but then it was decided to have some of her mixed emotions conveyed in a new song, "Lars, Lars."

Mr. Meehan wrote another new scene, an argument between the

mother and father over whether she should tell the children they don't really have a bank account downtown—a lie she had told them to make them feel secure. The scene was inserted early in Act One to show Mama's strong will, which plays an important part in the newly established story line.

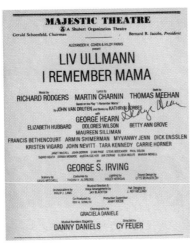

Choreographer Graciela Daniele retained her contractual billing, but replacement Danny Daniels is given more prominent treatment. Raymond Jessel was credited on the song listing page and given a bio as additional lyricist.

There were other big and little changes. For example, a scene in the first, Philadelphia, version showed how Mama's Uncle Chris, the head of the family, rejects a suitor for the hand of one of her sisters because he turns out to be Swedish rather than Norwegian. Mr. Meehan said he woke up with the idea for a later scene in which the suitor, who has been reinstated, then is rejected because he is a Methodist. Uncle Chris, who professes to be a freethinker, turns out to be a strictly Lutheran freethinker. Mr. Meehan told Mr. Feuer about it that morning and it was in the show that night. The scene served as a needed comic relief after a scene with one of the children in the hospital.

"Not every change we tried worked," Mr. Meehan said. "A musical is like a very complex Rube Goldberg machine. You can send the whole works clanking in the wrong direction. Ultimately what you're looking for is a Rolls-Royce engine."

Mr. Feuer said the stress and strain on the star and the company were considerable. They had to perform a presentable show for the preview audiences while learning new dialogue, stage business, songs and dances during daytime rehearsals. "After a week or two of working with Miss Ullmann I referred to her as Heifetz," Mr. Feuer said. "Any passage I would ask her to play she played just exactly, with astonishing facility."

Miss Ullmann, who had been working 12 to 14 hours a day without a Sunday off for two months, said it was totally unlike her previous experience. "Scenes are being thrown in and taken out. It's almost like a workshop. We get lines at 3 o'clock and go through blocking, finishing rehearsals at 6. God! I don't think I can do it anymore. I think I should get lines the night before and at least have time to sleep on them."

But Mr. Feuer told her, when she was given three new scenes and four others with minor changes in one swoop, "You're going to stagger around the stage and I'm going to get a lot of information from it. I can find out the same thing from an insecure performance as I can from a finished one."

When it came time to concentrate on the musical numbers, the focus shifted to Mr. Jessel, the new lyricist, and the redoubtable Mr. Rodgers, who composed six new songs in about two weeks. Mr. Jessel, who had written some of the words and music for Mr. Cohen's production of *Baker Street* a few seasons back, answered the telephone at his Los Angeles home at 8 A.M. and was told by the producer to catch the 9 o'clock plane to New York. He did make the noon plane, after getting leave from his job as story editor for the television program *Love Boat*. [Jessel was co-composer-lyricist of *Baker Street*. During that show's troubled tryout, director Harold Prince called in Jerry Bock and Sheldon Harnick (of the just-opened *Fiddler on the Roof*) to write four new songs.]

"My first feeling when I saw the show in Philadelphia," Mr. Jessel said, "was that it needed some energetic numbers, some brightness—it seemed all of one shade. It didn't really have any choral sound, it was just a bunch of solos and duets. There were other things, too. They already had reached the decision to go in a different direction with the character of Mama, which had not been sufficiently forceful. It was hit by the critics, possibly justifiably so, as being a little soft, a little pie in the sky. It was like the song "When You Wish Upon a Star." Now the point she's making is that you've got to struggle. It's a much more determined Mama."

He had just written a new song before the interview, "A Little Bit More," to show Mama's backbone. It was to replace a song called "Maybe, Maybe, Maybe" in which Mama says that "maybe makes things happen." In the new song she says, "If you really want something, give it all you've got, and when you've given it all you've got, give it a little bit more."

To get some choral singing into the show, Mr. Jessel introduced early in the first act a song called "Where We Came From," for a group of Norwegian immigrants, expressing some nostalgia for the old country but happiness at the opportunity in their new homeland. Another new choral number, "Easy Come, Easy Go," gives Uncle Chris and his cronies at McSweeny's Bar a chance to express their breezy philosophy of life. A song which revealed the hostility of Mama's sisters toward Uncle Chris, "He's a Most Disagreeable Man," has kept its tune but was given a new title, "Uncle Chris," and new words which express the sisters' two-faced attitude toward the head of the family, who might leave them money in his will. And to follow

Uncle Chris's deathbed scene with comic relief, Mr. Jessel wrote a duet for the maiden sister and her undertaker suitor, "I Don't Know How," which suggests he might be somewhat of a loss as a lover.

Mr. Rodgers, meanwhile, unflappably accepted his seventh lyricist in a line that includes Lorenz Hart, Mr. Hammerstein, Mr. Rodgers himself, Stephen Sondheim, Mr. Charnin and Sheldon Harnick. He said he liked the challenge of working with different collaborators because they stimulated variations in his music. As with most of the others, Mr. Jessel wrote the words first and Mr. Rodgers put them to music, working at a desk rather than a piano. "I just sit, fitting music to the lyrics for the purpose of the musical," he said. "I don't want to write a showy song." He said his favorite among the pieces he composed for Mama is a duet for Mama and Papa, "You Could Not Please Me More," with lyrics by Mr. Charnin. For a man whose 1937 musical *Babes in Arms* is currently being revived at the Goodspeed Opera House in Connecticut and whose first musical was the 1920 Columbia University varsity show *Fly With Me*, he projected youthful high spirits and confidence to the rest of the company during its passage through rough seas. [Actually, Rodgers was heard on Broadway a year earlier (see below).]

The heaviest emotional burden on the eve of the opening is carried by Mr. Charnin, who said, "I have nothing but tart optimism about the success of *Mama*." His work on the show, he feels, was aborted. "I think of a musical as being an armada, with each part a boat. Comes the opening on Broadway, all these boats will dock—it's a question of coaching and cajoling them into harbor. All I wanted to do with this show was simply stopped when I was relieved of my assignment. But I still see my *Mama*. My *Mama* goes on in my head every night and they stand up and cheer it every night."

I Remember Mama opened on May 31, 1979 at the Majestic Theatre to highly negative reviews. The show closed there on September 2, 1979 after 108 performances, with a total loss.

Showman Alexander H. Cohen (1920–2000) saw himself as David Merrick's chief (and sole) competitor. Cohen waged a never-ending publicity campaign from his aerie atop the Shubert Theatre, the roof of which Merrick looked down upon from his perch atop the

St. James across the street. The battle was solely in the eyes of Cohen, though. Merrick had his flops mixed among the hits, to be sure, but Cohen's record in the all-important field of musicals was disastrous. No contest.

Cohen came to town with enough money to buy in as associate producer on one of those pocket-sized, five-character melodramas, this one having the bad fortune to open two days before the bombing of Pearl Harbor. Nevertheless, *Angel Street* was one of the biggest successes of its time. Over the next fifty-eight years, Cohen was principal producer on almost seventy productions. He achieved his most notable success with a series of intimate revues, under the banner "Nine O'Clock Theatre." These included *An Evening with Mike Nichols and Elaine May* and the ground-breaking *Beyond the Fringe*. (These lucrative productions, tellingly, were privately financed and not open to regular investors.) Cohen also produced a handful of important plays, including the Broadway transfer of Harold Pinter's *The Homecoming* and the legendary Richard Burton *Hamlet*.

But musicals are where the money are. Cohen produced ten full-scale, big-budget Broadway musicals: *Make a Wish*, *Courtin' Time*, *Rugantino* (in Italian, mind you), *Baker Street*, *A Time for Singing*, *Hellzapoppin' '67* (starring Soupy Sales), *Dear World* (starring Angela Lansbury), *Prettybelle* (starring Lansbury), *Hellzapoppin* (1977, starring Jerry Lewis)[see page 70], and *I Remember Mama*. All were complete busts, financially. (Cohen's intimate musical revue, *A Day in Hollywood/A Night in the Ukraine*, fared considerably better.) At least eight of them underwent severe tryout trouble, with three of them shuttering out-of-town. Call it bad luck, if you will; or call it lack of artistic vision.

Tellingly, the creators of these shows included the composer-lyricist and director-choreographer of *Hello, Dolly!*; the director-lyricist and librettist of *Annie*; the producer of *Fiddler on the Roof*; the composer and lyricist of *Funny Girl*; and the great Richard Rodgers. Cohen didn't hire these people on the way up, mind you, nor did he hire them at the moment they (or at least, their shows) burst into legend. He hired them after they achieved greatness, ideally while their blockbusters were still running. Cynics might surmise that he signed up anyone whose name he could raise money on. The record shows that he did, indeed, raise money on these names; that he spent said money lavishly, on the shows and their promotion and limousines, etc.; and that the investors never saw said money again. Merrick had a roster of reliable angels who were glad to invest in each production as it came along, as did Hal Prince (for a while, anyway). The self-promoting Cohen attracted a different sort of investor, many of whom sent in their money, got burned, and never returned.

The inclusion of Rodgers in this last of the Alex Cohen extravaganzas was especially cynical. Broadway's most enduring composer had first reached the street in 1919, when he was sixteen (although half his score for *Poor Little Ritz Girl* was tossed out in Boston). He soon hit his stride, with major hit shows in the Twenties, Thirties, Forties and Fifties. His last strong score, though, came in 1962 with his first post-Hammerstein show *No Strings*. His four remaining shows were, each of them, sub-par, unhappy experiences marked by severe turmoil. (See *Rex*, page 290.) Trotted out for publicity for *Mama*, Rodgers was clearly an ailing old man. *I Remember Mama* staggered through Labor Day; an acclaimed revival of the ever-young Rodgers hit *Oklahoma!* opened on December 15; and Rodgers himself died as the decade ended, on December 30, 1979.

Charnin, a Jet in the original *West Side Story*-turned lyricist-turned director, has gone down in the record books for his blockbuster *Annie*. He came to *Annie* with a handful of flops, including *Hot Spot* and the legendary *Mata Hari*. He followed *Annie* with a similarly dismal string (including *Mama*, *The First*, and *Annie 2*). Librettist Tom Meehan seemed on the same track, with *Mama* and *Ain't Broadway Grand*, although I suppose you could say he rebounded with *The Producers* and *Hairspray*. *Mama* marked Cy Feuer's final Broadway credit, Ray Jessel never made any more emergency visits, and Liv Ullmann has—so far—never sung again.

Outside
Interference

Subways Are for Sleeping

Skyscraper

Flying Colors

On a Clear Day You Can See
  Forever

7 OUT OF 7
ARE ECSTATICALLY
UNANIMOUS ABOUT
SUBWAYS
ARE FOR
SLEEPING

HOWARD TAUBMAN ·········· "ONE OF THE FEW GREAT MUSICAL COMEDIES OF THE LAST THIRTY YEARS, ONE OF THE BEST OF OUR TIME. It lends lustre to this or any other Broadway season."

WALTER KERR ·········· "WHAT A SHOW! WHAT A HIT! WHAT A SOLID HIT! If you want to be overjoyed, spend an evening with 'Subways Are For Sleeping.' A triumph."

JOHN CHAPMAN ·········· "NO DOUBT ABOUT IT. 'SUBWAYS ARE FOR SLEEPING' IS THE BEST MUSICAL OF THE CENTURY. Consider yourself lucky if you can buy or steal a ticket for 'Subways Are For Sleeping' over the next few years."

JOHN McCLAIN ·········· "A FABULOUS MUSICAL. I LOVE IT. Sooner or later, every one will have to see 'Subways Are For Sleeping'."

RICHARD WATTS ·········· "A KNOCKOUT, FROM START TO FINISH. THE MUSICAL YOU'VE BEEN WAITING FOR. IT DESERVES TO RUN FOR A DECADE."

NORMAN NADEL ·········· "A WHOPPING HIT. RUN, DON'T WALK TO THE ST. JAMES THEATRE. It's in that rare class of great musicals. Quite simply, it has everything."

ROBERT COLEMAN ·········· "A GREAT MUSICAL. ALL THE INGREDIENTS ARE THERE. As fine a piece of work as our stage can be asked to give us."

Evgs.: Mon. thru Thurs.: Orch. $8.60; Mezz. $6.90; Balc. $5.75, 4.90; 2nd Balc. $3.60; Fri. & Sat. Evgs.: Orch. $9.40; Mezz. $7.50; Balc. $6.90, 5.75, 4.90; 2nd Balc. $3.60; Wed. Mat.: Orch. $6.60; Mezz. $4.30; Balc. $4.05, 3.60; 2nd Balc. $3.00; Sat. Mat. Orch. $5.92; Mezz. $4.90; Balc. $4.30, 3.80; 2nd Balc. $3.00.

MAIL ORDERS FILLED THRU JAN. 1963

ST. JAMES THEATRE   44th St., W. of B'way

Subways Are for Sleeping (1961)

Calling All Critics

Broadway producers are perennially hopeful, even in the face of impending disaster. What can you do, though, when you know that your show is hopeless? David Merrick simply closed *Breakfast at Tiffany's* in previews [see page 42]. But five years earlier—faced with a stinker of slightly lesser proportions—the "abominable showman" came up with an audacious plan, as related by his long-suffering press agent Harvey Sabinson in his 1977 memoir, *Darling, You Were Wonderful*.

David Merrick's infamous "Quote ad of the century."

"Seven Out of Seven"

by Harvey Sabinson

I arrived in Boston slightly unnerved and with little enthusiasm for the job at hand. The musical *Subways Are for Sleeping* had opened—to intense animosity—two nights before in Philadelphia. Like the New York City subway system it attempted to glorify, it was without apparent virtue, and in deep trouble. In less than four weeks, it would be inflicted upon the theatregoers of Boston.

Subways Are for Sleeping was "inspired," to use the word with supreme looseness, by a book of considerable charm and inconsiderable content by Edmund Love, a laconic man given to browsing through New York as if it were a secondhand bookshop. Having earned a bit of money from his writings, Love was now embarked on an extremely hazardous undertaking. He was eating his way through all the restaurants listed in the classified telephone books of New York City, one a day, from A to Z. This ambitious project, that could take at least a lifetime, or at the *very* least a life, intrigued me. When I asked him why, he merely replied, "Because they're there."

David Merrick realized he had acquired little more than a title when he bought the stage rights to Love's book. He commissioned Betty Comden and Adolph Green to flail it into an acceptable libretto, and Jule Styne to write the music. Michael Kidd was engaged to direct a cast that included Carol Lawrence, Sydney Chaplin (one of Charlie's boys), Phyllis Newman (Adolph Green's wife), and Orson Bean. The show was one of many Merrick entries during the 1961–62 season.

In blind obeisance to that threadbare theatrical code, "the show must go on," I was in Boston to alert its unsuspecting citizenry to the arrival of this expensive charade. Since Philadelphia is but 325 miles away, I had to move fast before the "word" beat me to it.

The Boston press usually plays it straight. They claim no prejudice because of a show's gloomy history prior to landing on the shores of Massachusetts Bay. Therefore I was greeted not as the advance man for a traveling leper colony, but as the emissary of a perfectly respectable enterprise. My stores of photographs and feature stories were accepted with grace and interest. All was going well until I reached the desk of Cyrus Durgin, urbane critic of the *Globe*.

Durgin and I exchanged the usual pleasantries as he sifted through my material, selecting what he considered appropriate for the drama pages of his paper. Shuffling my photographs, he looked up and said, "There is a conflict on the night your show opens. The Netherlands Chamber Orchestra is playing its only Boston concert that evening. After grappling with the problem, I have come to the conclusion that I will attend the concert. My assistant, Kevin Kelly, will cover *Subways Are for Sleeping*."

"Mr. Merrick won't like it," I said.

"That's tough," countered Durgin, biting down hard on his pipe stem, "I don't work for David Merrick. I'll cover the event I deem more important to the Boston cultural scene."

This convinced me that the bad news from Philadelphia had overtaken me in the homestretch.

"Then I take it you have no objection if I alert my master to this extraordinary state of affairs," I said. "He detests surprises—unless they come in the form of unexpected hit shows."

"Not at all," said Durgin. "Tell him anything you want. Also tell him that I consider Kevin a highly competent critic. Musicals try out in Boston year after year, but we don't often get a distinguished foreign ensemble like the Netherlands Chamber Orchestra."

The gauntlet was flung, leaving me no alternative but to pick it up and carry it back to Philadelphia, where Merrick was regrouping his demoralized forces urging them to dismiss from their minds all thoughts of defeat. "The show is a monumental disaster," he exhorted his troops. "Get it fixed before we open in Boston, or I'll close it here."

I reported my findings in the colony to the north. "How can Durgin send a second-string critic to review a half-million dollar musical?" Merrick lamented. "I consider it an affront to me and to the Broadway theatre. I won't have it. You can head right back to Boston and tell him that if he doesn't see fit to cover it himself, I will bar Kevin What's-His-Name."

Mounting my erratic steed, the New Haven Railroad, I returned to Boston to resume negotiations. They collapsed completely when Durgin, every part of him clenched, muttered, "The nerve of that man trying to tell me how to do my job. It's Kelly, and that's final."

Subways Are for Sleeping managed to survive the Philadelphia run. It arrived in Boston lightly buffed and begging for a fresh chance. On opening night Merrick set up a defensive perimeter in the lobby of the

Colonial Theatre. An outpost was to be manned by a lone, unarmed vassal—me.

"When Kelly gets here," said Merrick, "tell him there is no ticket for him. If he wants to know why, tell him I consider him incompetent. If he becomes difficult, throw him out bodily. If you need me, I'll be there in the lobby."

SUBWAYS
ARE FOR
SLEEPING

Sydney Chaplin puts co-star Carol Lawrence to sleep with his singing.

At 7:30 Kelly arrived, apprehensive but not exactly shaking with fear. I repelled him at the outer breastworks. To his rear was a general assignment reporter for the *Globe* recording every word of our brief volley. When the reporter requested an interview with Merrick, I summoned my peerless leader, who valiantly stuck to his guns. "Mr. Durgin has insulted me and my production by sending an incompetent to review it," he said.

Not since Marshal Foch uttered his famous rallying cry, "*Ils ne passeront pas*," has terrain been held with such fervor. Certain that he would never penetrate this wall of resistance, Kelly turned on his heels and retreated.

The skirmish won, Merrick and I entered the theatre. As the house lights dimmed and the overture began, I headed for the cozy confines of the manager's office. "Where are you going, son?" he asked. "Aren't you watching the show tonight?"

"I saw it in Philadelphia,' I replied. "I'm eligible for leave."

As I opened the office door, Merrick was right behind me. Discretion dictated that he, too, should seek refuge lest the audience become hostile.

"When we open in New York, I'd honestly prefer to have the second-string critics there," I said to him. "This show could bring out the killer instinct in Taubman, Kerr, and that gang."

Merrick offered no response. Pulling a Manhattan telephone directory from an overhead shelf, he sat down at the manager's desk and began to read. Within moments a smile creased his face. It was apparent that he was deriving great pleasure from reading the phone book.

He looked up and said, "Do you recall when I used to ask you weekly when Brooks Atkinson was going to retire as critic of the *Times*?"

"Yes," I replied, "and when it finally happened, you seemed

strangely overjoyed." [Former police reporter J. Brooks Atkinson (1894–1984) became drama critic of the all-powerful *Times* in 1925 and remained in his post until the end of the 1959–60 season. Upon his retirement, the Mansfield Theatre on West 47th Street was renamed in his honor.]

"I never told you at the time why I wanted to know," he said. "For a long time I've had this idea in the back of my mind. Now, with Atkinson out and Howard Taubman in, I'm convinced it can work."

"What can work? This show?"

"No, no, no. My idea." His voice dropped to a soft whisper as he divested himself of his great inner secret. "I think it is possible to find seven people with exactly the same names as the seven daily newspaper critics.

"Already I've found a Walter Kerr, several Robert Colemans, a Richard Watts, and loads of John Chapmans in the Manhattan book. I'm willing to bet that we can locate a Howard Taubman somewhere in the metropolitan area."

"Why was it so important for Atkinson to retire?" I asked.

"Because in all this world there is no other man with that name," he said. "I was hoping that his replacement would have a fairly common name... Now move your chair closer. I'm going to whisper the rest to you."

Rejecting my offer to sit in his lap, he resumed. "You mustn't breathe a word of this to anybody. Not to your wife, not to your partner, not to anyone on your staff. If it gets out, the idea is dead. I want you to contact seven people with the same names as the critics. Invite them to a preview performance in New York, as my guests. Take them out after the show to some expensive place like the Oak Room. Then get their written permission to quote them in an ad. I want to form my own critics' circle."

"It's absolutely brilliant, David," I said.

"Wait! I'm not finished. Do some research. Go through reviews of shows like *My Fair Lady, Oklahoma!, South Pacific*. Pick out the wildest praise from there and we'll attribute it to *Subways* from *our* critics.

"I've been dreaming about this for a long time. It wouldn't work with a good show, but with a dubious prospect like this, it just might come off. Now remember, not a word to anybody."

"Just one question, David," I said. "What if we get good notices in New York?'

"Don't talk nonsense," he replied.

The following morning I brought the Boston reviews of *Subways* to Merrick's suite at the Ritz-Carlton Hotel. Immaculate in his Savile Row pin-striped, hand-tailored suit, he said, "You don't have to tell me what fell apart today. I'm sure the reviews are dreadful."

"Most of the critics hated it," I said. "But I'm still in shock from reading the *Globe*. There's a rave in it and it's by Kevin Kelly."

"Impossible," said Merrick. "He didn't see it."

"Apparently he did. Last week in Philadelphia. After I warned Durgin that we'd bar the second-stringer, he sent Kelly to Philadelphia. Since we were sold out, he bought a standing-room ticket for last Saturday's matinee—and adored the show. He tells the whole story here in his review. There's also an accompanying item in which you're quoted as calling him incompetent."

Merrick smiled at this irony. "Doesn't his good review of this bomb prove him incompetent?"

With few tickets left for the Boston engagement because of a huge advance sale, my work there was done. Merrick suggested that I return to New York on the next plane to begin the quest for the "magnificent seven."

In 1961, before strikes and high operating costs whittled the number to three, Manhattan boasted seven daily newspapers. At the *Times*, Howard Taubman; Walker Kerr for the *Herald-Tribune*; John Chapman for the *Daily News*; Robert Coleman for the *Daily Mirror*; John McClain for the *Journal-American*; Norman Nadel for the *World-Telegram*; and Richard Watts for the *Post*.

PREMIERE PERFORMANCE, DECEMBER 27, 1961

ST. JAMES THEATRE

DAVID MERRICK
presents

SYDNEY CHAPLIN   CAROL LAWRENCE
in
The New Musical Comedy

SUBWAYS ARE FOR SLEEPING

ORSON BEAN

with

GRAYSON HALL   GORDON CONNELL   CY YOUNG
EUGENE R. WOOD   GENE VARRONE   JOHN SHARPE

and

PHYLLIS NEWMAN

Book and Lyrics by

BETTY COMDEN and ADOLPH GREEN

Music by

JULE STYNE

Suggested by the book by EDMUND G. LOVE
Settings and Lighting by WILL STEVEN ARMSTRONG
Costumes by FREDDY WITTOP
Musical Direction by MILTON ROSENSTOCK
Orchestrations by PHILIP J. LANG
Associate Choreographer MARC BREAUX
Dance Music Arranged by PETER HOWARD
Production Supervisor NEIL HARTLEY

Directed and Choreographed by

MICHAEL KIDD

The opening night billing page.

Within a few hours I managed to locate my surrogate critics. Kerr, Watts, Chapman, and Coleman were listed in Manhattan, Taubman in the Bronx, McClain in Old Tappan, New Jersey, and Nadel in Union, New Jersey. A typical phone conversation follows:

"Hello, is this Walter Kerr?"

"Yes, who is this?"

"My name is Harvey Sabinson. I'm the press agent for David Merrick's Broadway production, *Subways Are for Sleeping*."

"I hate subways. I always try to take the bus."

"It's a Broadway show."

"Never heard of it. We don't go much to the theatre."

"It hasn't opened yet. That's probably why you haven't heard of it. It's being produced by David Merrick. You must have heard of him?"

"I think I once saw him being interviewed on television. Funny fellow with a black moustache?"

"Yes, that's him. Let me tell you why I'm calling, Mr. Kerr. Are you aware that there's a drama critic with the same name as yours?"

"I understand there is. Fellow works for the *Tribune*? I read the *Times*."

"Well, Mr. Merrick would like to invite you and Mrs. Kerr to see a preview performance of *Subways Are for Sleeping*. Is there a Mrs. Kerr?"

"Has been for eighteen years. But we don't go much to the theatre. Last show we saw was *Oklahoma!* Cost us twenty dollars including dinner."

"Well, this won't cost you a cent. Free down-front orchestra seats. Supper after the show at the Plaza. We'll even pay for taxis to get you to and from the theatre."

"Yeah? What's the catch?"

"It's just a little joke we want to play on the critics. We're inviting seven gentlemen with the same names as the seven daily newspaper critics. You won't be alone. And there's nothing for you to do except enjoy the show."

"What if we don't like it?"

"Then there's no obligation. Nobody will pressure you."

"Doesn't sound right to me."

"Believe me, there's nothing wrong with it, and you'll have a chance to see a big Broadway musical before it opens."

"... I guess we have nothing to lose—except an evening at home. When can we go?"

"Any night that's convenient for you week after next."

"How's Tuesday?"

"Okay. Just look for me in the lobby of the St. James Theatre on West Forty-fourth Street next to the ticket taker. I'll be wearing a blue blazer with gray slacks."

"Do we ask for our tickets at the box office?"

"No, don't go to the box office. I'll have your tickets with me. Just look for me."

"What if there's another guy in the lobby with a blue blazer and gray slacks?"

"I'm the one who'll be frowning. Just ask the ticket taker for me. You have my name?"

"No, I didn't catch it."

"It's Harvey Sabinson."

"Okay, Mr. Samuelson, we'll see you a week from Tuesday."

"Don't worry about a thing, Mr. Kerr. I'll send you a confirming letter with all the details. Oh, one more thing. Don't breathe a word of this to anybody. Not even your best friends."

"I'll try not to. G'bye."

"Thank you and give my love to Jean... I mean Mrs. Kerr."

In a like manner I managed to secure the cooperation of the Messrs. Taubman, Watts, Chapman, Nadel, and McClain. Only Robert Coleman required a personal visitation. A financial public relations man, he was aware of all the chicanery of the business. After a few hours in his office on lower Broadway, I convinced him that his participation would in no way jeopardize his standing in the financial community.

With my seven "phantom" critics in tow and sworn to secrecy, I proceeded to research the quotes, selecting the most laudatory phraseology from reviews of a few of Broadway's biggest hits. Then I prepared carefully worded statements for each of my new-found friends to sign, granting permission to use their names and quotation in paid advertisements.

A pleasant week of previews was marred by a single recalcitrant. My John Chapman got up and left the St. James Theatre during the intermission one evening. As he passed me in the lobby, he growled, "I think it stinks."

Who needs him, I thought; the Manhattan phone book is full of John Chapmans.

As for the rest, they enjoyed the show immensely, much to my surprise. I suppose it was because the price was right. There was nothing wrong with our late evening suppers either; I was abundantly generous with Mr. Merrick's money.

One night, while sipping Scotch with the Taubmans and the Kerrs in the Oak Room, I was spotted by a colleague who came over to our table. When with a half smile I introduced my guests to him, he muttered something that sounded suspiciously like "Up yours," before withdrawing.

I accounted for this breach of etiquette by explaining than not even my closest colleagues were aware of our little caper. Taubman winced. A salesman of audio equipment in a Lexington Avenue shop, he said, "I hope I didn't spill the whole thing the other day."

Panic gripped me. "What happened?" I asked.

"Well, one of my customers is in show business," he replied. "I told him about your call and asked him what I should do. I wasn't sure if your invitation was on the level. He told me not to worry about it and to have a good time at the show."

"And your customer's name?" I inquired.

"Leland Hayward."

Hayward was a respected producer who occasionally joined Merrick in a theatrical venture. [The touring company of Merrick and Hayward's *Gypsy*, starring Ethel Merman, had closed earlier that month.]

I silently prayed that he would leave town for a month or at least develop a severe case of laryngitis.

With everybody signed up, I reported to Merrick that phase one of his ingenious plan had been carried out successfully. Now we had to take another person into our confidence. We went to see Fred Golden, Merrick's account executive at the Blaine-Thompson Advertising Agency.

Merrick closed the door to Freddie's office, peering around first for possible eavesdroppers. Then he outlined the plot, demanding that blood oaths of secrecy be obtained from all agency personnel who would be involved in the mechanical preparation of the ad. "Don't submit the completed ad to the papers until the very last minute before insertion," he insisted. "I don't want the copy acceptance departments to have any time to study it carefully."

Our three great minds blended to come up with a headline: "7 OUT OF 7 ARE ECSTATICALLY UNANIMOUS ABOUT *SUBWAYS ARE FOR SLEEPING*." Not particularly clever or well-said, but not exactly soft-sell either. The remaining copy was to consist of the names and the quotes:

HOWARD TAUBMAN—"ONE OF THE FEW GREAT MUSCIAL COMEDIES OF THE LAST THIRTY YEARS, ONE OF THE BEST OF OUR TIME. It lends luster to this or any other Broadway season."

WALTER KERR—"WHAT A SHOW! WHAT A HIT! WHAT A SOLID HIT! If you want to be overjoyed, spend an evening with *Subways Are for Sleeping*. A triumph!"

JOHN CHAPMAN—"NO DOUBT ABOUT IT, *Subways Are for Sleeping* IS THE BEST MUSICAL OF THE CENTURY. Consider yourself lucky if you can beg or steal a ticket for *Subways Are for Sleeping* over the next few years."

JOHN McCLAIN—"A FABULOUS MUSICAL. I LOVE IT. SOONER OR LATER EVERYONE WILL HAVE TO SEE *Subways Are for Sleeping*."

RICHARD WATTS—"A KNOCKOUT, FROM START TO FINISH. THE MUSICAL YOU'VE BEEN WAITING FOR. IT DESERVES TO RUN FOR A DECADE."

NORMAN NADEL—"A WHOPPING HIT. RUN, DON'T WALK, TO THE ST. JAMES THEATRE. It's in that rare class of great musicals. Quite simply, it has everything."

ROBERT COLEMAN—"A GREAT MUSICAL. ALL THE INGREDIENTS ARE THERE. As fine a piece of work as our stage can be asked to give us."

A few days before the official opening, Freddie submitted a layout to Merrick, who thought it lacked a single element. In the interest of

"integrity" he wanted it to include a photograph of each member of his personal critics' circle. A photographer was dispatched on a whirlwind tour of the Bronx, Manhattan, and New Jersey to shoot the portraits. Our critics had to admit they were enjoying the attention immensely.

The official opening night of *Subways Are for Sleeping* was filled with mixed emotions. The preview performances had gone so well that we began to harbor some faint hope that the show would be treated kindly by the real critics. At the same time, like children with a marvelous secret waiting to be shared, we wanted the gag ad to run.

The souvenir program, featuring Tom Morrow's sleeping straphanger.

The actual reviews were split down the middle. Chapman, Watts, and Coleman were affirmative. Taubman, Kerr, and McClain were negative. Nadel was on the fence, and only the slightest nudge would have made him drop on the negative side. Not even the ayes, however, were enthusiastic enough to deter us from our original course. Freddie was told to proceed as planned and to submit the ad to five papers for insertion on Thursday, January 4.

Late in the afternoon of January 3, Merrick, his general manager, Jack Schlissel, and I set up a night watch in Freddie's office. "Do you realize," he asked us, "that if all the papers run this ad, I'll be out twenty-five thousand dollars? It's worth it, isn't it? There's never been a more pointed comment on those boring quote ads. And who knows, maybe it'll help the show run longer."

As we savored what was to come, the evening wore on. We ran out of things to talk about, people to knock, show business jokes to tell. Then, at 7:30, the *Times* called to advise Freddie that they had caught on and would not run the ad. They considered it misleading. To protect the sanctity of the press in general, they had even alerted all the other papers. But it had been too late to catch the *Herald-Tribune*, which had already gone to press with its City Edition.

Freddie cajoled the man from the *Times*. "We make no claim that these seven people work for newspapers," he said. "We've even run their pictures so that there will be no mistaking them for the real critics. It's a clever comment, that's all. Where's your sense of humor?"

The *Times* wouldn't budge. But at least we had the first edition of the *Trib*. As soon as it was off the presses, Schlissel and I picked up an armful of copies. If nothing else, they'd be collector's items in the years to come.

Later we heard that the *Post* thought we had included the wrong photograph of Richard Watts. Our Watts was black; their's was not. As they were replacing our photo with theirs, the call from the *Times* came in. The *Post* immediately killed the ad.

As a publicity stunt, however, the hoax was a huge success. It was reported throughout the world. The saga of Merrick's clever ruse appeared in *France Soir*, the London *Times*, the Stockholm *Dagbladet*, and the Tokyo *Shimbun*. Within a few days, the *Trib* itself reran the ad, this time as editorial matter, together with an ad of their own creation that revealed what the actual critics had said. But they were not above pointing fun at themselves for falling victim to a splendid practical joke.

In its issue of January 12, 1962, *Time* reported: "...David Merrick has done it again. Last week, with a full-page ad that managed to run in an early edition of the New York *Herald-Tribune*, he perpetrated one of Broadway's most brazen jokes."

The *Time* article quoted Merrick's explanation for selecting his particular Richard Watts: "There isn't one critic who is a Negro, which I consider a violation of the Fair Employment Practices law. My group is more representative."

The reaction of the legitimate critics was mixed. John McClain wrote that it was "so original and funny, it warranted publication." Kerr, who found the show "limp," was not enchanted by Merrick's latest escapade. Taubman refused comment.

The Better Business Bureau sternly denounced Merrick's brainchild as "deceptive and confusing." When he learned of this, he said, "What is the Better Business Bureau? Something like the Diner's Club?"

Given a shot in the arm by all this publicity, *Subways Are for Sleeping* managed to survive until June, when dismal word-of-mouth finally caught up with it, and it came to the end of the line. But Merrick's reputation as a prankster was forever secure.

After the closing, he called me and said, "I've got an idea for the greatest publicity stunt in the history of the theatre. Want to hear it?"

Oh no, not again. But nothing in this world could keep him from telling me, so I dutifully said, "What is it, David?"

"It's an idea that's guaranteed to turn up long lines at the box office: *a great show that wins unanimous raves.*"

Subways Are for Sleeping opened December 27, 1961 at the
St. James Theatre, to mixed reviews. It closed there June 23, 1962
after 205 performances, with a partial loss.

Harvey Sabinson pretty much tells us everything we need to know.
Except that Merrick followed through on his idea for "the greatest
publicity stunt in the history of the theatre." His next musical at the
St. James did, indeed, win virtually unanimous raves. *Hello, Dolly!*
they called it.

Skyscraper (1965)

Thanksgiving Turkey

Unforeseen woes seem to pile up on musicals in trouble; when everything is going wrong, dire crises have a tendency to multiply. *Skyscraper* was such a musical, undergoing severe and continual rewrites. And then, as the show was laboring through an abnormally extended preview period—extended so as to allow more fixing— *Skyscraper* received a "low blow" from a theretofore respectful corner.

Jack Gaver, the drama critic for United Press International, gave a full account in his chronicle of the 1965–1966 season, *Season In, Season Out*.

The show art demonstrates more imagination than *Skyscraper* itself.

"*Skyscraper*"

by Jack Gaver

The preview performance, an ever-growing factor on Broadway in recent years, was brought into sharp focus in the case of *Skyscraper*, a $450,000 musical that stirred up considerable advance attention because it was providing dramatic star Julie Harris with her debut as a singing actress.

The late Dorothy Kilgallen, Broadway columnist for the *Journal-American* and other Hearst newspapers, started a fuss that was both annoying and humorous—at least, she enlivened the season for the moment—by writing a resounding rap of this show twenty-two days before its official opening. The following led off her column of October 22:

"I wish someone would pass a law making it illegal for a columnist to see a Broadway show before its official premiere…"

(I must interrupt here to comment that this seems to be a poor excuse for being some place where you don't belong.)

But to continue quoting:

"…Then we would all be spared the personality splitting question: to comment, or not to comment, when they still might be 'fixing.' *Variety*, and other papers, review shows the minute they rear their heads out of town, in any town, so it seems to me the divertissements are fair game when they come into my town and start playing previews to which people pay $50 a ticket for the privilege of sitting in the balcony…"

(This price is one that an organization can charge, if it desires, on an occasion when it buys out a house, or part of one, either preview or regular performance, to raise money for charitable purposes.)

Miss Kilgallen again:

"… I am referring, specifically, to *Skyscraper*, which I saw—saw the first act of, to be completely accurate—at the Lunt-Fontanne Theatre last night in homage to a worthy charity, the George Junior Republic, of which I am a patron. The street outside the theatre was jammed with Rolls-Royces and Cadillacs, the theatre was crammed with attractive and celebrated and polite people, but even the politest could not work up much enthusiasm for this new musical comedy. It contains Julie Harris, quite inexplicably, since she is not a musical-comedy performer; Charles Nelson Reilly, who does everything but set fire to his trousers to get laughs where none are written in the libretto; one marvelous construction-company ballet in the first act which should open the show but doesn't; no music to sing of; and a lot of costumes that imitate last year's Courrèges.

"I will be delighted—but astonished—if this one gets good reviews.

"However, in the case of the George Junior Republic benefit, the show was followed by the traditional glamorous supper party tossed by Lillian and Hubie Boscowitz at the Four Seasons, where the turkey served is far more enjoyable than that dished up at the Lunt-Fontanne."

That turkey bit was the insult supreme, completely gratuitous in view of the explicit nature of the comment that preceded it.

As you might expect, the Broadway community buzzed after that. The only silent spot seemed to be the office of producers Cy Feuer and Ernest Martin, old hands in the matter of musical-comedy hits. They couldn't have liked it, but they said nothing publicly.

[The highly combative Feuer and Martin were known for their heavy-handed ministrations. They had fired librettists, directors, and choreographers on such seemingly smooth-as-silk shows as *Guys and Dolls* and *How to Succeed in Business without Really Trying*.]

Miss Kilgallen brought up the matter again in her column of October 27, to wit:

"I have in hand a slap on the wrist from Howard Lindsay"—the celebrated actor-author-producer—"an acquaintance whom I have respected for many years, saying he thought I was 'way out of line' to comment on *Skyscraper* before it opened officially on Broadway. [Lindsay was Broadway royalty, best known as co-author and star of the long-running comedy hit *Life with Father*. His credits with co-librettist Russel Crouse included such musicals as *Anything Goes* (which Lindsay also directed), *Call Me Madam*, and *The Sound of Music*.]

"Perhaps I was. If so, it wasn't the first time I was ever out of line and I hope it won't be the last time.

"He wrote:

"'Sometimes what looks like a dull show can be changed into a success by changes in routining, by an additional scene or changes of dialogue already in the works, by cuts of numbers or by new numbers, and in many other ways. This can happen between one performance and the next.'

"Very true. I know this. We agree. He adds:

"'You know as well as I do that *Variety* is not read by the public, and that its opinions stay pretty much within the trade.'"

"I do know this too. But Howard conveniently left out the reviews by critics in Boston, New Haven, Philadelphia, Detroit, and wherever shows happen to try out. Their circulation is not confined to 'the trade.' They write for their readers... and they write complete reviews, whereas my comments were a brief opinion and billed as such..."

Miss Kilgallen also "conveniently" left out something. No New York playgoer, except someone in the business, is going to know what the out-of-town critics thought about a show any more than they are going to be familiar with the opinion of the out-of-town critics who write for a trade paper such as *Variety*.

Julie Harris as the dream girl, over chorines dancing on the beam of a skyscraper.

Back to Miss Kilgallen regarding Mr. Lindsay:

"...He also seems to forget the ticket brokers who go out of town to see plays and musicals, the scouts or producers of television shows who catch shows in their early stages looking for possible talent, and who can be the fastest spreader of the word—'It's a hit,' 'It needs fixing,' or 'It's a bomb'—since Marconi invented the wireless because they don't even have to wait for a weekly deadline, as *Variety* does. They are in Sardi's and other key places the same night, or the night after, and they influence important people ..."

They don't, however, influence the regular ticket-buying public because they never come in contact with it, which is a lucky thing for the public. Of course, some news-hungry columnist might print the opinion of some such Elmer Expert, but it is always well to bear in mind in this connection that the late producer Michael Todd, as expert as they come, returned from New Haven on a late winter night in 1943 with the opinion that *Away We Go* couldn't possibly make it because it wasn't enough of a girlie show. But they made a few

Outside Interference

changes in that one in Boston, although they didn't turn it into a girlie show. For one thing, they changed the title. When it reached New York it was called *Oklahoma!* Todd, of course, had had a lot of company in the matter of bum steers on a lot of other shows through the years.

It might be pointed out in this connection, too, that there are those who question that a show can be "fixed" in miraculous fashion, as Howard Lindsay intimated. *Skyscraper* wasn't right when the columnist saw it twenty-two days before its opening, and it had spent weeks out of town before it began previews here. How could anyone expect it to be turned around into complete effectiveness?

I do know that these miracles sometimes happen—in the space of a few weeks or within a couple of days. I had no first-hand contact with *A Funny Thing Happened on the Way to the Forum* before opening night, but I remember that the out-of-town reports had it floundering, and that it came into town a few days before the premiere still needing help. Choreographer-director Jerome Robbins answered an S.O.S., and according to those who should know, did a bit of this and a bit of that and, almost overnight, made it possible for the show to become a long-run hit.

Back to the Kilgallen report:

"...If *Skyscraper* had been playing to non-money-making invitational previews while in the throes of alterations, and I had chanced to see a performance, there would have been no word from me in this space... However, once *Skyscraper* had thrown itself upon the commercial market in New York and 'the public' was paying to see it, I felt that, as a reporter, I had a right to treat it as no great secret. This is not an apology, it is merely an explanation."

"Funny thing, as many times as I've written about a show, 'It got rave reviews in Philadelphia,' 'It's playing to S.R.O. in Boston,' or 'It looks as if you ought to order your tickets now,' I've never heard from Howard—or anyone—that I was 'out of line' in telling my readers what was happening, or about to happen ..."

As for that last paragraph, I think that it is just as wrong for any gossip columnist to tout an incoming show as surefire as it is to label one a certain failure. The record books are full of shows that looked like certain winners on their tryout tours and landed on Broadway with dull thuds. Any experienced producer, while he doesn't want the advance word to hint at disaster, would rather have his show "sneak into town" than to have it come in on a wave of ballyhoo such as might herald the Second Coming. Too much advance praise often has caused many playgoers to invest in tickets for shows that don't make the grade.

While it is my belief that Miss Kilgallen was wrong in what she did to *Skyscraper,* and that another Hearst columnist, Bill Slocum, didn't help matters a few days later by applauding her in print, I also don't approve of the way the preview thing is handled.

There has been a move in recent months by some producers to sell preview tickets at a dollar or so under what the regular box-office price is to be. I don't think that's discount enough. I believe that a preview ticket should sell for no more than half the regular price. That would go a long way toward eliminating much of the griping in this area. Also, I don't think preview houses should be sold out to organizations that, as per the case cited by Miss Kilgallen, resell the tickets for what the traffic will bear to raise money for charitable purposes. It's a wrench to pay that sort of money even for a proven show that you think you're going to like; it seems a bit much to pay it for something that is still in the laboratory. That sort of thing can't possibly make friends for the theatre.

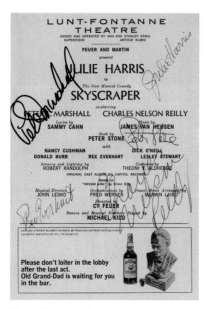

The billing page for the Lunt-Fontanne.

Producers will not appreciate the half-price suggestion. Not all even make the slight reduction cited. The *Skyscraper* previews were at the full price. In the case of shows with extended preview periods, the producers hope to turn a profit as well as to spend the time polishing the production. Because once the critics have turned in their reports, there may be no more show. Such a preview profit, of course, is only a drop in the bucket as measured against the huge production cost and the weekly operating expenses, but it is better than a deficit and, if the show does succeed, it has a head start toward that day when everything is paid off and the investors begin to make money.

A major reason behind the increasing popularity of the preview idea among producers is the desire to eliminate losses that almost invariably are incurred in touring prior to the Broadway opening. This is not a new problem; it has always existed. It's a rare production that comes into New York without a deficit to show for its road weeks. This is due to the fact that moving a show around is costly, and that there are many extra expenses involved making the changes hopefully undertaken to improve the attraction. For various reasons, it costs less to make such changes in New York. This situation has grown worse with the rising cost of everything in recent years, especially in the case of those big musicals. It was not unusual in the past for the producer of a musical to book tryout engagements in three or four cities in the East, almost certainly in two. Now, as an economy measure, there is an increasing tendency to confine the "tour" to one city.

There is not complete agreement among producers on the felicity of playing a lot of previews in New York, either on top of a brief tour or without touring at all. Even if this does cut costs, some feel that more can be learned about what repairs shows need by playing in other cities where the local critics review them and often make helpful suggestions. They feel, too, that it is good to get the reaction of non-New York audiences. Other producers think that since they are preparing a show for exhibition in New York, they can get a better reaction if the tryout audiences consist of New Yorkers. Also the players and stage crews have the advantage of getting familiar with their theatre long before opening night instead of having to settle into it with a few hours or days.

In any event, the preview seems to be here to stay, and there will be more before there are less.

Miss Kilgallen did not live to find out whether the critics agreed with her about *Skyscraper*. She died in her sleep on November 8.

The reviews were mixed, it is true, but the consensus was that it was a pleasant, tuneful affair in the main, as can be gathered from these brief quotes from a few of the reviewers:

"...It always looks alive and is often funny."

"...A reasonably entertaining show... It isn't too bad a buy."

"...A captivating musical... funny right from the beginning... packed with entertainment."

"...It turned out to be a bright, amusing, and imaginative entertainment... "

"...A light, gay show... a bouncy, fast-moving melodious affair."

John McClain, drama critic of Miss Kilgallen's *Journal-American*, felt that the show had sufficiently good ingredients so that it "could easily come home a winner" and added, "I believe they have a good chance to make it."

Skyscraper, based somewhat vaguely on Elmer Rice's comedy hit of two decades ago, *Dream Girl*, had about as extensive and intensive working over as any musical ever has had, according to co-producer Feuer, who also directed, and Peter Stone, who wrote the script. Changes went on almost daily during the six tryout weeks in Detroit and the four preview weeks in New York. Stone said there were six complete revisions of the script as well as seventy-five sets of revision pages. A new ending to one scene and some new dialogue went in a few hours before the opening-night curtain. Three days after the premiere, they put in an entire new musical number.

Miss Harris won no honors for her singing ability, but most of the critics felt that her skill at comedy, in her role of an admirer of old buildings fighting the real estate and construction interests, more than made up for that deficiency.

Skyscraper opened November 13, 1965 at the Lunt-Fontanne Theatre to mixed-to-favorable reviews. It closed there June 11, 1966 after 241 performances, with a total loss.

Skyscraper's troubles might well have been foreseen by its history. Back in 1957, Feuer and Martin came up with a project about a woman who refused to sell her brownstone to make way for a skyscraper. In 1959 they announced a musical version of the Elmer Rice comedy *Dream Girl*. (And no, they did not call it *Dreamgirl* or *Dreamgirls*.) The producers then signed a two-show deal with songwriters James Van Heusen and Sammy Cahn, best known for all those Sinatra hits: "Call Me Irresponsible," "Come Fly with Me," "Love and Marriage," "High Hopes," "My Kind of Town (Chicago Is)," "The Second Time Around," and more.

When the first Feuer and Martin/Cahn and Van Heusen show—the Mary Martin vehicle *Walking Happy*—was delayed due to the withdrawal of the star, Feuer and Martin combined their two leftover ideas into what became *Skyscraper*. (Rice retained credit for *Dream Girl*, although the links were tenuous.) Thus, you had a story without strong underpinnings. *Walking Happy*—which followed *Skyscraper* into the Lunt, which Feuer and Martin leased in 1960 and operated through most of the decade—had stronger source material and proved a stronger show. Not strong enough to withstand star trouble, book trouble, and other annoyances.

After all was said and done, and all the pre-opening changes and rewrites and fixings, *Skyscraper* was a poor musical. The show seems to have caught at least one lucky break; the Broadway critics—no doubt as a reaction to a lowly columnist intruding on their turf—appear to have been overly kind in their assessments of the show. It also couldn't have hurt that *Skyscraper* followed a parade of lousy musicals; here they were in mid-November, and look what the year had offered: *Kelly* [see page 328], *Baker Street*, *Do I*

Hear a Waltz? Half a Sixpence, Flora, the Red Menace, The Roar of the Greasepaint, Pickwick [see page 276], *Drat! The Cat!* and *On a Clear Day You Can See Forever* [see page 258]. Furthermore, two of the year's most awaited musicals—the Loesser-Fosse *Pleasures and Palaces* and the Merrick-Josh Logan *Hot September* (out of William Inge's *Picnic*)—had shuttered on the road. Broadway was more than ripe for a hit, and some of the critics seemed to be rooting for *Skyscraper*. But the favorable word didn't fool anybody. Broadway finally found a blockbuster hit the following week, as it happened, in the unlikely *Man of La Mancha*.

It should be added that for Ms. Kilgallen, the *Skyscraper* affair was merely an incidental distraction. Kilgallen (1913–65) had more important things on her mind. Daughter of a Hearst crime reporter, Kilgallen began working for a Hearst paper when she was eighteen. She had her first brush with celebrity when she and two other (male) reporters waged a "race around the world" as a circulation booster. Kilgallen came in second, following the *World-Telegram* but beating out the man from the *Times*.

She married Richard Kollmar, featured juvenile of Weill's *Knicker-bocker Holiday* and Rodgers and Hart's *Too Many Girls*, in 1940. Five years later, the Kollmars began a thirty-minute radio show called *Breakfast with Dorothy and Dick*, which remained on the air into 1963. Over the years, she watched her husband produce seven full-scale musicals, including the moderate hit *Plain and Fancy* and four full-fledged disasters—which is to say, she was no theatrical outsider innocently stumbling on *Skyscraper*.

Kilgallen became even more famous in 1950 as one of the original celebrity panelists on the television game show, *What's My Line?* With her popular newspaper column, weekly exposure on television, and her radio show, Kilgallen was one of America's most famous columnists of the era.

But Kilgallen, and her column "The Voice of Broadway," was not merely interested in fluff. While Broadway was a-titter over her "Thanksgiving turkey," Kilgallen was handling an even hotter story. A veteran crime reporter (having covered the trials of Sam Sheppard, Bruno Hauptman, and others), she was summoned by Jack Ruby—the man who killed Lee Harvey Oswald—for a jailhouse interview. In her column, Kilgallen claimed that she had information that would uncover the true story of the Kennedy assassination.

Then she went to see *Skyscraper*. She discussed the show in her columns of October 22 and October 27. Twelve days later, the fifty-two-year-old Kilgallen was found dead in her bedroom. A heart attack, due to "a combination of moderate quantities of alcohol and barbiturates," said the medical examiner. Conspiracy theorists, needless to say, think otherwise. Remember Marilyn Monroe? they say.

Which seems a strange way, indeed, to end the tale of *Skyscraper*.

LOUISIANA HAYRIDE

MAX GORDON presents

Clifton WEBB
Charles BUTTERWORTH
Tamara GEVA *Patsy* KELLY
in the new HOWARD DIETZ *revue*

FLYING COLORS

DESIGNED AND
LIGHTED BY
NORMAN
BEL-GEDDES
DANCES BY
AGNES
DE MILLE
AND WARREN
LEONARD
COSTUMES BY
CONSTANCE
RIPLEY
ORCHESTRA
CONDUCTED BY
AL GOODMAN

WORDS AND MUSIC BY

Howard Dietz AND
Arthur Schwartz

Alone Together
A Shine On Your Shoes
Smokin' Reefers
Louisiana Hayride
A Rainy Day

HARMS
NEW YORK
CHAPPELL & CO. LTD.

Flying Colors (1932)

Breakdown

While the method of this book is to include people and productions with which the reader is likely to be familiar, the tale that follows does not fit the formula (although cameo roles are played by Noël Coward and Harpo Marx). Even so, the tryout troubles depicted will, I feel, add something to the discussion.

Max Gordon (1892–1978) hailed from the streets of the lower East Side of New York City, or what they nowadays refer to as the teeming lower East Side. One of eight children of an $11-a-week pants presser, Gordon's eldest brother, Morris Salpeter, went into burlesque. By 1902, Morris—using the stage name "Cliff Gordon"—was successful enough to move the family out of the tenements. At seventeen, Max went out on the burlesque circuit as an advance man. In 1912 he formed a partnership with burlesque comic Al Lewis. Lewis and Gordon were artist's agents, booking vaudeville acts. Within two years they hit upon the idea of producing full-scale one act plays on the vaudeville circuit, with significant success. (Among the plays was Eugene O'Neill's *In the Zone*.) In 1920 they became associated with Broadway producer Sam Harris, as associate producers on a string of successful plays.

In 1926 Gordon left to become head of the New York office of the Orpheum Circuit. But the coming of talking pictures in 1927, the merger of Orpheum into Radio-Keith-Orpheum (or R.K.O.) in 1928,

This sheet music cover promises a bountiful entertainment, although the promises went unfulfilled. First-time choreographer Agnes de Mille was fired on the road.

and the stock market crash in 1929 put Gordon back on the street, wiped out. Groucho Marx, an old vaudeville buddy, has reported that Gordon called him up, and "in a voice that sounded as if it came from the grave, said 'Marx, the jig is up.'"

One morning in the spring of 1930, Gordon read that the producers of the successful 1929 intimate revue *The Little Show* were producing a sequel. The principal songwriters Arthur Schwartz and Howard Dietz were being retained, but the three stars, Clifton Webb, Libby Holman and Fred Allen were unfathomably bypassed. With nothing to lose, Gordon signed up the stars, as well as Schwartz and Dietz. On October 15, 1930—on borrowed money—Gordon presented *Three's a Crowd*, which set a new standard for the sophisticated, intimate Broadway revue.

Gordon and his songwriters immediately went to work on a successor, with the same quality but on a more lavish scale. Dietz and Schwartz wanted to write the entire score themselves, which was almost unheard of in a Broadway revue; and they insisted that all the sketches come from one writer as well. With George S. Kaufman as the writer and Fred and Adele Astaire as the stars, *The Band Wagon*—assembled in less than four months—was an even bigger hit than *Three's a Crowd*. Very few people are around who saw *The Band Wagon*, but they all seem to insist that it was the finest Broadway musical revue ever. (The 1953 M-G-M film *The Bandwagon* starred Fred Astaire and featured the songs of Dietz and Schwartz, but otherwise had nothing to do with the 1931 revue.)

Gordon's one-two punch did not escape the notice of Broadway's greatest composer of the time, Jerome Kern. With his former producers (Ziegfeld, Dillingham, Arthur Hammerstein) on the verge of bankruptcy, Kern allowed Gordon to produce his new *The Cat and the Fiddle*; another hit, and one that opened exactly one year to the day after *Three's a Crowd*. With other producers forced to cut back by the Depression, newcomer Gordon was suddenly the only success in town. Thus, Noël Coward—looking for an independent management to partner with him and the Lunts in his upcoming *Design for Living*—invited Gordon aboard for what was sure to be the most successful comedy of the year. Thirty years later, Gordon recounted what happened in his 1963 autobiography, *Max Gordon Presents*.

"Disaster, with Music"
by Max Gordon with Lewis Funke

Nothing endures, cynical poets wail. Certainly the state of euphoria induced by my triumphant encounter with Noël Coward did not. A few all too brief weeks of excitement, the Broadway buzzing, the ego satisfaction of sideward glances as I entered a restaurant, the sense of soaring onward and upward, the vain, deluding human assumption that what was happening to others around me would never happen to me—a few all too brief weeks and it was all over. The cloud to which I had ascended vanished into thin air.

In the joyous excitement following the opening of *The Band Wagon*, I had agreed to do another revue with Howard Dietz and Arthur Schwartz. In retrospect it was a foolish thing to have done. There is a saying about going to the well once too often. But there is also a fairly general tradition that a producer goes along with successful writers. My agreement was not only natural but almost obligatory. Dietz and Schwartz had given me two hits in a row—in the case of *Three's a Crowd* it was not their fault that conditions on the road were such that the show failed to make money.

In the spring of 1932, as the Depression slipped further and further into what was to be its darkest period, getting money for the new show, *Flying Colors*, was impossible. Bankrolls—what there were of them—had gone into hiding. Brokers on whom I had counted were in trouble. [*The Band Wagon* had been financed with a $99,000 "buy"; ticket brokers advanced the money in exchange for virtually all the prime seats for the early months of the run.] There was talk of surprisingly few new productions. Many producers who kept going figured that the only things to do were revivals. At least the royalties could be eliminated in the case of classics, and old sets were available.

My own personal financial position deteriorated. As a successful producer I had convinced myself that it was necessary to keep up appearances. At the same time I was intent on trying to protect stock market securities I had purchased on margin. The result was an accumulation of debts reaching close to one hundred thousand dollars. On the face of it my behavior appears now to have been the epitome of vainglorious folly. Actually, it was not an extraordinary or wildly illogical position.

I had gone into producing on borrowed money. There was nothing wrong with this. Businessmen frequently do, expecting to repay their obligations from profits. I had expected to begin repaying my debts with the profits from *Three's a Crowd*. This turned out to be a miscalculation. [The show closed in New York with a small profit, but deteriorating conditions on the road resulted in a brief tour with huge losses.] *The Band Wagon* did close its engagement with a ninety-thousand-dollar profit, half of which was mine, and *The Cat and the Fiddle* had just about cleared its investment at the time of my meeting with Coward. Running strongly, I figured it would go a long way toward my making good my intentions. But this was not to be. Instead, unable to raise the required capital for *Flying Colors* from outside sources, I was forced to use my profits.

THE IMPERIAL THEATRE

FLYING COLORS

Tamara Geva, Clifton Webb, Patsy Kelly, and Charles Butterworth before the curtain.

Because of the economic climate we decided that although we would try to do another sophisticated, modern revue for essentially the same audience that had admired *Three's a Crowd* and *The Band Wagon*, we could not afford to make it too restricted for the general taste. Hence the decision to present the revue on a somewhat larger scale than *The Band Wagon*.

We signed Clifton Webb, always good insurance. He could dance, act, clown, and sing. Indeed, one critic had said of him "little or no scenery is needed when Webb is on the stage—he is his own production." From *Three's a Crowd* we brought back the fetching and excellent Tamara Geva. We hired the incomparably funny Charles Butterworth, who could give the appearance of a man always in need of someone to help him cross the street, whose grasp of any subject could be as feeble and confused as an American tourist in a five o'clock Paris traffic jam. To round out an excellent cast, we signed Vilma and Buddy Ebsen. [This was a sister-brother team of eccentric dancers. Long after his dancing days, Buddy Ebsen went on to become a folksy TV star.]

Dietz decided, with my agreement, to seek a fresh talent for the large dance numbers. After watching some of the work of the able but, from a Broadway point of view, completely inexperienced Agnes de Mille, we gave her the job. We also decided, for a change of pace and because of his heralded flair for the spectacular, to give the scene designing assignment to Norman Bel Geddes. Dietz himself would handle the general direction.

We went into rehearsal in August. It was hot and I was nervous. Nor did it help my anxiety to discover that the mercurial Kern, reunited with his former partner Oscar Hammerstein 2d, had written a new show, *Music in the Air*, which, without a word to me, he had given to another producer. As I have indicated, there is a general tradition for producers and writers to continue their relationship after they have enjoyed success together, unless that relationship has been an unhappy one for business or personal reasons. Kern never had given me any reason to believe that whatever disagreements we had during the tryout period of *The Cat and the Fiddle* had lingered. On the contrary, he had sworn undying fealty to me following an incident that occurred in the Globe Theatre not long after the opening.

The theatre had been in the process of changing ownership. On the Saturday night of the week in which the transaction was made, I went to the box office to collect the show's share of the gross receipts and discovered that someone had appropriated the till. I had no money on which I could put my hands. Phone calls to the various members of the Erlanger firm, which had a forty-per-cent interest in the show, proved futile. The actors had to be paid, and I was determined not to stay a moment longer in that theatre.

In a white-hot anger I ran to Tillie Leblang, then one of the leading ticket brokers, and pleaded with her to lend me ten thousand dollars so that I could pay the cast and move the production to the George M. Cohan, which I knew was available. I signed a note for the money. On Monday I went to the Erlanger office and told them what had happened. Saul Baron and Marc Heiman listened with mild interest. When I suggested that the Erlanger firm ought to join me in the note to Tillie Leblang, Baron bluntly and with what amounted to tacit agreement from Heiman, refused. From Kern, at least, I gained praise. He called me his hero and blessed me over and over again. [It turned out that the money had been taken in desperation by Charles Dillingham, who was at that time running the production end of the Erlanger office. Dillingham (1868-1934) was Broadway's most respected producer of musicals for twenty-five years, with credits including Victor Herbert's *The Red Mill*, Irving Berlin's *Watch Your Step*, and Kern's *Sunny*. The Globe Theatre, which Dillingham built in 1910, closed the night that Dillingham stole the receipts. It returned to legit use in 1958, as the Lunt-Fontanne.]

Thus, Kern's action in regard to his new show was a bitter blow. The continuing slide in the nation's economy and the unsatisfactory rehearsals of *Flying Colors* did not help my state of mind. I had not been a sound sleeper for years. Now I began to suffer from insomnia and nerves. The slightest noise made me jump. I became increasingly irritable, and found myself screaming at Millie over minor incidents, something I had never done before. [Millie was vaudeville dancer Mildred Bartlett, whom Gordon married in 1921.]

Instead of matters improving for *Flying Colors*, they seemed to grow worse. Agnes de Mille, who was to distinguish herself so brilliantly in musical comedy choreography time and again, was unused to the pressures of preparing a Broadway show. Insecure in her handling of Broadway-type dancers, she was unable to organize rehearsals satisfactorily. Bel Geddes, overbearing and unsympathetic, insisted that some of the dances be made to fit what Miss de Mille regarded as unsafe sets. There were bitter arguments. Dietz tried to maintain the peace—fortifying himself with the help of a flask. Schwartz frequently lost his temper. Webb and Tamara, refusing to be caught up in the uncertainties of what was going on, proceeded to take care of their own numbers.

I was helpess. I shouted. But matters had gotten to the point where no one was paying any attention to me. "What's going to happen to me?" I wailed as visions of my indebtedness rose before my eyes. I began to worry about what would happen to Millie, to my mother, to Millie's mother and father, all of whom were dependent upon me for support. Fantasies leaped into my fevered brain. I saw myself working as a stage doorman, while Millie slaved in some department store—Millie, whose career I had clipped short out of my own selfishness.

Sleep now left me almost entirely. One day as I sat in the back of the theatre watching rehearsals, I began to sob. I knew that I was in deep mental trouble. In the succeeding days nothing anyone would say or do could calm me. Millie begged me to see a doctor. I refused. I was terrified at what the doctor might say. The crying continued. In the middle of ordinary conversations the merest hint of disagreement caused tears.

The night of the run-through was unbearably hot. It did not help me either to see what was in progress on the stage. I felt myself being pushed to the edge of panic. More than ever now a sense of impending disaster began to rise within me, like a swollen river fed by flooded mountain streams. Friends assured me that the show would be in shape by opening night; "it always is" are among the more famous words in the theatre. Tormented mercilessly in my mind, unable to sit still, unable to stand still, I headed for Philadelphia and the beginning of the tryout period.

The dress rehearsal in Philadelphia was my Inferno. I sat between Millie and Ben Boyar, my general manager. Nothing seemed ready— the dances, costumes, lighting—everything was out of joint. The rehearsal went on for hours. It was almost three o'clock in the morning. All that I had built and striven for in the last two and a half years was being washed away.

The Forrest Theatre, where the rehearsal took place, has a curving marble staircase. I happened to turn around, and it caught my eye. A thought flashed through my mind—at least Millie would have the insurance. I jumped from my seat and ran toward the staircase. Up the steps, up and around I ran until I had gained the top. Behind me came Millie and Boyar. They were calling me back. I began to climb the balustrade. I remember nothing else. Boyar told me later that I was threatening to jump. I hesitated. Boyar grabbed me.

When I regained a semblance of sanity, Millie and he persuaded me to return to my suite at the Ritz-Carlton. They thought it would be a good idea if we walked. They clutched me lest I break away. All the way back I cried, berated those associated with me, repeated mournfully that I was bankrupt, dishonored, that life was useless and no longer worth living. I wished I were dead.

The New York billing page.

As we entered the room, I found myself free and made a dash for the window. Boyar caught me again. He held me while Millie called a doctor. I was put under sedation. The next day they brought me back to New York, to the Leroy Sanitarium—behind bars. My lawyer and lifelong friend Abe Berman took over the management of my affairs and my interest in *Flying Colors*. My old and trusted friend Owen Davis protected my securities with his own funds. I was engulfed in what the doctors called a nervous breakdown.

Those first weeks in Leroy Sanitarium were one long, tormented nightmare. I made little progress. Actually, from a physical standpoint there is not much that doctors can do for a person whose nerve signals have become so jangled that they resemble the lights on a telephone switchboard gone wild. Sedation, warm packs, rest. That is all.

Suggestions that I submit to psychiatry seemed to upset me. In the end each case is individual and recovery depends to a considerable degree on the complexity of the disturbance and the patient's own will to recover and live. For what seemed like an eternity to those near me, I did not care. There was no use in telling myself that after a series of hits I was entitled to one failure. All reason, all sense of proportion had fled.

Millie kept her vigil at my bedside, devoted, loyal, understanding. I dared not look at her. When I did, I could only think of the predicament to which I had brought her, and tears would fill my eyes. I needed her there by my bed. Yet there were moments when the anguish of these nightmarish visions made me wish she would go away.

Through the long hours of the night, as the tears streamed onto my pillow, I would try to review what had happened, how I had come to this pass from which there seemed to be no return. Occasionally there cut through the hopelessness the recollection that I was to produce Noël Coward's play. But that did not help me either. Suppose Coward was to know that the man to whom he had entrusted his play was nearly out of his mind, a bundle of uncontrolled, jangled nerves, that this man was deep in debt? What would he do? Would I lose the play? Was there to be no relief from these burdens that had overwhelmed me?

The weeks passed. Rest and treatment had their effects. Raw nerves healed and quieted. My brain cleared. My body regained its strength, the crying became less frequent, less acute. Bleak despair gave way to cautious hope and gradually to determination.

Friends helped—those who would let few days pass without calling, without trying to give some word of cheer; those who wrote encouraging notes, who tried to say what I needed to hear....

There was a visit to the hospital by Harpo Marx that has been one of the more warming memories of my life. Harpo spent an hour with me, humoring me, showing me the promise of the future. As he arose to leave, he reached into his pocket and withdrew a roll of bills, threw it across the bed, and ran for the door. Four thousand dollars were strewn around—needed, helpful, reassuring. The following day Groucho called to tell me he knew what Harpo had done. "I want you to know," Groucho said, "that I've got fifty per cent and there is more where that came from."

I cried. But these were not the bitter tears. They were the warming, heartening, cleansing tears—in their own way now helping me back to reality and new life.

Flying Colors had opened, not the shambles I had dreaded, nor the disgrace. Agnes de Mille had been relieved of her assignment and

Albertina Rasch called to the rescue. [The uncompromising de Mille was also fired from her next Broadway musical, *Hooray for What!* Her 1942 ballet *Rodeo*, to a score by Aaron Copland, secured her one more chance at Broadway, on the similarly-set musical *Oklahoma!* Rasch had choreographed Gordon's first three musicals, although she is perhaps best remembered for George S. Kaufman's gibe while sitting through one of her dances: "I'm breaking out in an Albertina Rasch."] The reviews were mild, the comparison with *The Band Wagon* inevitable. There was praise for three of the songs: "Louisiana Hayride," "Alone Together," and "A Shine on Your Shoes." The company was hailed and yet there was a pallor and a kind of languor over it all.

Happily, as time passed, I succeeded in accepting *Flying Colors* for what it was, a chapter among the darker pages of my chronicle. Now, I told myself, I must look forward only. I must completely regain my health and work as hard as I could to repay the friends who placed faith and funds in me and my career. I prayed that *Design for Living* would be my lifeline, and was daily encouraged by the excitement it appeared to be generating. Coward helped stoke the simmering hub-bub by letting it be known that he had deliberately written the play for the Lunts and himself.

As *Flying Colors* neared the end of its engagement—188 performances at a cost of $125,000, none of which it regained—I received a call from John C. Wilson, Coward's American representative and business associate. Coward, Wilson announced, would shortly be on his way from England. I was to make arrangements for a theatre and an opening date.

Flying Colors opened September 15, 1932 at the Imperial Theatre, to mixed reviews. It closed there January 25, 1933 after 188 performances, with a total loss.

Gordon's breakdown in Philadelphia—which he wrote about so candidly in 1963, a time when such things were not openly discussed—appears not to have been his first experience with mental illness. Years before, brother Cliff had attained nationwide prominence with his vaudeville act "The German Senator." In 1913, impresario Martin Beck helped legitimize vaudeville by importing the living legend Sarah Bernhardt. (The Divine Sarah insisted upon being paid in gold.) On April 23, Cliff Gordon was programmed to follow Bernhardt on the bill at the Majestic in Chicago. At the matinee, his act received not a laugh. "Any comedian who tries to follow Bernhardt is bound to die," he said, coming off stage. Cliff Gordon did not show up for the evening performance. He was found dead, in the hotel bathtub. A heart attack was the verdict, but from Max Gordon's description one wonders whether it wasn't suicide. Cliff Gordon was thirty-three.

Cliff's death sent the twenty-one-year-old Max into a severe depression. He withdrew for months, with his weight falling from 150 to 118 pounds. It was then, somehow, that he hit upon the idea of producing one-acts for the vaudeville circuit, with good will from friends of Cliff helping float the idea.

By December 1932, Gordon was back on the road with the tryout of *Design for Living*. The show opened on Broadway January 24, 1933—the night before *Flying Colors* closed—to a completely sold-out run. It was indeed one of the theatrical highlights of the decade, although by no means a goldmine. The deals were, understandably, steep. Ten percent of the gross went to each of the three stars, with another ten to Coward as author; and Coward insisted on a limited engagement of only twelve weeks. "I get bored after that," he said, "and besides I've other things to do." In the end, Coward extended to seventeen weeks. After splitting the profits with Coward and the Lunts, Gordon wound up with $42,000. Not a fortune, but substantial in 1933.

In the 1933–34 season Gordon had four successes simultaneously. All told, he produced fifty-odd shows; some hits, some flops. His musical record after *Flying Colors* was spotty. *Roberta* was a hit, despite severe tryout troubles during which Gordon was forced to fire the director—Kern himself, who unaccountably insisted on trying to stage the show. Gordon's other six musicals failed, despite the presence of names like Porter, Moss Hart, Kern, Hammerstein, Kaufman, Ira Gershwin, and Weill. Gordon more than made up for it with his non-musical hits, including *Dodsworth*, *Junior Miss*, *My Sister Eileen*, and two of Broadway's biggest blockbuster comedies, Clare Booth's *The Women* and Garson Kanin's *Born Yesterday*.

Colonial
Theatre

PLAYBILL

the magazine for theatregoers

ON A CLEAR DAY
YOU CAN SEE FOREVER

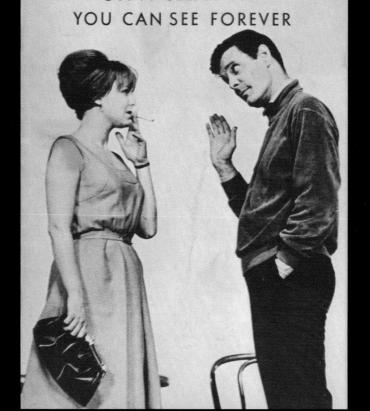

On a Clear Day You Can See Forever (1965)

A Shot in the Arm

Lyricist-librettist Alan Jay Lerner hired Doris Shapiro as his personal assistant in 1952, during the filming of *Brigadoon*. Shapiro remained with him through *My Fair Lady*, *Gigi*, *Camelot*, and into the troubled tryout period of *On a Clear Day You Can See Forever* in 1965.

Clear Day began life as a very different property. *I Picked a Daisy* was announced for March 1963, with Lerner joined by composer Richard Rodgers and director-choreographer Gower Champion (a year before his blockbuster *Hello, Dolly!*). Barbara Harris, the Second City alumnus who had dazzled the Broadway hierarchy in Jerome Robbins's production of Arthur Kopit's *Oh, Dad, Poor Dad, Mama's Hung You in the Closet and I'm Feeling So Sad*, was signed to star opposite TV-star Robert Horton.

By 1962, though, Lerner had grown impossible to work with. When Lerner disappeared to Capri—and stood up Rodgers—once too often, the composer pulled out of the project. Lerner eventually turned to Burton Lane, with whom he had written the score for the 1951 Fred Astaire movie *Royal Wedding* (containing the standard "Too Late Now"). Lane found Lerner as difficult as Rodgers had; but

The Boston *Playbill* features a rehearsal shot of Barbara Harris and Louis Jourdan.

not having written a Broadway musical since *Finian's Rainbow* in 1947, the opportunity of writing a show with the author of *My Fair Lady* was too good to pass up. As with *Camelot*, Lerner chose to serve as producer of *Clear Day*.

There were no doubt many reasons for Lerner's erratic behavior, but they were enhanced by the magical injections he received from society doctor Max Jacobsen. "Dr. Feelgood" (as he came to be known, derisively) offered what was apparently a concoction of enzymes, vitamins, zinc, calcium—and Methedrine (speed). Whatever was in his shots, they certainly had an effect. His patients, reportedly, ran the gamut from John F. Kennedy to Tennessee Williams, from Eddie Fisher to Howard Cosell. Lerner soon introduced Shapiro to the shots, and Dr. Max became such an integral part of *Clear Day* that he left his office in the care of assistants and accompanied the show to Boston. Shapiro relates the strange tale of *Clear Day* in her 1990 autobiography.

from "We Danced All Night"

by Doris Shapiro

Coming home in the car from the runthrough in New York, we brought Louis Jourdan with us. He was handsome, had an actor's gallantry, and already knew all his lines. Though he was not a trained singer, he had been taking voice lessons for the show. He was going to half sing, half act the songs the way he did in *Gigi*. [Robert Horton had withdrawn from the project when *I Picked a Daisy* was cancelled. Jourdan, who introduced "She Is Not Thinking of Me" and "Gigi" in the 1958 film, came in to play the male lead. Lane, however, expressed deep concern that Jourdan was unable to sing the booming ballads he had written for the character.]

"You'll sing, you'll see," said Dr. Max mysteriously.

"Okay with me," said Louis. "I'll try anything once."

The doctor didn't give him the big shot in the vein in his arm. He got the little one in his hip.

"How do you feel?" said Max gruffly, looking down at his hands.

Louis was a polite man. "Marvelous, Doctor, thank you," he said, tightening his belt.

"Let me hear you."

He let out a note.

"Can you hear your voice in your ears?"

Louis sang a phrase. "Yes, I can. Like an echo chamber?"

Max nodded wisely. "Now go back and tell me how you sing."

"Where's Alan?" It was Burton Lane in the darkened theatre.

"He's coming." Me, still being protective.

Louis Jourdan was singing onstage to the piano.

"Have you noticed," I said, "his voice seems to sound bigger?"

"I'm still worried," Burton said to Bud. [Stone "Bud" Widney, Lerner's "production supervisor," served as all around creative assistant. It was Widney who found and developed the idea for *Camelot*.]

"He sounds like the character to me," Bud said. "A little biting, impatient, almost bullying when it comes to the establishment. I don't think Alan intended him to stand still and sing a song."

"He may be all right in the patter songs, but he's going to need a voice for 'On a Clear Day.'"

"Do you notice," said Alan's voice in the dark—he slipped into a seat—"how his voice is improved?"

"He's not a singer, Alan."

"But listen to him. Don't you notice a change?"

"He's a sweet guy and a good actor, but I'm worried about him singing my score."

"Well, don't. He'll do it. He's a star, you know."

It was time for the fun part of the show, with the actors, orchestra, lights, audience. Time to watch a great big new Alan Jay Lerner musical get dressed up and move into the sets and come to life for the public.

The Boston Common was planted with September mums. The lake glistened; the sky was blue. I felt a slight foretaste of autumn when I opened the window. Such a civilized, small, pretty city.

There was no sign of Alan at the theatre. No messages.

"The singers are at the Hotel Victoria, the dancers are in the lobby, and the actors are downstairs reading their lines." The stage manager was steering me carefully over the dangerous boards and props backstage toward the front of the theatre.

"Where's Alan?" he said.

"He'll be here anytime. He's driving up in the car," I lied, guarding the secret of the chartered yacht. [Lerner had chartered an eighty-five foot yacht to sit in Boston Harbor, for trysts with his mistress, a member of a scandal-plagued political dynasty.]

I wandered toward the sound of piano music. Herbert Ross was conducting a dancers' rehearsal. "Where's Alan?" he said cordially. [Choreographer Herb Ross started the year with Kelly (see page 328), which he followed by doctoring the Richard Rodgers-Stephen Sondheim *Do I Hear a Waltz?* Ross was credited as choreographer (or replacement choreographer) on twelve Broadway musicals, from 1951 through 1966. All of the shows were failures, although Ross's work was usually praised.]

"He should be here anytime now. He's driving up in the car with the chauffeur. When I see him, I'll tell him you have something to tell him," I said politely.

I went downstairs. The two stars and the director were rehearsing a scene. I stood in the shadows and feeling self-conscious, started to leave.

"Where's Alan? I need him to see something." It was Bobby Lewis, the director. Small and bald and plump, he had no charisma that I could see, and I thought of the theatrical Moss Hart. [Robert Lewis, a co-founder of the Actors' Studio, directed twenty Broadway shows including Lerner's *Brigadoon* and *Kwamina* (see page 146). Moss Hart, who died in 1961, directed *My Fair Lady* and *Camelot*.]

"He's driving up in the car with Tony. He should be here anytime now."

As I tiptoed away, someone moved behind a pillar.

"What are you doing here?" I whispered to Tony. I pulled him away with me. "Everybody's looking for Mr. Lerner. He's supposed to be driving up with you. You'd better stay out of sight."

I hurried around the corner to the Victoria Hotel. The rehearsal was taking place in the old ballroom.

"There you are!"

It was Bud.

"Alan has been looking all over for you."

The sound of the chorus was enormous in the room, the melodies enlarged to the tenth power by the choral arrangement. I slid happily into a seat beside Alan. He was looking his working best, with a bit of windburn on his face. The music filled the room, exciting everybody.

"It's going to be great," I whispered.

He squeezed my hand.

"It does sound good, doesn't it?' he said.

The voices were building to the climax of "On a Clear Day You Can See Forever," and then, in big Broadway musical style, by repeating a word (the word was "forever-and-ever-and-evermore"), they climbed to the heights and ended at the summit. Everybody was smiling. Even Burton Lane.

"What time did the doctor get in?" Alan asked the chauffeur.

"Just half an hour ago, Mr. Lerner. I helped him with his bag up to the room."

"Good. We'll feel better now," he said to me.

Tony pulled up to the hotel. We got out.

The doctor had packed enough medicine for everybody. I had reserved a room for him on the same floor as ours. Alan wasn't waving a red flag, but he wasn't being overly discreet about the doctor either. For the moment it was more convenient to have him in the hotel. If people met and passed each other in the corridors, so be it. Alan was no longer in the mood to shield Burton Lane from an encounter. Burton wasn't about to quit at this stage.

In the absence of Max with the real thing, I had gotten in the habit of giving myself one of the small shots in my hip every time I felt myself getting ragged. They kept me from sleeping but didn't make me feel good. Now as the doctor slowly pushed the lever, I felt unbelievably clarified again, as though I had been living a half-life for the two days before he came. Alan was holding a piece of cotton to his arm and looking at me in the mirror. Our eyes met. He smiled. So did the doctor. I cast my eyes down. It was too intimate.

The front of the Colonial Theatre was milling with people dressed for the Boston opening. I ran around to the stage door. It was after eight. A few minutes to curtain time. I needed my shot. Backstage it was chaos.

"Have you seen the doctor?"

"I saw him going into Louis's dressing room about ten minutes ago," said Bud.

"Are you looking for that strange-looking man with the glasses?" It was one of the dancers.

"Yes, the doctor."

"He's looking for Barbara's dressing room."

Barbara Harris's dressing room door was ajar. Barbara was standing nervously in front of the mirror like a patient committed to surgery, while the hair man was adjusting her hair. Behind her, Max, looking a little wild in his haste, was bending down sticking a needle into her hip.

The top-billed Jourdan was replaced in Boston, with Harris moving into first position.

"Is this all right?" Barbara said to me in the mirror in a tense voice.

"Absolutely," I said, longing to hold out my arm.

"You'll hear for yourself if it's all right when you get out there," muttered the doctor.

Bostonians know they're a tryout audience. They can be tough. But opening night of an Alan Jay Lerner musical anywhere was a celebration. I could hear the bassoon and violin warming up when I showed the doctor to a seat and sat down in my own next to Alan's empty one in the last row on the aisle.

I saw Oliver Smith slouching long-legged and reassuringly casual and unworried nearby. He had designed hundreds of shows.

The lights were dimming. The conductor entered. Applause. It was an expectant audience, excited, a show-me audience. He raised his baton for the overture. Instruments up, and suddenly we were plunged into music. Brass. Woodwinds. A flood of strings sweeping over all and carrying us in the arms of Burton Lane's melodies, which were orchestrated into an opiate state of bliss. I felt myself go. I petted Alan's sleeve and smiled at him in the dark. I was in a kind of agonizing empathy for everyone. I felt for Alan, whose last three years of work were about to be laid bare for all to sample and criticize. Every word, every moment, was on trial, to be taken with delight or passed over unnoticed. No wonder he wore dark glasses.

I felt for the actors, who had to face the audience for the first time, with nothing but themselves to offer.

The curtain was rising, and there was applause for Oliver's set. A door opened, and out stepped Louis Jourdan. Irascible, impatient, irreverent, Alan's favorite kind of hero, he strode out, calling for his secretary with all the assurance of a lifetime of star performances. I slid down in my seat and relaxed.

That this big festive show was pouring out whole and effortlessly, with coherence and style, when only an hour ago it had been in pieces was a miracle to me. And although I could anticipate every word that was coming, tonight it was a new experience, for the last missing ingredient was there: the audience. Ready to give back its listening silence, its laughter and applause.

It was going to be a hit.

By intermission I had two pages of notes from Alan. Nothing big. Notes on performance, notes to the director, notes to the stage manager, notes to tighten the weave as much as possible, so that no sign of a seam showed; notes to trim, heighten, shape.

I wandered in the crowded lobby, trying to pick up people's comments. It was dense and noisy. People were smiling and talking a lot. Boston society was there.

"They love it," we said to Alan, bursting into the manager's office. "Did you hear the applause?"

Burton Lane was swiveling back in a chair; Bud and the general manager, Irving Squires, were there. Oliver Smith, tall and smiling, was leaning against a wall.

"They love the score," I said excitedly. "They're talking about the score—the lyrics."

"It's going to be fine," said Oliver simply.

Alan was pacing. I went to the typewriter and started to type my notes.

"Louis and Barbara play charmingly together, don't you think?" said Alan.

"We'll see how he sings 'On a Clear Day,'" said Burton.

We heard the bell.

"We'll see what time the curtain comes down is what we'll see," said Alan, clenching his teeth a little.

We waited for the lights to go out before we went to our seats. The orchestra was playing. The audience was part of the show now, involved, affectionate even, humming the tunes as they came back to their seats to live it out to the end.

But at ten of eleven, when there was no end in sight, they began to get a little restless.

Alan looked at his watch. We had to be out of the theatre by eleven o'clock or pay overtime. Enough overtime to make profits shrivel.

A man and woman walked quickly and embarrassedly up the aisle and out.

Alan got up and paced in the back. The jokes were still working, the songs were, but the scenes were losing shape.

Cutting, I thought. It needs to be cut. With the audience there, certain lines that nobody had ever noticed in rehearsal became superfluous. Somewhere in the middle the show became heavy and began to list.

But it wasn't anything that couldn't be fixed. I heard them laughing; I watched them listening. They were loving it. Applause. The audience and the actors had become old friends. They were still willingly following Alan to the end. It just needed to be cut. It was eleven-thirty. About ten couples had walked out. Baby-sitters had to go home. By tomorrow night it would already start to be trimmed. Alan had three weeks to get it down to size.

At around eleven-forty the last chorus ended. Daisy Gamble and Mark embraced, and the curtain came down. The applause was briefer that it would have been forty minutes earlier. The theatre was emptied within five minutes.

Much of the trouble was in the second act. It's the second act that tells you whether you have a show or not.

"It can be fixed," said Oliver Smith, biting into a sandwich. I never saw him lose his cool, even when the turntables in *My Fair Lady* wouldn't work.

Two carts with white linen from room service were piled with sandwiches and coffee.

But if collaboration means laboring together, that was not what was happening at this meeting after the show. Everybody was laboring on and for his own.

"I still would like to see a singer in the role," was Burton Lane's contribution. He had been huddling darkly with Bud Widney, talking about John Cullum. He was the singer whom Richard Burton had befriended in *Camelot,* who had become Burton's understudy. John Cullum was a name that some people in the theatre knew.

"That's not the problem, Burton," Alan said quietly. He had been sitting with his feet up on the couch, listening thoughtfully to everybody with an inner look on his face.

Irving Squires, the manager, said it cost thousands of dollars to pay overtime. He hoped some scenes could be cut out by tomorrow night. Bobby Lewis and Herbert Ross were there.

"Let me sit up with it and see what I can do," Alan was saying. Everybody was exhausted. They were glad to leave him to wrestle with it. He sat with Bud and me, and I waited for him to produce magic as he had in *My Fair Lady.*

At 2:00 A.M. Bud went off to bed. At 3:00, Alan and I went in search of the doctor. He was in his room, sitting on the bed, sleepily giving himself a shot.

"What do you think, Max?" Alan said, plopping down on the other bed.

Max nodded his head. "It can be all right."

The reviews weren't bad. They didn't harp on the obvious length problem.

Alan did radical surgery; he decided to cut out the psychiatrist's family. He and Bud had talked for two days about it. Painstaking work, but he hoped he would lose a big chunk of time. It meant giving up a whole comedic portion of the musical. He would try to rescue some of the gags, of course, but the family had to go. Bud was all for it. I felt Alan was being reckless, acting out of control. But I didn't say a word.

"Let's go to work," he said to me, clipping fresh yellow paper onto his clipboard.

With the doctor back in New York, Alan was not looking good. His eyes had begun to water. He had developed a cold sore on his lip. He couldn't seem to find a way to be comfortable. The skin around his eyes was raw from wiping them almost constantly for two days.

I had terrible palpitations. I sat frozen like a stone in a bamboo chair meant for luxuriant pleasure. The skin on my face was beginning to feel as if it were stretched.

"Page eight-seven," Alan said in a small, tight voice. "Cut from line nine, the rest of the page." He turned a page. "Page eighty-eight, cut to line... let me see... line sixteen...." He wiped at his eyes.

I was horrified. He was falling apart. So was I. What was keeping him from calling the doctor? What if we were hooked? Was this the time to quit? I ventured: "Do you think you might want to call Max?"

He looked up and eyed me suspiciously.

"You know," he said, "the shots may be all right for men, but I don't think they're the best thing in the world for women." He stared at me. "If I were you, I'd be careful."

Women? Careful? What's he up to? I thought. Are we having withdrawal symptoms? I couldn't believe it.

Another hour passed. Alan put down his script and said wearily, "I think I'm getting a migraine headache. Call the doctor." [Robert Lewis, in his 1984 autobiography *Slings and Arrows*: "It was particularly painful to be asked over and over by professionals, after the opening, 'Bobby, why didn't you get Alan to fix the book?' Marrying and divorcing might have been distractions from the work at hand, but the never-ending ministrations of the doctor were, in my layman's opinion, what seriously impaired Alan's creative potential.... As far as his marital affairs were concerned, they would have been none of my business, if it were not for the fact that his mind, and time, were frequently distracted by myriads of lawyers, his and those of the wife he was then divorcing, herself a French lawyer. Add to this the necessary activities connected with the wooing of the current lady friend, plus daily ministrations from the doctor, and you can figure how much time was left for work on the script and lyrics."]

Nobody may ever know what it was the doctor gave. But what we did know was that it took away Alan's headache instantly. His eyes stopped leaking at once. Within a few hours, the cold sore had healed. It worked. And he worked.

When Bud appeared in the doorway after breakfast, we were getting more shots. We weren't fooling around any longer. There was no talk of the doctor's going home.

"I think I may have the script licked," said Alan quietly, pursing his lips. "I've taken out the family." He delivered it resignedly.

"Great. It has to come out of somewhere."

Alan sighed. "It's too bad. They were funny."

Bud shrugged.

"I've managed to save some of the jokes. We'll put it into rehearsal today."

"The sooner the better. I suppose you want me to fire the five actors?"

"No. That's the manager's job. What I want you to do is get in touch with him so he can do it before the rehearsal starts. I don't want to come to the theatre and have to see people who are fired and don't know it yet."

Bud went to the phone.

"And be sure he knows, of course, that they have to play it once more tonight."

"Right."

I said to Alan, "It's amazing how the actors can do it; read the new pages today in rehearsal and still play the family version for the audience tonight."

"I work harder," said Alan.

That night we went to see the family's last performance. There they were, just as lively, quarrelsome, and funny as ever, though all day long they'd sat in the theatre watching themselves being wiped out of existence. Their bags were packed in the hotel, yet they played with all the enthusiasm of people in a snapshot at a party long gone by.

But the following night, despite their departure and all the cutting and manipulating, the curtain came down only ten minutes sooner. And with the family gone, the play lost color; there were some awkward transitions. Some of the texture had been loosened, leaving exposed moments that came

A herald for the Broadway production.

from the family. Mark was directing his dialogue to his friend Conrad. The stage seemed too empty.

"Let's work," said Alan. "The ending. Nobody likes it. I'm going to read the other two to the cast tomorrow, and put it to a vote. I'm tired of thinking about it. Let *them* decide."

"You're going to let the cast decide which ending to use?" I was being judgmental.

"Why not? Do you think it's sacred?"

"I dunno." I had assumed that after a whole evening of show there could be only one way that it could all come inevitably to rest.

"You're right," he said, "you don't know."

The next day he put it to a vote, as he said he would. The cast wanted Mark and Daisy to go off in a blaze of light in the airplane, no matter what the rational arguments against it were.

The director and the choreographer worked out a big walk toward the plane; it was decided the choral arranger should be called in New York to enlarge the music and put the changes on a plane that night; Abe Feder in New York redid the lighting by phone, and the whole cast was repositioned in the airport. We spend the afternoon in rehearsal. It wouldn't shorten the play, but it made everybody happier.

As Alan settled in for the siege, the yacht became a battleship. He almost never got up from his chair anymore. He had a grim look in his eyes, and when he moved, it was almost slow motion. He could concentrate only briefly and lapsed into little dozes.

Burton Lane never came to the boat, but the word from Bud was that Burton wanted Louis Jourdan out of the show and John Cullum in. If the play was going to go down, he wanted at least to rescue his score. Bud was beginning to go in Burton's direction.

I was aghast. They wanted to remove a big star and put in a singing actor. To be honest, I thought Louis's character, Mark, was not the most developed. But he did have charm. That was what Alan could write when all else failed. Louis Jourdan's charm was persuasive.

"We've taken the liberty of speaking to John Cullum. He could go in on two days' notice," said Bud, puffing on his pipe and looking deceptively casual.

"I wish you hadn't," said Alan.

"It wasn't my decision."

"I hope Louis doesn't suspect any of this."

"If he does, he hasn't indicated it."

"Burton wants to put John in the role."

Alan looked at me as he said it, and I knew he didn't want this.

"We'd have to pay off Louis. It would cost a fortune," Alan said.

"Burton thinks it's worth it. And who knows? Maybe with a big lyrical voice like John's the show would pick up some. It won't solve the job of cutting; you still have to do that. But this might help."

Alan said, "I wonder how Louis would take it?"

"Louis is a gentleman. I think he'd be the first one to understand. You know, he himself had doubts about singing the part."

"But I overcame them for him," said Alan. "I taught him how to deliver the songs."

He looked at me and the doctor, back at Bud. I kept my mouth shut. Alan looked down at his hands, and there was silence while he thought. When he spoke it was with resignation.

"I guess I'm the one who has to speak to Louis. Call him in his room," he said to me, "and see if I can come and have breakfast with him."

But Louis Jourdan didn't want to give up his part. He'd put a lot into it. He wanted more time to try harder. He asked for another week.

As Alan told this to Bud in the hotel room after breakfast with

Louis, he looked at me with concealed excitement. There was no doubt in my mind that he was delighted with Louis's position and that he would rescue him.

"I guess we have to give this guy a chance," said Alan to Bud. "We can't just sweep him out like dust."

Bud nodded noncommittally.

"Well," said Alan, getting up and squinting at himself in the mirror, "I told Bobby Lewis I'd stop by his room and have a chat. I'll meet you all at the theatre."

My attention lapsed (detachment that came with the shot). The next time I noticed, everybody had left, and I was lying on the couch alone in the room with Bud. Whether he saw me or not, he lifted the phone and called New York. It was Louis Jourdan's agent.

"Alan wants Louis out" is what I heard. "Speak to him—will you?—and explain it's not as if he'll lose anything. He can go off on vacation on full salary, for the good Lord's sake."

I was very confused. I was positive Alan had just told me he didn't want to switch leading men. But I knew Bud would never do this on his own. Alan must have said the opposite to Bud. I took it as another sign of Alan's giving in to pressure.

On Thursday night John Cullum went in and played Mark.

I felt it was a turning point in the disintegration of the musical. Alan was developing a bitter look around the mouth. Removing a big chunk that could come out had led nowhere. It looked as if the cuts were going to come from here, there, and everywhere.

Alan didn't go to rehearsals anymore. He was too busy writing. We went to the performances at night.

Performances were one step behind rehearsals, and because there was always enough new material to keep the actors slightly on edge and holding back in the new parts, the performances were uneven, sometimes shaky, tentative. They played what was left of the old play bigger, and the audiences seemed confused.

The actors brought their usual good-natured gallantry to the learning of the new lines, but people were being stretched to the limit. The grimness around Alan's mouth stayed.

"At this point all I want is to get through this decently." His mouth slackened, and he added plaintively, "If I ever get out of this alive."

The rest of the stay in Boston slipped by for me in a dim, punishing miasma of monotony. I remember one night at the theatre during a particularly tedious part of the performance, when I slipped out into the empty lobby to sit on a bench. Oliver Smith strolled up. I admired him; he was a cool, always good-natured professional. He had designed all of Alan's shows that I had worked on.

He smiled and sat next to me, with his long legs out in front of him.

"One day, Doris," he said, "we'll have lunch and talk about what happened to this show."

So it wasn't just my imagination. "It's been destroyed," I said. He nodded. We didn't talk about it anymore or ever. It was enough said.

On a Clear Day You Can See Forever opened at the Mark Hellinger Theatre on October 17, 1965 to mixed-to-unfavorable reviews. The show closed there on June 11, 1966 after 260 performances, with a substantial loss.

Alan Jay Lerner (1918-86) continued to struggle to recapture the magic of *My Fair Lady*. *Clear Day* was followed by the Chanel bio-musical *Coco* (with music by Andre Previn), which despite its many problems managed to eke by thanks to the box office strength of Katharine Hepburn. A Civic Light Opera adaptation of *Gigi*, for which Lerner reunited with Frederick Loewe for five new songs, made an unsuccessful Broadway visit in 1973. (The Tony Award eligibility rules, however, were bent to allow Lerner and Loewe to receive that season's award for Best Score.)

Lerner's final four new musicals were bonafide disasters, one more spectacular than another. *Lolita, My Love*, with music by John Barry, closed in Boston during its 1971 tryout; *1600 Pennsylvania Avenue*, with Leonard Bernstein, lasted one week in 1976; *Carmelina*, which Burton Lane undertook with understandable misgivings, lasted two weeks in 1979; and *Dance a Little Closer*, a musicalization of *Idiot's Delight* written with composer Charles Strouse, shuttered the night it opened in 1983.

These shows, from *Clear Day* on, were all mightily flawed—flaws that stemmed in great part from Lerner's erratic behavior. But each show contained stretches of wonderful writing; it almost seemed as if Lerner's finished work was still brilliant *but* he was only capable of finishing a quarter of what went on the stage. All the while, the once and future classic *My Fair Lady* continued to entertain audiences throughout the world.

As for Dr. Max, he eventually lost his license and disappeared from view—although his legend lives on the pages of every unflattering biography of John F. Kennedy.

Battle Stations

Pickwick

Rex

The Red Shoes

Nick & Nora

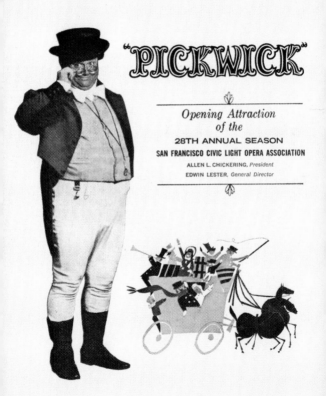

"PICKWICK"

Opening Attraction
of the
28TH ANNUAL SEASON
SAN FRANCISCO CIVIC LIGHT OPERA ASSOCIATION

ALLEN L. CHICKERING, *President*

EDWIN LESTER, *General Director*

Pickwick (1965)

A Case of Mumps

The following tale pits an outspoken actor against his vitriolic producer. It was played out after-the-fact, but still might prove illuminating. Jack Gaver, the drama critic for United Press International, gave a full account in his chronicle of the 1965–1966 season, *Season In, Season Out*.

Beloved British star Harry Secombe looking askance at the Broadway stage.

"Pickwick"

by Jack Gaver

One of the more diverting of several controversies destined, fortunately, to enliven a season that needed all of the extracurricular help it could get was, unfortunately, missed by the general public.

This was because (1) it came to light after the show at issue, *Pickwick*, had closed and was no longer news, and (2) its delightful details were confined to the pages of the weekly theatrical paper *Variety*, a not inconsiderable forum, but which is, after all, a trade paper. Since it constitutes an item in the growing list of Merrickiana, which is rapidly becoming a major part of the history of the theatre of our time, this tilt between producer David Merrick and British actor Peter Bull should be preserved in the archives.

The incident was the anticlimax of a promising venture involving a musical version of Charles Dickens' *The Pickwick Papers*. Wolf Mankowitz, one of England's more prolific, versatile, and successful writers, had sifted a workable string of incidents out of the prolix original. There was music by Cyril Ornadel, well known in London, if not here, and lyrics by Leslie Bricusse, already prominent on this side of the Atlantic as co-author with Anthony Newley of *Stop the World— I Want to Get Off* and *The Roar of the Greasepaint—the Smell of the Crowd*, both Merrick productions, by the way. It also had intricate and tricky settings designed by Sean Kenny, a *wunderkind* of recent years whose work seems to attract almost as much attention as that of the authors and stars of his shows. [Kenny made three Broadway appearances, all under the auspices of David Merrick: the two above-mentioned Newley-Bricusse musicals and the scenically astounding *Oliver!*]

Furthermore, in the title role was Harry Secombe, possibly the most popular singing actor-comedian in the British theatre, a hefty, hearty Welshman of operatic training with a rousing tenor voice as robust as his body.

This combination worked well enough for the show to have a lucrative eighteen-month run in London under the production banner of Bernard Delfont. Merrick, who tries to nail down any foreign production that seems to have possibilities, gained the American rights to this one, complete with Secombe, Kenny scenery, and the other assets of the British operation. [This was Merrick's third and final Newley-Bricusse-Delfont importation.]

The producer played a gambit that had worked for him before, and, as things turned out, it was well he did. In 1962 he had brought over another Dickens, British-made, Kenny-designed musical extravaganza, *Oliver!*, and toured it profitably for months before opening it on Broadway. Even had the original cast album made and on the market well before the New York premiere, a rare procedure.

That tour included the fourteen "golden weeks" of playing time divided between Los Angeles and San Francisco for the subscription season of Edwin Lester's Civic Light Opera operation. This is guaranteed-capacity-money-in-the-bank. A show fortunate enough to be scheduled by Lester can't avoid making a lot of money with him.

So, Merrick went back to Lester with *Pickwick*, and the money rolled in, to the tune of $125,000 weeks in Los Angeles, where there is much greater capacity than in San Francisco. Capacity business did not ensue at subsequent touring stops in Cleveland, Detroit, and Washington, D. C., en route to New York, and notices were mixed along the way. Efforts were made, especially in Detroit, to make some alterations with an eye to bolstering the show for Broadway.

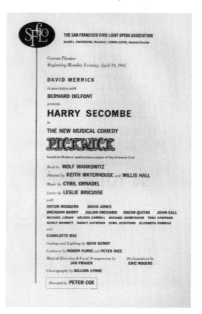

The production opened at the 46th Street Theatre to a fair, but by no means overwhelming, advance sale such as some much-publicized (even if not eventually successful) musicals run up. The premiere occurred during a strike that had closed all New York newspapers except the *Post* and the *Herald Tribune*. Incidentally, there was a total strike blackout of newspapers when *Oliver!* opened in New York in January 1963 and, in the scramble to get any sort of notices to the public via radio and television, one radio station let Merrick review his own production. He said he liked it. ["The greatest musical of all time," said WNEW's guest critic. "A truly great classic of the theatre: transcendent, unique, incomparable, prodigious, stunning." The non-partisan reviews, when they finally appeared, were almost as laudatory.]

The San Francisco billing page. Two of the three main featured players were gone by the time the show reached Broadway

The *Pickwick* review in the *Post* was mildly favorable, with major praise for Secombe, while the *Herald Tribune* notice was discouraging. [Walter Kerr: "*Pickwick* ran for eighteen months in London, and while it is too soon to say how it will do here, I did feel that it was taking up most of the eighteen months last night." Howard Taubman of the *Times*, when his review was finally printed, called it "cheap, comic-strip Dickens."] The show's capacity was slightly over $75,000 a week, but it never reached that. The top gross, and for only one week, was $60,000 plus. Merrick closed it on November 20 and, at last, we come to Mr. Bull's document of disagreement.

A friendlier shot of Secombe graced the Broadway program.

Peter Bull is a large, in all directions, British character actor of fine reputation. He is witty, and he writes well, as several books of theatre memoirs attest. He actually looks like his name: like the popular cartoon conception of that symbol of Britain, John Bull. At this stage of his career, he admits quite frankly that he seeks those jobs that pay him handsomely while requiring only a minimum of time on stage. Which is the sort of role he had in *Pickwick*, that of Sgt. Buzfuz, with one highly effective appearance in the second act's courtroom scene. Although he had the role in the original London *Pickwick* production, Bull did not join the American version until its final weeks prior to the New York premiere, due to previous commitments. Two seasons previously he had had the same sort of showy, short role in *Luther* for—who else?—David Merrick.

The actor aired his feeling about *Pickwick* and Merrick in a letter to the editor of *Variety* published in the December 22, 1965 issue, which printed alongside an itemized rebuttal by the producer. [Merrick's missive bears evidence of having been written by his long-suffering press agent, Harvey Sabinson.]

"A small item in the show business obituary column of *Variety* recently caught my eye," Bull wrote. "It read, '*Pickwick* folded after 56 performances at an approximate breakeven or, perhaps, a slight profit, as a personal investment of the producer, David Merrick.'

"I wonder how many eyebrows were raised at this announcement, and I hope that some of the backers of the show, to say nothing of the members of the public who actually enjoyed the entertainment, will be surprised at the sudden withdrawal of *Pickwick*, as most of the acting profession appears to be. Was it not fairly common knowledge around Broadway that, in spite of rough critical handling and a shaky start, it played to around $50,000 every week? Was it not agreed that most, if not all, of its production costs were paid off on the road? And, above all, was it not maintained by the most skeptical people that it would clean up at Christmas, to say nothing of Thanksgiving?"

(Merrick: "While true that *Pickwick* played to around $50,000 every week it was open, it sold discouragingly few tickets after the New York premiere. The average daily take was $900, and, had we run one more week, we would have grossed an appalling $25,000 for that week and less thereafter.")

"Indeed," to resume with the Bull indictment, "special matinees and prices were being quoted in the press until a few days of the closing..."

(Merrick: "Naturally, our ads quoted holiday prices and schedules because we in the theatre, for some strange reason, live with hope.")

"...At the last matinee (SRO, natch, as were most matinees), the theatre was packed with children, who not only gave the cast the most astounding ovation after the show, but crowded around the stage door afterwards to ask why *Pickwick* was being withdrawn. A good question, as it happened to be the ideal Christmas fare, with its jolly, unsexy, knockabout run, real ice skating and riveting changes of scene.

"I am no clairvoyant, but I would hazard a guess that the backers and, indeed, Merrick himself would have reaped a rich reward eventually if he had not seemingly lost complete interest in the enterprise. It is certain that the depressing sight of angry mums and gritty children demanding refunds at the box office would have been avoided Thanksgiving week.

"Merrick will point out that the advance was small. And that is, indubitably, a fact, but the size of the advance was probably due (a) to the almost negligible promotion for the show after the first few weeks and (b) the curious behavior of the gents in the box office, who were refusing, presumably on orders from someone, to take any telephone orders on the grounds that the theatre was sold out on any future night that a customer was requiring seats for. This bewildered the poor old general public, as well it might, for they had been reading in the papers that seats were available as far ahead as New Year's Eve."

(Merrick: "The post-opening publicity was not negligible, despite the fact that for two weeks thereafter the newspaper strike persisted. Over $30,000 was spent on the purchase of TV and radio time, and the show's principals appeared on most of the local and network radio and TV programs, such as Ed Sullivan and Merv Griffin. Bull himself appeared twice on the Griffin show, and my publicity department offered him extraordinary aid in the American promotion of his book, including placing an article in the *New York Times*, which appeared after *Pickwick* had closed. [The book in question was called *I Say, Look Here! The rather random reminiscences of a round actor in the square.*] The box office of the 46th Street Theatre impressed me as one of the most cooperative, informative, truthful and polite groups of treasurers it has been my pleasure to work with.")

"Merrick will doubtless point out to his angels that the operating 'nut' for *Pickwick* was high. Again, absolutely true, but will he tell them that no effort was made to cut it down before the closing notice? It is believed that no discussion was held about possible reduction in royalties, percentages or even salaries to tide over the losing weeks before Christmas. The only suggestion, for a cut in the size of the chorus, was made after the opening performance."

(Merrick: "Attempts were made to activate reductions in royalties, percentages and salaries, but to no avail. Three days after the New York opening, requests for reductions were made directly to London, but were rejected.")

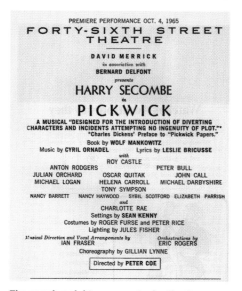

PREMIERE PERFORMANCE OCT. 4, 1965

FORTY-SIXTH STREET THEATRE

DAVID MERRICK
in association with
BERNARD DELFONT
presents

HARRY SECOMBE
in
PICKWICK

A MUSICAL "DESIGNED FOR THE INTRODUCTION OF DIVERTING CHARACTERS AND INCIDENTS ATTEMPTING NO INGENUITY OF PLOT."
"Charles Dickens' Preface to "Pickwick Papers."

Book by **WOLF MANKOWITZ**
Music by **CYRIL ORNADEL**   Lyrics by **LESLIE BRICUSSE**
with
ROY CASTLE

ANTON RODGERS   PETER BULL
JULIAN ORCHARD   OSCAR QUITAK   JOHN CALL
MICHAEL LOGAN   HELENA CARROLL   MICHAEL DARBYSHIRE
TONY SYMPSON
NANCY BARRETT   NANCY HAYWOOD   SYBIL SCOTFORD   ELIZABETH PARRISH
and
CHARLOTTE RAE
Settings by SEAN KENNY
Costumes by ROGER FURSE and PETER RICE
Lighting by JULES FISHER
Musical Direction and Vocal Arrangements by   *Orchestrations by*
IAN FRASER   ERIC ROGERS
Choreography by GILLIAN LYNNE

Directed by PETER COE

The opening night program trades the "new musical comedy" label for "a musical designed for the introduction of diverting characters and incidents attempting no ingenuity of plot." The critics slammed the book anyway.

"The star of *Pickwick*, Harry Secombe, was powerless to make any suggestions (a) because he was ill with mumps when the decision to close the show was reached and (b) because Merrick did not speak to him from a few days before the opening until after the closing had been settled. Secombe got his notice the day before he was due to return to the show. It arrived at his hotel, delivered, by a Third Person.

"Now, Secombe, who is not only the biggest musical star in England, but also, far and away, the most loved and respected member of the theatrical profession there, is, I submit, entitled at any rate to a show of good manners, however insincere, and particularly from an impresario who, on the first night, had sent (in absentia) a message which read, 'I am proud and privileged to present you in your first New York appearance.'"

(Merrick: "I didn't speak to Harry Secombe because, as a child, I had never had the mumps, and I understand it is quite serious in adult males, which might not be of concern to Bull…. Secombe's personal manager, Robert Kennedy, was advised, well in advance of the closing, of the strong possibility that we could not continue. The exact closing could not possibly have come as a complete surprise to him.")

"Another star from England, Roy Castle, made a big personal success in the show, and his experience was even more impersonal. Merrick did not speak to him from the day he opened until—well, he hasn't spoken yet!

"'Actors are children,' Merrick keeps on saying, but surely even he must realize that children must be spoken to once in a while. But I fear the Personal Touch, which has successfully and beneficially been a feature of the theatrical world for so long, is fast vanishing from the business.

"My own theory about Merrick's conduct of this particular production is that he never really liked *Pickwick*. He certainly didn't take up his option after seeing it in England. His interest was only kindled after seeing the big profit it was making in London. He lost interest when his sweeping structural alterations didn't work out in Detroit and Washington.

"His approach to 'improving' the show during this period was arbitrary and, I think, just a tiny bit irresponsible. I personally think it was unwise to employ a 'play doctor' who actually confessed, after submitting a few scenes of appallingly un-Dickensian flavor, that he hadn't really read *The Pickwick Papers*.

"Merrick also wanted to pep up the show with new numbers. A great many were rushed into rehearsal and the artists concerned broke their backs trying to get them right. Most of them were anachronistic and had to be abandoned after a few performances.

"After a short lapse, fresh demands for new songs were heard in the wilderness and, though nobody appeared to be commissioned to supply them, members of the cast, their relatives and friends flooded the market and two new items were culled from this source, though I gather there was a bit of trouble about payment for them. It had, indeed, become a 'Do It Yourself Show,' and the morale of the company reached a new low.

"It was particularly curious as Merrick had allowed the show to play for three"—(four)—"months to enormous takings on the West Coast with hardly any alterations. But after the pre-Broadway shakeup, certainly the older members of the company were alarmed at the lack of faith in the original merits of the production."

(Merrick: "Attempts were made all along the tryout route to insert revisions by a top playwright, Sidney Michaels, but cooperation from the director and principals were negligible. New songs were even written by a talented young composer, but the director and the principals refused their cooperation in inserting these changes. Bull did not join the show until it had played San Francisco, Los Angeles and Cleveland.")

"On reaching the promised land, in this case Broadway, *Pickwick* played a few moderately successful previews, and Merrick, perhaps wisely, disappeared to Vietnam to give Ambassador Lodge a severe drubbing for not inviting the chorus of *Hello, Dolly!* to 'chow' with the stars. [Due to Cold War tensions, the Moscow engagement of Mary Martin's touring company of *Hello, Dolly!* was canceled at the last moment. Merrick used his State Department connections to reroute the cast—already airborne—to Vietnam, where *Dolly* wowed the U.S. troops. When U.S. Ambassador Henry Cabot Lodge invited the featured players (only) to dinner at the Embassy, Merrick loudly complained—and garnered widespread, international publicity for the show.] It is interesting to note the producer's sudden concern for the lower theatrical strata, as it seems only yesterday (actually 1963) when I, as a principal in his production of *Luther*, had to decline his offer to supper after the first night because he had omitted, doubtless by oversight, to invite the entire cast."

(Merrick: "I had no opening night party for *Luther*. When I do have opening night parties, every member of the cast and crew is invited.")

"Anyhow, his absence around the opening of *Pickwick* passed almost unnoticed. The absence of the scenic designer was far more serious. It is rumored that the management refused to pay his fare over. This seemed false economy, as not only should Sean Kenny have ensured that his intricate sets were displayed to their best advantage, but he also could have averted the series of mishaps caused by falling scenery, etc., which could have had fatal results. One member of the cast had to be rushed to the hospital."

(Merrick: "Sean Kenny's work on the show was completed before the premiere at the 46th Street Theatre, and the sets functioned smoothly at the opening.")

"But that, of course, is part of the lunacy that attacks an enterprise which has so much money at stake. Suddenly, there is tightening of the pursestrings just when it seems silliest. A serio-comic incident of this type occurred towards the end of the run when Secombe caught mumps.

"The others of the company were summoned to the stage and told that the management would have those of the cast who had not had mumps inoculated against the disease. There was a large showing of hands, and we never heard another word on the subject, though my doctor informed me that each injection would have cost around $20 a whack."

(Merrick: "As regards the mumps inoculations, my physician advised me that there is no medical proof that the shots are in any way an effective deterrent.")

"Fortunately, none of the company of *Pickwick* has caught mumps to date, but they were all out of work Thanksgiving week and realized only too clearly whom they had to thank for that. An extra week could not have denuded the management to the bone.

'There are few things less attractive than the sound of a visiting actor criticizing the organization which has given him employment and provided him with a living, which he may have taken from a native artist. But I cannot leave this country, which I admire and like so much, without a small word of exhortation. I have made a survey of the conditions under which the average actor lives, and I am appalled by them.

"Rapidly, the entire industry appears to be passing into the hands of producers, to whom the whole thing is a desperate fight for huge grosses. The personal touch or love of the theatre has almost completely disappeared, and one can only exhort everyone from the creative side to refuse to work unless they have contracts that will prevent them being completely in the power of the operator.

Nick Nappi's artwork promises a jolly olde time.

"It is all wrong that every pre-Broadway show must be engulfed in the panic that seems to seize every producer at the absence of an instant rave notice from the first out-of-town critic they come up against. 'What has gone wrong?' they hiss and scream at each other.

"'Someone must go,' they continue. And out goes the director, the choreographer and/or the leading gent or lady, but never, unfortunately, the producer himself. The latter, impelled by insecurity and lack of courage and imagination, is certain that the fault cannot be his because he has spent all the money on getting the show in front of an ungrateful public.

"But, of course, he has probably left out the most valuable factor of all, faith in what he must have once believed.

"This generalization does not only apply to musicals. In a straight production of Merrick's, the leading man (not the one who is reported to have given him a tiny biff in downtown Philadelphia) was replaced recently." [Bull is referring to Joseph Campanella, who was replaced by Barry Nelson during the tryout in *Cactus Flower*. Elsewhere, during the Philadelphia tryout of *Inadmissable Evidence*, Nicol Williamson tossed Merrick into a trash can in the alley of the Locust Street Theatre (see *Rex*, page 290).]

"Now, Merrick and the director were possibly perfectly right in this instance, but I can only hope that the actual dismissal was dished out with the utmost courtesy and tact by one of them and not by a Third Person. It was Third Person who informed the English artists during the last week of *Pickwick* that the final salaries and air tickets would be handed to us at the last performance. [Bull is presumably referring to Jack Schlissel, Merrick's hard-nosed and pugnacious general manager.]

"That was to ensure, I imagine, that we didn't do a midnight flit. I must point out that we were usually paid on Thursdays. It is this sort of thing that has made me feel that I don't like to be an actor much any more.

"I think conditions are slightly better in my native land, where the personal touch hasn't entirely vanished from the theatrical profession. But over here it does appear to me to be bogged down by bullying, fear, and possible humiliation, and leaves the performer at the mercy of an unscrupulous and egocentric employer.

"There seems to me far more security and friendly atmosphere in a bank, a post office or even the subway, where there is, at any rate, a cop on hand to try and see you don't get killed or maimed in the jungle."

Merrick wound up his rebuttal with this:

"By now the whole matter has become a total bore to me. As the producer, it was I who took all the risks. It was all the salaried and royaltied people who earned the money, and my decision to close when we did was not capricious but, rather, sound in the face of the public apathy toward the show."

Whatever merit there may be on either side in the above, the exchange is a most enlightening one as to theatrical matters in general, as well as in this particular, and a vote of thanks is due to *Variety* for providing it with an outlet.

Pickwick opened October 4, 1965 at the 46th Street Theatre, to mixed reviews. It closed there November 18, 1965 after 56 performances, with a slight profit.

Pickwick marked British actor Peter Bull's fourth of five Broadway visits. His final appearance occurred fourteen months after his *Pickwick*ian departure, supporting Lynn Redgrave and Michael Crawford in Peter Shaffer's one-acts *Black Comedy* and *White Lies*. He died in 1984, at the age of seventy-two.

Keith Waterhouse and Willis Hall, British authors of the 1960 play and 1963 screenplay for *Billy Liar*, were announced as adaptors of the American *Pickwick*, but their billing was subsequently removed. Sidney Michaels was a promising young American playwright, albeit very briefly. He arrived in New York in 1961 and, we are told, managed to option five plays within five days for $8000; none of these efforts seem to have arrived on Broadway. His first produced play was a translation of the French hit *Tchin-Tchin*, which Merrick presented in 1962. The show failed, despite Anthony Quinn and Margaret Leighton in the leads. *Dylan*, a 1964 biography of Dylan Thomas, was a moderate hit starring Alec Guinness. Two star musicals failed, Bob Preston's *Ben Franklin in Paris* (1964) and Joel Grey's *Goodtime Charley* (1975). Michaels's biggest break came in 1970 with *Applause*, but Betty Comden and Adolph Green were rushed in to replace his libretto. His final Broadway play was *Tricks of the Trade*, which lasted a single performance in 1980, despite a cast headed by George C. Scott.

The details of the doctoring of *Pickwick* seem lost to history; at least, to anyone I could think of asking. Or so I thought. As I was editing this, at least one answer came my way. In talking to Ellen Stern, who wrote the pieces on *Mack & Mabel* and *Cry for Us All* included in this book, I learned that her husband was a former Broadway stage manager—and, yes, he did *Pickwick*. Peter Stern remembered that songs were coming from all sides; at least one piece of "special material" was written by John Strauss for his wife Charlotte Rae, *Pickwick*'s featured comedienne. Stern also told me the reason for the show's extended and lucrative pre-Broadway tour: Merrick used *Pickwick* as bait for preferential bookings of his freshly-minted blockbuster *Hello, Dolly!*

Pickwick was the seventh musical Merrick imported from England. All were financially successful, two of them—*Stop the World—I Want to Get Off* and *Oliver!*—enormously so. Merrick continued to import British plays until 1975, including some of the most memorable production of modern times, including Tom Stoppard's *Rosencrantz and Guidenstern are Dead* and *Travesties*, and Peter Brook's *Marat/Sade* and *A Midsummer Night's Dream.* The forced-though-profitable runs of *Roar of the Greasepaint* and *Pickwick* marked Merrick's final foreign-born musicals.

Rex (1976)

Knockout

Richard Adler, co-composer-lyricist of back-to-back Tony Award winners *The Pajama Game* and *Damn Yankees*—absent from Broadway since *Kwamina* in 1961 (see page 146)—reappeared in 1973 as co-producer of a revival of *The Pajama Game*. (He had almost been to Broadway in the interim, but the 1968 Bea Arthur musical *A Mother's Kisses* kissed off in Baltimore.)

The interracial revival of *The Pajama Game*, starring Barbara McNair, Hal Linden, and Cab Calloway, had little to recommend it other than the recreation of Bob Fosse's original choreography. (It did possess one of the only twenty-year-old stage managers ever on Broadway. Did you ever try to fly in a blackout drop when the star comedian was inebriatedly weaving back and forth under the curtain line? I did—too many times.)

In the course of the revival, our eighty-six-year-old director mentioned to the composer-producer that he was writing a musical version of *Twelfth Night*. Adler signed on to compose and produce George Abbott's final Broadway musical *Music Is*, which ultimately reached Broadway Christmas week of 1976, and closed before New Year's.

Edward Colton, the veteran theatrical lawyer who represented both Adler and Abbott, mentioned that he had yet another fabled client

Gilbert Lesser's vacant portrait of Henry VIII unintentionally mirrors the underwritten character at *Rex*'s center.

who was interested in doing one more show. Did Adler have any ideas for Richard Rodgers? Adler did—and he was suddenly producing two new musicals—which were to open and close within seven months.

Sheldon Harnick, whose partnership with Jerry Bock had ended with the unloved and unsuccessful *The Rothschilds* in 1970, was signed to do the lyrics. (A musical comedy *Arsenic and Old Lace*—with a score by Rodgers and Harnick, book by Mike Stewart, and direction by Hal Prince—had been announced for the spring of 1973, but never went any further. Starring Mary Martin and Ethel Merman, no less.) Jerome Lawrence and Robert E. Lee, authors of *Inherit the Wind* and *Mame*, were signed as librettists of *Rex*, although they were eventually replaced by Sherman Yellen (of *The Rothschilds*).

Most importantly, Adler lined up Broadway's hottest new director-choreographer. Michael Bennett, of *Company* and *Follies*, had just worked wonders in Detroit, transforming *Seesaw* from a shambles into an almost-hit. Bennett's time had come, and he was eager to direct his first musical on his own. (*Follies* was co-directed by Harold Prince.)

Before things could proceed, though, Adler and Bennett came to an impasse over money. Bennett demanded the Princely sum of ten percent of the profits, the sort of slice received by folks like Robbins and Champion. "Ten percent!" said Adler. "Who does he think he is? I don't need Michael Bennett."

So Bennett passed on *Rex*. He had another idea, anyway, a musical about chorus dancers on the line, auditioning for a new musical. Adler went through the list of potential directors, and the best he could come up with was Ed Sherin. Whose only musical had been *Seesaw*, before he was sent packing by Bennett (see page 28). Caryl Rivers went to Boston to cover the tryout for the *New York Times*.

"Hal Prince's Rx for *Rex*"
by Caryl Rivers

Rex, the Richard Rodgers-Sheldon Harnick musical about Henry VIII which opens tonight at the Lunt-Fontanne, sailed into the port of Boston a month ago. The new show was laden with more treasure than the flagship of Sir Francis Drake of the Spanish Main: golden tapestries, a king's ransom in velvet and lace, a gilded throne and a seasoned crew that had seen these particular waters many times before.

It was one Broadway-bound musical that seemed to have it all. *Rex* had the melodies of Richard Rodgers, lyrics by Sheldon Harnick (*Fiddler on the Roof*), a book by Sherman Yellen (*The Rothschilds*), a star, Nicol Williamson, acknowledged to be one of the better actors of his generation, and, for a setting, the colorful panoply of Tudor England.

Yet when it arrived in Boston, *Rex* seemed to be foundering. There were rumors of trouble with the show's book and with its star. Williamson, it was said, might walk out at any time. The *Boston Globe*'s Kevin Kelly said *Rex* lacked "impact" and complained of a "now-you-see-them-now-you-don't" shuffle of Henry's wives.

Rex, it seemed, was suffering from lumbago in its first act. Part of the problem was the sheer time span it had to cover, since the show opens with Henry married to his first wife, Catherine of Aragon, and ends with his death nearly 30 years—and five wives—later. Still, there was healthy optimism. Richard Adler, the show's producer (and the composer of *The Pajama Game* and *Damn Yankees*) was certain all the ingredients were there for a smash. "Look," he said, shortly after *Rex* settled into its Boston engagement, "this show has a cough, it hasn't got cancer."

But Adler was taking no chances. He had called in Harold Prince, one of the classiest "doctors" around, to treat *Rex*'s ills. As director or producer, Prince has been involved with some of Broadway's splashiest musicals—*Fiddler on the Roof*, *Cabaret*, *West Side Story*, to name a few. [Prince, like Adler, began his Broadway career with back-to-back Tonys for *The Pajama Game* and *Damn Yankees*.] If Hal Prince couldn't cure the pain-in-the-Rex, who could?

The therapy had actually begun before Prince's arrival, during the show's engagements in Wilmington, Del., and Washington. The character of Henry had already changed considerably. Nicol Williamson had felt waves of hostility coming across the footlights: Why was this nasty man killing those nice ladies? He complained that the audience didn't understand Henry's desperate need for a male heir, his fear that without a strong king, England would plunge back into the civil strife of the Wars of the Roses. Scenes were rewritten, and then some members of the company complained that the revisions turned Henry into Mr. Nice Guy.

Queen Catherine had also undergone a sea change. At first, she was young and gorgeous and no once could figure out why Henry wanted to leave her. So she was turned into a dowdy housewife who busied herself mending Henry's shirts. [Catherine was played by thirty-seven-year-old Barbara Andres.] Unfortunately, *that* incarnation took the oomph out of her final confrontation with Henry.

The stage is set for Prince, who arrives on a cold Sunday in March, with the chill winds swirling the trash in eddies on the deserted street in front of Boston's Shubert Theatre. While the cast rehearses onstage, Prince meets with members of the show's creative staff. He is no stranger to *Rex*, having seen the show in Washington.

Prince tosses out ideas and suggestions. The blue silk tent that unfolds in the first act isn't coming out fast enough. In Washington there was a rippling effect, like a breeze. Can that be restored? The gold lamé nightgown on the doll that is supposed to be the baby Prince Edward is too gaudy, it has to go. A mat used for a scene in which Henry wrestles with the king of France looks like a piece of rubber. Prince suggests it be covered with a tapestry fabric to disguise its modernity. He is concerned about the scene in which Henry rages at his second wife, Anne Boleyn, who has just presented him with a daughter, Elizabeth. Henry's rejection of both baby and mother makes him seem too churlish, Prince says. Sherman Yellen agrees to rewrite the scene so that Henry, after his outburst on discovering he does not have a son, returns to Anne's room and tenderly cradles his baby daughter.

Yellen, who is writing under conditions reminiscent of the Tet offensive, talks about a new scene that will bring the very young Elizabeth onstage in the middle of a quarrel between Henry and Anne. That means a new child actress will be needed, and the casting will take valuable time. The New York opening has been postponed a few days, but time is short.

Someone remembers that a member of the chorus is traveling with her 5-year-old son, who has curly red hair and freckles and would make a perfect Elizabeth. But as it turns out, the boy—Sparky—is bidding to outdo Nicol Williamson in artistic temperament. He absolutely refuses to wear a dress. Richard Adler coaxes him; so does the director, Edwin Sherin. Sparky holds firm, happily sailing paper airplanes through the lobby. After tricky negotiation, a compromise is reached. Sparky will do the part wearing a nightgown. The word goes out to the cast. Nobody is to tell Sparky he looks "cute," let alone beautiful.

After his first rehearsal, Sparky gets a round of applause from the cast. Williamson gives him a wry look and says, *"That's* the part I must have." [Sparky Shapiro retired from the stage, as far as I can tell, after *Rex*.]

In another meeting in the lounge, Prince talks about the new persona for Catherine of Aragon and her new costume. She is to be regal and pious, with a strength that comes from the certainty of being right in the eyes of God. "Simple, simple, simple, like a nun's habit. Not hanging loose, that looks just terrible. I just want her to look close to a literal nun. I could see against the white a big jet black cross. I think it's worth the trouble rushing in a new costume for the life it'll give."

By Tuesday, major changes are in the works for the first act, and the cast is rehearsing the new scenes whenever it can. Barbara Andres, slightly schizophrenic after all the changes in the character of Catherine, is onstage with Williamson, rehearsing the scene in which Henry asks her for a divorce so he can marry Anne Boleyn. She is working with Ed Sherin to find a way to play the scene. Sherin is in an awkward position. A show in which a "doctor" comes in is something like a ball game where a relief pitcher trots in from the bullpen—but the old pitcher doesn't leave the mound.

"You're getting into the frail woman thing," Sherin tells her. "But the fact is, you know you hold all the aces. You're strongest in the scene not when you're operating out of anger, but out of certainty. You believe Henry would rot in hell if he divorced you. It's inconceivable that he would do that. Don't look at him so much. Don't need him so much."

With the new characterization, Sherin says, Catherine's song comes as a surprise to the audience, which makes the scene more effective. Now, he says, the audience will think, "Look at the love she once had in her life, look at what she once felt."

The song is, like most of the music Richard Rodgers writes, rich, melodic, romantic. [Andres stopped the show with "As Once I Loved

You," according to orchestrator Irv Kostal. "Ed Sherin couldn't stand it. He called a meeting, and opened up with, 'It's against my religion to allow a song to interfere with the progression of the story line by causing the audience to unnecessarily applaud.' And Dick answered, through his difficult-to-control voice box, 'It's against my religion to take out a song that stops the show!'"] Rodgers is keeping a close eye on things. At 74, his walk has been slowed by a stroke, but he works as hard as ever.

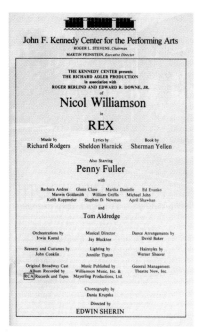

John F. Kennedy Center for the Performing Arts
ROGER L. STEVENS, Chairman
MARTIN FEINSTEIN, Executive Director

THE KENNEDY CENTER presents
THE RICHARD ADLER PRODUCTION
in association with
ROGER BERLIND AND EDWARD R. DOWNE, JR.
of

Nicol Williamson
in
REX

Music by | Lyrics by | Book by
Richard Rodgers | Sheldon Harnick | Sherman Yellen

Also Starring
Penny Fuller
with
Barbara Andres Glenn Close Martha Danielle Ed Evanko
Merwin Goldsmith William Griffis Michael John
Keith Koppmeier Stephen D. Newman April Shawhan
and
Tom Aldredge

Orchestrations by | Musical Director | Dance Arrangements by
Irwin Kostal | Jay Blackton | David Baker

Scenery and Costumes by | Lighting by | Hairstyles by
John Conklin | Jennifer Tipton | Werner Sheerer

Original Broadway Cast | Music Published by | General Management
Album Recorded by | Williamson Music, Inc. & | Theatre Now, Inc.
RCA Records and Tapes | Mayerling Productions, Ltd.

Choreography by
Dania Krupska

Directed by
EDWIN SHERIN

The billing page for the Washington tryout.

"He's amazing," says Penny Fuller, the actress who plays both Anne Boleyn and Elizabeth. "He writes a song, and if they don't like it, he goes up to his room and writes another one."

Rodgers watches the audience very carefully. "You can sense what the audience is up to. Are they silent when they go out, or do they seem happy to be where they are? Are they paying attention in the quieter scenes? If they are rustling, reading their programs in the middle of a scene, you know that scene is in trouble."

He thinks the feedback from *Rex* audiences is very good and getting better. "I remember," he says, sitting on a bench in the Shubert lobby, "when we opened *South Pacific* in this theatre. We knew we had a smash, but we kept working on it."

When he plays a new song for other members of the company, if they don't like it, they are silent. One doesn't, after all, say to Richard Rodgers, "That one doesn't hack it, Dick." Rodgers knows what the silences mean. So he goes to his room and writes another song. In the copyist's room in the Bradford Hotel the pile of music that has gone out of the show is higher than the music that stays. When a scene changes, a mood changes, and a song—no matter how lovely—no longer fits. A writer for *Saturday Review* saw the show in Wilmington and called one song, "The Pears of Anjou"—about getting old—Rodgers' finest work. The song vanished from the show in Boston.

Irwin Kostal, who is doing the orchestration for the show, has felt some pressure to play around with the Rodgers melodies, to make them sound more Elizabethan. When he first heard the songs, they were Broadway, not Tudor. In orchestrating them, he played a few tricks with tempo and pacing to get the flavor of the era. He was encouraged to do more. He took one song and gave it the full Tudor treatment. Then he put it back in his suitcase and locked it. "The name on that marquee is Richard Rodgers," he says. "If they want Elizabethan music they can go hire an Elizabethan."

By the middle of the week the show is undergoing major changes. Richard Adler says he can't remember any show that has been more thoroughly revamped on the road.

Hal Prince is working on more first act changes. He doesn't mince words about what he doesn't like but he is not stingy with praise. He tells Sherman Yellen that one new scene "loses me on the first line" but the ending, he says, is "marvelous, absolutely marvelous!" Sheldon Harnick is working on lyrics for a new song for Henry. As the matinee audience files in, Prince and Harnick perch on a pair of theatre seats and discuss the lyric. Prince likes the idea, but thinks it is too prayerful, especially a line that asks, "Haven't I obeyed your laws, God?'"

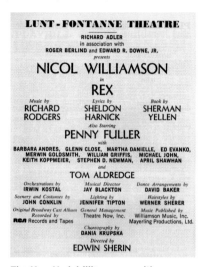

The New York billing page, with no mention of replacement director Harold Prince.

"That disturbs me," says Prince. "The man I see on that stage has been a breaker of rules—he's switched churches, taken women at will."

Harnick explains that the real Henry always believed in his righteousness.

"That may have been true in real life, but not on that stage. I'm seeing him as a member of the audience and I see him as a breaker," Prince responds.

Prince goes on. "It isn't that I don't like the lyric; you know I wouldn't fool around with you. I just think at this spot it may not be appropriate. Tell you what. Let's go to Joseph's and get something to eat. And let's yap at each other, the way we used to. Let's talk it out."
[Rex marked Prince and Harnick's sixth show together.]

Sherman Yellen finds Prince "a marvelous catalyst for me." He takes the changes in stride. "I don't mind the harshest cut as long as it's just and intelligent."

One of his problems is making Tudor reality palatable for modern audiences. "It's hard to make their behavior seem rational. What seems cruel to us was reasonable to the Tudors." He has read the last statements of people executed by Henry. They did not find his sentence unjust. "They had broken the rule of their world by offending the monarch and they knew the consequences." The play, he says, "moves from scatology to grief very sharply. That's the kind of world it was. Cruelty next to laughter."

The actors who will recreate this world are being coaxed though grueling days of rehearsals by Ed Sherin. "I'm surprised it's working as well as it is, with so many personalities under such great strain," Sherin says. Friends have called him from New York saying, "Gee, I'm sorry you're not directing the show anymore."

"The rumors in New York were that Prince was going to take over direction, but I wouldn't permit that. He's managed to make it very easy for me to work with him. He has been very smart in a tough situation." [Ed Sherin began his Broadway directing career in 1968, with the remarkably powerful *The Great White Hope*. He has gone on to direct twenty Broadway shows, plus others that never reached town; six of them starred his wife, Jane Alexander. None of Sherin's work other than *Great White Hope* is particularly memorable, except perhaps for the twin disasters *Goodbye Fidel* (1980) and *Prymate* (2004). His third musical, a 1979 attempt at *Seven Brides for Seven Brothers*, starring Howard Keel and Jane Powell, folded on the road. Sherin cut "Lonesome Polecat"; he said he didn't like it.]

Often, the actors are rehearsing the new scenes during the day and performing the old ones at night. "The actors can't act viscerally if they can't remember their lines," Sherin laments. "It's mind boggling. It's the hardest work I've ever done in my life. I was under fire in Korea and that was simple to compared to this. I've never had more of a challenge. I have to keep cool, keep an easy flow of laughter going. If I had been directing this play twenty years ago I couldn't have done it."

During the rehearsal—which would be followed by a matinee—Penny Fuller and Nicol Williamson, exhausted, keep missing lines and giggling. Williamson keeps saying one line as, "Madame, you *dimish* the throne that I *thit* on." He jabs the air with a finger and says, "I've had it with this kingdom. What I need is three brandies."

But they get through the matinee without mishap. On Thursday, Sherin is rehearsing the cast in a scene that will end the first act. Henry's third wife has died in childbirth and rival factions in the court are pushing Anne of Cleves and Catherine Howard at him.

"You must choose, Majesty," says an earl, pushing forward the lovely Catherine. Nicol Williamson looks at Catherine and then around at the court. He claps his hand on the arm of a handsome male dancer.

"I choose him!"

The lords and ladies crack up.

The Thursday audience is a good one, and the weekend performances are sold out. Spirits in the company are high. One staff member says, "I heard bells for the first time tonight."

On Friday, the cast is rehearsing the new opening number which features a song by Tom Aldredge, as the jester, which will wind through the opening dialogue between Henry and his court. [This number was subsequently cut.] In the middle of the rehearsal, Williamson marches off to his hotel room. He does not show up for a scheduled interview but does return for the show that night.

The new opening number is to go into the Saturday matinee. Williamson does not appear at the orchestra rehearsal before the show. The cast is blowing lines all over the stage. "Your Majesty, I— Oh forget the line!" says Cardinal Wolsey. Williamson must play the scene in an hour.

"Is he going to wing it?" asks an observer.

"You're learning," says the producer.

They stumble through the opener at the matinee. The orchestra strikes up at one point, but Williamson keeps talking. The orchestra stops.

Williamson is adding to his reputation for being mercurial and temperamental. "You don't know if he's going to be nice to you or punch you in the mouth," says one cast member. [This statement turned out to be prescient, as discussed below.] The company tends to regard its moody star as a lovely, expensive, intricate piece of machinery that just happens to have a time bomb in it. Williamson's unpredictability adds a current of tension to the whole affair. So much of *Rex* rides on his shoulders that no one wants to risk getting him upset.

Despite what one cast member called his "temper tantrum" on Friday, Williamson is back in form by Saturday night. *Boston Herald* critic Elliott Norton, seeing the show for the second time, writes that Williamson could play Henry with one hand tied behind his back and says that's exactly what he might do if he isn't in the mood to go all out. But, says Norton, this time Williamson was brilliant, and the show has a new, dynamic spirit.

When *Rex* packs up to leave Boston that night, it is still, in Richard Adler's words, "a work in progress." Two new songs will go in during rehearsal in New York. But *Rex* now seems to have the wind at its back. And the bells—were they really ringing, or was that only the tinkling sound of hope? The answer is waiting, in New York.

Rex opened April 25, 1976 at the Lunt-Fontanne Theatre, to a chorus of pans. It closed there June 5, 1976 after 49 performances, with a total loss.

"One of the most interminable musicals in years," said Clive Barnes in the *Times*, saluting Rodgers's many years of service to Broadway but pointing out that "even Othello went wrong... . *Rex* has almost everything not going for it."

Rex went wrong from the very beginning. Adler went after Richard Burton, Peter O'Toole, Albert Finney, and even the aging Rex Harrison; he wound up with the fiery but non-stellar Williamson, who appeared to be extremely uncomfortable on stage and off. His acting performance turned anemic when he started singing, in a not unpleasant but very different voice; and he refused to participate in anything so lowly as publicity.

Williamson did tell columnist Liz Smith, during the tryout stop in D.C., that "I feel as though I'm dying. Every single moment is like being taken away in an ambulance." The star finally garnered headlines late in the run, when he bashed a chorus boy in the face during the curtain calls. (The lad whispered to another actor "It's a wrap," but the hypersensitive Nicol heard "It's crap.") *Rex* closed after a mere six weeks, although the ailing Rodgers quickly geared up for one more severely troubled musical (see *I Remember Mama*, page 204).

The last word might as well come from lyricist Sheldon Harnick, who had this to say about the title song, one of many that were lost on the road. "Nicol was up there bellowing "Rex! Rex!" It sounded like he was calling his dog."

The Red Shoes

A NEW MUSICAL

GERSHWIN THEATRE 50th STREET & BROADWAY

The Red Shoes (1993)

The Secret Vision

The 1948 British film *The Red Shoes* is a minor classic, as these things go. A combination of dance, emotion, atmosphere and melodrama, it seemed a reasonable choice for Broadway musicalization. As it turned out, the adaptation lacked inventiveness or style, and quickly became Broadway's new money-losing champ (at a reported eight million).

Lyricist-librettist Marsha Norman and director Susan H. Schulman, from the impressive-though-problematic 1991 musical *The Secret Garden*, clearly couldn't handle the material. Or perhaps they knew what they were doing, only to be shunted aside by an inexperienced producer. (*The Red Shoes* was Martin Starger's fifth Broadway offering, but he had not been controlling producer on his previous ventures—only one of which, Larry Gelbart's *Sly Fox*, was profitable.)

The Red Shoes turned into a battle between a group of contemporary, youngish free-thinkers (feminists! their opponents shouted) and a bunch of old white men (chauvinists!). Which is no way to create a hit Broadway musical. Bruce Weber covered the musical for the *New York Times*.

Stylish artwork for a style-less musical.

"What Went So Very Wrong with *The Red Shoes*"
by Bruce Weber

The song that opened the second act of *The Red Shoes* was called "*Do Svidanya*," Russian for "goodbye," and singing it during the Sunday matinee on Dec. 19, the fifth and last performance of the show at the Gershwin Theatre, cast members were nearly numb.

"There was such sadness," said Margaret Illmann, who played the lead role, the ballerina Vicky Page. "We never imagined we'd be saying goodbye so soon."

There was, as it turns out, a great deal of bitterness, too. Indeed, if some of the raw emotion that had erupted backstage during the rehearsals and endless previews of *The Red Shoes*—there were 51 of them—had ended up in front of an audience, the musical might still be running.

Instead, because *The Red Shoes* had survived a host of travails on the way to the stage, and because it had been more or less revamped in the frantic final weeks, it was presented with the kind of relief that begets false hope. And when the show, which was based on the 1948 film about ballet, received uniform, stake-in-the-heart critical pans, it became one of the greatest calamities in Broadway history, with nearly $8 million lost in a finger snap.

How could some of the theatre world's most illustrious figures produce such a disaster? [This is journalistic hyperbole; the only "illustrious figure" involved with *The Red Shoes*, in Broadway terms, was composer Jule Styne.]

The answer is that it's hard to imagine a starker example of what happens when collaboration goes awry. By opening night, Dec. 16, the disagreements between the producer, Martin Starger, and much of his creative team, which had resulted in his dismissing the original director, two featured players, the male lead and the production stage manager, had become dishearteningly public. And of course the show hadn't been ready for its scheduled opening on Dec. 2, which had forced Mr. Starger into a costly two-week postponement.

Less public, though, was the nature of the backstage upheaval, a struggle for artistic control that involved nothing less than which "vision" of the show to pursue, and the factions that had developed, largely along generational lines, as a result.

On one side were the 61-year-old Mr. Starger, the composer Jule Styne, who turns 88 tomorrow, and the eventual director, Stanley Donen, who is 69. They more or less wanted to put on a staged version of the film; they saw the story of a young ballerina driven to suicide by the conflicting demands of the men in her life as a classic melodrama. In the other camp were the original director, Susan Schulman, who is 47; the playwright Marsha Norman, 45, who wrote the book and lyrics; the choreographer, Lar Lubovitch, who is 50, and the set designer, Heidi Landesman, 42, all of whom felt that to hew so closely to the vision of what they felt to be a cultural artifact would produce a dated, dull show.

Which explains why the critics unanimously saw the show as a hodgepodge. If they liked the dancing or the set, and many did, they found the story a treacly rehash of the film, the score uninspired, the language of the book and lyrics mundane: all in all a stitched-together effort, its seams in embarrassing evidence.

It was astonishing, really, considering the creative minds involved. But it seems they agreed on nothing. In fact, given the principals' willingness to parcel out blame in recent interviews, it's hard to know who, if anyone, was a weak link.

The billing page for the early previews.

"The amateurism of the producer and the director ultimately sunk the show," Ms. Norman said. "They didn't know what they were doing."

Mr. Styne said, "Marsha's a talented lady, but she doesn't know how to write lyrics."

Mr. Donen railed against what he called "a secret vision" of the play, shared by Ms. Norman and Ms. Schulman, which he said Ms. Norman kept trying to perpetuate.

And Mr. Lubovitch defended Ms. Schulman. "What was apparent early on," he said, "was that Mr. Donen's lack of stagecraft was acute."

Ultimately, of course, the fate of a show is the responsibility of the

The Red Shoes

producer, in this case Mr. Starger, most of whose résumé has to do with Hollywood, and who, unusual for Broadway these days, sat in the producer's chair alone. Mr. Starger raised the money, contributing a sizable chunk of his own, and from the beginning was in on every decision, on both the creative and business sides. This of course made him the biggest target of all the carping, much of it aimed at what was perceived to be his insensitivity to the creative people he hired. There was particular resentment of his swift closing of the show before it had run long enough to qualify for any Tony nominations. [Choreographer Lubovitch and set designer Landesman were generally considered likely to have received nominations, and might well have won; both awards were taken by the Lincoln Center Theater transfer of the Royal National Theatre's *Carousel*.] "Obviously people who are replaced are going to be disgruntled," Mr. Starger said. "But what happens in this situation is that everything that's good about the show, that has noting to do with the producer. What they find fault with is the producer's fault."

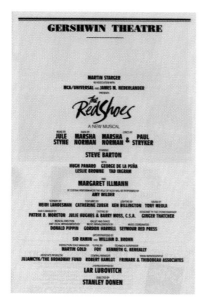

The final billing page, with Steve Barton replacing Roger Rees in the starring role.

The day the reviews were published, box-office sales dwindled to $20,000, Mr. Starger said, a death knell for a show that cost more than $400,000 a week to run. It might have lost $200,000 to $300,000, he said, if he had kept it open another week and invited the Tony voters, fulfilling the award requirements. [One of the criteria for eligibility is that the Tony Voters be given a reasonable chance to judge all potential nominees, which would have meant inviting them before the opening. At the time, this would have been interpreted as a clear admission that the producers were contemplating closing the show even before the reviews hit. Since *The Red Shoes*, it has become accepted practice for shows with minimal advance sales to invite voters prior to opening.] It would have taken an infusion of $1.5 million to allow the show to run through January, thus giving it a chance, however slim, to go on. He decided not to take it.

The project's troubles actually began long ago. Mr. Starger acquired the production rights in 1989, the year after Mr. Styne won permission from Michael Powell, one of the film's original directors, to go ahead with a stage score. Two book writers preceded Ms. Norman, who was hired in late 1991. Her friend Ms. Schulman—they had worked together, along with Ms. Landesman, on *The Secret Garden*—signed on the following spring. A workshop of the show was put on during the summer of 1992 in Saratoga Springs, N.Y. A year later, a second workshop was done, in Manhattan in the downtown rehearsal studios at 890 Broadway, and that, by most accounts, is what accelerated the show's troubles.

The second workshop was either well received or not, depending on whom you ask. Days after it ended, and three days before the show was to begin Broadway rehearsals, Mr. Starger dismissed Ms. Schulman.

"I was told: 'The show is yours, I want it to be mine,'" she recalled. "He felt I had a secret feminist version. But I think we're talking about chauvinism, in the sense of adhering to things in the past. There was an unwillingness to discuss how the original story might be perceived in 1993."

Mr. Starger, for his part, conceded that he wanted the show to adhere more faithfully to the movie. But he added that the main reason he made the change was that he didn't think the work was good enough. [If Starger was convinced by the second workshop that the show wasn't good enough, then why did he immediately go ahead with the Broadway production?]

"The vision of the play I had in mind was not simplistically one thing: do the movie," he said. "The vision I had was of a show beautifully written, beautifully composed, beautifully acted, beautifully danced."

Whether the version that ended up at the Gershwin was better than what Ms. Norman and Ms. Schulman put on in August is a matter of debate, but everyone agrees that the spirits of the two were drastically different.

"I didn't want to write an ending where a girl couldn't choose between two men and jumped in front of a train," Ms. Norman explained. Instead she wrote an ending in which Vicky is killed, accidentally, onstage. After witnessing a fight between the two men, she has a momentary loss of concentration in the performance of a dangerous stunt.

"It was a lapse, not a girl going crazy," Ms. Norman said. "It was the idea that you could die in the perfection of your craft.

"The idea was that our passion and self-sacrifice, this is what is so ennobling and grand about us as artists."

The other main difference was the use of Ms. Landesman's sets. As directed by Mr. Donen, every scene was played directly at the audience, more or less at center stage. Ms. Schulman's staging, however, was based on old drawings that Ms. Landesman had turned up, depicting the interiors of European opera houses from a variety of skewed angles. Her version allowed the audience a variety of perspectives, many providing a look at the stage and backstage at the same time.

Reactions to this in the workshop ranged from excitement to confusion, and in the end, Mr. Starger opted for a simpler idea. In any case, when cast members reassembled at the Gershwin to begin rehearsals on Aug. 30, they were greeted by Mr. Starger's introducing them to Mr. Donen, which took many by complete surprise. [A complete surprise, and for good reason. Donen, whose Hollywood directing credits included *Singin' in the Rain* and *Seven Brides for Seven Brothers*, had never directed a stage musical. He had last been on Broadway in 1942, as a seventeen-year-old chorus boy.]

"I know the company, with a couple of exceptions, loved Susan Schulman," said Hugh Panaro, who played the young love-struck composer, Julian Craster. "I think that was the saddest moment. We did a wonderful workshop, came back after vacation, and our leader was gone."

By most accounts, the next weeks were chaotic, as Mr. Donen and Mr. Starger began forging a version of the show that would more closely echo the movie. Ms. Norman was making daily changes in the book and lyrics, as per instructions, and then grappling with criticism from Mr. Donen and Mr. Starger. Finally, Mr. Starger hired the veteran lyricist Bob Merrill to pitch in. Mr. Merrill, writing under the pseudonym Paul Stryker, never saw the show; he faxed in his lyrics from his home in California. [Merrill had been Styne's lyricist for *Funny Girl* and *Sugar*. He was also a composer in his own right, with the charming *Carnival* and the disastrous *Breakfast at Tiffany's* (see page 42) to his credit. As for the pseudonym: Styne landed his first Hollywood job in 1941, writing cowboy songs for Roy Rogers at Republic Studios. (Head of the music dept.: Cy Feuer.) Jule Styne did not sound like a good name for a writer of cowboy songs, so the studio suggested he change it to Paul Stryker. Styne didn't.]

As the new version took shape, some early decisions had to be painfully reversed. Roger Rees, the actor who had first been hired to play the impresario, Boris Lermontov, was dismissed because his singing voice, never his forte, couldn't fill the capacious Gershwin. A better voice was particularly necessary because the show had become virtually bankrupt of singers. [The role was taken by Rees's understudy, Steve Barton. Barton gained prominence creating the role of Raoul in the London and Broadway productions of Andrew Lloyd Webber's *The Phantom of the Opera*, although he was never able to successfully follow up that performance. He worked extensively regionally and abroad, but

The Red Shoes was his only other Broadway credit.] Ms. Illmann, a principal dancer with the National Ballet of Canada, had not been cast as Vicky for her voice (in the end, all but half a song was taken from her); meanwhile, Ms. Norman had written a number of songs for Irina, the ballerina Vicky replaces, but in the new version the role was diminished, and the part evolved into more of a dancer's. So the original Irina, René Ceballos, a strong singer, was dismissed and replaced by Leslie Browne, a former principal with American Ballet Theatre. [Another featured performer, actor Timothy Jerome, was replaced by Tad Ingram in the role of Sergei Ratov.]

One thing everyone was pleased with was Mr. Lubovitch's choreography, which was crowned by an 18-minute "Red Shoes Ballet." As the show evolved, however, and the story changed, Mr. Starger and Mr. Donen wanted to move the ballet from the beginning of the second act to the finale, turning what most people conceded was the artistic high point of the show into a climax, the proverbial 11 o'clock number.

"Though none of the choreography was changed, it was re-ordered," said Mr. Lubovitch. "The result, as I see it, is that it no longer matched the show."

All of this is what led to Mr. Starger's postponing the opening from Dec. 2 to Dec. 16, and when the curtain finally went up, it seemed, for a brief moment, a triumph.

"Such a struggle but here we are and I think we can be quite proud," Marsha Norman wrote in a note to Mr. Starger that night. "All my best."

The Red Shoes opened December 16, 1993 at the Gershwin Theatre to a chorus of pans. It closed there on December 19, 1993 after 5 performances, with a total loss.

The Red Shoes marked a sad farewell for composer Jule Styne (1905-1994), the final remaining member of his peer group (which included Rodgers, Loesser, Loewe, Weill and Bernstein). Styne was clearly past his prime; his last true success had been in 1964, with *Funny Girl* (although he won a Tony with the 1967 *Hallelujah, Baby!* [see page 134] and the 1972 *Sugar* had turned a profit). But despite the failures of his shows, Styne's music itself had remained vibrant and bright. *The Red Shoes* score, though, was neither; it gave the impression of being patched together out of scraps of old Styne tunes, some of which were clearly identifiable. In a nod towards the competing Gregory Hines musical *Jelly's Last Jam*, the ill-fated *Red Shoes* was dubbed "Jule's Last Jam." And it was; he died on September 20, 1994.

PLAYBILL®

MARQUIS THEATRE

NICK & NORA

Nick and Nora (1991)

Ten Big Boys in a Room

Our various behind-the-scenes-adventures have taken us through many of the perils of producing a Broadway musical. Relatively unexplored is that most hidden, yet arguably most critical, step: Raising the money. Ellen Stern of the short-lived magazine *Manhattan, Inc.*—who two decades earlier had told the tale of *Mack & Mabel*—relates the strange, sad, and ultimately futile saga of Broadway's other ampersanded, alliteratively-titled musical, *Nick & Nora*.

This graphically intriguing *Playbill* title treatment is intended to convey... just what?

"Show Biz Whodunit"

by Ellen Stern

890 Broadway: a new musical is in rehearsal. Singers, dancers, singer-dancers, a dog. They're marking their steps, learning their moves. Once there were as many as 23 new Broadway musicals announced each fall, but this season there is only one—this one. *Nick & Nora*, based on Dashiell Hammett's *The Thin Man* and opening on November 10. [As the show underwent continual changes, the opening was postponed to December 8 (after a near-record-setting total of 71 previews). It was the only "new" Broadway musical to open between May 1, 1991 (*The Will Rogers Follies*) and April 26, 1992 (*Jelly's Last Jam*).]

A pond, Alcadian National Forest, Maine: the guy who dreamed up the show 11 years ago is fishing from a row boat—and thinking about where it all went wrong.

In the spring of 1980, Jim Pentecost from Queens is an off-Broadway stage manager with a Broadway dream. At 29, he's working at the Hudson Guild on *Madwoman of Central Park West* with Broadway types Phyllis Newman and Arthur Laurents, and spending his odd hours watching and waiting for the elusive idea that will take him to the big time. [Phyllis Newman's one-woman show, *The Madwoman of Central Park West*, transferred to the mid-Broadway house 22 Steps (on the site of the old Latin Quarter) on June 13, 1979, for a run of 86 performances.]

Theatre 80 St. Marks is a grungy little revival house in Greenwich Village, and on the rainy April afternoon Pentecost goes there to see *The Thin Man*, it's drearier than ever. But on that black-and-white screen, the guy sees his musical. "The characters danced," he says. "I could hear them sing."

The Broadway theatre, for all its impact and huge grosses, being essentially a closed shop—10 Big Boys in a room and everyone else on the outside—Pentecost knows that without illustrious coattails to ride, he'll stand no chance of even getting the rights. But with

Phyllis Newman as Nora—or better yet, her husband, Adolph Green, and his partner Betty Comden as the show's writers—he has a shot. He rents 16 mm reels of the first two *Thin Man* movies and lugs them uptown to Comden and Green. No go. They pass in favor of musical-izing Ibsen's *A Doll's House* (*A Doll's Life*, five performances). [*A Doll's Life*, with music by Larry Grossman, and directed and copro-duced by Harold Prince, opened September 23, 1982. Comden and Green's *Will Rogers Follies* also opened before *Nick & Nora* reached Broadway.]

Five years pass. The idea percolates. Pentecost moves to Broadway as the production stage manager of *La Cage aux Folles*, directed by Arthur Laurents. He and Laurents become close. In May 1985, he approaches Laurents about the *Thin Man* project. Laurents says yes.

Arthur Laurents is legendary for having written such Broadway shows as *Gypsy, West Side Story, Anyone Can Whistle, Hallelujah, Baby!* and such movies as *The Way We Were, The Turning Point, Rope* and *The Snake Pit*. Small and taut at 73, he plays tennis in the Hamptons all summer, skis in Switzerland every January, admires the mysteries of P.D. James and Ruth Rendell but not Dashiell Hammett, relishes word games and loves to dish. A passionate and opinionated figure, he leaves no uncommitted acquaintances: he is either worshipped or loathed. "He's brilliant," says a Broadway roller, "but Wagner was brilliant too. And he was a Nazi."

With Laurents as his certified Big Boy—and having joined forces with a young production assistant named Charles Suisman (Goodspeed Opera House, *Dreamgirls*)—Pentecost begins serious negotiations with the Hammett estate for the rights to *The Thin Man*. He's a player at last. The game is afoot.

Three years go by. When the papers are finally signed in 1988, Pentecost and Suisman own a one-year option on the literary rights to the novel (cost: $5,000) and (for another $5,000) a one-year option from Ted Turner for rights to the movies and characters. Now to write the show. [Turner Entertainment had purchased the M-G-M catalogue, which included the *Thin Man* movies.]

Laurents says he's interested only in directing, not writing, the book. So arguably the best book writer in the history of Broadway musicals is on board, but not as the writer. Who then?

In the summer of 1987, A.L. ("Pete") Gurney—author of *The Cocktail Hour, Love Letters* and other small, WASPy plays—is selected. Why? Gurney doesn't know. "I have kind of a reputation for writing sophisticated dialogue, I think," says he. "Arthur and I hammered out a plot, but most of the ideas were his. Finally, I said, 'Arthur, I think this is yours. You should do it.'"

Laurents agrees. No argument from Pentecost and Suisman. After four months of slogging along with Gurney ("Pete didn't know anything about writing a mystery," Laurents says now, "or a musical"), he's eager. "That click!" he says. "The bell rang! I was ready to *get* at those people."

Pentecost now has the great Arthur Laurents writing his *Thin Man* musical. Laurents begins by disregarding *The Thin Man*.

Using Hammett's basics—Nick is the hard-drinking gumshoe, Nora his perky helpmate; he's called in to solve a murder between martinis and repartee, she and Asta the dog assist—he plops the characters in Hollywood, devises an original mystery and renovates their relationship.

"I didn't use the original story because I thought it was boring," he says.

One thing a musical needs is music. So the search begins for a composer. After turning down or being turned down by the usual suspects—Stephen Sondheim, Jule Styne, Cy Coleman, Jerry Herman—Pentecost and Suisman settle on a composer who isn't going to turn them down: Charles Strouse (*Annie*; *Bye Bye Birdie*; *Come Back, Birdie*; *Applause*; *All American*; *A Broadway Musical*; *Golden Boy* [see page 178]; *Superman*; *Charlie and Algernon*; *I and Albert*; *Mayor*; *Rags*; *Dance a Little Closer*)—a man who, it seems, has never met a show he wouldn't write.

Now for the words. Lyricist Sheldon Harnick (*Fiddler on the Roof*) doesn't like the show. "I don't want to put clever words in the mouths of amoral people," explains the guy who won a Pulitzer for doing exactly that in *Fiorello!*

Next? Laurents considers Richard Maltby Jr. (*Baby, Song and Dance*) the second-best Broadway lyricist after Sondheim. Onlookers wonder how the bespectacled, rumpled and languorously wry Maltby will get on with the ship-shape Strouse. It's not a marriage made in heaven. "We didn't get along at *all*,'" says Strouse. "He's totally unfocused, he's consistently late, he's disorganized. His attention span is a little less than my son's—when he was 11."

"I have a lot of idiosyncracies," Maltby allows. "I drive Charles crazy with them. My first drafts were terrible. I over-rhyme, I go for cleverness to no purpose. When I don't have a clear idea of what I'm doing, I'm really second-rate.

"Funnily enough," adds the lyricist, "I was more interested in doing a show with Pete Gurney than with Charles or Arthur."

This then, in May 1988, is *Nick & Nora*'s writing team.

The work underway, Pentecost and Suisman start trying to raise the money, having budgeted their show at $6.5 million. Starting with

$125,000 from Suisman's family, they get lists of investors on other shows and hit the phones.

February 1989

Laurents, Strouse and Maltby have a first act and four songs. They do a reading at the Dramatists Guild with a pick-up cast featuring two Tony winners—Joanna Gleason (*Into the Woods*) as Nora and Christine Baranski (*Rumors*) as her chum—who have been Laurents's choices from the beginning. [Both remained with the project through the Broadway opening (and closing).]

Reaction? "It's okay," says a relatively enthusiastic member of the audience. "But it's not a strong book. I don't think they've set up the mystery part of it."

Pentecost is unfazed. "Charlie and I feel it's on track." He sets the next goal: the first backers' audition will be on June 26. A backers' audition is an extremely edited presentation for potential investors. It aims to highlight the show's strengths and skirt its weaknesses. The producers' job is to invite as many deep pockets as possible.

"It's not that difficult," says an optimistic Pentecost. "There are certain people who invest regularly. They're always invited to these things." He means Terry Allen Kramer (*Sugar Babies*, *Me and My Girl*, daughter of the investment firm, Allen and Co.), Marty Richards (*Grand Hotel*, *La Cage aux Folles*, widower of Band-Aid heiress Mary Lea Johnson), Jimmy Nederlander (the Nederlander theatres), Rocco Landesman (the Jujamcyn theatres) and the Shuberts (all the rest of the theatres). We're talking Big Boys here.

June 26, 1989

The Rainbow Room. The invitees have shown, and Pentecost and Suisman are hopeful. (It must be remembered that they are making no income at all during this time, so they're anxious to get to the ticket-selling phase.) Standing tall, they introduce themselves and their show, Laurents and the actors, the first act and the now 13 songs.

And? "Good response from a lot of people," says Pentecost. No money, however. Smiling brightly, Laurents compares it with the first backers' audition for *West Side Story*. "We raised not one penny," he recalls. "They said it was a f—king *opera*."

The reaction may not appear to trouble the creators, but suddenly they're elsewhere. Strouse goes off to work on *Annie II*, Maltby on *Closer Than Ever* and *Miss Saigon*. As for Pentecost and Suisman, they're treading water. [*Annie II*, a sequel to *Annie*, was one of the biggest flops of the decade; it shuttered in January 1990, during its Washington tryout. *Closer Than Ever*, a 1990 off-Broadway anthology revue featuring the work of Maltby and David Shire, ran for 288 performances. *Miss Saigon*, which opened April 11, 1991, played 4,092.]

October 1989

The troops are reconvened for three more backers' auditions. Still no money.

Pentecost realizes that he and Suisman need other money-raisers. This will entail giving up part of the store (their percentage) and billing. First aboard, for $500,000, is Daryl Roth, the coproducer of Maltby's *Closer Than Ever*.

February 1990. The producers sequester Strouse and Maltby in one of Laurents's beach houses. Provided with a rented car, rented piano, food that Strouse calls "little tidbits, which I think of as largely cheeses") and sweatshirts reading Camp Quogue, the two spend a concentrated week at work, having dinner every night with, and altogether too much of, Arthur Laurents.

He's everywhere. As mediator, meddler and muse, he's reviewing every song word by word, note by note, as it's written. "I'm known in the trade, as it were, for my musical acumen," he confesses. "Fortunately I'm in the position of saying that Leonard Bernstein trusted me and Stephen Sondheim trusted me, so… that's pretty good credentials. I have no musical knowledge—I can't tell the difference between a diminished fifth and love-40—but I have a very good ear."

The billing page at the beginning of previews. Note the miniscule credit given to originating producers James Pentecost and Charles Suisman.

On a musical, the ultimate authority is known as the "muscle." On a Richard Rodgers show, the muscle was Richard Rodgers. On a Sondheim show, it's Sondheim. On a Jerry Herman-Arthur Laurents show, it's Arthur Laurents. And in Quogue, he's muscling all over the place.

The result is an almost entirely useless week.

More backers' auditions and more backers' auditions. "Too many," says Joanna Gleason. "You start to take it personally. Will they get it? Will they love it? Will they give us lots and lots of money?"

By March 1990, Pentecost and Suisman are actively wooing Big Boy coproducers. Terry Allen Kramer likes the show but not them; she's accustomed to a slicker breed. James Nederlander temporizes.

Marty Richards talks a deal but won't cut it. The Big Boys just aren't playing ball.

More backers' auditions. More no money. What's the problem? *City of Angels* doesn't help; another murder-mystery musical set in California. And there's the recession. Whatever, *Nick & Nora* is a tough sell. "I'll tell you what else it is," says a Broadway bigmouth. "Arthur Laurents being both writer and director, Arthur Laurents being in his seventies, Arthur Laurents not having written a Broadway musical since *Hallelujah, Baby!* back in 1967." [See page 134.]

May 10, 1990

Things suddenly look up. A deal is struck with Rocco Landesman, president of Jujamcyn theatres, for over $1 million and the St. James Theatre, contingent on their raising the rest of the capitalization. Dates are announced for a New York opening in February 1991, following an out-of-town tryout in Baltimore.

The producers are confident that the Rubicon has been crossed and finish putting *Nick & Nora* together. Dog auditions are held for Asta, and Barry Bostwick (George Washington in *George Washington*, the miniseries) is signed as Nick.

Ready to go. All that's needed is the remaining $4.5 million. A last round of backers' auditions is scheduled. This time the producers won't rely on the authors' describing the show; they'll get actors to perform it and call it a "workshop." They feel they can't miss.

They miss. Here's how:

August 9

Laurents starts rehearsing the actors, Bostwick and Gleason are wonderful as Nick and Nora.

August 17

Bostwick comes down with malaria.

August 20

The workshop proceeds anyway with Nick played by the bespectacled, rumpled and decidedly unglamorous Richard Maltby. A catastrophe.

Everybody blames everybody. "I wanted the producers to cancel, but they said no," gripes Laurents.

"Everything we did was in collaboration," insists Pentecost.

"It was a terrible mistake," says a Broadway insider. "When Barry got sick, they should have cancelled."

"It was too long," offers Suisman. "It ran a little over two hours."

"That's because Arthur was adverse to scaling it down," says Pentecost.

"How else could we judge it," snaps Laurents, and then, "I *knew* it was going to be a disaster."

Variety quotes Pentecost, "If we don't get the rest of the money, we will have to put the show off until we do." A major no-no. The Big Boys never admit the sky is falling.

September 18, 1990

Last gasp time. One more backers' audition at the Dramatists Guild. Back-patting friends, whatever potential angels are left, a knuckle-cracking Strouse—they're all there. They get the usual laughs. They raise zilch.

"I'm beginning to get a bad feeling," says an agent in the audience.

Rocco Landesman pulls his investment and gives the St. James to *The Secret Garden* (produced by Mrs. Rocco Landesman). [*The Secret Garden*, produced by Heidi Ettinger Landesman and others, opened April 25, 1991 at the St. James for a not-quite-successful run of 709 performances.] "They were coming to us for more money, more than our $1 million," he says. "They were saying that if we really wanted the show to happen, we'd put more money into it. But even if we put in another half-million, they'd be short.

"The only reason we invest in the first place," he adds, "is to get shows into our own house. We essentially pay for tenants. It's wild. I can't think of any other real estate business that does that." Real estate business?

By November 12, 1990—after two years, six months and four days of trying to finance the show—Pentecost and Suisman have raised only $3 million. It seems over.

November 27

Arthur Laurents attends a meeting at Jimmy Nederlander's office, ostensibly to discuss a musical version of *The Scarlet Pimpernel*. And what to his wondering eye should appear there but ... Big Boys: Nederlander! Charlene (Mrs.) Nederlander! and Terry Allen Kramer! He claims they ask, "So what's going on with *Nick & Nora*?" (although Nederlander says Laurents called *him*).

By the end of the meeting, Pentecost and Suisman are effectively out. That afternoon, Laurents's agent, Shirley Bernstein (sister of the late Leonard), calls them to say that Kramer and Nederlander want the rights. They're going to produce the show, in association with Daryl Roth, and will leave the day-to-day duties to one Liz McCann, a producer in her own right (of such bygone non-musicals as *Nicholas*

Nickleby, Amadeus and *Elephant Man*) and more importantly, a friend of Nederlander's. (For her expertise, she'll get $2,000 a week and a piece of the pie.)

Pentecost and Suisman desperately turn to the writers from whom they receive varying amounts of sympathy. "I just think it's a shame," says Strouse. "They worked very hard and they cared." Adds Maltby, "They worked their little tails off but didn't raise the money. And there *is* a bottom line."

Strouse offers them a piece of his share if they'll retire gracefully. "I've been f—ked. Everybody's been f—ked," he tells Pentecost. "But let's try to make it amicable."

But they have one card yet to play. They still own the rights to *The Thin Man*, which they promptly renew for another year.

January 23, 1991

Negotiations begin in a tense meeting at Jimmy Nederlander's office, with the once and future producers and attorneys.

"Charles and Jim wanted us to pick up their attorney's fees," complains Terry Allen Kramer. "*We* felt they were a little out of line. But we're not mean. I thought we were extremely fair. We offered them $35,000 for expenses out of pocket—not reimbursing them for the $306,000 they'd put up for backers' auditions.

The opening night billing page. Despite the innumerable tryout troubles, the producers made only one personnel change, replacing featured actress Josie de Guzman with her understudy Yvette Lawrence.

"Listening to all this back and forth, $5 here, $10 there, after two hours I got up and said, 'Jimmy and I can't be bothered.' I got tough, and I said, 'We don't need you anyhow. We'll wait till the rights expire.' They said, 'We just picked up the rights.' They'd picked up the rights to renew six months before they were even up!

"These stinkers, who were crying poor mouth," she snarls, "had had the $5,000 for rights—and wanted us to reimburse them! That was it. I called Arthur Laurents, said, 'Jimmy and I have done our best, but we can't continue this way.'

"And Arthur Laurents said, 'Then there will be no show.'"

May 1, 1991

The final divorce papers are signed, allowing Pentecost and

Suisman a small share and smaller billing. "And that's the end of *them*," says Mrs. Kramer.

"Never," says Laurents. "I've never been through anything like this. Devastating. Just devastating. It's the worst experience I've ever had in the theatre."

The show is reannounced to open in November at the Marquis Theatre (co-owned by Nederlander and Kramer) after a Baltimore tryout. The budget is trimmed to $4.8 million.

June 21, 1991

Apparently that's not trim enough. Baltimore is canceled.

So the show will open cold in New York, where, if you're in trouble, everybody knows all about it. And how to fix it. As Strouse says, "There are three major drives in man: food, sex, and rewriting somebody else's musical."

August 12, 1991

10:30 a.m. The doors of Studio 3 at 890 Broadway are thrown open, and the *Nick & Nora* company meets for the first day of rehearsal. Laurents, in a pink shirt and white slacks, stands on tiptoe to kiss Liz McCann, in a pink shirt and white slacks. Strouse mumbles nervously, "We're still rewriting. By this point, I'm usually prepared." Mr. and Mrs. Nederlander are in Europe. Mrs. Kramer is in the Bahamas. Maltby is in California with an ailing relative. Bostwick, Gleason and the dog are posing for photographs.

And 486 miles north, sitting in a boat in the middle of a pond in Maine, Jim Pentecost casts his line and thinks wistfully about 10 Big Boys in a room.

Nick & Nora opened December 8, 1991 at the Marquis Theatre, to negative reviews. It closed there on December 15, 1991 after 15 performances, with a total loss.

"The worst experience I've ever had in the theatre," said Arthur Laurents, in his forty-fifth year in the theatre. And this statement came even before the first rehearsal!

Nick & Nora went on to a typically stormy production-and-preview period; given the sentiments the creators expressed above, it should be no surprise that they were unable to work together when the pressure *really* started. The rest of the *Nick & Nora* story parallels the saga of other musicals that pepper these pages, but the gory specifics needn't be chronicled. Ms. Stern's hair-raising piece spotlights an all-important but little-discussed aspect of producing a big-budget Broadway musical, and we'll leave it at that.

Did James Pentecost and Charles Suisman encounter so much fundraising difficulty because they were Broadway novices, unable to break their way through into the ranks of the Big Boys? Or was their problem, more simply, that *Nick & Nora* was from the start an ill-fated musical with little chance of success?

One might opt for the latter explanation, except that *Nick & Nora* did, ultimately, attract those same Big Boy investors. Despite (or because) of such expert productorial guidance, the show nevertheless went down the hopper. Would *Nick & Nora* have fared better, artistically, with the original producers retaining creative control? Possibly so; certainly, under the auspices of Mrs. Kramer, the Nederlanders et al., *Nick & Nora* veered seriously awry through its preview period, with every collaborator for himself.

And not only the collaborators. This was a musical comedy in which the central married couple become estranged, with the heroine having an affair with a featured character. It was apparent from the auditorium that the on-stage chemistry between the two stars was lethal, while the leading lady—as was much reported in the press— was having an affair with the actor playing the featured character. While this was beside the point and had nothing whatsoever to do with *Nick & Nora*, the audience in the theatre was clearly not pulling for Nick and Nora to get together.

A producer friend, having been approached for participation, sent over the materials. My observations were: Arthur Laurents hadn't written a successful musical or play since 1959, and not without trying; yes, he directed the 1983 hit *La Cage aux Folles*, but I didn't much like *La Cage*.

Charles Strouse had written seven failures since *Annie*, including two 4-performance flops, two 1-night wonders, and one that folded out of town. Strouse's music during this time was becoming stronger and more adventurous, but his collaborators all seemed on a different page.

Lyricist Richard Maltby had found no Broadway success in his first three efforts, two of which closed out of town. The third—*Baby*, of which I was a big fan—had failed to meet its potential, which I ascribed to an indistinct point of view that was at least partly the fault of director Maltby. He had also done the American adaptation for a fourth musical, Andrew Lloyd Webber's *Song and Dance*. Yes, Maltby had directed the superhit *Ain't Misbehavin'*; but he had not written that show's lyrics, nor was he directing *Nick & Nora*.

Getting past the personnel, I was left with a core question. I enjoyed the *The Thin Man* films, but I saw them as episodes of a situation comedy (with a delicious situation) rather than a story. Not conducive to musical comedy, although not impossible.

And while it is unfair to judge one show against another, *City of Angels*—which opened in December 1989—posed an enormous obstacle. It would not be enough for Laurents & company to come up with an entertaining, witty, clever and off-beat musical; in order to win the critics and an audience, it would have to be *more* entertaining, witty, etc. than *City of Angels*. Not impossible to accomplish, mind you. But Larry Gelbart's wildly funny book, David Zippel's uncannily clever lyrics, Cy Coleman's smokily jazzy score, and Michael Blakemore's ingenious production, set *Nick & Nora* scaling four treacherous slopes.

My verdict: good luck to *Nick & Nora*, but don't hold your breath. And don't invest.

The Nadir

Kelly

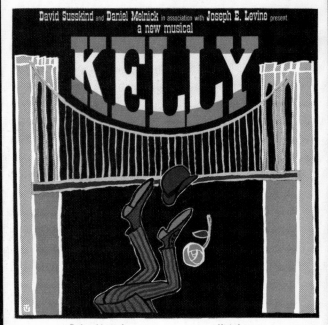

Kelly (1965)

"Heeeeeeeeeeeeeeeeelp"

Kelly was just another musical comedy, coming along during the last throes of the so-called Golden Age of the Broadway musical. *Hello, Dolly! Funny Girl*, and *Fiddler on the Roof* were the big musicals in town. Theatregoers could also choose Bea Lillie in *High Spirits*, Sammy Davis in *Golden Boy* (see page 178), Robert Preston in *Ben Franklin in Paris*, Chita Rivera in *Bajour*, and Buddy Hackett in *I Had a Ball*—not to mention the long-running Pulitzer-winner from 1961, *How to Succeed in Business without Really Trying*.

David Susskind, the lead producer of *Kelly*, saw fit to invite the *Saturday Evening Post* to send a reporter along to observe the birth of the show. "With any luck," said co-producer Daniel Melnick, "you will be able to write a textbook on how to produce a play in the American musical theatre."

A textbook study it is, certainly. Because the reporter had unlimited access, and because *Kelly* turned out to be a legendary case of musical comedy gone wrong, the resulting article—printed at length in the April 24, 1965 issue—allows us to sit in and calmly watch a classic case of Second Act Trouble. And because the reporter did such a very good job, the saga of *Kelly* makes remarkable reading. Lewis H. Lapham has been editor of *Harper's Magazine* since 1976, but back in 1964 he spent three months living with *Kelly*.

A view from the bridge.

"Has Anybody Here Seen *Kelly*?"

by Lewis H. Lapham

PROLOGUE

The musical comedy *Kelly* opened at the Broadhurst Theatre on Saturday, February 6. The New York drama critics unanimously condemned it as one of the worst musicals they had ever seen. Walter Kerr, writing in the *New York Herald Tribune*, spoke of it as "a bad idea gone wrong." Howard Taubman, the critic for the *New York Times*, called it "wooden and hollow…without freshness or imagination."

It closed after a single performance, costing the investors roughly $650,000. Nobody on Broadway could remember such a spectacular disaster within the recent history of the theatre.

On Monday, February 8, the morning of the play's collapse, David Susskind, the television impresario and the most eloquent of *Kelly*'s three producers, spoke to newspaper reporters of his grief. To the *New York Herald Tribune*, he said, in part:

"I have never been so shocked, so surprised in my life. I believed in *Kelly*. I believed in the cast. I believed in the staging…the songs. Then I saw the reviews. They raised a huge unanswered question mark in my brain. What happened to my taste? Did I put on something crass? Could I be this wrong?"

Such a confession would have seemed improbable to him in October 1964, when, prior to the first rehearsals, Susskind's press agent came to the *Saturday Evening Post* with a proposition for an article about the making of a Broadway musical. The press agent, Jack Perlis, announced that Susskind would welcome the presence of a writer during all phases of the production. No producer had ever before suggested such a thing, Perlis said, but no producer had as much courage as Susskind.

Considered in retrospect, the events leading toward that last catastrophic weekend in New York possess a dramatic form that divides, without any pedantic unities, into four acts.

ACT I

The Brooklyn Bridge, Sunday, October 25, 1964, Early Afternoon

Seen from a distance in the clear light of an unseasonably warm afternoon, the men and women grouped on the pedestrian walk of the Brooklyn Bridge seem as luminous figures in a Renoir painting. The chorus girls, dressed in costumes of the 1880's, carried parasols. The men in striped blazers and derby hats had brought picnic baskets and mugs of beer.

They stood in a small circle, listening to a trombone player try the opening bars of a tune called "Everyone Here Loves Kelly." When he had got it right, the girls put aside their parasols and danced, kicking their legs high in the air. The press agents, who had arranged the entertainment for the benefit of newspaper photographers, then began to push everybody else out of the way.

"Behind the cameras, please," they said, "everybody behind the cameras."

Joseph E. Levine, a heavy man with alligator shoes and a dark silk suit, smiled fondly at the dancing, pleased that he had managed to borrow the Brooklyn Bridge for a publicity stunt on behalf of his new play. Derived from the legendary exploit of Steve Brodie, the play was about a young man who jumps off the bridge around the turn of the century.

"Showmanship," Levine said, watching some bewildered pedestrians walking across to Flatbush. "This is what I call showmanship." [Joseph E. Levine had started as an importer of low-brow foreign films in the late Fifties, with titles including *Godzilla, King of the Monsters!*, *Hercules*, *Jack the Ripper*, and *The Last Days of Sodom and Gomorrah*. He started to move into more classy fare with the Katharine Hepburn-Ralph Richardson *Long Day's Journey into Night* in 1962, but it wasn't until 1967 when he hit the A-list, as executive producer of *The Graduate*.]

Levine had been brought into the venture by David Susskind and Daniel Melnick, Susskind's partner in his television enterprises, and between them they had raised $450,000 for the play's production, a sum they then thought adequate to the purpose. Of that original money Levine put up $250,000; Susskind and Melnick persuaded a small group of investors to put up another $150,000; and Columbia Records, in return for the rights to the record album, had advanced $50,000. None of the producing partners had ever before attempted a Broadway musical. [Television producer David Susskind had produced three Broadway plays. The first two, in 1956 and 1958, had lasted 5 performances each; the third, Peter Glenville's production of *Rashomon* (1959) starring Rod Steiger and Claire Bloom, achieved a certain degree of prestige though it lasted only twenty weeks. He moved into films with greater success, co-producing Lorraine Hansberry's *A Raisin in the Sun* (1961) and Rod Serling's *Requiem for a Heavyweight* (1962).]

When the photographers had taken enough pictures, the chorus girls put on fur coats, and everybody went back to the yellow tent set up on a traffic island at the Manhattan end of the bridge. The press agents, among them Jack Perlis, encouraged any stragglers with promises of more music and beer.

"Titans," Perlis said, speaking of Susskind and Levine, "these men are titans, giants of the entertainment industry, the Barnums of today. Whatever they do, they do big. I promise big action."

The Amsterdam Roof, Six Weeks Later

The first rehearsals took place in an old theatre on the seventh floor of the New Amsterdam movie house at Broadway and 42nd Street. Drafty and dimly lighted, the theatre had once been used by Florenz Ziegfeld for some of his smaller productions. Herbert Ross, the director and choreographer, sat in a wooden chair placed on an old burlesque runway. A tall, lean, awkward and flatfooted man, he sat with his right leg folded under his left, wearing a loose sweater and steadily smoking cigarettes. Although he was well-established as a choreographer of television shows and Broadway musicals, *Kelly* was the first musical that he had ever directed. [*Kelly* was Ross's tenth of thirteen credited Broadway musicals. Ross almost always received strong personal reviews, but each of his musicals failed. While *Kelly* was the first new musical he directed, he had already earned a reputation as a play fixer. "If Herb is such a great show doctor," his wife Nora Kaye once asked, "why do all the patients die?"]

During those first weeks, gradually giving substance to his visions of space and movement, he seldom raised his voice, preferring to speak to the company with light sarcasm. His horn-rimmed glasses and the deep lines in his gentle face gave him the appearance of a university professor.

"You're doing this like a bunch of drunken old ladies, for heaven's sake," he would say to the dancers; or, "Don't just sit there like an Equity member, Leslie, *react*." Other than Ross's bored, calm voice, the only sound in the theatre was that of the rehearsal pianist playing the same tunes over and over again on the upright piano to the left of the stage, and the dancers counting to themselves as they waited to make their entrances. The girls wore their long hair pinned up in brightly colored scarves.

Moose Charlap and Eddie Lawrence attended every rehearsal, both of them pacing nervously up and down the aisles, watching their play from different angles. They had written *Kelly* five years before, in nine days and nine nights of fierce inspiration. They had been unable to get it performed, however, because the producers to whom they brought it had wanted to make unacceptable changes in the script.

Conceived as an ironic farce, the play concerned a young Irish immigrant (Hop Kelly) who, before the opening curtain, has tried and failed in three attempts to jump from the Brooklyn Bridge. The action takes place along the Bowery during the late 1880s. A sarcastic and cocksure youth, Kelly had offered to jump from the bridge in a moment of braggadocio. A group of gamblers took him up on the offer and squandered large amounts of money on his three losses of nerve.

As the play opens the gamblers are ready to bet on him once again, but this time, to insure their investment, they intend to make him party to a fraud, by means of a complicated scheme to throw a dummy off the bridge. In his first appearance on stage, however, Kelly sings a soliloquy in which he reveals hope of regaining self-respect by honestly risking death. The dramatic action depends on the ensuing conflict between Kelly and the gamblers. (The action also involves several subplots, including Hop's love for a gambler's daughter.)

At various intervals the characters pause, in the tradition of Bertolt Brecht, to sing songs intended as commentaries to the audience. These dealt with such themes as social injustice and the falsity of romantic love.

Both Lawrence and Charlap thought of the play as an artistic statement about modern life, not as a Broadway entertainment. They were thankful that in Susskind and Melnick they at last had found producers with the courage to present such a play.

"Those other guys," Lawrence said, referring to other producers, "wanted to change the kid into some kind of knight in shining armor, like a crummy love story."

A man in his early 40s, nearly always dressed in a well-fitting tweed jacket and a soft hat slanted jauntily across his eyes, Lawrence had a cold and self-contained manner, as if he never quite heard what anybody said to him. Although known principally as a nightclub comic and as an author of comedy sketches for television, Lawrence had also studied painting for four years after the war with Fernand Léger in Paris, and he believed that an artist's work was inviolable. *Kelly* was his first full-length play. [Lawrence was best known on Broadway for his role as Sandor, the featured comic, in the 1956 Styne-Comden-Green-Robbins-Fosse musical, *Bells Are Ringing*.]

Charlap, more excitable and intense, had composed the music for three Broadway shows, among them *Peter Pan*. A small man, almost bald, he walked with a bounding gait and spoke in a quick and husky voice, generally accompanied by violent chopping motions in both hands. [Charlap had indeed composed *Peter Pan* for Jerome Robbins and Mary Martin in 1954, but half of his score was thrown out during the tryout (and replaced with new songs by Styne, Comden, and Green). Charlap's retained tunes included "Tender Shepherd," "I Gotta Crow," and "I Won't Grow Up." His other two musicals, written with lyricist Norman Gimbel, were the quick failure *Whoop-Up* and the even more disastrous *Conquering Hero*.]

"The play is something I believe in," he said "It thumbs its nose at cliché. I'm not attempting to speak to the 12-year-old mind.... This is 1964; so it's against sentimental.... Give it the bitter chop; no perfect fifths or octaves.... At least let me be wrong on my own terms.... I hope I still believe in it when it gets to Broadway."

On the afternoon of the third day, Daniel Melnick came confidently forward out of the gloom of the darkened theatre, his overcoat draped across his shoulders. On his way across the stage he paused to kiss two chorus girls lightly on their foreheads. Under the overcoat, the collar of which was trimmed in fur, he wore a double-breasted cashmere sweater with suede buttons.

"Ask any question you can think of," he said, introducing himself. "With any luck you will be able to write a textbook on how to produce a play in the American musical theatre."

Although Levine had contributed the major amount of money, he had entrusted the production to Susskind and Melnick. At the age of thirty-two, Melnick had been Susskind's partner for the past year in Talent Associates-Paramount Ltd., a company that packages and sells television shows and which, as he explained, concerned itself with "all media on both coasts." Of Lawrence and Charlap, he said: "Eddie and Moose, of course, are insane."

He intended the remark as a high compliment, meaning to suggest that the richness of their talent surpassed the understanding of ordinary people. Susskind appeared later that evening. He wore an old raincoat and walked with the rolling gait of a sailor or a prizefighter. "We're not remote, entrepreneurial figures," he said, "we're gutty, rich, virile, accessible." Laughingly he remembered the numerous auditions for prospective investors, many of whom had been confused by the unconventional aspects of the play. "Overbred society people," he said, "...the critics had not yet told them what to think."

The Cort Theatre, A Week Later

On Monday, December 14, the company moved to West 48th Street because Ross wanted to try the dance numbers on a larger stage. The scene was nearly identical to the one on the Amsterdam

Roof: steam pipes against a brick wall behind the stage, the same harsh light, the same drafts. The cast, after a month of rehearsals, had become bored. When not called upon to perform, the dancers and actors sat listlessly on folding chairs, reading newspapers, working crossword puzzles, talking about clothes and love affairs. "What do you mean, does she know him?" said a blond girl waiting to sing, "of course she knows him, she's been living with him for a week."

The stage had been marked out with strips of tape to indicate the eventual placing of the props and scenery. Randy Brooks, the stage manager, was beginning to note the necessary timings; how long for platforms to rise into place; how long for each scene, each crossover, each song. Susskind and Melnick now came to every rehearsal. Often Susskind sat by himself in the back of the theatre, staring at the stage with fierce concentration. Late one afternoon he confessed to a suppressed ambition to become a choreographer. He spoke also of his fondness for the timelessness of the theatre, a remote and far-off place wherein only the imaginary was real. "The musical comedy is the only generic American art form," he said. "I would like to have one continually in rehearsal. It's great therapy to come and watch the singing and dancing, away from Madison Avenue and the money worries and the bureaucrats."

The Philadelphia billing page. Top-billed Ella Logan was fired from the show, reinstated, and then fired once more.

Melnick had taken to sitting directly behind Ross, whispering in his ear, giving advice about the movements of the dancers, or the placing of the sets, or the reading of particular lines. As the rehearsals continued, Ross sometimes spoke to the company with a harsh edge in his voice.

"Listen, people," he would say, "this is not important dialogue, so please just don't let it lie there."

The actor with whom Ross was most concerned was Don Francks, a Canadian nightclub and television entertainer playing the role of Hop Kelly. Although not much past the age of 30, his gaunt face was marked with deep shadows. He had quit school at a young age and wandered around the world, shipping out as a seaman on a freighter to South Africa, working in an iron foundry in British Columbia, traveling to Mexico on a motorcycle. Melnick had promised him that with *Kelly* he would be discovered as a sensational star in the United States, another Robert Goulet. [Goulet, also of Canadian stock, was launched to stardom in the 1960 Broadway musical *Camelot*.]

Usually he came to rehearsal dressed in soft leather boots and tight-fitting suits of his own design. He seldom spoke to his colleagues, preferring to inscribe his passing thoughts and fancies in the large black notebook that he carried with him everywhere. Waiting his turn to perform, he would decorate the pages of the notebook with drawings of flowers, like illuminations in a medieval manuscript. At times Francks put his inspirations into prose, and at other times into poetry.

At the end of the rehearsal on Thursday night, Ross, Melnick, Susskind, Lawrence and Charlap gathered in the 11th row to consider the possible elimination of a song sung by two actors playing the parts of Frank and Jesse James. (One of Lawrence's subplots involved the robbery of the Bowery Savings Bank by the James brothers.)

"Let's be realistic, gentlemen," Melnick said, "it's not coming off, and we cannot hold onto the dream."

As soon as Charlap understood the intent of the conversation, he began to twitch nervously. Susskind put his arm around him, seeking to comfort him.

"Moose, Moose," he said, "stop that nonsense. Nobody's going to hurt you."

"I won't cut it," Charlap said, "I'm sorry; I simply won't do it."

So saying, he got up and walked out of the theatre.

By the following afternoon, Susskind and Charlap had temporarily resolved their differences. But thereafter, if ever Susskind put his arm around Charlap's shoulder, the color would drain from Charlap's face, and his eyes would assume a glazed expression.

The rehearsals proceeded without incident for the rest of the week, and on Sunday the cast presented a run-through of the entire play for an audience of about one hundred friends and relatives. The friends and relatives did not laugh much, nor did they applaud in a way that could be thought heartening.

"I remember in Paris once, after a performance like this," Lawrence said without explanation, "the audience yelled 'author, author,' and the actors brought out a gorilla."

The audience's lack of enthusiasm had a depressing effect on Ross, who sat slumped in his seat in the last row, his face in his hands.

"There isn't a page of dialogue that works," he said, "not a line."

Melnick, however, managed to interpret any apparent failure as an inconsequential illusion. Of the audience's response on this occasion, he said:

"They're interested. They're intrigued, but they're too respectful. Like it was a poetry reading or an evening at the Ninety-Second Street Y.M.H.A. The love scene is too honest."

Much later that night, after long and involuted conversations in the men's room, everybody agreed that except for a few minor troubles in the first act, the play was in remarkably good shape. Ross, having regained his composure, expected slight changes in Philadelphia. "For what we have got to say," he said, "maybe we could cut twenty minutes; nothing's so good that it can't be cut."

"The wonderful thing about this show," Melnick said, "is that everybody is working together. There is none of that terribleness, that viciousness, those cliques common to most musicals. What we have here is a unity."

En route To Philadelphia, December 22, 1964, Late Morning

The talk in the car, a long Cadillac with two telephones, devolved largely on deals: for books, movies, plays, people, television rights and common stocks. Joseph E. Levine, his hat placed firmly on his head, his hands spread motionless on his knees, sat on the back seat with Susskind. Melnick sat in front with the driver. They talked with the largesse of Monopoly players exchanging railroads and utilities.

Levine was in a contented mood. His most recent film, *Marriage Italian Style*, had opened the day before in New York to rave notices and was expected to gross several million dollars at box offices across the country. *The Carpetbaggers* continued to earn record sums, and in London everybody said that Carroll Baker would attract additional millions in *Harlow*. For a man who had started out in Boston fifty-nine years ago with no money and no prospects, and who had, among other things, sold plastic statuettes of Daddy Grace on the streets of Harlem, Levine had come a long way. ["Sweet Daddy" Grace was a flamboyant evangelist and founder of the United House of Prayer for All People.]

As the car moved slowly through the Lincoln Tunnel, Melnick explained that they might have trouble selling tickets to *Kelly* because Don Francks, in the lead, was an unknown name.

"He's not a star, Joe," Melnick said, "in Kansas they never heard of him... Jesus, what am I talking about, Kansas... they don't know him on Forty-Second Street."

"So I'll give him three pictures," Levine said.

Susskind reminded Levine that he was to appear the following week on Susskind's television show, *Hot Line*, together with Isaac Stern, the violinist, and Risë Stevens, the opera singer.

"It's a classy guest list, Joe," Susskind said, "you could talk about *Kelly*."

"Will Isaac play 'Hearts and Flowers' if I tell him the story of my boyhood?" Levine asked.

During the rest of the trip Susskind seldom spoke. Levine and Melnick, however, continued to talk about money. Levine said he had just bought the movie and television rights to Romain Gary's new novel, *The Ski Bum*.

"Did you read the book, Joe?" Melnick asked.

"What do you mean, did I read it? I didn't have to read it. I bought it."

As the car approached Philadelphia, edging through the suburbs on the north side of town, Levine asked a series of questions about *Kelly*. Being a novice at producing for the stage, he wanted to know about costs, renting theatres, unions, advertising procedures. At the end of this conversation, by way of a joke, he asked, "So when do we close?"

Everybody laughed at that, and Levine said that no matter what happened on Broadway, he would make the play into "a helluva movie."

In the lobby of the Barclay Hotel on Rittenhouse Square, waiting for the bellboy to bring his luggage from the car, Susskind looked with mounting doubts and suspicion at the potted palms.

"I hope we're going to be happy here," he said.

ACT II
Philadelphia, The Shubert Theatre, The Following Night

The marquee outside the theatre looked like the marquee on a suburban supermarket. The cold and efficient lettering advertised, as if it were the day's special grocery offering, A SMASH NEW MUSICAL COMEDY. The phrase was conceived by Nat Dorfman, a New York press agent assigned by Perlis and Susskind to promote *Kelly* on the road. The show was to play a preview performance on Saturday, December 26, and on the following Monday, December 28, it would open for the Philadelphia critics and the beginning of a three-week engagement.

At 7:30 P.M. Wednesday, as a few people stood in line at the box office, the company began its first run-through with costumes, lights, scenery and orchestra. Ross sat in the 14th row, dictating notes to his assistant. Susskind and Melnick took their accustomed positions, directly behind him. To Ross's right sat Freddy Wittop, the costume designer, and Oliver Smith, the set designer. [Wittop and Smith had performed the same jobs on Broadway's then-reigning hit, *Hello, Dolly!*, which also took place in and around New York in the 1880s.] To his left, five rows farther back, sat Charlap and Lawrence.

The run-through required the better part of two days. Randy Brooks, the stage manager, stopped the performance every few minutes until he had satisfied himself that the sets worked properly and that the actors knew their exits and entrances precisely.

The revelation of the sets and costumes inspired Susskind and Melnick to elaborate compliments. "Smashing, Freddy, absolutely gorgeous," Melnick would say to Wittop. "Ravishing, Oliver, perfectly ravishing," Susskind would say to Smith. The sets had cost almost $100,000.

Because several scenes took place in the Bowery, in a lower-class milieu, many of the costumes, which cost another $90,000, had been made to look poor. "They look so good," Melnick said, "as if they came from an Army-Navy surplus store for $3.98."

"My rags are chiffon," Wittop said, "otherwise they wouldn't float that way. The idea is poetic dirt, not just a dirty look."

Charlap and Lawrence, however, disapproved of both sets and costumes. They would have prefered a bleak stage and abstract sets, something more in the tradition of Bertolt Brecht.

"This is too real, too materialistic, too rich," Charlap said. "The imagination droops, and suddenly you're competing with *My Fair Lady*. In East Germany they would understand how to do this play."

"Well, if it's a stiff," Lawrence said, "we can always charge admission to let the people see the sets and costumes."

Ross, although pleased with the visual effects, worried about the music. He wasn't happy with Sandy Matlovsky, the conductor, and he thought some of the orchestral arrangements lacked style. Matlovsky had been hired at the insistence of Charlap, partly because the two men were friends and partly because Matlovsky had conducted the first New York performance of Brecht's classic *Threepenny Opera*. [Matlovsky did not conduct the first performance, which was at the Empire Theatre in 1933; he conducted Marc Blitzstein's long-running 1954 off-Broadway adaptation. The orchestrations for *Kelly* were by Hershy Kay, whose credits included Leonard Bernstein's *Candide* and the 1963 musical *110 in the Shade*.]

Upon hearing the orchestra play a dance number called "Tough Neighborhood," Ross said, in an aside to Susskind and Melnick, "That's the worst thing I ever heard...it's as if they never saw the parts and telephoned it in!"

In a louder voice, to Matlovsky, he said, "Stop it, Sandy, stop it, I'm sorry, but I want it my way, now...it's just terrible."

The rehearsal ended at 11:30 P.M., the run-through having progressed as far as the last scene in Act I. Ross and the two producers then summoned their authors to a meeting in the basement of the theatre. They had begun to suspect that the character of Hop Kelly was not sufficiently sympathetic or heroic. Earlier that day they had decided to ask Lawrence for three new scenes and Charlap for at least one new song.

Although the authors agreed to these requests, they did so with heavy reluctance, doubts obviously beginning to cloud their minds. When they had left, Melnick, who had been a vice president of the ABC television network and there had established *Ben Casey*, said, "You've got to be a Jesuit or a rabbi to justify all the changes and satisfy the emotional needs of these people... Authors are like children."

Susskind thought Lawrence and Charlap ungrateful for his and Melnick's advice.

"They ought to be down on their hands and knees for all the creative collaboration they're getting," he said.

The Same, Three Nights Later

Levine, who had gone back to New York after a press conference that first day, returned to Philadelphia for the first preview. Before the performance he stood unobtrusively in the lobby, watching the audience come into the theatre, listening to the customers talking about their Christmas presents and the unusually warm rain that season.

"This week in New York," he said, "I've already had a flop and a hit. *Marriage Italian Style* is big. Everywhere there are lines, long lines at the box office."

The flop was Eugene O'Neill's *Hughie*, with Jason Robards Jr., a play that Levine had produced with the hope of improving his image among the literati.

"I mean, it was art for Chrissake," he said. "The critics are supposed to go for art, aren't they?? I always knew that movie critics hated movies, and so from now on I know that drama critics hate plays."

He was especially troubled by the knowledge that the success or failure of a play depended on the opinions of only five or six men in New York.

"It's a crap game," he said. "You could take $500,000 to Las Vegas and do as well."

He watched the performance from the back of the theatre, leaning against the rail behind the last row of seats, together with Susskind, Ross and Melnick. They watched the audience with the fascination of children looking at lions and tigers in a zoo.

Charlap and Lawrence stood off to one side. Of all the people in the theatre they were the ones who most enjoyed the show. Lawrence, who had bought a new hat for the occasion, carried his script under his arm. He laughed at all the jokes and listened complacently to the songs.

Charlap, more nervous, paced excitedly back and forth.

"They [the producers] complained that the book doesn't hold," he said. "Well, it holds, it holds like nothing you ever saw before."

The audience, however, reserved its warmest applause for the sets and costumes. If the customers had arrived discussing Christmas or the weather, they left talking about the same subjects except for a sympathetic lady in a veil who, expressing the majority opinion, said to a friend on her way through the lobby:

"I feel sorry for the cast."

Ross, Susskind and Melnick walked back to the Barclay Hotel in the rain, all of them trying to think of something reassuring to say.

"I know it's there somewhere," Susskind said.

"I hope we don't get good notices," Ross said. "Eddie will be more difficult if we do... it's a question of major rewriting."

"At least we now know the things we thought were bad are really just as bad as we thought," Melnick said.

An hour later, at the Variety Club, a bar frequented by traveling actors, the members of the cast comforted themselves with Scotch and variations of the maxim that Philadelphia audiences were always wrong. They ignored the Christmas tree and the messages of good cheer pasted on the walls.

"In Philly," somebody said, "they hated *West Side Story*."

"If they liked it," said somebody else, "then we'd really be in trouble."

The Philadelphia program used one of *Playbill*'s generic cover photos.

The Barclay Hotel, The Morning of December 29

In a room overlooking Rittenhouse Square, Ross, Melnick and Susskind sat staring gloomily at the Philadelphia newspapers scattered on the floor.

Ross sprawled gloomily on a couch too small for his angular figure; Melnick and Susskind lounged in armchairs. In a corner of the room, suffused in cold, bright sunlight, a table had been set up with pastry and coffee.

The play had opened the night before, and the reviews were mixed. The Philadelphia *Daily News*, the least important of the local papers, thought *Kelly* "a thing of quality… rowdy in humor and blessed with memorable music and engaging dance." But the critic for the Philadelphia *Bulletin* spoke of "a tedious story torpedoed by indecision and the easiness with which it is led up blind alleys." He described Hop Kelly as "a one-dimensional oaf." The producers chose to believe the worst of the reviews.

"This show is an accumulation of non sequitors," Susskind said, "for a hero we have an oaf, a passive iconoclast, a whiner, a cardboard social protest. There is self-pity implicit in his every speech and move."

"We have to get a line to the story," Ross said, "and then try to fill in the motivations. It happens all the time, just a matter of making the kid heroic."

After an hour of anguished conversation, they decided to cut Frank and Jesse James from the script, to move a successful dance number from the second to the first act and to insist that Lawrence write whatever they told him to write. They also wanted to cut the opening soliloquy, a song for Francks called "Ode to the Bridge."

Charlap and Lawrence, accompanied by Matlovsky, the conductor, arrived about noon. They took chairs at the opposite end of the room and refused all offers of pastry or coffee. They looked wary.

Susskind began by reading aloud the sentence of the review about "a tedious story torpedoed by indecision." He then said, "Eddie, I agree with that review 100 percent."

Lawrence merely stared at him, saying nothing, his mouth drawing into a stubborn line. Charlap and Matlovsky looked at the paintings on the walls.

To interrupt the awkward silence, Melnick brought up the subject of the "Ode to the Bridge."

"It's no good, Eddie," he said, "it's Gotterdämmerung."

"Of course, like a bad poem," Lawrence said, "that's the whole point of the joke."

"Eddie," Susskind said, "it's a humorless rumination."

"I think it's funny," Lawrence said, "and my friends all think it's funny."

"Your friends are wrong, Eddie," Susskind said.

"I'm not willing to give it up," Lawrence said, "at least not for now."

At that, discouraged by the inflexible expression in Lawrence's face, the producers dropped the subject. They proceeded to the faults in Hop Kelly's character.

"You've got to make the kid more lovable, Eddie," Ross said. "We've got to understand why the girl loves him."

"Have you got that, Eddie?" Susskind said. "Get to the love."

"I'm beginning to see the reason for all that love stuff in those old Metro movies," Melnick said.

Lawrence then read the three new scenes that he had written over the past two days. The others listened in noncommittal silence. When nobody said anything, Lawrence said. "I don't know what I'm writing anymore."

"Eddie," Susskind said, "don't talk like that. You've got a hero, you've got a mission, you've got enemy forces."

"Next time," Lawrence said, "we tryout in Hudson's Bay. They haven't seen an actor there in thirty years." [*Foxy*, a Bert Lahr musical that opened in February 1964, had tried out in the wilds of the Yukon Territory. Even so, the show failed in Canada and New York.]

Having thus disposed, at least temporarily, of the writing problems, the producers turned their attention to the music. To Matlovsky, Melnick said, "Sandy, let me level with you. I'm not comfortable, I'm worried, I don't think we're on top of the music."

"It's not the kind of music that plays itself," Matlovsky said, "the score is like a dead animal."

"We've got to have the result, Sandy," Melnick said.

From Charlap the producers also wanted a second new song, this one a ballad for the newly lovable Hop Kelly.

"It should be a song of self-revelation, discovery, recognition," Susskind said, "the 'I've Grown Accustomed to Her Face' of our show."

Although Susskind and Melnick wanted to put all these changes into effect as soon as possible, Ross refused to let them give the new material to the actors until later in the week.

"Don't mess around with these people, Danny," he said to Melnick, "they're tired. I'm not going to see the show for the rest of this week, and I don't care what happens on stage. This is only Philadelphia. Who cares what happens in Philadelphia?"

As the meeting adjourned, just after two o'clock, Lawrence permitted himself a last wistful remark: "I liked my own show better. It was intimate and small, and now I see it turning into a lavish Broadway spectacle."

"Eddie, there's a big hit here," Susskind said. "This is the show you intended to write."

"I hate it," Lawrence said.

The Shubert Theatre, Five Days Later
The first rehearsal with Lawrence's three new scenes, rewritten

since the meeting in the Barclay Hotel, and Charlap's two new songs, took place on the evening of January 3. The company would perform this "new" show on the following night.

The actors playing the James brothers had been fired on Saturday and already had gone back to New York. On the same day Susskind had gone to London to supervise the filming of a television spectacular, thus leaving the production to Melnick. During its first week in Philadelphia the play had earned $44,000, about $16,000 less than its expenses over the same period.

In the revised version of the play, Hop Kelly approached his jump from the Brooklyn Bridge as if for the first time, not the third. He had gained an additional reason for the jump. As he explained to his girl-friend at the end of Act I, "because it's there. If I was in England, maybe I would want to swim the Channel, or if I was in Buffalo, go over Niagara Falls in a barrel."

Lawrence, although he had written the lines himself, disliked them. He still came to the theatre every day, not as a matter of inter-est, but for fear that the producers would change lines without asking him. Watching the new love scene, he said:

"Smug, smug. My God, that's what I can't stand, that smugness.... Never again, no more Broadway producers. They want to run the the-atre like a bargain basement in a department store, trying to sell only what the public will buy. In France we used to sit around and laugh about things like this, but the trouble is that nobody here is laughing except me."

Melnick was pleased with the changes. He thought that now the play had begun to take shape, to tell a believable story that people could enjoy and understand.

"We took out the hostility," he said to Ross. "It's sensational. Herb, sensational...it moves so fast that if anybody in the audience stops to sneeze, they're lost."

The Barclay Hotel, The Morning of January 5th

The new material had proved as disappointing as the old. The audi-ence on Monday night laughed weakly at the new jokes and failed to demonstrate any additional sympathy for the new Hop Kelly. Susskind, informed of this disappointment on the telephone to London, demanded improvements; Levine called later in the day from New York giving similar instructions. Sitting in the same chairs as on the previous Tuesday, Ross, Melnick, Charlap and Lawrence shared a common anxiety. They felt a need for strong and decisive action. Ross, who looked cold and tired, sat with his hands concealed in the sleeves of his sweater.

"I have something very dramatic," he said, "...it's Ella."

Nobody said anything. Ella Logan had last appeared on Broadway in 1947 as the lead in *Finian's Rainbow*, and her role as the mother of Hop Kelly was to have served as the vehicle for her triumphant return to the stage. "She's a cantankerous lady," Ross said. "She's so vulgar I can't stand it. She's hurting us, and she will definitely have to go."

"She's a cancer," Melnick said, "a Trotskyite."

Both Charlap and Lawrence, surprised by this suggestion, pointed out that Miss Logan was the nearest person they had to a star, that so far she had received the loudest applause, that many tickets had been sold because of her name, and that, without her, the already small business at the box office might diminish even further.

"That's a chance we must take," Melnick said. "If she were fabulous, we might not have the guts to get rid of her, but her part is irrelevant. We can give her lines to the father. She's hurting us, and we've got to be ruthless, just as if she were a song or a dance."

"You get a lot of laughs with the mother," Lawrence said.

"Two laughs, Eddie," Melnick said.

"Nobody understands my jokes," Lawrence said.

Without further argument it was agreed to do away with Miss Logan: Melnick said he would tell her on Wednesday night after the performance. Then, taking advantage of this new surge of self-confidence, he telephoned Nat Dorfman, the press agent.

"Nat, Nat sweetheart, I'm very disappointed in you.... I'm unhappy, Nat. The word of mouth is not good enough. Not enough people know that we have a very exciting show. Nat, I'm not interested in sympathy. Nat, I want it on the radio."

The Variety Club, Wednesday Night

The miasma of collective depression settled, like a mist in a swamp, along the bar. The members of the company exchanged rumors, saying that a screenwriter from Hollywood (some said it was the man who wrote *The Carpetbaggers*) would come east to rewrite the script. Others said that after Boston the show would travel to Toronto in hope of gaining additional time in which to make improvements.

Anita Gillette, a small, brown-haired girl with large, soft eyes, sat at a table among several dancers. To Tony di Vecchi, a dancer who kept his money in his shoes, she said, "Tony, am I on the way up or the way down?"

"If it's a big hit, honey,"' he said, "you're on the way up." [Anita Gillette first came to prominence in 1961 when she subbed for Anna Maria Alberghetti in *Carnival*. (Producer David Merrick, who was battling with Alberghetti, made sure that the press was in the house for Gillette's "triumphant" debut.) Gillette quickly moved into ingénue roles in two big 1962 Josh Logan musicals, *All American* and *Mr. President*. Both were dire failures. *Kelly* came next; Gillette was definitely on the way down.]

At around midnight Don Francks passed silently and wonderingly through the room, a riding crop under his arm and his familiar black notebook clutched in his left hand. As the character of Hop Kelly gradually became sentimental, Francks's performance became less convincing. This confused and alarmed him, and so, on this particular night, leaving the Variety Club without saying more than a few words to anybody, he went back to his hotel room and wrote of his disillusion in his usual cryptic style. (The relevant entry in his notebook later read: "Thank you for your plastic flowers; thank you for your rubber fern... the bubbles in my pink champagne have burst.")

On his way out of the bar Francks smiled bleakly at Charlap, who, with his wife, sat drinking in the corner of the room under the Christmas tree. [Charlap's wife was the pop singer Sandy Stewart.] Charlap was brooding about the transformation of the play and the arguments won and lost with producers.

"The job of the creative man," he said, "is not to let the money men vitiate his work."

And then, growing more excited with the liquor and the late hour and the enormity of the injustice he felt inflicted upon him, he quoted at random from the work of Ezra Pound, savagely cutting the air with his hands and mixing up the verses of several poems.

"O helpless few in my country," he began, "O remnant enslaved, thwarted against the systems.... Go my songs.... I have weathered out this storm; I have beaten out my existence."

Ella Logan came in at about two a.m. Round-faced and sly, a woman in her early 50s, she wore a Hawaiian blouse and looked around the room with the exaggerated melodrama of a conspirator in a Shakespearean play.

Talking softly among her supporters in the corner of the bar opposite to Charlap, she reported Melnick's visit to her dressing room. That night, she said, he had come to her and told her that her part was being reduced to five lines in the first act and six lines in the second. She interpreted this maneuver as an attempt to humiliate her and thus oblige her, for reasons of her own pride, to quit the show. If she quit the producers could say that she had violated the contract and therefore they were under no obligation to pay her.

"But I ain't moving," she said. "I told him very politely I'd speak to my lawyer, and I ain't moving."

Mickey Shaughnessy, a tall and florid man playing the part of a prizefighter who befriends Kelly, gave voice to the troubled emotions of everybody present. Although successful as a nightclub comic and a character actor, Shaughnessy had never played in a Broadway musical, and he was unfamiliar with the rules of behavior out of town.

He pounded his fist on the bar, glaring at the crowd with fierce, direct eyes. Several people tried to quiet him, but he ignored them, his anger that of a passionate and simple man first encountering intrigue.

"I'm sorry, I'm raw," he said. "I'm nightclub. I'm used to telling something to a man's face. We know the play's a bomb. But what is all this whispering and calling everybody 'darling'? If this is Broadway, I don't want it… it's untruthful. We've heard rumors of a new writer and new director. Let's go ask Mister Ross or Mister Lawrence or Mister Melnick…. Let's talk to each other."

The speech was received in embarrassed silence. Although accustomed to treachery, the other actors were not used to talking about it, especially in the presence of strangers in a bar. Eileen Rodgers, an actress who was cast in the role of a dance-hall queen, began to cry behind her dark glasses, the tears streaming down her face.

"I wish I was back in *Tenderloin*," she said. "It was a flop, but at least people were friendly." [Featured actress Eileen Rodgers had prominent roles in the two Abbott–Bock–Harnick–Prince musicals, *Fiorello!* and *Tenderloin* (see page 188).]

Philadelphia, The Lu Lu Temple, Thursday Afternoon

Ross had called the actors together for a line rehearsal in the grand ballroom of the Masonic Temple down the street from the theatre. The uneasiness and anxiety of the night before had now communicated itself to the entire company. It was another unusually warm day. Through the open windows on the south side of the room, a few birds could be heard singing over the noise of the traffic and the rain.

Halfway through the third scene in Act I, Jesse White, an actor in the role of Stickpin Sidney Crane, the principal gambler attempting to corrupt Kelly, slammed his script on the floor and addressed Eddie Lawrence. As a younger man White had played in several Broadway plays, but lately he had been working as a movie and television actor, his most famous role being in a series of television commercials for Chun King Chow Mein. [White was best known on Broadway as the asylum attendant in the long-running 1944 hit *Harvey*, a role he repeated in the 1950 film (with James Stewart) and the 1970 revival (with Stewart and Helen Hayes). Character man White hit it big in 1968 when he was hired for a commercial as the Maytag Repair Man, a recurring gig which lasted until 1989.]

"How can I say a *line* like that, Eddie, for God's sake. What does it mean?" he said. "It stinks. It's not funny. If we go to Boston with this stuff, the critics will kill us. We keep hearing that you're going to write new material, but all you do is bring the same old stuff warmed over. I'm out on the stage and nothing happens."

"If you don't like it." Lawrence said, "you can quit."

He then stood up and walked stiffly from the room, his script under his arm, his mouth set in the familiar obstinate line. He was followed by Eileen Rodgers, again in tears.

"I can't stand the screaming," she said, "I can't stand it anymore."

Ross allowed the company a ten-minute break and went to comfort Miss Rodgers in the hall. Lawrence had gone back to his hotel.

Waiting for the rehearsal to resume, Ella Logan, now frankly outspoken about the faults of the production, whispered to a dancer that Ross had lost control of his actors.

"Too many ears," she said, "Herbie has too many ears.... There's something frightfully fishy going on; you can't trust anybody around here. With most plays you never see the producers, but these guys do everything but come in rehearsal clothes." From that moment on she was always to refer to Melnick as "the smiling killer."

When the company again assembled for the reading, Ross and Melnick both made short speeches, seeking to reassure the actors. "I know the script is bad," Ross said, "but changes will be made. You must not deteriorate under the emotional strain. It's rough, but that's why we are out on the road."

"At this critical moment," Melnick said, "we must not lose faith in Herb. We cannot behave like animals, snapping and snarling to protect individual interests. All of us have to recognize one thing. Eddie may be a son of a bitch, but he's *our* son of a bitch."

He went on to tell Miss Logan that she was a destructive influence, and he asked her to please cooperate.

"If the show's a flop," he said. "we'll all go back to television."

"You'll go back," Miss Logan said. "Some of us belong in the theatre."

The Shubert Theatre, The Next Day

Lawrence came to the theatre shortly before noon, expecting to watch the actors rehearse a scene that he had written the previous night. Despite his objection to the producers' intentions, he had agreed to more revision.

Before he arrived, however, Ross, acceding to the actors' requests and to his own intuition, had discarded the scene. Instead of following the script, he was conducting an experiment in improvisation, asking the actors to invent their own lines.

As Lawrence entered from backstage, a small, precise and well-dressed figure, he saw Ross sitting among four or five actors on folding chairs, all of them staring expectantly into the rafters. He sat down in the third row.

"I would like you people to say anything that comes into your heads," Ross was saying. "Don't worry about what it means; just respond to whatever is said to you."

Lawrence listened incredulously to the ensuing dialogue. After he had heard a minor actor say, "I don't know how the kid is going to jump off that monster and live," he turned and walked silently away.

A few minutes later, however, he could be heard shouting at Melnick in the lobby of the theatre.

"This is a disgrace," he said. "These lines will never reach the stage, never. This is worse than *Young Doctor Malone*, this is sentimental slop. This is abominable."

Although his exact words were not distinguishable, Melnick's voice, much softer, could be heard mumbling appeasement. When he returned to his seat in the third row (Lawrence had again withdrawn to his hotel), Melnick was handed a telegram from an associate in his New York office.

NOTES FROM THE IVORY TOWER. WORD IN NEW YORK IS KELLY BIG HIT. TEASERS UP. LOOK GREAT. HAVE SEEN ADVANCE SUNDAY AD. SENSATIONAL.

The telegram partially restored Melnick's self-confidence. Never again, he said, would he produce a musical comedy under the conditions now imposed on him. He particularly resented the contract he had signed with Lawrence and Charlap; under its clear, Dramatists' Guild terms, not a word of the script could be changed without their consent.

Although conceding that Lawrence had seemed a little upset just a few minutes before, he nevertheless thought that both authors would listen to reason at the meeting scheduled for that evening in his hotel room. What with all the money involved, and the chance for a hit and everybody's name in lights, he could not imagine that reasonable men would argue about a few lines of dialogue.

"For five hours I'll listen to the charade," he said. "I'll let them catharsize. They'll go along. We'll all be happy together in Boston."

INTERLUDE

Lawrence and Charlap never went to Boston with the company. On Friday, January 8, the same night that Melnick predicted reconciliation, he received a second telegram, this one from the authors' lawyers, threatening "appropriate action" if he and Susskind continued to permit unauthorized changes in the script. Over the weekend and through the following week the dispute became increasingly bitter. During this period the producers became furtive and shy.

Susskind returned from London on Monday, January 11, and rescinded the decision to abandon Miss Logan. Lawrence accordingly proceeded to write her part back into the play.

Lawrence's third and last revision went into the play on the evening of Tuesday, January 12. Although satisfactory to the authors, it failed to encourage the producers. During the intermission that night, in a bar adjacent to the theatre, Ross, Susskind and Melnick, their faces strained and tense, avoided looking directly at one another, like suspects waiting to testify before a grand jury. Later that night they confronted their authors in the Barclay Hotel, and presented an ultimatum. Melnick reported the substance of the conversation at breakfast the following morning.

"We told Eddie he was written out, that he was dry and had reached a dead end. The hero is still a petulant, mean and whining kid. We told Eddie he needs help, another writer."

Lawrence refused the offer, still maintaining that the character of Hop Kelly should be hostile, an anti-hero that the audience comes to admire despite his unattractive manners. On Friday, Melnick reported that he and Susskind were determined to do whatever they wanted to do with the show, even if it meant getting rid of Lawrence and risking trouble with his lawyers. The play had continued to suffer at the box office, and they already had been obliged to raise another $100,000 to pay the show's expenses, first to Boston and thence to New York.

"It's incredible," Melnick said, "that guys like Levine and David and myself can be frustrated… wrecked… by these small-time maniacs…. I mean, it's unheard of, fantastic…. The time for pleasantries is past."

On January 16 Lawrence and Charlap left Philadelphia. The next morning Charlap telephoned from New York and said that he and Lawrence were through with *Kelly*.

"It's not our show anymore," he said, "it's tenth-rate television jazz."

He reported that on Friday his lawyers had filed a demand for arbitration of the dispute. Levine had come to a meeting that night and there had been an unpleasant scene.

"The whole thing was like a sordid German movie," he said. "Levine shouted a lot. He wanted to know who the hell did we think we were, for Chrissake, Shakespeare and Beethoven? So I made a speech, sforzando, triple f's, and told them all they really cared about was money, and they didn't care what they put on the stage as long as some sucker paid $9.90 to see it…. These men are not human beings to me anymore, they're beasts. These are the men who will blow up the world."

On Monday, January 18, while stagehands were hanging the scenery in the Shubert Theatre in Boston, Lawrence and Charlap asked their lawyers to seek a court order that would enjoin the producers from bringing the show to New York.

ACT III
Boston, The Shubert Theatre, Wednesday, January 20

The tedious, familiar business of a dress rehearsal with stagehands, lighting crew and orchestra began at 1 p.m. The stage was smaller than the one in Philadelphia, and Randy Brooks, the stage manager, had some trouble making the necessary adjustments. The play was to open that night for what was scheduled as a three-week engagement. The cast already had learned a new opening scene written by David Goodman, a comedy writer and a friend of Melnick's, who had secretly been with the show for almost a week. The new scene introduced Hop Kelly as a frankly sentimental Irish kid trying to make a success of himself in the tradition or Horatio Alger. Whereas in Lawrence's play the boy had been booed and jeered at by a crowd of townspeople when he first came onstage, he was now welcomed with friendly cheers. His father proudly announced him to the people milling around on the Bowery as an idealistic young man. The father's line read: "Clear the road for Hop Kelly, clear the way for the hero of the world."

Kelly—with derby and rose—takes a dive from the Brooklyn Bridge in the artwork by Tomi Ungerer.

Melnick, sitting in the middle of the theatre with Ross and Susskind, explained that the tangled affairs of the production had assumed "nightmare proportions."

In order to forestall the authors' demand for arbitration he and Susskind had sought and won a temporary stay in Supreme Court in New York. This stay would postpone the court hearing until the following week. Throughout the rehearsal he was called away to the telephone, presumably to talk to lawyers, and he begrudged the time thus wasted. "The worst of all this," he said, "is that it prevents me from doing the creative work on the show."

Both he and Ross thought that the new scene, together with some other dialogue supplied by Goodman elsewhere in the play, immensely improved the character of Kelly.

"Until I heard these new lines," Ross said, "I never realized how dreadful Lawrence's stuff was."

He half expected Lawrence and Charlap to appear at the theatre that evening and to come running down the aisles, yelling that this was not their play. "I've been through that kind of scene before," he said, "and it's not particularly pretty." [Ross is presumably talking about *Hot Spot*, which he doctored in 1963. Ross's highly-praised assist on that show might well have led to the Kelly assignment; *Hot Spot* composer Mary Rodgers was Melnick's sister-in-law.]

Nat Dorfman arrived about 3 p.m., his arms filled with press releases. He squinted in the dim light, looking for Eddie Lawrence. The producers usually informed him of events three or four days after the fact, perhaps on the theory that if a press agent knows too much he becomes confused and ineffective.

At the end of the rehearsal, on the way to his hotel for a vitamin shot, Melnick said that the advance sales had been disappointing and that other prospective investors were coming up from New York that evening to look at the play. [Could these be the same "vitamin shots" that Alan Jay Lerner was taking during the creation of *On a Clear Day You Can See Forever* (see page 258), which opened later that year?]

"We desperately need good reviews," he said. "If not… Acapulco."

The Shubert Theatre, Later The Same Evening

Levine arrived only a few minutes before the opening curtain, accompanied by a retinue of his vice presidents carrying dispatch cases. Throughout most of the performance he remained in the lobby, seated heavily in a red-plush chair, receiving bulletins from Susskind and Melnick. He had come from Hollywood that afternoon, and he looked tired.

"This is not a business for sissies," he said. "This is much tougher than the movie business, and that ain't no lead-pipe cinch."

Although he had originally promised the cast a large party in Boston to celebrate his triumph in his home town, he felt obliged to cancel it for fear that the show might fail. He did not want to stand around among a crowd of old friends, all of them obviously struggling to think of some hopeful remark.

"Like those terrible Hollywood previews," he said. "Everybody knows the movie's awful, but nobody knows what to say." A look of remembered pain drifted across his face. "Someday I'd like to try to produce one of these musicals by myself. You know…without any partners."

Every now and then Susskind or Melnick came out of the theatre to inform Levine of the developments within. Toward the middle of the first act, Melnick appeared and said, "They love it, Joe. It's great, it works."

Two scenes later, Susskind said, "If only we had thrown those nuts out three weeks ago; now the script illuminates the characters instead of obscuring them."

Levine remained of the opinion, however, that the play should be funnier. "More jokes," he kept saying, "there ought to be more jokes."

When it was over, and before they went back to their hotel to talk to the prospective investors, Levine stood in the lobby with his arm across Melnick's shoulders.

"Mister Melnick and Mister Susskind have done a lot of fine work, and they have a lot at stake," he said, carefully avoiding the word "we," "and Mister Melnick, I'll tell you something, you put this show in shape in three weeks and get some laughs and you'll be the new boy wonder."

Melnick smiled at that and said that if the play was the success he thought it was, he would gladly give some of the profits to charity. Enchanted once again by his own euphoria, he left the theatre in an elated mood, explaining that he had to go back to his hotel to "juggle the balls in the air" among the investors from New York.

The actors and dancers, however, returned to their hotels, feeling depressed. To them the applause had sounded thin and perfunctory. Only a few of them bothered to stay up for the reviews. To her agent in New York, Eileen Rodgers sent a postcard on which she had scrawled the single monosyllable, "HEEEEEEEEEEEEEEELP!"

Boston, The Ritz Hotel, The Afternoon of January 21

The reviews were as bad or worse than those in Philadelphia. Although three of the critics faintly praised the show, calling it "colorful" and "appealing," the most influential critics in Boston, Elliot Norton on the *Record American* and Kevin Kelly on the *Globe,* damned it unequivocally. Norton described it as "the noisiest musical of the season, a rattling cover for emptiness." Kelly spoke of "a conventional piece of razzmatazz."

Again, as in Philadelphia, the producers had chosen to believe the worst. In the room overlooking the Boston Public Gardens, the trees already blurred in the gathering dusk, they sat around in the familiar attitudes of defeat and disillusion, Ross on the sofa, Melnick and Susskind in armchairs. On a tray against the wall were the glasses and the liquor bottles left over from the preceding night.

"I'll give you the bottom line first," Melnick said. "We close here

Saturday and open in New York a week from tomorrow night."

He explained that the reviews in the *Record American* and the *Globe* foretold financial disaster in Boston. The investors from New York, after staying up to read the papers, and having learned of the impending lawsuit, had refused all offers of a deal. Levine had declined to advance additional money, and at 10 o'clock that morning he had departed for a week's vacation in Jamaica. To Susskind he had said, "David, this is Chicago, and I get off at Chicago."

Levine's defection left Susskind and Melnick in an embarrassing situation. Lacking sufficient money to support the play for its three-week run, they finally decided to fold the show and accept their loss. But then, after long and complicated discussion, they reversed the decision on the ground that if they failed in Boston the gossips back in New York would say that *Kelly* had been the worst disaster since the Chicago Fire. Whereas if they could at least survive for a few weeks in New York, everybody would forget about it and dismiss it, in Susskind's phrase, as "just another rotten show." [This turned out to be a grave miscalculation. In the prior decade, dozens of musicals had folded on the road, some of them far worse than *Kelly*. By coming into town so spectacularly, *Kelly* became Broadway's most legendary flop ever. For twenty-two months, that is, until *Breakfast at Tiffany's* (see page 42) made a brief appearance next door at the Majestic.]

Having reached this conclusion, Susskind had been on the telephone all afternoon in search of $50,000, enough to pay their costs for another week. To raise this money, Susskind had determined upon a plan to promise, for the same investment, equal shares in several of his other productions.

"These money worries sap the creative juices," Susskind said. "I mean, you're always asking yourself if you can get out of town alive. What kind of life is that?"

"If we believed in God," Melnick said, "we'd pray a lot."

The telephone continued to ring throughout the rest of the evening. First it was Don Francks. Melnick spoke to him in his most ingratiating voice. "You were beautiful, sweetheart," he said, "touching, great, terrific, very moving.... Goddard Lieberson (the president of Columbia Records) saw the show last night, and he says you are the best talent he has seen in the last ten years."

After he hung up, Melnick said, "I thought I'd better come on strong before he had a chance to complain about anything. If he leaves, we're dead."

Balanced on a desk was a design for the cover of the record album that would be issued if the show was to have even a modest success in New York. Susskind looked at it accusingly.

"Someday that could be a collector's item," he said, "the only one of its kind in the world."

The longer he considered the possibility, the more depressed he became.

"We haven't got a Chinaman's chance," he said. "I don't believe in miracles or fantasy or magic. There is only truth, and the truth is that this is a bad show. If I thought I could fool Kerr and Taubman and the other critics so easily, I would lose all respect for the American theatre."

Melnick, still possessed by his vision of fortune and success, wanted to rewrite the entire show in a week. Two television comedy writers were on their way from California, and he thought the miracle might yet occur. Lying on the floor, his hands behind his head, staring up at the ceiling, he said, "This is wild, this is radical, but what about a new number for the opening of Act Two? Let's fantasize for a second."

Ross, looking at his shoes, said, "There's no content, Danny, nothing. Just a lot of sweat and movement to conceal a lack of content."

"I keep asking myself," Melnick said, "how could these two schlemiels conquer us? It must have been colossal ego on our parts to think that we could work with these people."

At this point the telephone rang again, and it was Charlap. He and Lawrence had come to Boston that afternoon, and they wanted to see the performance that night. Susskind told him he could go to the theatre, but he must not speak to anybody in the company and he could not speak to Susskind or Melnick.

"All communications must be in writing, Moose," Susskind said on the phone. "I don't want to talk to you... nothing verbal, Moose." Hanging up, he said, "The profundity of this experience, this trauma, this holocaust... the reason that the world will go up in a puff of smoke is because people don't love each other, they enjoy each other's misery. Moose and Eddie no doubt have their arrogance intact. All that stuff about Brecht, for God's sake. If they wrote *My Fair Lady*, Eliza Doolittle would have a cleft palate and a limp."

A few minutes later his daughter called from the University of Wisconsin. Susskind told her that the reviews in Boston had been mixed, that the schedule had been slightly changed, and that the play would now open in New York two weeks sooner. When he put down the telephone, he said, "You know what she told me? She told me, 'Don't worry, Daddy. You can always come here and teach English!'"

Shubert Theatre, 20 Minutes Later
Half an hour before the opening curtain the cast assembled back-

stage to hear their fate. Their faces already made up for the performance, the girls wearing partial costumes or old dressing gowns, they gathered in a circle around Susskind, Ross and Melnick. The bored stagehands listened from a distance.

"Well, I guess I'm elected because I'm on a panel show and should be used to this kind of thing," Susskind said. "…you all open in New York next Friday. We believe there are enough individual excellencies to warrant opening where it counts."

Susskind then nodded at Ross.

"I think the producers have made an extraordinary decision," Ross said. "They are… we are, out of money. It will cost another $50,000 to open in New York. I can only admire them for their decision."

"Which really means," said Eileen Rodgers, "that we don't have a fighting chance."

At that several people began to talk at once, arguing with one another, their voices beginning to get loud and edgy. Almost everybody, impressed by Susskind's courage and generosity, thought Miss Rodgers unappreciative.

"Please," Susskind said, holding up his hand for silence. "I would hope this is what you want, if not.…" He was interrupted before he could finish, everybody pressing forward to congratulate him and shake his hand.

"Elliot Norton hated *Oklahoma!*" somebody said. "Who cares what they think in Boston?"

The Ritz Hotel, The Next Night

Mel Brooks and Leonard Stern, the television writers from Hollywood, had arrived that afternoon from California; that evening they had seen the show for the first time. Neither of them had read the script. At 11:30, their observations scrawled on large sheets of paper or the backs of envelopes, they went up to Susskind's suite to suggest improvements.

Brooks, a small, energetic man with thinning hair, sat in a chair in front of the fireplace. Stern leaned against the mantelpiece. Taller and heavier than Brooks, wearing a goatee and elaborate gold cuff links in his silk shirt, he chewed gum and spoke with slow solemnity. Both men enjoyed reputations as writers for such comedians as Jackie Gleason and Steven Allen. [Brooks had served as a writer for Sid Caesar's Show of Shows, among other television programs. He had written the libretto for two musical failures, *Shinbone Alley* (1958) and *All American* (1962). In between, Brooks had joined with Carl Reiner for a series of comedy sketches which were recorded as *The 2,000 Year Old Man*. Stern had written for *The Honeymooners* and *The Steve Allen Show*.

In 1958, Stern and Roger Price created the word game *Mad Libs* (while sitting in Sardi's). With an early on-air boost from Allen, *Mad Libs* became wildly successful, and directly resulted in the formation of the publishing house of Price Stern Sloan. Stern was also, with Susskind and Melnick, a partner in Talent Associates.

As one of his first ideas when joining Talent Associates in 1964, Melnick decided to produce a sitcom capitalizing on the James Bond craze. Brooks was hired, and later joined by Buck Henry, to develop the script. Eventually, Stern joined the team; the result was *Get Smart*, which went on the air in September 1965—eight months after Kelly opened and closed—and continued until 1970.] Ross, Susskind and Melnick sat at the other end of the room, like schoolboys waiting for the headmaster to decide their punishment.

"OK, you want it straight," Brooks said, "you've got a Chink's chance. As cloying, as horrible, and as saccharin as some of the scenes are, the audience seems to forgive."

He recommended getting rid of Ella Logan. "I didn't believe a mother's tears wouldn't work," he said, "but it doesn't. She softens the show. She's out there selling torn rubber raincoats."

Ross and Melnick nodded enthusiastically, looking at Susskind with expressions of triumph, reminding him of their opinion in Philadelphia.

"She's just dreadful," Ross said. "Everybody who has come from New York says she's killing the show."

"It'll be a pleasure to fire her," Melnick said.

"OK," Susskind said, "so Ella's out of the show."

Brooks and Stern then proceeded to the principal weaknesses of the play. "What we are up against, fellas," Brooks said, "is grievous errors in the structure of the book; too many extraneous characters sing extraneous songs. Moose and Eddie wrote some marvelous stuff, but they only brought you to the five-yard line. No touchdown."

"The end of Act One," Stern said, "I don't know where is the commitment."

"The first three numbers in Act Two," Brooks said, "are the worst, seventy-five miles an hour into a stone wall. Death. Three losers back to back."

"That song," Stern said, "that awful song... what's the name of it?"

"'Home Again,'" Ross said.

"Yeah, right, 'Home Again,'" Stern said. "Well, it's terrible. What should be an enchanting lyrical moment is a pedantic horror."

With these observations everybody expressed wholehearted agreement. Ross slouched deeper into his chair, peering out at Brooks through his fingers.

"You have a very incisive mind, Mel," Melnick said "It's fabulous, Mel, fabulous."

Susskind asked if there was anything good about the play, and, if so, what to do about it. "The best thing in the show is Don Francks," Brooks said. "What you're bringing to Broadway is a new boy, a new face…. Go all the way with the kid. The love for the kid is the tickets. More love, more tickets."

"The boy delivers such a strength, such power," Stern said.

Stern wanted to cut three or four songs from the score, but the producers resisted because they then would have a very short musical with little music.

"So what," Brooks said. "Light the blaze under Don Francks. A few happy moments for the tired businessman watching some girls jump around onstage, and everybody goes home at ten o'clock. They'll be glad to get the first cabs."

As of 2 a.m., after eleven pots of coffee and much more conversation, the producers had agreed to cut Ella Logan and to engage a songwriter to write a song replacing "Home Again." This, with Miss Logan's other song, was the ninth of Charlap's seventeen songs to be cut.

The producers also wondered if Kelly's leap from the Brooklyn Bridge at the climax of the second act was properly staged. He accomplished the jump by means of wires, and Susskind had doubts as to the theatrical effectiveness of the stunt.

"Sure. Leave it in," Brooks said, "the hippies know he's on wires, but the Hadassah don't know." Ross departed at five a.m., carrying a Napoleon to his wife and leaving Brooks and Stern with instructions to write two scenes in addition and several comedy routines.

Stern wandered aimlessly around the room, and Brooks, lying on the sofa, reflectively smoked a cigarette and looked at the first light of a cold, Saturday morning. "Isn't it fantastic," he said to Melnick. "You see things in the last six days that you should have seen a year ago… fantastic. It's the same with all shows in trouble. The same sad tune but different lyrics."

ACT IV

New York, A Dance Studio on Sixth Avenue, Monday, January 25, Noon

The squares of sunlight on the polished floor gave the room a cheerfulness inappropriate to the mood of the people present. Dispirited and resigned, they had returned from Boston in a snowstorm the day before. Nobody expected a long run in New York. Mickey Shaughnessy had engaged a hotel room through Saturday morning. Ross arrived at 12:30, his face announcing him as the bringer of dismal news. He addressed the company from a folding chair placed in the center of a semicircle.

"OK," he said. "Almost a total rewrite of the play will be available at four P.M. According to my latest information, we will open this Saturday instead of Friday. Maybe Danny and David can raise an extra $50,000. If so, we can pay for another week of rehearsal, and we will open on Saturday, February 6, but we've got to figure for the twenty-ninth."

He announced the elimination of Ella Logan, and then outlined the new play as written by Brooks and Stern. They had begun writing it that Saturday morning in Boston, and had finished late Sunday night in New York.

In it Hop Kelly had become the boy next door: fearful, sweet and shy, a kid trying to do something for his sweetheart and his dad. The new comedy routines scattered through the play depended on exchanges such as the following, between two gamblers:

First gambler: "You can't welsh on an Englishman."

Second gambler: "Why don't you English on a Welshman?"

The cast received Ross's information with skepticism, knowing that if there was too much new material, they would not have time to learn it properly, and must therefore give shaky performances on opening night. A few of the actors also complained about the quality of the new lines.

"It's Jewish nightclub humor," somebody said, "Catskill stuff."

Before any of these objections could develop into extended arguments, however, Susskind and Melnick arrived with more words of hope and assurance. They took chairs on either side of Ross.

"I hope this is our last chat," Susskind said, "but I want to tell you the facts of life. At the end of our run in Philadelphia we had used up all our money. We have had, as you know, quite a number of troubles, particularly with Moose and Eddie, who thought they had written the Holy Scripture. But I want you to know that I believe in miracles, and that I am working around the clock to raise another $50,000 so that you people can have an extra week of rehearsal. I believe that with the new script we now have a strong show."

When the producers had left, and while they waited for the new scripts, everybody talked about the departure of Ella Logan. Mickey Shaughnessy, who had become extremely fond of her, had already talked to her that morning on the telephone. He had learned that instead of telling her themselves, the producers had instructed the stage manager to telephone her and tell her not to come to rehearsal. He thought this an abrupt way of firing a person, lacking in courage or courtesy.

"I'm a very torn-up guy," he said. "I liked that woman very much, and I wanted to do something to show how I felt about it. But she told me to forget it, that's the way it is on Broadway."

The Same, Two Nights Later

The afternoon rehearsals took place in an atmosphere of profound discouragement. At about 3 P.M. Ross, together with Susskind and Melnick, had gone to the Dramatists Guild for a meeting at which they hoped to reach a conciliation with Charlap and Lawrence. The authors' demand for arbitration was to be presented the next day in Supreme Court, and the producers feared the judge might close the show before it opened. The company, having heard wild rumors about the court action, half expected the arrival of federal marshals ordering them to quit work. Whenever the telephone rang or the elevator doors opened, everybody looked nervously over his shoulder.

Susskind came in about 8 p.m. and reported that the conciliation had failed, that Charlap and Lawrence, although willing to return to work for the show, had remained adamant in their request that the script be restored to what it had been on the opening night in Philadelphia. "How much endurance is a man supposed to have?" Susskind said. "I wish you could tell what somebody was like by looking at his face. I don't understand what they want. If it's a hit, they get their royalties; if not, they can take a big ad in *Variety* and call me a lot of nasty names. We now have got as many lawyers as actors."

Room 130, New York County Courthouse, The Next Morning

In the passage outside the courtroom, Ella Logan, accompanied by her lawyer, said she had come not to testify but merely as "an interested spectator." Speaking of the producers, she said "Amateurs, darling. Dilettantes."

Justice Samuel Gold elected to hear "the matter of Susskind" as the last case of the morning, when only Miss Logan and a few men in shabby overcoats remained on the hard wooden benches of the courtroom.

Harry J. Halperin, Susskind's attorney, moving to prevent the arbitration, began his statement by saying that his clients had invested nearly $500,000 in the play. This was his strongest argument. He reminded the judge that it was customary for authors to accept help if their plays received mixed reviews out of town.

"Even a genius must be practical, your honor," he said; "if Shakespeare were alive and behaved like Eddie Lawrence, then Richard Burton's *Hamlet*, one of the greatest productions of all time, but one that modified the script, could never have reached the stage."

[The highly acclaimed Richard Burton production of *Hamlet*, directed by John Gielgud, opened in April 1964. It remains Broadway's longest-running *Hamlet* with 137 performances, having broken the record set by Gielgud in 1936.]

The judge asked Edward Schlesinger, the attorney for the authors, whether the matter could not be resolved in a peaceful manner, perhaps at a meeting in his chambers.

Schlesinger shook his head.

"Opposing counsel would have us weep for the producers' plight," he said, "but it was they who created this situation, willfully, deliberately and villainously. They want to take the play and do whatever they want with it, and we think the play will be a disaster. They are interlopers and vandals."

For several minutes Justice Gold examined the briefs presented by both attorneys, and then, addressing himself to Halperin, he said: "These people are vain about their work. They feel you'll mess it up in such a way as to make it commercially successful, but not something they wish to lend their names to. Being normal men, I'm sure they're acting according to the noblest motives their minds can conceive."

"But $500,000, if your honor please," Halperin said, gesturing desperately with his hands, "$500,000 and they want to see it down the drain."

Justice Gold said he would consider the matter and would hand down his decision in a few days. On her way out of the courthouse, Ella Logan, who was smiling, remarked on the unusually fine weather. "Almost like spring," she said. "I think I can hear birds singing."

The Broadhurst Theatre, Monday February 1

The despair of the previous week had given way to a new hopefulness. Susskind had borrowed another $50,000, thus delaying the opening until Saturday, February 6. Justice Gold, although he had ordered the dispute to arbitration, had not specified an exact date, and he had denied the authors' cross-motion to enjoin the opening.

Even Melnick's wife, who had never liked the play and who had come to the dress rehearsal with serious doubts, expected a limited success. As the younger daughter of Richard Rodgers, the composer of *Oklahoma!* and *South Pacific*, her opinion was considered valuable. [Melnick was married to Linda Rodgers, who did not go into show business. Her sister, Mary Rodgers, was the composer of *Once Upon a Mattress* and *Hot Spot*.]

"The jokes don't seem like insults anymore," she said.

"They're generic," Melnick said. "I think it's on the way to something terrific." He thought the smallness of the Broadhurst Theatre would contribute to the sympathetic effect.

"It's an intimate house," he said, "not much bigger than our living room."

"We should have done the play in our living room," his wife said. "It would have been cheaper."

Although hopeful of success, Susskind still was troubled by the threat of an eventual lawsuit. On the telephone Charlap had referred to Melnick and himself as "money men," an epithet that he considered the unkindest of all possible insults. "How can he say that?" Susskind asked. "We contribute to this thing on all levels. Those slobs," he said again, "ought to be down on their hands and knees to all the people working to save this show. They can't be right if it means eighty people out of work and $500,000 lost." [What goes unmentioned is that producers Susskind, Melnick and Levine were otherwise occupied. Their import of the British play *All in Good Time*, by Bill Naughton, opened at the Royale on February 18—one week after the originally-scheduled opening of *Kelly*. I suppose you could call it a major hit, in comparison; it lasted six weeks.]

Of all the people associated with the show, however, the most optimistic was Nat Dorfman. For several days the newspapers had been printing stories about Ella Logan's dismissal, about the lawsuit, about opening two weeks before the date originally announced. Dorfman had been fending off reporters with assurances that these apparent troubles merely foretold a more dramatic success.

"I have never told so many lies in my life," he said. But he reasoned that even the disparaging publicity must do the play some good. "The people will be surprised," he said. "They'll like it because they'll come expecting so little."

The Same, Five Days Later

The bulletin board backstage was decorated with the usual opening-night telegrams, among them one from Leonard Stern, who, since rewriting the show in Boston and New York, had returned safely to California. The telegram read: MAY THIS BE THE FIRST OF 1,000 PERFORMANCES.

Wandering across the stage, en route to their various dressing rooms, the members of the cast stopped to embrace and wish each other good luck. Half an hour before the curtain Ross and Melnick, both in evening clothes, came around to thank everybody for their time and trouble. On behalf of the company the dancers presented Ross with the gift of a Japanese tree in a pot.

Susskind, who had suddenly become superstitious, stayed away from the theatre. On his television program that week he had entertained a group of soothsayers, among them a palmist, an astrologist, a lady with tea leaves, a man with playing cards and a handwriting analyst. In response to his question "Will *Kelly* be a big, fat hit?" each of the five had consulted his respective sources and returned with the unanimous answer, "a smash."

The night before, at the last of the five days' paid previews, Susskind had been absent, eating dinner with friends at "21." Ross and Melnick believed that the show had gone especially well that night and so, for good luck, Susskind had returned to "21," where, as the opening curtain went up, he was sitting at the same table with the same friends, ordering the same meal.

In the crowd outside the theatre, jostled by arriving celebrities, Levine, tanned and healthy after his week in Jamaica, overheard a conversation between the box-office manager and twelve people who had tickets to the show that had closed the preceding week at the Broadhurst. [David Merrick's successful transfer of the British hit, *Oh What a Lovely War.*] They wanted their money back.

"So do I," said Levine.

Together with Ross, Melnick's wife and a few of his vice presidents, Levine sat out the performance at Sardi's, the theatrical restaurant directly across the street from the theatre. Melnick watched most of the play standing up behind the last row of seats, and loudly applauding at all appropriate moments. Whenever the strain became too severe he walked across 44th Street to Sardi's and ordered another drink. At the intermission he told Ross he had heard a conversation between a blonde girl and Jean Kerr, the playwright and wife of Walter Kerr, drama critic for the *New York Herald Tribune*.

"Jean Kerr is crazy about Don Francks," he said. He considered this a good omen, because he once heard a rumor that Jean Kerr exerted an influence on her husband's opinion.

Charlap and Lawrence saw the play from the balcony, Charlap holding a tape recorder and accompanied by his lawyer, Lawrence making notes on sheets of yellow paper. Ella Logan sat with friends in the orchestra.

The play went as well as it ever did. The actors and dancers gave their performances all the verve and energy at their command. Nobody dropped a line. But although the applause sounded loud and hearty in the orchestra, where most of the people had free seats, the balcony remained ominously quiet.

While the audience drifted out of the theatre at the end of the performance, Charlap, Lawrence and Ella Logan stood on the sidewalk among friends sympathetic to their respective causes. "I could write better than this when I was eleven years old," Lawrence said. "The most shocking dialogue I've heard in the theatre in twenty years.... They're going to jail for this."

"Cornball," Charlap said, "one of the ugliest things I ever saw, like a horse with three legs. The work of hucksters."

Miss Logan smiled peaceably. "A lovely night," she said, "just the kind of night to go for a ride in the park." [The lead paragraph of Howard Taubman's review in the *New York Times*: "Ella Logan was written out of *Kelly* before it reached the Broadhurst Theatre Saturday night. Congratulations, Miss Logan."]

Sardi's, A Few Minutes Later

Because it was Saturday, the newspaper reviews would not come out before Monday but everybody went to Sardi's anyway, partly because it was the customary thing to do and partly because at least they could wait for the television reviews.

The tables downstairs had been reserved for members of the company and their friends, and when each of the principal actors arrived, there were gusts of applause. At a large table near the center of the room Levine sat with his back against a pillar, surrounded by his family, his friends and his vice-presidents. He entertained them with magic tricks, balancing forks and spoons on his forehead.

When Charlap came in, defying a tradition that forbids outcasts at such celebrations, he stopped at Levine's table and offered to shake hands.

"You still going to sue me, are you?" Levine asked.

"Yes, sir," Charlap said.

"Well, I'll tell you something, you little punk," Levine said, batting aside Charlap's hand. "I'll fight you in every court in the country, you and that crummy partner of yours."

The job of watching and then reporting the television reviews fell to Fred Segal, the man whose advertising agency had designed the posters and billboard publicity for *Kelly*. He had been with the production since the beginning at the Amsterdam Roof. Although never fond of the play, he liked many of the people associated with it, and it pained him to bring unhappy reports.

"NBC thinks it's a musical by committee," he said, returning from his first trip to the television set.

Thereafter, as he continued to come downstairs with less and less hope, he walked through the room with increasing slowness. Upon his last return he sat quietly at the table for five minutes before saying anything, moodily stirring his drink.

"Monumental bore," he said eventually, "AP."

After that word from the Associated Press, Segal didn't bother going upstairs anymore. Instead he explained his theory of *Kelly* as the ugly debutante. "You know what *Kelly's* like," he said, "it's like an ugly awkward girl at a coming-out party she doesn't want. Her parents have bought her a new dress, hired the most expensive ballroom, taught her to sing and dance, all this in hope of impressing the right people, in this instance the New York drama critics. But the parents don't love her. They did it for reasons of their own, and that's why she's still a dumpy, awkward girl. Nobody loves her."

The Broadhurst Theatre, Monday, February 8

The reviews, of course, were ruinous. Norman Nadel, writing in the *New York World-Telegram*, exceeded even Kerr and Taubman in the harshness of his judgment.

"There is some virtuoso tuba playing in the otherwise common-place overture to *Kelly*," he began his column, "...mark it well, because nothing else that entertaining happens during the next fifty-five minutes."

Lacking even one moderately kind adjective, which they could per-haps take out of context and use in advertisements, the producers decided that morning to close the show. They had no money to pay for another week. During the afternoon Susskind's office telephoned or sent telegrams to the cast, informing them that there would be no second performance.

At 8 p.m. Susskind came to the theatre to say good-bye to the actors and dancers. Melnick did not appear. The company gathered in the first five rows of the orchestra, all of them stunned, some of them crying. "I had to see you again," Susskind said. "You're marvelous people. I'm heartbroken. The notices bore no relation to the things that I had come to love in the show. Those were death notices." As he talked he swayed slightly. Accompanying himself with broad, circular gestures, as if trying to shape his feelings of sorrow and loss into a round ball.

"I will never forget any of you," he said. "I will stay in this business forever, I intend to come back to this theatre and beat its brains out. We just thought we had so much going for us. If there had been only one review, even one phrase that we could have taken out of context, we would have borrowed more money to pay for ads to keep the show open, but there was nothing. I'll never know why or how...."

His voice weakened, subsiding into vague and helpless sounds.

Eileen Rodgers cried out, "May your next show be a good one, David," she said, "you deserve it."

At that everybody applauded, and Susskind, smiling wanly, continued with his farewell.

"One last word about Moose and Eddie," he said. "I hope they come to their senses. I hope all this ugliness passes away in a cloud of mercy and understanding. But... if not... maybe we'll have to call on you to testify."

Nat Dorfman, who had listened to the speech with awe in his face, was himself almost moved to tears.

"In all my days," he said, "I have never seen a scene so beautiful as this, nothing so poignant, so true."

McKay's Dump, Secaucus, New Jersey, Four Days Later

Under a railroad bridge, beyond a soap factory hidden in a veil of yellow smoke, at the end of a winter road worn deep with ruts, an almost illegible sign mounted in a jumble of wrecked automobiles marked the entrance to McKay's Dump. A heavy mist reduced visibility to less than thirty yards.

Randy Brooks, the stage manager, had said the sets would be burned at 10 a.m. The man at the gate, however, said he had heard nothing of any such play, and besides, they didn't burn stage sets anymore: He pointed toward a road leading to the center of the dump and said maybe at the end of it somebody might know something.

The road, paved with the tar-paper shingles of ruined houses, ran in a wide semicircular curve, along the crest of a mound of debris. In the hollow of the curve, rising out of the rank and fetid mud flats, marsh grass swayed in the wind. Every few hundred yards along the edge of the temporary road, the old men living in makeshift shacks were lighting their morning fires. In answer to questions they, too, pointed vaguely down the road.

Where the road finally stopped, at the brink of a new excavation, a man wearing high rubber boots stood leaning against a bulldozer. He said he had broken up some stage scenery about an hour before and then had buried it in the muck. No, he said, nothing could be seen, not even the edge of a flat or a drop; he had already buried something else on top of it.

"A play, huh," he said. "Yeah, we get a lot of plays out here."

Kelly opened February 6, 1965 at the Broadhurst Theatre, to unanimous pans. It closed there that same night after 1 performance, with a total loss.

And with that, my friends, I think we can safely close our book on *Second Act Trouble*.

Credits

The following publishers, authors, and their representatives have generously given permission to reprint articles, book excerpts, and other material. Every effort has been made to contact copyright holders of other material contained in this volume.

"In the Act, the Drama Backstage Is Not an Act" by Cliff Jahr. Copyright © 1977 by The New York Times Co. Reprinted with permission.

"The Fight to Save *Seesaw*" by Patricia Bosworth. Copyright © 1973 by Patricia Bosworth, reprinted with the permission of The Wylie Agency, Inc.

"Lainie's *Seesaw* Side" by Lainie Kazan. Used by permission of Lainie Kazan.

"The Million-Dollar Misunderstanding" by John Gruen. Copyright © 1966. Used by permission of John Gruen.

"Why Holly Went Badly" By Lewis Funke. Copyright © 1966 by The New York Times Co. Reprinted with permission.

"An $800,000 Disaster" by Patricia Bosworth. Copyright © 1972 by Patricia Bosworth, reprinted with the permission of The Wylie Agency, Inc.

"Starlight, Starfright," excerpt from *Darling, You Were Wonderful* by Harvey Sabinson. Copyright © 1977 by Harvey Sabinson. Used by permission.

Excerpt from *This Bright Day* by Lehman Engel. Reprinted by the permission of Russell & Volkening as agents for the author. Copyright © 1974 by Lehman Engel, renewed in 2002 by the Estate of Lehman Engel.

"*No, No, Irene*" by Chris Chase. Copyright © 1973. Used by permission of Chris Chase.

"Irene a Financial Hit to All But Its Backers" by Mel Gussow. Copyright © 1974 by The New York Times Co. Reprinted with permission.

"Getting the Show off the Road" by Ellen Stock (Stern). Copyright © 1974. Used by permission of Ellen Stern.

Index